FRANK AND ME
AT MUNDUNG-NI

FRANK AND ME AT MUNDUNG-NI

A KOREAN WAR MEMOIR

JOSEPH DONOHUE

iUniverse, Inc.
Bloomington

Frank and Me at Mundung-ni
A Korean War Memoir

iUniverse books may be ordered through booksellers or by contacting:

iUniverse
1663 Liberty Drive
Bloomington, IN 47403
www.iuniverse.com
1-800-Authors (1-800-288-4677)

ISBN: 978-1-4620-7283-5 (sc)
ISBN: 978-1-4620-7285-9 (hc)
ISBN: 978-1-4620-7284-2 (ebk)

Printed in the United States of America

iUniverse rev. date: 04/12/2012

CONTENTS

MAP OF KOREAN PENINSULA

ACKNOWLEDGMENTS

For their precious time, suggestions, and insights reading my first draft I thank the following people in no particular order. My loving wife and lifetime partner, Christine, who was my literacy expert, editor, and supporter par excellence. Although she died prematurely, Christine had already helped me through the final draft, for which I am most grateful. I'm sorry that Frank Milisits, my neighborhood pal and wartime buddy who was my inspiration and partner in crime, had only the promise of a story being written. I miss them both dearly. I'm beholden to my three sons Jody, Christopher, and in particular, Terence Donohue and his wife, Irene, for listening to my stories ad nauseam and offering their computer savvy and incredible patience, without which this book would never have been published. I'm grateful to Wendell Cunningham Fleming, James Forrestal, Donald Fulton, John Ryan, and Kevin O'Donoghue for their precious comments, time, and energy in going over my manuscript. I'm also appreciative of the robust enthusiasm displayed by Robert Kirin during my writing, and in particular of his indefatigable wife, Tabatha, for her thoughtful research and creative ideas. I'm also indebted to my colleagues from the Lawrenceville Creative Writing Group for their great perceptive suggestions, involvement, and constructive criticism. Last but not least, I thank my foxhole buddies, machine gun platoon sergeant Lyle Olson, Mike Company commander Lieutenant Ron Gotshall, and all the guys who made this story possible and provided me with an experience of a lifetime. To all those helpful people whose names I have inadvertently left out, my sincerest apologies.

INTRODUCTION

(The following article was printed in our St. Ann's "STANNER" high school, now Archbishop Molloy, newsletter in 1992. I thought it was an apt introduction to Frank and me for this memoir.)

Frank J. Milisits   Joseph E. Donohue

The Inseparables

Frank J. Milisits and Joseph E. Donohue, both from the class of 1949, grew up together in Yorkville, pals and grammar school classmates. In 1945, it was inevitable they "walked through the black iron gates of St. Ann's Academy together." It was the beginning of "four wondrous and unforgettable years with the Marist Brothers." But adolescent life was soon jolted by the realities of the adult world. The misery of the Korean War was about to shatter the silence of their serene world of friendship. Drafted into the regular army, they reported on the same day to 44 Whitehall Street. Processing revealed that their army serial numbers were but one digit away, but alas, separation sent Frank to Fort Knox, Kentucky, for basic training and Joe to Fort

Jackson, South Carolina. They wrote often to each other, and the master plan for reunion was for both to volunteer for airborne. A long shot came to be, and they were reunited on a chow line in Fort Benning, Georgia. With tough training and five jumps later, less than a half of the class of 423 graduated but Frank and Joe received their "wings." They assumed their graduation had to do with a Marist philosophy of "Fight Blue and White, Fight and Never Give Up." They went from Georgia to San Francisco and on to Tokyo for their final orders to Korea. And then Frank reported to the Forty-Fifth Infantry Division and Joe to the Fortieth Infantry Division. Both were born in September 1931, and each celebrated his twenty-first birthday "in bunkers buried deep into the hillsides of Korea." Writing to each other became the order of the day, although during the fighting, their companies were not more than yards apart, and they never knew it. "We pulled a lot of triggers there on 'Heartbreak Ridge' and the 'Punch Bowl' and lost a lot of good men . . . *who shall never be forgotten.*" A chance six-hour reunion behind the lines in a place called Mundung-ni was followed months later by the sweet sounds of rotation home. They heard the words separately but were going home together. Thirty-nine years later, each is a godfather to the other's first son. Frank is a retired actor, artist, and gentleman farmer in Maine, and Joe is a retired school supervisor and university professor who lives in New York. They still stay in touch. Certainly, God's providence has been with them, and they are truly thankful. "Non Scholae Sed Vitae." Not school but life.

AUTHOR'S NOTE

I always wanted to write what it was like being drafted at age twenty in 1952 and going to the war in Korea. The fact that I was drafted with my best friend gave it more meaning as an odyssey of shared moments between veterans and lifelong buddies.

The heart of this memoir goes back to 1937. It was the year that I met Frank Milisits in the first grade at St. Stephen's of Hungary grammar school on Eighty-Second Street in Yorkville. We became great pals as kids. During World War II, as ten-year-olds, we kept scrapbooks on the war, lived the battles, became junior air-raid wardens, gathered scrap metal for the war effort, and went to the block parties for the veterans coming home.

In 1948, our junior year at St. Ann's Academy High School, we joined the Seventh Regiment, the "Silk Stocking" Regiment of New York City. We played basketball at the Eastside House, roller hockey at Carl Schurz Park, baseball underneath the Fifty-Ninth Street Bridge, and went to all the neighborhood dances. In 1950, everything suddenly changed. Communist North Korea invaded the Republic of South Korea. Our Seventh Regiment was not going to be activated for the war, so Frank and I decided to opt out of the Guard and become eligible for the draft. We were inducted together and went to Camp Kilmer, where we started on our venture to war.

My perception of that journey, which started more than sixty years ago, is told as I remember it. All the moments are in sequential order as they happened. The accuracy of times and places and the inevitable exaggeration of retold moments have been considered, so I chose to write this memoir in the genre of creative nonfiction to give me the leeway to visualize and write the kind of dialogue and language that was commonly used by soldiers at that particular time and in that particular situation.

BACKGROUND

During World War II, President Roosevelt and Premier Stalin agreed at the Yalta Conference that at the war's end, Korea should be liberated from the Japanese and become a united country. On August 8, 1945, just days after the first atomic bomb was dropped on Hiroshima, Russia declared war on Japan and sent troops south from her border into northern Korea. On August 15, 1945, Japan surrendered, and zones of occupation were set up, establishing the Thirty-Eighth Parallel as a demarcation line between the United States and the Soviet Union, creating a military partition of the country.

On June 25, 1950, North Korean troops invaded South Korea, and a week later, General Douglas MacArthur sent American troops from occupation duty in Japan to help the South Korean government. The war in Korea had begun.

The first two years of the war in 1950 and 1951 were characterized by invasions, retreats, attacks and counterattacks. Battle lines were constantly changing. By the summer of 1951, the Cold War had become a hot war between South Korean and North Korea, drawing other countries into the conflict. By April, President Truman dismissed General MacArthur as Far East commander for wanting to escalate the war after Chinese troops crossed into North Korea and attacked American forces. General MacArthur wanted to retaliate by bombing China. No one wanted to blunder into a third world war. It was agreed that talks should be held to end hostilities.

By October, some progress had been made at the negotiating table. A thirty-day cease-fire froze the battle zone across a 155-mile line from the Yellow Sea to the Sea of Japan. Both sides took advantage of the lull in the fighting to fortify their positions. The Chinese and North Koreans carved caves deep into the bowels of mountains for protection against heavy bombers and artillery. American and United Nations troops built log cabin—like bunkers on the tops of ridges both in front and back of the Main Line of Resistance (MLR) and depended upon massive firepower to keep the enemy in check.

In the United States, the draft was reinstated to provide manpower for what had become a nasty war of attrition. When I arrived in Korea as a replacement in September 1952, I thought the war would soon be over. General Eisenhower was running for president and promised to come to Korea and bring the war to an end. The peace negotiations at Panmunjom, however, took on a somber note of "who would blink first." The Communist forces had an endless supply of manpower and were willing to trade lives for real estate.

The chances of becoming a casualty were one in nine for the soldiers in combat. Survival depended on the coordinated firepower of heavy automatic weapons to keep the enemy in check. Bunkers and other fixed positions were zeroed in on and vulnerable to attack. The haunting thought of "death today and peace tomorrow" weighed heavily on everyone's mind. For the troops, it was a tough psychological burden to carry around.

While negotiators dickered over demarcation lines and how war prisoners should be repatriated, patrols were going out daily into no-man's-land, dodging booby traps and minefields, risking their lives to keep the enemy at bay. Nobody wanted to be the last casualty of the Korean War.

PROLOGUE

Frank and I had arrived in Korea in a time of chaos and uncertainty. Communist prisoners of war on the small island of Koje-do, west of Pusan, had recently rioted. Embarrassingly, they took the American commander of the camp hostage for a few days until he was finally freed by determined GI prison guards who kicked some ass with fixed bayonets. To make matters worse, some Korean guards at the camp opened the compound gates to thousands of prisoners of war who claimed to be anticommunist and didn't want to return to their homeland in either North Korea or China. The result was mayhem. The Communist top commanders at the Panmunjom Peace Talks claimed all sorts of atrocities were committed by "mad dog" American soldiers and angrily walked out of the negotiations. All hell broke loose along the entire battlefront.

At the end of August 1952, Frank was assigned to the Forty-Fifth Infantry Division, a National Guard outfit from Oklahoma called the "Thunderbirds." I was assigned to the Fortieth Infantry Division, a National Guard outfit out of California called the "Fighting Fortieth." My 224th Regiment was referred to as the "Gallahad Regiment," which just happened to have the "mad dog" American soldiers who were the prison guards at the Koje-do Island prison camp at the time. Our Fortieth and Forty-Fifth Infantry Divisions were frontline outfits. They burrowed themselves into the mountains like all the other combat soldiers in Korea, pointing their machine guns, mortars, and artillery at the enemy across from them. Fighting took place in rat-infested trenches that connected to a maze of fighting and sleeping bunkers, command posts, and first-aid medical stations.

Patrols dodged minefields and tried to ambush each other on mountain ridges and in valley floors. Over time, each side had their weapons zeroed in on each other so that few rounds strayed far from their intended targets. Casualties mounted, and nerves were frayed. Our job was to hold the line until the war ended.

Frank and Me at Mundung-ni: A Korean War Memoir is the story of childhood pals growing up in Manhattan and being drafted in 1952 as replacements for the war in Korea. It's a story about naïve, enthusiastic, twenty-year-old kids sharing their journey to war. It's about friendship, sadness, and joy during twenty months of service to their country. It's about growing up and facing the realities of war. It's about the boredom and routine of living on the front lines, which could suddenly turn ugly and become a hair-raising, deadly, heart-thumping moment of terrifying fear and exhilaration. It's a memoir of unforgettable personal moments, written in a creative nonfiction genre, which hopefully captures the full-circle journey of going to the war in Korea in 1952 as replacements and returning home in 1953 as combat veterans.

PART 1—CIVILIANS

CHAPTER 1

THE PROMISE

Frank died. It was early February when I got the phone call. Although I was expecting it, I still wasn't ready for the call. I felt my body go numb. I leaned against the door with the receiver in my hand long after Sue had hung up. I couldn't believe it. After sixty-two years, I had lost my best friend to throat cancer. I remembered the last time I had seen him and the promise I had made.

I knew he wasn't well. He had diabetes, and his drinking had gotten out of hand. He had gained an awful lot of weight and wasn't doing anything about it. I fought back tears as another wave of sorrow engulfed me. I remembered the last time we had been together, and a grim smile came to my face.

Frank had been on a waiting list for weeks and had finally been admitted to a veteran's hospital in Boston. He was pleased with that. He thought maybe his luck was changing. Times had been tough on an unemployed, aging actor with a young family to support. He had no money for private care. His teeth had to be pulled before he could receive any more treatment. His throat had been burned raw from the radiation. He could barely talk, and he was under heavy medication. The doctors gave him weeks to live, a few months at the most.

Frank was much older than Sue. He had been her idol since she was a teenager. Now she was more like a daughter caring for an aging, ailing father than a wife who was also raising a young son and working to make ends meet. When she called in October to say how downcast Frank was, I knew I had to get up to see him right away.

On an overcast Sunday morning, I took the early shuttle out of LaGuardia and flew to Boston. I hailed a cab from Logan Airport to the VA hospital. Frank knew I was coming, although he insisted it wasn't necessary. "I'm doing okay," he said. "You have better things to do." The hospital inside was typical government issue—dull green walls and dark white ceilings. Metal-framed flower prints were spaced above the long, checkered linoleum floors. As I walked past open doors, I caught glimpses of beds, patients, and the sudden whiffs of rubbing alcohol and strong detergents. I was so caught up in the dismal atmosphere of institutional oppressiveness that I barely heard the uniformed attendant reciting directions to Frank's room.

An empty elevator took me to the fifth floor. It was church-mouse quiet except for the metal taps on the soles and heels of my old cordovan jump boots. Frank would get a kick out of me wearing them, I thought. They would bring back some fond memories of our paratrooper jump days. If that didn't boost his spirits, I had some miniature bottles of Johnny Walker Red tucked inside my blue blazer as a backup.

The place looked abandoned. Where was everybody? I didn't see any doctors or nurses or visitors for that matter. I felt like an intruder, like I wasn't supposed to be here. With each step, I became more aware of the sharp clicking sounds emanating from the toes, heels, and soles of my boots.

"Whoa!" I cried, turning a corner and almost bumping into a male orderly who was as startled as I was at the presence of another person.

"I'm sorry. I'm looking for the east wing."

"Go through the double doors and straight ahead to the far end of the hall. You can't miss it," he assured me.

As I went into the east wing, I entered a shadowy, U-shaped ward of cots. Outlines of bodies were sprawled in all sorts of contorted shapes and positions on the beds. The only light came from a solitary, double-framed window stationed on each side of the room. Strong odors of dried perspiration and urine hit me immediately. Leftover food was scattered about on cluttered, dirty trays.

"Who ya looking for?" a rumbling voice cried out.

I almost jumped out of my skin. I turned around to a dark figure sitting on a chair next to one of the beds. "I'm looking for a Frank Milisits," I said in a low tone.

"Who? Speak up. I can't hear too good." I stood silent for a moment, afraid I might wake the ward. I walked gingerly to his chair and repeated, "I'm looking for a buddy of mine, Frank Milisits."

"The actor?" he asked.

"Yeah," I replied, "the actor."

The heavyset, unshaven watcher leaned forward and pointed across the room. "He's over there," he growled, "on the other side by the window."

"Thank you," I said and tiptoed to the beds on the other side of the ward. I walked past three beds and peeked at each of the occupants. Because of the poor light and dim haze, I couldn't make out the handwritten nameplates at the foot of the cots.

"Ya missed him," boomed the voice.

"No, I don't think so," I whispered.

"Whadyasay? Speak up! You won't wake 'em. They're all doped up."

"I don't see him!" I said in a voice louder than I had intended.

"Ya missed him. Ya missed him," he insisted impatiently. "Look behind ya. That one! That one over there," he gestured.

I looked down at a complete stranger. I saw a long body curled up in sleep. *This isn't Frank*, I thought. *The old man is nuts.* I kept staring at the face. The person I was looking at was way too old. *This guy is probably a World War II vet*, I thought. I kept looking at the face. This guy was ancient. A hawk's beak of a nose protruded down a gaunt, wrinkled face. The eyes were

5

closed and recessed in deep, hollow, creviced sockets. The mouth was pursed tightly together like a witch sucking on a lemon. There was no sign of his thick, blue-black dyed hair. There was only grayish fuzz spread sparsely over a faded pink scalp. The body was emaciated, almost skeletal.

This couldn't be Frank, I thought. Frank could weigh close to three hundred pounds on his six-foot-two, big-boned frame and joyfully crush you in an exuberant bear hug of an embrace. I was getting strange feelings. I was getting goose pimples. I tried to picture a once-gargantuan body on this now-gaunt, thin, and delicate frame. *Maybe . . . maybe*, I thought.

I looked at the hands clasped together under one side of the face. They were big and gangly. They were the right size—the huge ham hocks that could effortlessly palm a basketball in each hand or swaddle the graceful, thin handle curve of a thirty-six-ounce Louisville slugger or delicately cradle a quarter-inch fine-hair paintbrush. Slowly, the image of my best friend began to take shape, as if he were materializing into his old self right before my eyes.

It's Frank, I nodded to myself. *My God, it's Frank. It's really him*. I reached out and lightly stroked the side of his face. Eyelids fluttered and briefly opened and then closed again. Long seconds later, they twitched open again and a lopsided, ghoulish smile creased his face.

"Hello, old buddy." The faint whisper was followed by a long moment of silence, as if he were struggling for the right words to say. A tear appeared out of nowhere, glistening uncertainly in the dim light of the ward.

"Good to see you, old-timer," he said.

Frank strained to raise himself up and give me an embarrassed smile. I bent over to lend an arm, but he waved me off, and with great deliberation, he brought his skinny legs over and onto the floor. He showed more energy than I had expected. He stood up uncertainly, and in a bent-over position, he confessed gleefully that he hadn't taken all the pills he was supposed to take this morning because he wanted to be sharp for my visit. He said it

6

with pride, like a classroom cutup who was cheating on a test and getting away with it.

He gave me that crooked, dopey smile, which I was quickly warming up to. With a wink, he slyly uncovered a half-filled pint of scotch whiskey from the bottom of his half-filled laundry bag. "First, I got some clothes to do," he said. "I got a bladder problem. Piss all over myself. It's embarrassing as hell, but I can't help it."

Frank was weak but determined. With some soap and water, we used a slop sink in the shared bathroom outside his ward. I helped him soak and rinse out a pair of socks and urine-stained khaki pants. We laid them out on a long metal wall bar next to the sink. We left them there to dry and went back into the ward. The putridly powerful smell hit me again. "Let's get out of here," Frank said. "I thought we'd hang out on one of the benches outside. It's a little cool, but it's a hell of a lot better than this morgue."

I smiled at my old friend. He was trying hard to show that he was still in control and that he had things to do and choices to make. "Absolutely," I said. "I couldn't agree with you more." Frank got dressed in a heavy wool robe over his blue hospital gown, which came down to his knobby knees. It fell short of his fur-lined slippers but managed nicely to meet the tops of his high, athletic, ribbed socks. Covering his almost bald, peach-fuzz head was a navy blue baseball cap with USS Saratoga printed in gold lettering across the front. He was ready. He looked at me for approval, and I nodded. As we walked toward the hall, we passed the snoring figure of the ward watcher slumped into the chair. We looked at each other and smiled.

"Ain't he a pisser?" Frank said.

We took the elevator downstairs to the cafeteria and filled up a plastic container with ice cubes. At the front desk, Frank had to sign himself out. We found a bench in a small garden off to the side of the main entrance, near the spot where my cabbie had dropped me off. What a relief to be in the fresh air. Anything was better than that sickening ward.

On this hazy, overcast day, the sun was so high in the sky that it was too weak to provide any real warmth. The Styrofoam cups filled with ice chips and scotch had been a stroke of genius. They did the job of taking the nip out of the air and making us very comfortable. We just quietly sat there for a while until Frank broke the silence.

"I'm dying, Joe," Frank said, looking straight ahead at the cars going past the garden fence. Neither of us spoke. Agreement was in the silence that followed. Sue had told me the cancer had spread from Frank's larynx to his tongue and into his jaw. He had a hard time speaking, and it was difficult trying to understand him; however, it didn't stop us from talking. It was like old times. We were together again, enjoying each other's company as we had been doing since the first grade in grammar school.

"Marky's in the third grade now," Frank rasped. "He's a good boy and a good little athlete, and he can hit a ball pretty hard. I pitch to him all the time. I keep telling him, 'Marky, you must always keep your eye on the ball,' and he would whack that ball a country mile." Frank beamed. "He's very popular. He's got a ton of friends. His teachers love him, and the girls in his class think he's cute."

"He is lucky," I said. "Especially the good looks part. He's definitely got his mother's good looks."

Frank leaned closer to me and gave me that lopsided, ghoulish grin again. He looked at me like the cat that had just swallowed the canary. "I wasn't too bad with the ladies myself, and I don't mean just because I had three wives," he said, nudging me with his elbow.

"Come on, old buddy. I was just kidding," I said.

"I know you were," he said, leaning back on the bench. "I also know that I made some mistakes in life that I can't change. I'm grateful for Sue and glad that she has a job . . . that she likes . . . and is good at. I have a little pension money coming in, which helps some. I know Sue will marry again. She's still young. She's attractive. She's got a good head on her shoulders, and she's a good woman. It's been tough for her," he whispered.

The afternoon slipped away in good conversation. We were not chilled at all now. Sipping scotch through mounds of crushed ice warmed us up and helped soothe Frank's aching throat.

"Joe, I want you to do two things for me," Frank said, suddenly sitting up straight and looking at me dead in the eye. "I want you to do my eulogy, and I want you to scatter my ashes in New York over the East River and Central Park. That would be nice. I would like that."

"Yeah, I could do that. You're going to be cremated, right?" I smiled ruefully. "The ashes part will be easy, but the eulogy part will be hard. What do you want me to say?"

"Say whatever you want. Say whatever you think is best. I trust you," he said with a nod.

I smiled an evil smile. "Are you sure you want to trust your reputation to me?" There was just the slightest pause, but it was so obvious that we both picked up on it and enjoyed a good belly laugh. The scotch was starting to kick in.

"Okay, so how do you want to be remembered?" I asked.

Frank got deadly serious and a bit maudlin. He paused dramatically, and in a choked, barely audible voice, he said, "Tell them . . . tell them he was just a man who always tried to do the *fright* thing."

We looked quickly at each other and froze for what seemed like an endless moment in time. Frank realized that we had both caught what he had garbled. Fright instead of right brought uproarious, loud laughter from the two of us. There was no doubt about Johnny Red now.

"Shit, Joe, say whatever you want to goddamn well say and get it over with," he giggled.

We put our heads back on the bench, still chuckling, and crossed our legs. The soles of our shoes touched, and the obvious incongruity of slipper next to paratrooper boot brought another outburst of laughter. We were getting close to losing it. The image of my dark, leathery, cracked, forty-year-old, spit-and-polished jump boots under razor sharp pressed blue jeans next to his new, floppy, fur-lined slippers started us reminiscing. We talked about jump school and going to Korea. We rehashed old stories that we had told a million times before, but they were never quite the same as before. We listened to each other's tales knowingly, sometimes with humor, sometimes with sadness and wonder, but astonishingly, we always listened as if we were filling some unquenchable need to hear them again.

"You got my tapes?" Frank asked.

"I got your tapes, and I put them with mine," I answered.

"Joe, we got to tell the story. Nobody ever really asked what it was like going to Korea, and we never really told them."

"That was because nobody cared," I said bitterly

"Yeah, well, I cared. You cared. I'd like Marky to know about our war. I wish we had saved all the letters we'd sent to each other when we were there. That would have told the story."

"Yeah, that would have helped. Think of the times when we could have walked the letters over to each other, if we would have known how close we were on the line," I mused, a smile of remembrance coming to my face.

"I wish I had more time. I wish I could do it now," he lamented.

"Wishing isn't going to do it," I said. "When you get out of this cuckoo's nest, we'll work on it together. That's a promise. We'll write a 'Willy and Joe *Up Front*' kind of a book—only we'll call it *Frankie and Joey in Korea* or something like that. What do ya say?"

"Hey, that sounds good," said Frank, perking up. "It could even be a movie. Do you think I'm too old to play my part?" he asked, laughing at his own joke and showing a toothless mouth and bare gums. "If I can't get a good makeup artist, then maybe I could write a screenplay." His laughter got louder and louder and suddenly turned into a wheezing, wracking, choking cough. "Who's kidding who?" he gasped, his sallow face turning a beet red. "I'm not going to make it out of here, old buddy. It's up to you to write the story. We put up with a lot of shit in a short period of time," said Frank, breathing deeply and catching his breath. "It may not have seemed like much to others. It wasn't very glamorous, and there was no glory. There was no 'welcome home' parade, and maybe people didn't really care. But it sure as hell meant something to me. I know I will never forget it, and neither will you."

"That's because it was our war, Frank. We lived through it. How many soldiers have actually seen combat? Would you guess one out of ten? I don't know, but I do know that not too many wear the infantryman's badge. Unless you've been there, it's pretty hard to relate to it. Anyway, people were tired of war back then. Korea came along too soon after WWII. People were still afraid of a third world war. They wanted to forget the past. They wanted peace. I can understand that. But what gets me is the fact that there was a war that nobody wanted to admit to. Calling it a 'police action' was a joke. It always drives me nuts when people talk about World War II and then jump right over Korea to the Vietnam War. What an insult. It's like it never happened. What about all the guys that got killed and wounded humping hills and fighting in their bunkers?" I asked, working myself into a dither. "There sure as hell are a lot of memories for a war that didn't exist," I said and smirked.

"That's why you gotta do it, Joe," said Frank, soothingly trying to calm me down.

"You're the only one. You went to college. You wrote a dissertation. You have all the tapes. You have to do it," he said convincingly, clutching my arm like a politician at a clubhouse gathering.

"Yeah, but remember you're the creative one. You're the artist, the big movie actor," I countered. "How am I going to do it without you? No way, pal. It's got to be done together. When you get home, that will be the first order of business," I said firmly.

"I'm not going home, Joe. I'm leaving here a dead man. I know that."

The words exploded in my ears. They were harsh but true. "Promise me that you will do it," he said, and his voice betrayed a hint of desperation. "One more favor for ole Watashi."

The words caught in my throat. I nodded my head solemnly. "I'll do it, Frank. I promise."

A cab pulled up at the bottom of the hospital stairs. The door flung open, and two young boys about the same age jumped out, jostling each other, and without waiting for any adults, they raced each other up the long hospital stairs. Frank and I watched them without speaking. "Did you call a cab, Joe?" Frank asked nonchalantly. "That cab is still there. You'd better grab it, Joe."

He turned to me with a Mona Lisa smile on his face.

"What's up with you?" I asked with a mocking grin.

"Nothing," said Frank, shaking his head. "I was just thinking how good it is seeing you again, Joe."

"Same here, pal. Hang in there. I'll keep in touch."

I stood up and motioned the cab to wait.

I turned to Frank, who lifted himself unsteadily from the bench. Hunched over, he still towered over me. We stood looking at each other for a brief moment, and then he lunged and hugged me as usual but without the jarring crunch that I had grown so accustomed to over the years.

"Take care of yourself, old-timer," he whispered.

"You too," I said. "Let me walk with you inside."

"Nah! I'll be all right. Go ahead. The cab is waiting."

"Yeah," I replied. "Love ya, babe," I croaked, feeling the thin, fragile bones through his hospital robe. "Be good now," I said, breaking away and bounding down the stone steps, my boots crackling a sharp cadence as I walked to the waiting taxi. When I turned around to wave, Frank was gone.

I scanned the front garden where we had been sitting and in back of the hospital, but there was no one there. *He couldn't have gone very far*, I thought. *Where the hell could he be?* I felt uneasy and hesitant about what to do when a bent figure emerged from the revolving door and stiffly walked to the top of the stairs. He made a show of straightening up to his full six-foot-two height. With his powder blue gown peeking out from under his short, striped robe and his white wool socks standing tall above his slippers, he proceeded to give me the smartest and snappiest of all airborne salutes. His eyes focused on my eyes and held them. In slow motion, his right arm came up and extended long, bony fingers as they touched the peak of his USS Saratoga visor. With his slender, fragile body gently rocking back and forth, I acknowledged him by returning the gesture with great exaggeration and flair. Tears welled in my eyes. I dropped my salute sharply and turned quickly. Through the lump in my throat, I rasped to the cabbie, "Logan Airport please."

CHAPTER 2

GROWING UP CITY KIDS

On the plane ride from Boston back to New York, I closed my eyes, tilted my head back on the cushioned headrest, and tried to get comfortable. I could see Frank lying on the bed in the VA hospital, curled up in the fetal position, snoring like a wizened, withered, toothless old witch. That's not the way I would ever want to think of him. Frank was too vibrant, too vain, too adventurous to be remembered that way. I would remember him in my own way.

It was the first day of school, and a boy was crying. I thought he was a big baby, but I was wrong about him. His name was Frank, and he was a good guy. We grew up in the same neighborhood and became good friends. We got drafted together and journeyed to the war in Korea.

The tan brick school was built around a tiny church entrance squeezed in between rows of four-story tenement buildings. If it wasn't for the neon cross proclaiming St. Stephen's of Hungary in bold block letters, you would have walked right by it.

My mother had me champing at the bit. It was the first day of school, and my mother kept assuring me how much I was going to love it. "Children stay home with their mommies," she said. "Big boys go to school and make lots of friends and have fun. They have books and desks and classmates and teachers who teach them lots of new and wonderful things."

Sister Immaculata, my teacher, had a flowing black gown with a knotted cord tied around her waist. Her starched white bib bunched under her chin like a bow tie and then continued upward to encircle her face like a mirror. A black veil covered her head and trailed down her back. I wasn't afraid because my Aunt Mae was also a nun but dressed differently. She belonged to another religious order.

Sister Immaculata brought me to one of the wooden desks and told me it was mine. I couldn't believe it. In an instant, I was Tailspin Tommy in a dogfight, putting my double-wing fighter plane into a dive and shooting everything in sight. In the next moment, my desk was a racing car speeding around a crowded track with the other desks in the room. My mom was right. School was fun.

Sister Immaculata clapped her hands loudly. She told everyone to stop what they were doing and to stand up. In walked another nun. Sister Immaculata showed the boys how to bow and the girls how to curtsy. The boys placed their right palms on their stomachs and folded their left arms behind their backs with their palms facing out and bowed slowly. The girls held out both sides of their dresses and bent their knees. We had to repeat this after our teacher: "Good morning, Sister Agnes."

The principal held the hand of a boy who lagged behind with his head down and rubbed his eyes with his free hand. All eyes were fixed on the sobbing boy, whose chin was buried in his chest. I remember noticing how big he was, especially his hands. He looked like a second grader, and I remember how small and tight his checkered shirt and blue short pants looked. He was different.

Sister Immaculata said something to him in words I didn't understand. Everyone snickered at the way she spoke. It didn't make any sense to us, but the new boy didn't think it was funny because he ran to the empty desk behind me, flung himself into the seat, and buried his face in his arms over the top of his desk. His ears burned red against his shiny black hair.

"Children, do not turn around. Just ignore him," admonished Sister Immaculata. It was hard not to look back. Everyone sneaked peeks. Eventually, the crying stopped, and the boy sat up in his seat; however, he didn't say anything. I turned around and smiled. "Hi," I said, "my name is Joe."

Years later, Frank told me what had happened. In 1937, he and his mother along with his brother and sister were staying with his grandparents in Hungary. His father was working in New York and made arrangements for the family to come back to the United States. War fever was running high in Europe, and even though Frank was born in Pennsylvania, his family was born in Europe. And there was a possibility that his older brother, Steve, would be conscripted into the Hungarian Army. They came back to the United States as quickly as they could. A few days before Frank's sixth birthday, he landed in New York, which was a strange place to him, with people he didn't know and a language he had pretty much forgotten.

"When the principal spoke to me in English, I could make out what she was saying, but when I tried to answer her, nothing came out right," he had said. "I would move my lips and squeal a jumble of Croatian, Hungarian, and English gibberish. When she spoke Hungarian, I knew enough to get along. When she spoke English, I was scared. I thought I was going crazy, so I just kept my mouth shut and cried. I wanted to make myself small and disappear. I understood the name Joe because that's my middle name. Although I couldn't say it, I knew I had made a friend that day, and his name was Joe."

Another thought popped into my head during the plane ride. I remembered the time when on a dirt-covered field under the Fifty-Ninth Street Bridge on the day of our graduation from high school, Frank's zombie eyes stared at me in disbelief. The ball came off the bat into right field like a rocket with the base runners circling the paths. I charged the line drive at full speed and heaved the ball to first. Frank darted over from the hole between himself and the second baseman to cover the bag. He scooped the ball on a short hop, legs split and face twisted in pain. We nipped the startled runner by a stride.

"You're out!" could be heard throughout the borough of Manhattan.

The place went nuts. Frank ran out to me and put his arm around·my neck in a stranglehold.

"I don't believe what you did. You looked like a madman!" he wailed.

"I thought you were having a conniption. You should have seen the look on your face!" I howled. "And after that split, you'd better check your jewels while you're at it."

We had just won a game against our neighborhood rivals and were graduating from high school that same night. We were full of piss and vinegar with the rest of our lives ahead of us.

Even in the plane's restroom, there was no escape. I was haunted by the images from the VA hospital. I cringed at the thought of what lay ahead. I pressed the button and a loud swoosh flushed the toilet. I steadied myself against the stainless steel sink and bent closer to the metallic, mirrored wall. I traced the jagged crescent scar from my bushy left brow right up and into a receding, gray hairline. It was a grim reminder of our trip to Canada before we had been drafted.

We were on vacation. The sun kept popping in and out of thick clouds, casting fast-moving shadows on the surrounding Canadian hills. The black canvas top was rolled down around the rear seat of our borrowed white convertible. A steady wind pushed against our faces and through our hair. We sang at the top of our lungs, accompanying Tommy Dorsey as he played "Embraceable You." We had the northbound lane to ourselves. Homeward travelers filled two lanes of weekend traffic coming from the Laurentian Mountains into the city of Montreal. We were on vacation and going in style.

We pulled over and buttoned up the hood as the first drops of rain turned into a mild shower. We moved back onto the highway slowly, winding into a long bend in the road, when a car appeared in our lane and then cut back into its own lane several hundred feet ahead of us. Frank cursed him out and shouted in his exaggerated and bastardized high school French, *"Polly vouz eng-less? Son ze beetch bass-tard."* We cursed and laughed and gave him the Italian salute.

Frank saw the first car pull out into our lane and then squeeze back into the passing lane. He never saw the second car accelerate into our lane. I shrieked, "Frank, watch—" and closed my eyes as I braced myself for the head-on collision. Screeching brakes and the explosion of crashing steel thrust me forward into the windshield. The recoil threw me back and launched me through my side of the door onto a dirt embankment. I rolled into weeds and lay on my back, feeling warm blood and cool rain dripping down my face into my eyes and mouth. I don't know how long it was before I saw the tense faces of men peering down at me. They talked to me, but I couldn't make out what they were saying. They lifted me up and placed a cloth over my forehead. Strong arms half-walked and half-dragged me up the embankment toward a house across the road halfway up a hill. I passed the twisted wreckage of our convertible, where Frank was slumped over the wheel. People were administering to him. He wasn't moving.

They sat me down in a rocking chair that was in somebody's living room and asked me simple questions I couldn't answer. I tried answering; however, the words kept swirling around in my brain, and I couldn't put a thought together. I was able to say Frank's name.

"Frank? How is Frank? Where is he?" I kept asking. They kept telling me that he was okay. Then I remembered his head lying over the wheel. With a sudden burst of adrenaline, I jumped up and broke away and bolted out the door, crying, "He's dead. He's dead." Again, arms grabbed me and led me stumbling on wobbly feet to a taxicab. I was eased down into the front seat. Frank was seated in the back, holding a blood-soaked handkerchief to his ear and another to his mouth. His glassy eyes kept opening and closing. He was looking over at me. "Are you okay?" I asked.

He nodded but looked like he couldn't hold his head up. He was fighting to stay awake. "How about you? How are you doing?"

His words were metallic. He was looking at me but not really seeing me.

"Okay. I rapped my head pretty hard," I said. "But I think I'm okay." I turned around and took the towel from my bloody head and looked into the rearview mirror. "Holy shit! Frank, look. I can see the inside of my head," I said, turning around to look at him with the blood streaming down my face.

Frank's face was expressionless. He was calm and gave me a blank stare. "It's not so bad, Joe."

"Hold on," said the driver of the cab who slid into the front seat and started the engine. "The ride to the hospital will be quick. We have a police escort."

The newspaper account the next day about the two vacationing Yanks showed a picture of the Plymouth convertible twisted into a roofless, tangle of steel on wheels. It was impossible to think that anyone could have survived that scene. We walked the halls of our hospital, named Hotel Dieu, in patient gowns with wide bandages wrapped around our heads. Two nurses kidnapped us on their day off for an afternoon brunch, insisting that it was necessary for our successful convalescence. Frank was always able to turn adversity into something positive and make a silk purse out of a sow's ear.

Coming back from the plane's restroom, I plopped down into my seat and tried to get some sleep. I closed my eyes, but the images immediately popped into my head.

"Jane's pregnant," he blurted out. I could still see the anguish in his face when he told me about his girlfriend. The guilt and the shame he felt hiding it from both families was devastating. It was our second year home from Korea. Frank was a budding artist at Norcross Greeting Card Company, and I was a junior in college.

"I'm going to marry her. I love her," he said firmly in a low, assertive voice. "We'll get by," he assured me, nodding his head. "We'll raise a family. It's the right thing to do. I like kids. Maybe it will be a boy. It's good to have a boy as a first child. Don't get me wrong. I love girls, but you know it's nice if they have an older brother. Someone to protect them," he said with a quick, nervous smile. "I'm looking forward to it. I'm going to be a papa. Can you believe it, Joe?" he said, searching my eyes for approval.

I nodded and smiled and looked away.

"What can I say, Joe? I fucked up," he said with a smile, tears trailing down his cheeks.

The plane started its descent. "Flight attendants, get ready for landing."

I straightened my seat into the upright position and shook my head. *The memories of youth*, I thought. *Or were they the memories of an old man?*

CHAPTER 3

GUNG HO AND READY TO GO

The beer was flowing. Gildea's Bar went wild with couples dancing and singing George M. Cohan's patriotic songs. Frank and I caught the fever. We were ready. We were going to war, baby!

The draft had been going on for two years. Frank and I were in the National Guard, so we had been exempt from going into the army. They called us weekend warriors because we stayed at home and served our country at the same time. We went to weekly drill meetings at the Seventh Regiment Armory, attended weekend shoots several times a year at Camp Smith in Peekskill, and did our annual two weeks of summer training at Pine Camp in northern New York. We had it made in the Guard.

The Seventh Regiment had a proud old history going back to 1838. It was the first regiment called upon to protect Washington, DC, after Fort Sumter had been fired upon by Southern troops. Its formal uniform became the model for West Point Academy. The humor of the day was that the terminally ill, crippled, blind, and insane would be called into active duty before the majestic "Silk Stocking Regiment" of Park Avenue.

It was an honor to serve in the regiment, but Frank and I had toyed with the idea of not extending our enlistment and instead making ourselves eligible for the draft. We were young and eager and not very patient. There was a war going on, and we wanted in. We even fantasized about volunteering for jump school and becoming paratroopers.

One hot August evening after the regiment returned from its two weeks of summer training, I stood chafing on the faded Persian rug in front of my polished wood locker, listening to the boring performance reports from I Company's executive officer. Tiffany lamps cast muted shadows over the oak-paneled company room. Tobacco smoke mixed with the smell of linseed oil and boot polish. It had been a long day, and I couldn't wait for the meeting to be over so I could go to Donohue's Steak House with the guys for a bite to eat and some cold beers.

"I want every man to hear this loud and clear," said I Company commander, Captain Irsay, lighting up a delicate, white meerschaum pipe that sent smoke gyrating up into the dark recesses of the carved wood ceiling. "You all know there's a waiting list of eager volunteers wanting to join the regiment. Well, I have a waiver for anyone who wants to get out of the Guard effective immediately. May I remind you, gentlemen, that you will also become eligible for the draft, effective immediately. The selective service board will be notified of the change in your deferment status. May I see a show of hands?"

Not believing what I had just heard, I turned around to Frank. It was now or never. I waved and caught his attention. There was a slight hesitation before his head gave an imperceptible nod and our hands shot into the air. Faces turned with quizzical looks of disbelief. I heard murmurings and mutterings: "You guys are crazy. You don't know what you're doing."

I was grateful for the other show of hands. Next to me, Jimmy Freehill grinned as his hand went up, and John Schramel did the same. There was Blake and more hands. I smiled. At least we weren't the only gung-ho screwballs in the regiment.

The next day started the long Labor Day weekend. I was going to my folk's summer bungalow at Rockaway Beach on Long Island. In the summer, Rockaway was the place to be. Its boardwalk and bars were alive with Irish and American music, and the dancing attracted hordes of young people from Brooklyn, the Bronx, Queens, and Manhattan. Frank and the guys and girls from Yorkville would be coming down, and we planned to meet on Saturday at four o'clock in Gildea's, the most popular Irish bar in Rockaway.

Gildea's was like a Wild West, dance-hall saloon. Swinging doors opened to an endless, scarred wooden bar that divided the room between drinkers and dancers. Dark mahogany high chairs lined the bar. Sawdust partially hid the white tiled floor, which glistened from the afternoon sun streaking through the rafters. On the other side, a veneered dance floor led to an elevated bandstand opposite the entrance doors on the far side of the room. A rainbow-lighted jukebox played a mix of big-band sounds, romantic ballads, and jaunty Irish tunes. A boisterous bar crowd jabbered away in animated conversation. Small groups that were all in their late teens and early twenties laughed and bantered at tables scattered around the dance floor.

Early in the evening, jukebox music was replaced by a small five-piece band. All band members, more or less, wore black pants, white shirts, black shoes, and white socks. There was an accordion player, a drummer, a piano player, a bassist, and a fiddler who would get the attention of the crowd with warm-up squeaks and speaker feedback. Squeals morphed into a tune of "The Wild Colonial Boy," and the evening entertainment began.

Toes and heels tapped steadily to the likes of the "Stack of Barley," the "Beer Barrel Polka," and the "Tennessee Waltz." Energy levels rose with lindy hops and savoys, waltzes, and two-steps. Guys reinforced with beer courage and confidence peeled off from the bar crowd to cut in on the girls. At the end of the numbers, they returned to the bar, remained with their dance partners on the floor, or joined friends at their tables. Pitchers of beer, glasses of cokes, and black plastic ashtrays adorned the bare tabletops. Gildea's was revving up, and Big John, the owner, and his sidekick bouncer went into action.

Wearing his black-and-white uniform, Big John Gildea worked the room. Strands of black hair stuck to his sweaty forehead as he lunged from table to table, clearing the empty glasses with the zeal of a man possessed, pink cheeks flushed against milk-white skin. Beady black eyes darted from group to group. Squarely built with a broad chest, he was ready to pounce at any sign of trouble.

Six-foot-six with some inches to spare, Finbar Devine was a giant of a man. He was Big John's trusted lieutenant and enforcer. A moonlighting cop, bartender, and bouncer, he kicked off the annual St. Patrick's Day Parade for New York City's finest. Adorned in plaid kilts with a dirk tucked into his argyle socks and wearing a three-foot-tall, black, bearskin Busby, he proudly led his contingent, waving a five-foot baton to the lively tune of a piper's band. During the summer, he manned the entrance doors to Gildea's, inspecting everybody's ID for proper age and identification.

Frank sat at the bar with a soldier whose khaki uniform sported a blue shoulder patch in the shape of a shield. White wings sprouted from a red circle with the number eleven in its center and the word "airborne" printed above it in capital letters. I worked my way through the crowd and came up behind them. I tipped the soldier's airborne cap, and it slid down onto his nose. The flattop, crew-cut guy whipped around and smiled. It had been almost a year since we had seen each other. "Frank told me what you guys did. Welcome to the club, you crazy bastards," said Bobby, shaking my hand. "Good to see you, Joe."

"You know it's really your fault, Bobby," I said accusingly. "Telling us all those wild stories about jumping out of airplanes and being so bad and looking so good, you really sold us on that jive."

"He's right, Bobby," chimed in Frank. "It is your fault. Joe and I decided to get drafted and volunteer for jump school all because of you."

"You won't be sorry. You'll love it, man. It's great fun. You earn extra money. The uniform is sharp, and the women think you're cool. What else could you ask for?"

Frank looked at me and winked. "I told you we made the right decision, Joe."

Through the bar mirror, I spied three sailors walking through the swinging doors. I didn't know the two tall ones, but the short guy had been the third baseman on our neighborhood team. I waved and made faces in the mirror.

A puzzled sailor looked with uncertainty, and then came a smile of recognition. We turned from the bar and shook hands. "You look fantastic, Jimmy," said Frank, punctuating the word and faking a punch at Jimmy as he put his arm around him.

"This is like a team reunion," Jimmy said to his buddies as he introduced us to them.

"It's been a while, and the navy definitely agrees with you," said Bobby. "Where are you stationed?"

"Our ship's at Norfolk. We got a week's shore leave. You look terrific yourself. So how do you like jumping out of planes?" asked Jimmy, smiling broadly.

"Keeps me in shape," said Bobby modestly.

"How's your brother Ray? He's in the Eighty-Second Airborne, right?

"Yeah, he's doing fine. He's got thirty jumps to his credit, and he loves it."

"Ah, wouldn't mind tryin' that, but I'm 'fraid of heights," drawled one of the sailors, making everyone laugh. The beer and the bullshit flowed as the afternoon wore on. More people kept coming into Gildea's. Soon, we were at a table that grew to two more as some girls from the neighborhood came and joined us.

"Oh, no, I don't believe it," cried Bobby, rising up from his chair with his airborne cap folded over his belt and his dark brown tie tucked through one of the epaulettes on his form-fitting khaki shirt. "Aaa . . . ten . . . shun!" he cried, a little unsteady, trying to be heard above the din of the music.

"At ease, everyone. At ease. As you were," said and saluted the figure in his blue air force ROTC uniform.

"You're out of uniform, soldier," he said and smiled, shaking Bobby's hand to the jeering and laughter that greeted him from the tables. George took a deep bow. He was our great arm, the no-hit, fleet-footed center fielder on our team and a former member of the Seventh Regiment before he had enrolled in Manhattan College as a full-time student and cadet.

"What's it like being a Boy Scout leader?" asked Jimmy derisively, bringing more hoots and howls.

"They think you're an officer and a gentleman?" Bobby smiled.

"Damn right they do. You girls love a man in uniform, right?" quipped George.

"We love you, Georgie Porgie," cried Alice, whose boyfriend was a soldier stationed in Germany. "We think you look beautiful. Don't we, girls?"

Nods and smiles and a loud falsetto, "My hero," came from a tall, redheaded girl who feigned a swoon.

"See, they love me. What can I say? So how are you guys? How was summer camp? How did the regiment do without me?" George asked in rapid-fire fashion.

"We're not in the Seventh anymore," replied Frank nonchalantly.

"Yeah, and I'm in the Foreign Legion," smirked George facetiously.

"It's true," I said. "Frank and I had a chance to get out, and we took it."

George's mouth dropped open. "Get out of here. You're putting me on," he said, causing heads to turn.

"Frank and I quit the Guard."

"Well, you guys can be gung ho and get drafted if you want," crowed George. "If it's all the same to you, I'll just stay at home and spread myself out as best I can for these ladies until you guys get back."

Uncertain laughter cut through the sarcasm. "Man, George, you have no shame," Jimmy said.

"Yeah, none at all," I said, playfully slapping George on the back. "We really appreciate that, George. Don't we, Frank?"

Frank gave a look somewhere between a sneer and a grin, and we turned our attention to the music and the dance floor.

The band played Cohan's "I'm a Yankee Doodle Dandy," and the stirring music brought about an immediate sing-along from the couples already on the dance floor. "Yankee doodle do or die, a real live nephew of my Uncle Sam. Born on the Fourth of July—" The dancers started to savoy, which was a combination of the lindy hop and the jitterbug to the pronounced beat of the martial music. The tables and the room joined the singing, and the place started to rock.

"You're a grand, old flag, you're a high flying flag, and forever in peace may you wave. You're the emblem of . . . the land I love . . . the home of the free and the brave—"

More couples jumped up and bounced their way to the dance floor, keeping to the rhythm and singing along with abandon. Some of the patrons who were standing by the door listening and singing to the music joined in the dancing. There was dancing in between tables and in the bar.

"Pack up your troubles in your old kit bag, and smile, smile, smile. What's the use of worrying? It never was worthwhile. So, pack up your troubles in your old kit bag, and smile, smile, smile."

Gildea's became a menagerie of moving bodies and color. Uniforms and boots mixed with sport shirts, pistol-packin' pegged pants, and blue suede shoes; low-cut sneakers and ballerina slippers joined khaki pants and pedal pushers. It was a swarm of gyrating bodies. Without missing a beat, partners joined the singing and stomping to the beat of the next patriotic song. Gildea's was hopping to the fervor of another war.

"Over there! Over there! Send the word, send the word . . . over there! We'll be over, we're coming over . . . and we won't come back till it's over . . . over there!"

Applause, cheers, and whistles exploded after the last tune. Exhausted and sweating, the band took a well-deserved break, and the jukebox suddenly sprang to life with Johnny Ray's "Little White Cloud that Cried."

"Where do you think we'll be next Labor Day, old buddy?" asked Frank haltingly with his arm draped heavily over my shoulder.

I couldn't resist the pun. "Over there?" I asked impishly.

Frank winced at my response as Tom Davis, one of our I Company platoon sergeants, stood on a chair, all six-foot-four of him, and started singing with imperious dignity. Everything stopped as Seventh Regiment veterans rose to their feet, held up their beer glasses, and sang with gusto.

"Hail to I Company, the flower of the gallant Seventh glittering in gold and gray. We go marching in proud array. Our spirits carry us through the day, unfaltering; though our tasks be mighty . . . We'll win the Day with *toujours pret*, marching on with company I."

"Here's to the Seventh!" shouted Tom. "First in war! First in peace! First in the hearts of our countrymen!" Pouring sweat, we thumped our beer glasses in a staccato bump . . . bump, bump, bump, bump . . . bump, bump. It was a fitting way to end the evening. Frank and I were ready to go.

CHAPTER 4

A GREETING FROM YOUR NEIGHBORS

**Frank and I got the same cryptic message. We were to
report to the induction center on Whitehall Street, the one
across from Battery Park, on the same day. We were being
drafted together:**

Greetings:

Having submitted yourself to a local board composed of your
neighbors for the purpose of determining your availability for service
in the armed forces of the United States, you are hereby ordered to
report to the armed forces induction station at 44 Whitehall Street
at 9:00 a.m. on the 17th day of January 1952 for induction.

> Otto J. A. Grassi
> Member of Local Board

January 17 came soon enough. Leaving the house took
a while. It wasn't as bad as I thought it would be though. My
mom cried and tried to be cheerful, and my dad, not showing any
emotion as always, was calm and practical, asking me how I was
going to get to Whitehall Street. Did I have enough money? All
in all, it was pretty painless.

I hurried up the block to Frank's sister's apartment building.
It wasn't far. We lived on the same street. Smoke billowed

from the doorway. Eyes half-closed, Frank was hunched with a cigarette dangling from his tightly pressed lips. He stamped his feet together and moved from side to side. Both hands were buried into his blue-and-white high school jacket. Two canvas strap handles were cuffed around his right wrist, which was still half in his pocket. His overnight bag tilted upward, exposing its worn, scuffed bottom. "You look like one of those Holy Rollers shaking and baking with the spirit of the Lord," I crowed as I looked up and saw Frank's sister and brother-in-law duck out the window to wave to me. I smiled and waved back.

"About time," he shivered. "What took you so long? You only live down the street."

"Good-byes took longer than expected. I'm four minutes late—big deal," I said, took the stoop two steps at a time, and lit a cigarette from Frank's smoke.

"Let's go," Frank said and flipped his cigarette into the gutter. We bounded off the stoop and turned around and waved back to the two heads that popped again out of the window. Frank's brother-in-law was a World War II combat veteran, and he grinned from ear to ear, giving us the thumbs-up sign.

"Let's get out of here," said Frank, backing away quickly from the sidewalk.

"Jeez, not so fast," I said. "Turn around and look across the street, third-floor window."

Frank looked up and gave a big wave to my aunt Anna, who blew us kisses and threw a crumpled piece of paper out the window that spiraled lazily down to us. I circled under it, which caused cars to stop and honk. Frank used his height to snatch the ball of paper before it hit the ground. I had to smile. Amid the horn honking, Frank never lost his concentration, and his bag hand never came out of his pocket. He flipped the paper ball to me, and I slipped the rubber band off.

Two five-dollar bills were tucked into a folded envelope. The outside message simply said, "Behave and take care of yourselves and have a beer on us." It was signed, "Love, Aunt Anna and Uncle Tom."

We mouthed "thank you" and headed toward York Avenue. We looked the way we had when we had been in high school and walked to Saint Ann's every day. Only then we carried books instead of toiletries in our bags.

"That was nice of them," I said. "How did it go with you?"

"It was rough. My mom was crying, and my father was smiling, proud and teary-eyed. Steve came over to the house last night with Elsie and the kids. They broke out a bottle of Four Roses, and the toasting started. You've been to my house on special occasions. This time, it was to the saints. 'Here's to Saint Anthony. May you always find what you are looking for. Here's to St. Michael. May he bring you victory over your enemies.' This goes on until it's time for the kids to go to bed, and then Steve brings me into my room for a heart-to-heart, brother to brother meeting. He grabbed me by the back of the neck and looked me right in the eye. 'Listen to me. Don't be a hero. Whatever you do, don't volunteer for anything. Be smart. I want you to take care of yourself.' He's got me in Korea already. Sometimes he acts more like a father to me than a brother. I told him to lighten up, that I was only taking the subway downtown, but he didn't think it was funny."

"Come on," I said. "How did you expect him to act? You're his kid brother. He's trying to clue you in. He's a wounded combat veteran. He knows the score. He's ten years older than you."

"Try thirteen," said Frank as we turned into the subway.

"I know how he feels. I'm thirteen years older than my brother too, and I'd do the same thing. He can't help it. He almost lost his leg winning a Bronze Star, and he doesn't want you to get hurt."

"I'll probably end up being a cook stationed in Germany," Frank chuckled.

We changed for the train to Bowling Green, and the platform was packed with guys carrying satchels just like us. When we got to the street, we became part of a mob scene with crowds of guys spilling onto the streets, dodging and stopping traffic. Twenty-year-old New Yorkers were going to 44 Whitehall Street to be inducted into the army for two years of service.

Chattering young men in hooded parkas, checkered lumber jackets, windbreakers, fur-collared bomber jackets huddled in line outside the induction center and waited in the cold. I took out my draft notice with shaking hands to see if there was something I had missed about reporting instructions.

"Hey, Frank, check this out," I said in a loud voice and then read, "These two years constitute a goodly portion of the best years of your younger life—years you cannot buy back for any amount of money. You will realize that as you grow older——"

I couldn't finish with a straight face, and we both had a good laugh over it.

The line moved inside, and the processing began. It took hours. We lined up and urinated in a bottle. We covered one eye and then the other and read from a board chart. We repeated numbers whispered into our ears for our hearing test. We went from station to station and carried our induction papers with us. Frank and I followed each other everywhere. At the section-eight station, I waited outside the curtain and heard Frank's voice say, "What do you mean do I like men? Sure I like men, but I love women."

Frank came out from behind the curtain. He looked at me sternly. "Do you like men, Joe?"

I knew what to expect at this station.

At our last processing station, Frank received his army serial number, US 51160950, and his bus seat number, and his papers were put into a wire basket. I was next in line. I sat down, and a clerk walked by and leaned over me and emptied the contents from the basket. My serial number, US 51160951, began a new basket of documents and a new bus. As much as we had tried to stay together, the act of emptying the basket at that particular time put us on different paths after the induction process. Frank and I were no longer together.

Joe in center in white shirt with Frank in front at birthday party on roof of St. Stephen's School (1944)

8th Grade school graduation (1945) Joe, Jean, Joan & Frank

Yorkville Eagles Joe D.,Frank M. & Jimmy W

7th Regiment N.Y. National Guard (1948)

St. Ann's High School graduation (1949)

Rockaway Beach (1950)

Brother Richard, mom and dad

Teen's graduation from Cathedral High School (1951)

Head on collision driving in Montreal, Canada (1951)

Bungalow porch at Rockaway Beach summer before being drafted

With Aunt Mae week before induction (1952)

PART 2—RECRUITS

CHAPTER 5

BUSES, BARRACKS, AND BRAWLS

Because I had been in the National Guard as a teenager, I had never dreamed that twenty-year-old draftees were nothing more than a bunch of anxious, homesick kids in their first day of the army. They were funny, and they were serious. They were loud, and they were serious. They laughed, cried, and fought over the silliest of things. In my case, the fight was over dropped sheets, a pillow, and some blankets.

Frank was on one side of the induction center, and I was on the other. We waited to be transported to Camp Kilmer for several more days of processing and to receive our assignments to a basic training unit. I had a gut feeling that Frank and I were not going to be together much longer.

"Pop, there's no need to stay. Thanks anyway. Mom, please go home now. Everything is fine."

The dark curly haired recruit seated a few rows ahead of me got up and smiled awkwardly. He was visibly upset. He stole quick glances around to see who was watching.

"You and Mom should go home now. You don't have to be here," he hissed again, looking quickly around him. "I'm good."

The plump lady was holding an umbrella in one hand and a bulging shopping bag in the other. She looked completely oblivious to her surroundings. "Ah, no one will pay a bit of mind," his mother said and smiled reassuringly, looking at her son and then over to her short, bespectacled husband for confirmation.

"For sure, we're fine," he mumbled, nodding his head in assent.

Her forced smiles said it all. She wasn't to be denied. She and her husband were staying put. Inductees filed into the aisles and became instant spectators to the scene. They had to be wondering what kind of a guy would allow his parents to come with him to an induction center. The first day in the army had to be one of the most macho moments in the world. Was this kid nuts?

My section filled up quickly. Two sergeants led us downstairs to charter buses lined up along the sidewalk across the street from Battery Park. Once on board, roll call was taken. I had a chance to test my memory by yelling out my new army serial number. I threw my canvas satchel on the rack over my seat and waited while the head count was taken. The sergeants bounded in and out of the bus several times, checking names and numbers. I chatted with the guy next to me. We sat. We talked, and we waited. *It's just like the National Guard*, I thought. *Hurry up and wait!*

"Michael! Michael! Where are you, Michael?" came a distinct Irish brogue.

Heads turned and brought people up in their seats. A voice mimicked, "Michael, your mommy wants you," and brought an instant outburst of laughter. All eyes went to the woman at the front steps of the bus. Michael leaped from his seat and skipped down the aisle to the front of the bus, and in a desperate voice of exasperation, he exclaimed, "Mom, for cripe's sake, what are you doing? Get off the freaking bus."

"Let her come along," a voice suggested.

"Mommy wants to come to camp!" someone intoned in a little girl's voice, which was followed by hoots and smart-aleck remarks.

Although I felt for the guy, some of the things being said were pretty funny.

"Ah, now, Michael, you forgot your snack and your book," said his mother admonishingly.

"I don't need it. Okay? I don't need it. I don't want it," said Michael, steering his mother impatiently down the aisle toward the front of the bus.

"But you'll be wanting a little something later on," his mother persisted, oblivious to the noise and derision around them.

"It's time to go. Now!" said Michael through gnashed teeth. "I'll call you later."

"Make sure you do now," she warned as the bus driver took her gently by the arm and escorted her off the bus.

Michael whirled around and looked down the aisle. A red face flashed dark blue eyes, and in a halting voice fighting for control, he hissed, "Anybody have a problem with my mother?"

The bus fell silent. All eyes were on Michael.

"We ain't got no problem with your momma," piped the squeaky voice of a recruit slouched low in his seat.

"You got a problem with me then?"

"At ease! At ease, and knock it off! Everybody in your seats and face front," demanded a gruff old sergeant coming onto the bus. He turned to the driver and said, "Okay, let's move."

Twenty minutes into our ride to Camp Kilmer on the other side of the Holland Tunnel, our crusty sergeant stood up, swaying gently with the steady movement of the bus. "We're gonna make a pit stop."

The announcement was met with hoots and loud applause. "You can hit the head and grab some smokes. Fifteen minutes is all you get, so make it quick."

We pulled in behind another one of the other buses. Red and blue neon lights flickered on and off, advertising Pabst, Schlitz, and Rupert Beer. Pictures of models in swimming suits with beautiful white teeth looked out at us from signs reading, "The Smile of Pleasure."

"Remember . . . fifteen minutes."

The energy level in the bus soared. I stepped down into the shadow of two overhanging bridge girders that looked like giant lobster claws ready to pounce and devour the grimy tavern. Recruits formed lines outside the men's and women's rooms.

The smoke-filled bar was packed and smelled of stale beer. Frank came out of one of the toilets. "I had a beer on your aunt and uncle," he grinned as he was moved along by the flow of traffic heading back to the bus.

"Great," I said and smiled. "See you at Kilmer."

The white helmet and belt stood out in sharp contrast to the heavy wool overcoat that fell to the top of polished boots. White-gloved hands pointed us smartly through the gate. Our little convoy of buses formed a line on the macadam and came to a stop. A bevy of olive drab cadre in winter overcoats that looked like glorified horse blankets with brass buttons scurried about to meet us. They reminded me of the chant we used as kids marching on Maypole Day every time we passed a policeman in uniform: "Brass buttons, blue coats, stink like a nanny goat." We thought it was so daring and funny. I found myself singing it to myself as I hurried off the bus and tried to decipher the orders being barked at us.

A steady cadence marched us to our barracks, and we kept skipping steps to keep in step. It wasn't pretty, but for recruits, it was the best we could do. I was assigned a bunk and a bedding number and marched off again, trying to keep in step, to a large, barn-like building of stalls and cubicles where I waited to draw my bedding.

Numbers were called out, "Four-eleven . . . four-twelve." A dozen soldiers worked furiously behind a thirty-foot counter, emptying cubicles and dispensing bundles of bedding. Every man was given a white linen pillow, pillowcase, sheet, mattress cover, and two army blankets.

The next number called was, "Four-thirteen!"

I shouted, "Yo!" and nimbly dodged bodies as I made my way to the counter.

I showed my number and picked up my bedding. Numbers continued to be called. It was a busy scene.

"Hold it," said the soldier. "This isn't yours. He has your bedding. Check his number," he said, pointing to a soldier who had just left the counter with his jaw buried deep in a pillow that lay on top of the pile.

"Hold on!" I said. "I think you have my bedding."

The soldier scowled and eyeballed his tag and said, "Oh sheet, yeah," and dropped the pile of bedding.

I did a double take, staring down at my spilled linen and blankets on the warehouse floor. "Hey you dropped my stuff all over the floor," I said incredulously as he walked back to the counter.

"It's not mine," he shrilled. "It's yours," and he picked up another pile.

"I know it's mine, but *you* spilled it on the floor," I said, trying to keep my voice even.

"Hey, man, it's not my problem."

I stood in front of him, fighting off the anger and indignation I felt welling up inside me. "You're not going anywhere until you pick up my bedding."

"You wish," he scoffed. As he brushed past me, I thrust out my arm and swept the bundle of bedding from his arms onto the floor.

"Mother—" he yowled. A look of utter disbelief turned to rage as he came toward me. "Okay, man, let's go," the soldier snarled, bobbing and weaving like he was Sugar Ray Robinson.

I backtracked, not sure what to do. Was this guy kidding? He took a swing at me, and I went into a crouch. I took a quick step toward him, and the soldier jumped back.

"Come on. What you gonna do?" he taunted.

A circle of recruits formed around us. Some had bedding in their arms and peered over their piles to watch the action and egg us on. Nobody tried to break it up. They were enjoying the bout. It was like being back in the neighborhood and having an old-fashioned street fight, kids yelling and hollering and telling you what to do. I stepped forward again and feinted a punch, my shoulder aimed at his stomach. The soldier dropped his guard, and before he could bring it back up, I swiped my left fist across his mouth and grazed a part of his lip. The soldier touched his face with the back of his hand and saw his own blood. His eyes ballooned wide, and a frenzy of swings sent me scurrying backward and outside of the warehouse. He came after me, and we drew a bigger, noisier crowd.

"Freeze and stand at attention!" commanded a smartly uniformed lieutenant breaking his way through the circle of bodies surrounding us.

We stopped and looked at each other warily, not knowing what to expect.

One of the barrack sergeants came rushing out and saluted the lieutenant.

"Get everyone moving, sergeant, except these two men."

"Okay, break it up, everybody!" said the sergeant, briskly turning the gawking crowd into a disarray of milling soldiers who reluctantly dispersed but didn't wander so far away that they could not see what would happen next.

"What's the matter with you, men?" demanded the lieutenant. "You're still in civilian clothes and behaving like children. Is this any way for soldiers to behave? I could court-martial you two men for this behavior. Do you understand what I'm saying?"

I didn't know if the lieutenant was bluffing or not, but I felt embarrassed enough standing there being scolded like a schoolboy by the principal for fighting in the school yard.

"Sergeant, I want the names of these men. I want them double-timed back to their barracks, carrying their bedding. If they drop anything, give them push-ups and put them on a detail. Maybe I can arrange a little KP for these fearless fighters."

I found a towel tied to the end of my bed when I came back from evening chow. I was on KP for the next day. I would be awakened at four in the morning to report to the mess hall. When I passed the double-deck bunk of my bedding brawl buddy at the entrance to my barrack floor, I didn't see a towel tied to his bed. I wondered if we were on kitchen police together.

The only thing I saw was that he and his friend on the cot beneath him were obnoxious. Sporting nylon stockings pulled tight over their hair, they made silly comments that provoked just about anybody who passed them. Granted, they elicited smiles and a few laughs, but most of the recruits didn't react. They just wanted to be left alone after a long and hectic first day in the army. The talk and laughter were annoyingly loud and became a distraction.

"Hey, give us a break," drew even louder laughter.

"Can it, you guys. I'm trying to write a letter," an annoyed recruit chimed in.

The two friends continued to joke and horse around, oblivious to the requests.

"It's almost lights out. Keep it down," another voice pleaded.

"Oh, let's all be quiet and say our prayers. Ready everybody? Now I lay me down to sleep." And a burst of uproarious laughter and wisecracking followed.

"Shut the fuck up!" cracked like a bolt of lightning through the room. The sudden, harsh words brought a stunned silence to the barrack.

"Oh, that sounds bad" came out low and slow, followed by a harsh, loud, "Why don't you shut the fuck up, man?"

Hairy legs flashed over the side of my top bunk and slowly slid down to the floor. They walked unhurriedly but deliberately over to their bunk. I got up and followed and was joined by several others recruits. The two stocking heads were mesmerized. They lay on their bunks, not moving or saying a word. They just stared at the hairy legs coming toward them. Michael never hesitated, never broke his stride. He went right up to my sparring partner and yanked him from his top bed, sending him crashing hard to the barrack floor.

"Oh, shit. Watch you doin'? Oh, man . . . I'm hurt. What you do that for?"

Michael bared his teeth. "I don't want to hear from you two assholes again tonight. Understand? Not a fucking peep."

There was stunned silence as Michael waited and watched. He turned around, and we followed him calmly to his bunk. Minutes later, our barrack sergeant appeared to announce lights out. I closed my eyes and wondered where he'd been during our little ruckus. He reminded me of the cop on the beat who walked in slow motion to a disturbance in the hope that it would end before he got there. Sleep came quickly. I had kitchen police in the morning.

My eyes shot open. I thought I heard something. I closed my eyes. There it was again. It was a low groan. "I want to go home. Mommy . . . I want to come home."

It was a low-wailing voice. I couldn't tell whether someone was talking or moaning in his sleep. It wasn't coming from my top bunk. It was too dark to see anything.

"Mom, I'm coming home."

Another voice joined in from across the room, and it didn't sound like fooling around. Guys were talking in their sleep. "I miss you, sweetheart. I truly miss you. I love you so much."

"Hey, give us a break for Christ's sake," chimed in another voice.

"Good night, sweetheart. I love you."

"Kiss her good night already. You're waking everybody up."

Giggles were mixed with moans and laughing. I couldn't believe what was happening. I checked my watch, and the luminous dial showed 1:30 in the morning. *I'm wide awake, listening to guys who are talking in their sleep, giggling, crying, and fooling around*, I thought. *They're tired, sleeping in a strange bed, homesick, scared, and cranky.* In the past twenty-four hours, I had been separated from my best friend, had felt sorry for a kid, had been threatened with a court-martial, and had been put on KP to start my second day in the army. Unbelievable!

CHAPTER 6

First Sergeant Knox

Usually, recruits hated basic training, and they dreaded their first sergeants. Strangely enough, I liked both. Memories of my first sergeant were unforgettable. To this day, they still bring a smile to my face. I think of them as "Knox moments."

Lights and loud voices woke everyone up. Bodies unwound and stretched amid yawns and groans. Car doors slid open, and a blast of cold air jolted everyone into gear. A cranky, complaining, disheveled group of recruits hoisted duffle bags onto their shoulders and filed off the train. Vapor-spewing army trucks were lined up in a convoy waiting for us. Through rattling teeth, I answered the roll call, pleased to have remembered my serial number, while a helping hand hoisted me up onto the carrier.

Inside the fort, we took the main road past rows of neat, white, two-story, wooden barracks. Tank Hill was steep and caused us to slide down in our seats and get into each other's face. In the midst of good-natured elbowing and horsing around, our truck grinded to a halt.

"Hit the deck! On the double! Move it out!"

A group of soldiers shouted commands to us from behind the truck. Stiff and chilled, we staggered onto the road, bumping clumsily into one another, trying to make sense of the instructions being barked at us.

A slim, baby-faced, black corporal with an imperious look of importance stood in front of us. The name Bacon was stenciled over his breast pocket. A tall, light-skinned sergeant with a long face and a neatly trimmed mustache stood front and center of the formation, waiting impatiently for everyone to get into place. The command came from deep inside the chest of the tall sergeant. We automatically straightened to attention behind our duffle bags.

"Stomach in. I want your navels to hit your spine. Chest out, and eyes straight ahead," bellowed the tall sergeant.

"Don't move. Freeze!" hissed the stone-faced Bacon in a hushed undertone that reinforced the tall sergeant's order. "Now hold it." Satisfied with what he saw, he swiveled around quickly and executed a smart about-face.

All eyes were fixed on the granite-like figure on the top of the white-painted podium. Squinting eyes moved unhurriedly from one end of the formation to the other. You could hear the silence, it was so quiet.

"At . . . ease!" shattered the drama of the dream-like moment. "Welcome to Fort Jackson, home of the army's Eighth Infantry Division, the Golden Arrow Division. My name is First Sergeant Knox. I am the sergeant of 'B' Battery, which is a training company of the Forty-Fifth Field Artillery. I am the first of all your sergeants. I am the top. I own you. Your soul may belong to God, but here in basic training, your ass belongs to me. And with the help of God, I will make soldiers out of you."

He started out in the staccato voice of a big-city easterner using short, quick sentences and ended up sounding like a Southern preacher on a Sunday morning. "You will be the best trained soldiers in this man's army. You will be proud infantrymen ready for combat, ready to serve your country, and ready to come home to your family and friends when your job is done. It's going to happen here at Fort Jackson with the loving care from your cadre of trainers, who you will address at all times as *suh!* Do you hear me?"

"Yes, suh!" came the response.

"I didn't hear you."

"Yes, suh!" came the deafening roar.

White, even teeth flashed under a prominent nose topped by an unbroken line of dark, bushy eyebrows. A jagged line slashed down the left side of his cheek to his chin. It was hard to tell if the first sergeant was happy, gleeful, or maniacal. He was a cross between the actors Lee Marvin and James Coburn in their prime. He was right out of central casting.

For the next sixteen weeks, Sergeant Knox played the soldier's soldier. He was the star of the show. He could do anything better than anybody else, and he loved to prove it. He demanded excellence in himself, his cadre, and us. Fifty years after basic training, I can still recall the specific incidents of my first sergeant, those "Knox moments."

"I don't like slackers and goof-offs, and I don't like what I saw in the field today, so we're going to fix it . . . now! We're going back into the field, and we're going to do it right. Anybody have a problem with that? I don't hear anything. Anybody have a problem with that?"

"No, suh!" boomed the company in one solid voice.

"Somebody want to disagree?"

From the ranks, hands stayed locked behind backs as heads stared straight ahead. There was no movement. Not a sound was heard from the formation.

"You want to see me later in private, that's okay. You want to go across the road into the woods right now and settle your problem with me man-to-man, that's okay, too."

It was hard not to smile at this theater, but if you did and you got caught, then shit would hit the fan.

"Dresner! Wipe that childish, gooney grin off your pimply face. Now throw it to the ground. Step on it goddamn it! Step on it!" I said. "Grind it into the ground."

Poor Dresner was jumping up and down, crushing and stomping his smile into the ground.

"Faster, Dresner. Faster! Hurry it up before someone rams a size-ten, metal-heeled, spit-and-polished, paratrooper's jump boot up your cotton-pickin' sorry ass!" ordered Knox. "Now get back in rank."

No one moved. Smiles were fought back with determination. No one said a word. If Knox could read our minds—and maybe he could—he knew that every man in the ranks would have loved to see someone step forward and challenge him. I fantasized about the thought of some skinny recruit kicking his ass. To me, Knox was an authority figure to respect. It would have been unthinkable to take him on. It would be like committing a mortal sin. You didn't hit priests, cops, teachers, or first sergeants.

I found out he was a kid from Queens, New York. Rumor had it that he was called "Little Jimmy" at home because he was the youngest in his family. In whispers, the nickname was often used in the company but never to his face. He joined the army in World War II and saw action with the Big Red One Division in Europe. The story going around was that after he was discharged he re-upped and joined the Eighty-Second Airborne Division. After a hitch as a paratrooper, he went into civilian life and worked in construction. I didn't know if he was ever married, but when the Korean War broke out, he reenlisted with the rank of sergeant with the intention of becoming a twenty-year man and retiring with an army pension. Guys respected that, and they respected him.

His philosophy was Darwinian. He believed in the survival of the fittest. Jogging, push-ups, and squat jumps were the key to getting in shape and staying alive. He lived by the credo that to become a good soldier and to make it through combat, you had to be physically fit. Two refrains from basic training will always remain with me: the howling commands of "double-time!" "march!" and "leaning-rest position . . . ho!" Running and push-ups were the name of the game.

Knox's mood changed moment to moment. It was predicated on the complicated love-hate relationship between leaders and followers. When he was tough, we accepted it begrudgingly. When he went overboard, we despised him. When he was fair, we appreciated it and even liked him. He knew how to be human without breeding contempt and how to play the clown without losing respect. He was a leader.

One day in May, I left the mess hall after dinner and started jogging back to my platoon barracks. Shouts of "formation . . . 1900 hours . . . T-shirts and caps" filled the company street.

"What's going on?" I asked a soldier running by.

He turned quickly around and hissed, "Who knows? Fucking Knox has a bug up his ass."

I took the flight of stairs outside our barrack two steps at a time. Inside, I hung my fatigue shirt up and tried to find out what was happening. Nobody knew.

Whistles blew, and the cry of "fall out!" brought us into the company street, and we lined up by platoon in front of our barracks, not knowing what to expect. On the gazebo's podium, wearing a spotless white T-shirt and tailored, faded fatigue pants tucked into spit-shined, cordovan jump boots, was the incomparable "Little Jimmy" Knox.

"Today was not a good day for 'B' Battery. There were too many sick, lame, and lazy. Too many men falling out to the rear and slowing us down 'cause they're tired. Need to know who needs to be motivated. Who needs special attention . . . so we can fix that," he said, jutting and raising his jaw defiantly over the company. "If we're to be the best, we have to work harder. I know that and you know that, so we'll do it together, like a team. It's for our own good. Isn't that right? Let me hear it!"

Everyone shouted in unison. "Yes, sir!"

"One more time!" demanded Knox.

"Yes, sir!"

A tight, sadistic grin played over his mouth. He strutted back and forth. The smile quickly disappeared. "Com . . . pa . . . nee . . . ah . . . ten . . . shun!"

A barely audible moan was lost in the sharp click of boot heels coming together. A long, deafening silence fell over the group. "Cad . . . re . . . dis . . . missed!"

My face dropped in disbelief. It hit me that Knox didn't want to include his non-coms because it was their free time. This was between him and us. It was personal.

Knox gave the lonely commands, "Left face! Forward march! Dub . . . bull . . . time . . . March!"

One hundred and forty crew cuts in tees, fatigue pants, and boots double-timed down to the end of the street and turned right onto a main road. Minutes later, we turned into a secondary road and started passing small, private houses with gardens and nicely kept lawns. I didn't notice the black-and-white sheriff's car until it was cruising along side of Knox, who was jogging proudly in front of his formation. Words were exchanged. I could see Knox's head and arms moving and jerking like a puppet on a string. The patrol car edged in front of him, and the rear door flew open. Knox ducked his head and hopped inside. The car shot ahead, stopped, made a U-turn, and then passed us by.

A roar went through the company. We were now a leaderless, smiling, unstoppable juggernaut of motion. When we came to a fork in the road, a thin, piercing voice cried out from up front in the ranks. "I don't know, but I've been told," an energized company repeats the refrain.

"Stay to the right, and you'll never go wrong."

"Stay to the right, and you'll never go wrong," comes out in laughter and loud guffaws. The company never looked better, smiling and jogging in unison along a quiet, country road to who knew where.

A second unknown voice asserted itself, "I don't know, but I've been told."

An echo bellowed, "I don't know, but I've been told."

"Our first sergeant is a big asshole."

"Our first sergeant is a big asshole," brings a burst of cheers and laughter.

The shrill wail of the sheriff's siren brought me back to reality. It sped past the columns and slowed to a crawl at the head of the company. It was what I imagined jumping out the door of an airplane would be like. First, the head appeared, and then a crouched body leapt out of the car door. Paratrooper boots hit the road, picking up the step of the jogging troops. There was instant recognition and admiration. One hundred and fifty pairs of hands clapped. Men whistled and cheered while they double-timed in step as if nothing had happened. A new cadence swept through the buoyant ranks. "Left, right, left" became "Knox, Knox, Knox."

It was a typical "Knox moment," an unpredictable, unrehearsed scene, a smooth, final take for the cameras.

Shortly after our evening jog through that delightful small community of country homes, where Sergeant Knox had almost gotten himself arrested, I experienced another one of Knox's moments that brought pride and recognition to our company.

We were pumped up for the day of our Third Army physical-training tests. It was our last week of basic training. Knox had us convinced that we were the best rookie company in Fort Jackson, and we were eager to prove it to him. The battery of PT tests we were given were varied and brutal and performed on an exceptionally warm day at the end of May.

Sweat rolled down my face and soaked through my shirt. I had just finished the last exercise and gratefully flopped down on the ground and waited anxiously for the last guys to come in. Scores were being posted on chart boards. Corporal Bacon, Sergeant Anderson, and Sergeant Harris scurried from table to table, checking tabulations and conferring with Sergeant Knox. Our cadre assisted in the testing and scoring of performance along with Third Army personnel. Notes were compared, checked, and rechecked. Their body language told us that something was happening. Suddenly, Sergeant Knox and a master sergeant wearing the circled patch insignia of the Third Army got into a heated discussion. A red-faced Knox stormed over to us in exasperation.

"All right, now listen up, men." All eyes went to Knox. "I have good news, and I have bad news," he growled. "The good news is that you broke the physical training record for the entire Third Army area." Hoots and howls were silenced with a raised arm. "The bad news is that they don't believe you. You're going to have to do it all over again. They want to do it tomorrow. I want to do it now. I know you're bushed. I know you're hurting, but goddamn it, nobody . . . nobody calls me a liar. And nobody calls my men cheaters. We broke this record fair and square, and they don't believe it. The scores are too high to be right, so they're bringing in more scorers. I don't know who they think they are, but we'll show them who we are. We are 'B' Battery, the best training company in Fort Jackson. We're going to go out there and do it again, no matter who keeps score. Just one more time, men," snarled Knox, pausing and gazing slowly around at the men sitting on the ground in rapt attention. "One more time," he whispered.

This was a Knox moment, and nobody seized it any better than he did. It was pure shtick. The reaction was explosive. "One more time . . . one more time" became a chant and drew the looks and attention of the Third Army cadre. Like a screaming wave of banshees, we attacked the exercise course. High on adrenaline and bursting with energy, we grunted and moaned as we shimmied up poles, did pull-ups, climbed ladders, ran with sweat pouring down our faces until we shattered our last scores. We broke our own unofficial physical-training record, bringing polite applause and apologies from our stunned detractors. There was no question about our performance level. First Sergeant Knox had accomplished his mission. We were the most physically fit company in Fort Jackson, motivated and prepared for the hardships of combat.

His face was set hard. It was a dissimulating look blending both rage and pride. Knox was pissed and seven feet tall. He didn't know whether to shit or go blind. We jumped like jacks-in-a-box to his bellowing roar. We snapped to attention, responding to the moment by marching our aching bodies past the scorer tables, giving them a surprised and resounding "eyes right!" which clearly translated itself to "up yours," and another "Knox moment" was etched in my memory for a lifetime.

CHAPTER 7

CRIME AND PUNISHMENT

In basic training, the rules were simple. You did good, and God would reward you through your first sergeant. You did bad, and God would punish you through your first sergeant. Case closed.

The word going around was that Knox would be holding a meeting in the field and that he was ballistic. We had been on the range in the midst of a long, hard day setting up, aiming, and firing 80-millimeter mortars when the dastardly deed had been discovered.

"I want to know who did it. I want the man or men to come forward and to admit what they have done. I want them to apologize to the company and to take their medicine like men. I want to know who shat on the range," fumed a livid Knox.

The moment of silence lasted for minutes. I bit the inside of my cheek, feeling a smile coming on. Someone or some of the guys had shat out in the field. It was hard to believe. I wasn't sure if I was reacting to the absurdity of the moment or nervousness from seeing Knox so pissed off.

"If no one comes forward, then we all pay. We are a company that has been disgraced," he rasped, his voice shaking. "Somebody shit on us! Do you understand that? Somebody shat on me. They shat on you, and they shat on our company . . . on 'B' Battery . . . Forty-Fifth Field Artillery . . . the Golden Arrow.

They shat on the US Army! I want him or them to come forward now before we leave this site. Do I make myself clear?"

We were stunned into silence. Did Knox really expect anybody to come forward and confess to what had been done? I didn't think so. Either nobody knew who the guy or guys were, or if anybody knew, they weren't going to say anything. The guys themselves were probably scared shitless, too afraid to come forward. So what would we do now? In Knox's eyes, a crime had been committed, and it had to be paid for. The question was how? The answer didn't take long in coming.

We lined up outside the mortar pits, waiting to fill our steel pots with sand. When our helmets were filled, we individually quick-timed to the spot where the feces was discovered and dumped sand on it. We then double-timed back to the pits, which were hundreds of feet away, to refill our steel pots with sand. One hundred and sixty helmets of sand hustled to and fro. We did this over and over and over again. Knox was wild-eyed. I never saw him like that before.

"We keep doing this until I find out who it was," said Knox with a menacing grin. "If you know who it is, you owe it to yourself, to your buddies, and to the company to tell me."

The situation had been blown out of all proportion. Now we were all getting resentful. We were sweating and cursing, climbing up this dune of sand that was being created on top of this pile of shit that was buried and gone. We became robotic dumpsters. The pyramid of sand had now grown to a height of six feet, and it was fast becoming a monument to a shitter or shitters. Back and forth, back and forth, we would double-time to fill our steel pots with sand and then double-time and empty them. We did this until there was a ten-foot pyramid of clean, white sand standing as a monument to the sin of filth. It was clear that Sergeant Knox saw it as the deadliest of all sins. He was determined to get his man. From the bitching and moaning that was going on, most of us were beginning to agree with Knox. Why didn't the little shitter come forward and save us from this unnecessary, embarrassing nonsense? At twelve feet, he called a halt to our burgeoning mountain and gathered the company around him.

"I'm sad for what's going on here," he intoned solemnly, although I didn't detect any tears rolling down his cheeks. "We're at the end of our training on the way to being the best battery of trainees in all of Fort Jackson, and we've been reduced to coolie labor. For what!" asked Knox. "Paying for another man's wrong? It's not fair to you. You men deserve better. If they were men, they would come forward. If they were good buddies, they wouldn't do this to you. They're only thinking of themselves. They're willing to have you pay the price for what they've done. Think about that. I want those boys to become men and to take their medicine like men. I'm waiting, gentlemen."

After several minutes of suspenseful silence, he continued, "Okay, if that's the way you want it, helmets, T-shirts, and rifles on the double, and fall in!"

We made a mad dash to where our rifles laid across our helmet liners in squad rows. We stripped off our fatigue shirts, quickly slung our rifles, put our liners inside our steel pots, and lined up at attention. Sergeant Anderson, Corporal Bacon, and other cadre marched our platoons in a column of four with our nine-pound M-1 rifles raised above our heads. Sergeant Knox raced to the front of the company, carrying an 80-millimeter mortar in his arms. He looked deranged as he balanced the fifty-plus-pound mortar tube over his head and shouted the infamous words, "Dub . . . bull . . . time . . . march!"

He led us out of the range and across the main road into the woods. We followed him up a steep hill, our legs buckling and out of sync. The nine-pound rifle seemed to triple in weight as my arms started to waver and shake and come down involuntarily.

Drill instructors screamed at us to keep our rifles straight up over our helmets. Sweat rolled down my face and stung my eyes. My nose itched, and my eyes burned. Soldiers were called out of their ranks to do squat thrusts as punishment for not keeping their arms above their heads. Squat thrusts with rifles over your head were the most strenuous and difficult punishments. This meant holding your rifle over your head while jumping up and genuflecting in place. As one knee hit the ground, you leaped up immediately and came down with your other knee hitting the ground. You had to yell out the count. When you reached ten, you had to run to catch up to the column, take your place, and fall into step with the rest of the company.

Ranks in the company would bunch up from time to time. Guys banged into each. Others stumbled and fell, causing mayhem. "This is bullshit," I said to no one in particular, and I stopped. I didn't even try to jog in place. I waited for the guys to untangle themselves. Suddenly, from behind, I got my bell rung hard. A helmet slammed down onto mine. My head exploded from the vibrations of steel crashing into steel. "Fuck!" I yelled, and I swung my arm around. I thought someone was trying to be funny. "Keep your fucking hands to yourself!" I shouted angrily, looking into the stunned face of Corporal Bacon.

"Drop out, Donohue. Give me twenty squats, and you be insubordinate. Insubordinate," he snarled in his high, soft voice.

"Just keep your hands off of me." I tried to control the quiver in my voice. Of all the goddamn people I had to mess with, I ended up with Bacon. He was the leanest, sharpest, spit-and-polish soldier in the company. He was a superb gymnast and athlete. Under six feet tall, he was the strongest 140 pounds of muscles I had ever met. He challenged us to beat him during the Third Army physical-training tests, running the fifty-yard dash backward while we sprinted forward. He would do push-ups on his index fingers. He was an agile, vain prima donna in perfect condition.

I was in trouble. Some guys shat on the range, and I was going to pay for losing my cool in an out-of-control situation that was straight out of the Bataan Death. I was going to pay because I thought being punished for someone else's crime was bullshit.

CHAPTER 8

INTEGRATED JUSTICE

IN THE SEGREGATED SOUTH

I was punished by a black corporal who had to ride in the rear of the same bus that I took to go into the city of Columbia, South Carolina. In 1952, the army was integrated, but the South wasn't. Race was like the elephant in the corner. Everyone knew it was there, but they tried not to pay attention to it.

I knew it was coming. I just didn't know when. I was going to pay for my little altercation with Corporal Bacon after I had been clonked on the head by his helmet during our crazy, chastising run through the pine woods of South Carolina. Despite the chaotic situation, I didn't think he would understand my emotional state by telling him to literally "fuck off."

"Joe, you're wanted downstairs in Corporal Bacon's room."

The voice out of nowhere brought home reality. I shuddered, but I was glad to get it over with. The thought of what was going to happen to me was driving me crazy. I was apprehensive but relieved at the same time. I took a deep breath and knocked on his door and barked, "Private Donohue asking permission to enter, sir!"

It was several moments before the door opened. My heart was pounding. The door swung open. Bacon stood there with his stern black face contrasted sharply against his spotless white T-shirt, which was molded to his prizefighter's torso. Crisp, iron-pressed gray fatigue pants barely touched black Japanese zori slippers. An army manual was cradled in his arm as if it was the holy Bible and he was a preacher ready to give a sermon. I stood motionless at attention, surprised to see Sergeant Anderson behind Corporal Bacon, relaxing in a chair tilted against the wall.

"At ease, Private Donohue," said Bacon in a squeaky whisper, looking me straight in the eye. "Come in." I entered, grateful for the chance to break eye contact. I wondered if I looked as scared as I felt.

"I could court-martial you, Donohue," he said bluntly. He came right out with it. "What you did yesterday was insubordination. Swinging at your drill instructor and talking back in a threatening manner is a very serious offense. Sergeant Anderson here is a witness to what happened and to the conversation in this room. He agrees with me. I am duly apprising you of your misconduct under the US Code of Military Justice. What is your say to that?"

"Sir, Sergeant Anderson was not present when you hit me with your helmet. Sir, I did not swing at anybody. I raised my arm to protect myself."

"Come on, private. I saw what happened. I could see the whole damn thing," said Sergeant Anderson in a huff. "It was no way proper for you to act the way you did."

"Sir, it wasn't proper for Corporal Bacon to bang his helmet on top of mine."

"You stopped running soldier, and with all that was happening, Corporal Bacon tried to get your attention. Your swearing and swinging at your drill instructor was uncalled for. It was unnecessary. It was insubordinate . . . clearly."

I looked at Anderson in disbelief and then at Bacon. Were they kidding? Where did Anderson come in on this? I never saw him there. I didn't like what was happening. Was I being set up?

"Look," I said, "Plain and simple, you hit me with your helmet. I stopped running because there were guys in front of me who had fallen down. That's no reason to whack me."

Bacon quickly turned a page and then another and another, tracing with his finger until he triumphantly announced in his alto voice, "Here we go. The uniform code of military justice defines being hit as . . . closing of the fingers . . . striking with force."

"I never said you hit me with your fist. I said that you hit me with your helmet. The point is that you hit me. You admit it yourself!"

"Okay, okay." says Anderson, "Simple enough. The book says you weren't physically assaulted. You were tapped on top of your helmet with another helmet, and you reacted inappropriately by taking a swing and cursing at Corporal Bacon. Now that's a fact, and that's a big deal. That's a serious court-martial offense. The way I see it, we can go there, or keep it here," said Sergeant Anderson, looking judiciously at Corporal Bacon and me. "I'm thinking barracks discipline with a warning on your record."

Bacon took the prompt and looked at me discerningly. "Considering it's your first time in trouble and you're soldierin's good, I could consider a break. You have to shape up. Be on your best behavior. Any sign of trouble or bad attitude would go against you. I didn't hit you, Donohue. Sergeant Anderson here will testify to that. Right, Earl?"

"Right, Ross," echoed Anderson. "Saw the whole thing. Donohue swung at you."

"And a court-martial don't set good with your getting into jump school." Bacon smiled knowingly.

An awkward silence followed that comment. I could see my plans for meeting Frank at Fort Benning and getting airborne going right out the window. I could feel the tension in the room. It was as if things were moving in on me and the room was getting smaller. Here were two black noncommissioned officers, drill instructors, God in the eyes of recruits, paying too much attention to me. Why? I looked at Bacon, who was looking at Anderson, and thought I detected a glimpse of uncertainty in their faces. Something was going down that I wasn't getting.

In the few months since I'd been in Columbia, my eyes had been opened to a lot of things. It was not the same learning about the Civil War, segregation, and civil rights in class as it was to learn about it firsthand. I remember the brawl we had on the chow a few weeks into basic training. The soldiers were from another company. Most of the guys in my company came from New York and Ohio. The other companies had more Southern soldiers. It started with comical remarks about accents and drawls, went into bantering, and ended with slurs about Yankees, Rebels, and Negroes. I thought it was all in good fun until it turned nasty. Words turned into shoving and pushing, and we ended up fighting the Civil War all over again.

The first time I took a bus into the city of Columbia, the driver refused to move until I came to the front of the bus and sat in a proper seat. When I got off the bus and asked for directions from a black man old enough to be my grandfather, he removed his hat and bowed his head. When he spoke to me, he stepped off the sidewalk into the gutter and hardly looked at me. Downtown, there were separate bathrooms, fountains, and eateries for Negroes.

I couldn't help but think that maybe I was caught up in a race situation with Corporal Bacon and Private Donohue. I now understood that I lived and trained on an integrated army base in a segregated city where there were different rules for blacks and whites. One Sunday afternoon on post, I saw black soldiers turned away from a dance by GI chaperones from the Dixie Division after buses of young ladies arrived from a local college. The chaperones had said there was no more room in the hall, but my buddies and I had gotten in with no trouble at all.

The reality was that the vestiges of the Civil War were stamped on the city's streets. Iron plaques on the sidewalks memorialized the fire and destruction of the city caused by General Sherman's march. I ate in restaurants and walked in parts of the city where Corporal Bacon or Sergeant Anderson would not be welcomed. I was sure they had considered the possible consequences, namely how it would look to a court-martial committee in a Southern state that had fired the first shot in the Civil War at Fort Sumter trying a case of a black drill instructor assaulting a white private during basic training.

"So what do you want to do?" the booming voice snapped me out of my reverie. Anderson was now on his feet, looking down at me with a questioning look. I liked Anderson. He was a regular guy and very popular with the troops. He was a combat veteran and well respected. He was older than Bacon and seemed like an odd sidekick. I had the impression that he was kind of acting like a big brother to him.

"You don't have to think it over. It's a no-brainer. It's either a court-martial or company punishment. You're a smart kid. You went to college."

I thought Anderson was pressing a little too hard. I could see he was getting impatient. I thought he might be more anxious and annoyed with himself than with me. He didn't look comfortable in the role he was playing. He looked like he wanted to be somewhere else.

"You know what I'm goin' to do Earl? I'm goin' to give Donohue here a break," he said, coming over to me and smiling. "I'm goin' to make his decision for him. He knows he's done wrong, but I'm goin' easy on him. I'm not going to put him up on charges. He's gonna do punishment. He's gonna peel paint. Gonna scrape off the shower walls of this barracks with this." Bacon walked over to a dirty mess tray on a side table next to his cot and produced a stainless steel knife from the mess hall. "This will be your tool for Saturday's work party, and no weekend pass."

"You're lucky, Donohue," said Anderson, shaking his head like he couldn't believe what he had just heard. "You one lucky soldier," he repeated. "Anybody else and you would have been court-martialed. Corporal Bacon could have thrown the book at you."

I stood there with a resigned look on my face and slowly shook my head. I knew it was bullshit, and so did they. They didn't want it to go to a court-martial because it would draw attention to them, so they tried to scare me. Bacon had to do something to save face. All the guys in the barracks would be watching to see what would happen.

I wondered if Sergeant Knox knew about this. Somehow, I didn't think so, because he would have gotten involved if he had known. I was about to ask but thought better of it. I knew what they had in mind. I didn't know what would happen if it went to a court-martial. I would fight the charges and bring in my own witnesses. It would escalate. There could be things drawn into play that I couldn't imagine. It could blow up out of control. From what I could see, they had more to lose than I did. How certain were they that justice would be done in an army that had been segregated up to 1948? Who had more to lose? Their careers could be affected. What could they do to me? I was a buck private. Were they going to bust me to a civilian?

Basic training would be over in a couple of weeks, and the only thing that would really hurt me was not being able to go to jump school. I had my heart set on that. I didn't want to push the envelope. Bacon looked at me, waiting for my reaction. I wasn't going to thank him if that was what he was expecting.

"If that's my punishment, then that's what I'll do," I said resignedly. "As long as we understand each other," I said, trying to convey that I knew the score and hoped that my response didn't come off too lamely. I was getting screwed for blowing my cool at someone else's indiscretion. I was paying for it, going without a weekend pass, and scraping paint off a flaking shower wall with a dinner knife.

"I think we do understand each other," said Bacon with a relieved smile. "We understand each other just fine, don't we?"

Justice had just been served. A white northerner had been found guilty by two black noncommissioned officers in the segregated South. Until a few months ago, prejudice, discrimination, segregation, and racism were words that I had read about in the newspaper. Now I was a part of a personal and ugly confrontation that could jeopardize my hooking up with

Frank at Fort Benning. I understood Corporal Bacon. I got the message. I took my sentence and my punishment without making a big deal out of it. I kept my mouth shut. My case was closed. I was glad that I was at the end of my basic training. I could only have imagined what it would have been like to have had Corporal Bacon as my enemy for those sixteen weeks. As it turned out, everything ended well.

During our last week of basic training, a curious event took place. One late afternoon, we were unexpectedly loaded onto trucks to take us to our training site. This was odd because the preferable mode of transportation was marching, so it was a bit of a break from our normal routine. We off-loaded in the woods not far from our barracks where the road had become little more than a trail extending into a pine forest. We hiked to what could debatably be called a clearing and were given specific instructions. We unbuckled our cartridge belts and folded them down on the ground in front of us. We removed our helmet liners and leaned our rifles across them. We moved out in single files by squads along a crude path to a barnlike structure in the middle of nowhere. Now my curiosity was piqued. I saw the barn doors open up, and Knox stepped out with a cigar in his mouth. "When the Saints Come Marching In" was blaring from a record player inside.

"Step lively, men, and find your tables. Refreshments will be served shortly."

Wearing aprons and big grins, cadre manned trays of food with a cigar-smoking Anderson and smiling Bacon sitting on wooden kegs and pouring beer into Styrofoam cups. It was a shocker, a complete psychological turnabout. How could a surprise party to celebrate graduation from basic training be given by all-knowing, mother-loving, by-the-book, soldier-taunting drill sergeants for lowly, cotton-picking, city-slicker, dumb-ass privates? It wasn't possible. It was pure Knox.

The fun lasted into the evening. One of the party highlights was seeing the tough, little Sergeant Harris, a jet-black, Southern, World War II and Korean combat veteran bopping to Bill Haley and the Comets' "Rock Around the Clock" only to be joined by

Private Murray, a dark-haired Jewish twin from Brooklyn. Their wild swinging and jitterbug romping, with guys bouncing around clapping, stomping, and roaring the words to a rock 'n' roll beat, brought the house down. The day ended in "can you top this?" bull sessions at each table interrupted by intermittent songs and boisterous laughter.

The needle came off of the record. The knock-it-off voices of our cadre demanded silence and brought the room to a halt. "Gentlemen, the party is over," Knox announced in a slightly slurred voice. "I speak for all your drill sergeants and cadre trainers when I say congratulations for a job well done. You trained hard. You took everything we threw at you . . . and more. On the physical-training course as well as the rifle range, and in the heavy weapons pits, you broke all kinds of Third Army scoring records. You proved yourselves. On Saturday, the lead training company in the parade will be 'B' Battery Forty-Fifth Field Artillery, the best goddamn graduating infantry company in Fort Jackson."

The place erupted with a burst of hoots and hollering. Knox held up his arms and quieted everyone down. "Saturday, we're all going our different ways—airborne, mountain-climbing school, whatever. After that, most of you will go to the Far East Command in Korea. That's a fact. Remember what you've learned here. Fire your weapons. Keep them clean. Keep your eyes open and your butts down, and you'll be fine. Wherever you go, be a team like you were here."

A slow grin spread across Knox's face. He held it and looked over the room before he spoke again. "It's important that you know that I know," he said, again pausing for effect, "who shat on the range!"

The hall broke out in wild cheers and applause. Knox again raised his hands above his head. "I found out on my own, and it will stay with me." There was a loud groan as Knox continued, "I will personally see to it that this traitor to our battery will be punished in a way that he wished he had never been born," he said in a low, quivering voice.

68

"Now on your feet and grab a drink!" ordered Knox.

Chairs scraped the floor as the entire room stood up.

"A toast to you," said Knox. "Good luck! God bless, and may we meet again."

"Hear, hear!" roared the troops.

In this crazy, leader-follower, love-hate relationship, love definitely won out.

Although the basic training party was over, a gratifying incident occurred the following week on the day before graduation. A twilight softball game after chow became an enduring and fond memory of my last moments at Fort Jackson. I was playing second base when Corporal Bacon hit a single and then decided to stretch it into a double to show off his speed. Don Grauweiler, who was playing center field and also happened to have been a minor league ballplayer with a great arm, rifled a perfect throw just to the right of the bag, where I caught the ball and swiped my glove across the bag, slapping Bacon smack in the face as he was sliding into second. He was stunned as I whipped the ball around the infield like it was a routine play. Bacon got up slowly, holding his nose, and if looks could kill, I would have been a dead man. It was a wonderful moment. I knew I would cherish that for the rest of my life.

Graduation was an emotional day. Our training unit received a number of awards. I was a member of our company's honor guard during the ceremonies, and we marched for the last time as a group in Saturday's parade. The excitement was catching. We felt good, and we looked sharp. Marching behind the band playing a Sousa medley was something special. As I passed the reviewing stand, the command "eyes right!" was given, and I realized how tough it would be saying good-bye to these guys. I didn't know if it was sadness or love. I knew it wasn't hate. I was looking forward to seeing Frank at Fort Benning and beginning paratrooper training, but I never thought I would be leaving Fort Jackson and "Little Jimmy" Knox with such sad and tender feelings.

CHAPTER 9

WAITING FOR FRANK

Frank finished basic training a week ahead of me and went home for a week's furlough. I went straight to Benning. I wrote him a letter telling him I thought we had a good chance of being in the same airborne class. I told him that I wasn't looking forward to jumping out of airplanes by myself in very descriptive, bawdy language. When he finally did arrive, I didn't expect him to bring me such upsetting news from home. Now he gave me other things to worry about more than just jumping out of planes.

The first thing that struck me on the bus ride from the Columbus train station was the suffocating heat. The other thing was that it was such a macho soldier's town. Crew cuts were everywhere. They dominated the streets. Colorful T-shirts proudly proclaimed airborne, sky soldiers, rangers, or some other exotic branch of service.

Shoeshine stands were busy with boot blacks, slapping cloths on boots and shoes. Sporting goods stores, used car lots, pawnshops, diners, and bars catered to the needs of garrison soldiers and their families. Dry cleaning stores seemed to be on every street. Starched dress shirts hung on racks displayed in store windows. Creased summer uniforms and crisply laundered fatigues showed off their golden chevrons, stripes, and patch designs to the outside world. You couldn't help but feel the excitement of downtown Columbus.

I felt a rush when the bus went through the gates of Fort Benning. White-gloved MPs saluted smartly and waved us through the entrance under an arch that read, "Welcome to Fort Benning. The finest soldiers in the world pass through these gates." I wished Frank had been here to see this.

Inside the gates, my excitement mounted. It was a military wonderland. Bareheaded trainees in baggy fatigue pants double-timed to a sergeant's singsong cadence. "Left . . . left . . . left . . . left, right, left. Who are we?" asked the sergeant.

"Airborne!" replied the troopers.

"Airborne who?" pressed the sergeant.

"Airborne all the way!" cried the troopers.

"Are we gonna jump?" demanded the sergeant.

"Yes, sir!" came the reply.

"Without a chute?" asked the sergeant.

"No, sir!" came the response.

"All the way?" asked the sergeant.

"Yes, sir, all the way!" shouted the troopers.

The humorous exchange brought smiles to several riders in the bus, including me. From my window, I could see parachutes in the distance being slowly drawn up to the top of a cross-beamed, circular dome by an invisible puppet master. When the parachutes were hauled up to the top and their canopies touched the dome, they collapsed momentarily only to inflate once again and float gently down to the ground. It looked very much like the "Parachute Jump" at Coney Island. Here the chute was airborne and didn't mechanically come straight down.

We passed open sheds, and I saw soldiers grasping bundles to their chests as they jumped off two-foot platforms onto sawdust-thickened floors. A little later, I caught a glimpse of a hovering helicopter dangling a jeep by a cable hook. This was a place of continual movement and action. *Frank would love it here*, I thought. *Where the hell is he?* I had to write a letter to my girlfriend, Teen, and share this with her:

June 12, 1952

Dear Honey Child,

Well, I have arrived in Georgia and what a lucky state. Just think. They now have me. I'm afraid New York will have to wait until I come home.

The truth is, Teenie, the stories I hear down here, I'm scared to death. I know you're shocked to hear that, but just imagine me. I'll have some consolation with Frankie coming down here, though—excuse the shaky writing—the guy up above me is a very restless sleeper. He's either thinking of the 250-foot tower or the 1,200-foot jump, the sissy.

I bet ole Rockaway is jumping now. I hope I can get home for some part of the summer, but I guess I'll be lucky to get home for Christmas. It looks like I may have to send you a picture, or you'll forget what I look like. Ouch! I hear that comment. Just because they shaved my head! (That's the truth.) No wise remarks please.

My greatest enemy down here is the heat. I've only been here three days now, but it has hit a hundred degrees or more every day so far. The natives tell me that this is nothing. You can get sunburned by eight o'clock, scalded by nine o'clock, and in the hospital by ten o'clock and probably lose thirty pounds as well.

Oh, I forgot to mention the fact that the first and second platoons of my basic training B Battery guys went to Korea, or did I tell you that in my last letter? I think maybe I did now. When I think of all my buddies home on leave and you, I wish I was there. It seems like years since I've been home. I try not to think of it, but I just can't help it. When Frank comes down and starts shooting his mouth off about New York, I think I'll slug him.

Are you finished with school yet? I hope you make it all right.

How's my girl, Mary? Did she or didn't she? What did she have? What's the scoop?

Give my regards to everyone and be good. I've got KP tomorrow, so I'll be saying good night.

Love,
Joseph

After writing the letter to my girl, I walked over to the Airborne Gardens, a tavern on post. It was more like an old German beer garden back in Yorkville rather than a bar on a military base. The Gardens looked out onto a veranda that was surrounded with white rose-trellis fences and planted flowers. I expected potbelly bartenders in lederhosen, wearing high wool socks and feathered fedoras.

Sitting in the shade of a tree and drinking beers were two old friends from the Seventh Regiment back in Manhattan.

"*Toujour pret!*" I yelled with delight.

Mike Rice and Jack Squizzy were flabbergasted. All smiles, they leaped up, and we pummeled each other. It was unbelievable. Who would have thought that buddies from the Seventh Regiment Armory in New York City would be sitting at the same table in the Airborne Gardens in Georgia going to jump school?

Mike and Squizzy were like the Mutt and Jeff cartoon characters. They were always together. Mike was taller, a little older, and more laid-back, a blond, balding, long drink of water. Squizzy was short, dark, and a bundle of energy. They joined the army and were lucky enough to have stayed together through basic training and now jump school. They were delighted to learn that Frank was on his way to Benning. We bullshitted and drank beer for the rest of the afternoon.

The next day was Sunday. I went straight to the mess hall after mass, hoping that Frank may have come in last night. On the chow line, I couldn't help noticing the soldier ahead of me. His arm was in a sling and a bandage wrapped around his neck. I overheard a couple of guys knowingly talk about what had happened. The conversation was grim. They talked about jumping and tangled static lines, nasty neck burns from flapping risers after the opening shock of an unfolded parachute. A twinge of fear tugged in my gut. I wondered if I had bitten off more than I could chew.

Someone mentioned that a new batch of trainees had come in last night. My spirits soared. I knew Frank was here. I just knew it. I scanned the room from wall to wall. There was no sign of him. I stepped out of line and looked in the back. He wasn't there. My heart sank down to my boots. I didn't want to go near the thought that he wasn't here. I walked along the line and breathed a sigh of relief. His big head poked out above the rest. I was giddy. I could barely contain myself. I took a deep breath and tried not to run. I walked up behind him.

"Where the hell have you been?" I asked sternly.

We shook hands and pounded each other on the back like a couple of morons.

"I got in last night. I'm in Company E. They told me I'm in the next training cycle."

"We're together. Class 49-52," I said, beaming. "Frank, I can't tell you how glad I am to see you. I didn't want to go through this by myself, but I met two guys from the Seventh. Mike Rice and Jack Squizzy are here. There in a different company but the same cycle of training. We'll go through training together."

"That's great," said Frank. "We're going to have a ball." And then he stopped smiling. His face grew serious, and he started to talk in a low, apologetic tone. "Joe, your mother read the letter."

I looked at him for a moment, still smiling, and then the realization of what he had said brought shock to my face. I shook my head in disbelief. "Can't be," I said. "I sent the letter to you at your home address. You're putting me on," I said, looking at him expectantly.

Frank winced and looked straight at me. "No, it's true," he said, shifting his eyes away from mine. "She read it."

"What do you mean she read it?" I exploded. "How could she read it?" I asked demandingly.

"Look, I'm sorry, Joe."

"What do you mean you're sorry?" I rasped, almost losing my voice. "I wrote that letter to you. How did my mother get it?"

"You know my mom's English isn't good. She can hardly speak it, never mind read it. She got your letter in the mail while I was on my way home from Fort Knox. My mother puts the letter in her pocketbook and goes to the food store. Guess who's in the store? Yes, your mother. My mom gets all excited and tells her in her broken English that I'm coming home and that she just got a letter from you. She knows we're supposed to go to Fort Benning together, so she takes the letter out and hands it to your mother and begs her to open it."

"And my mother read it? I don't think she would do that," I said uncertainly.

"My mother would," said Frank sympathetically. "She would think that she would be sharing something special between the two of them from us. She would be insistent. She meant no harm. She would be happy. Look, it was a freak encounter. It shouldn't have happened, but it did. I'm sorry, Joe."

"What did my mother say? Do you know?"

"I don't know. She said that you were waiting for me to begin jump school together. That was it. No big deal."

"What am I going to do? What can I tell my mom? I never used language like that at home. I'm disgraced."

Frank shrugged. "Look, what are you going to do? That's the way soldiers talk," he said fatalistically, a slow grin playing across his face as he reread the letter in his head. "I thought that was the funniest, foulest letter I ever read. I thought it was a pisser. It was witty and ugly, and I laughed like hell. I enjoyed it."

"You would. Thanks a lot, but where does that leave me? It's okay for you, but I have to go home and face my mother. It's not my father so much but my mother. Man, what am I going to do? I can never go home again," I said, only half joking.

A flash of the letter shot through my mind. The opening alone was revolting. It was a clue to the rest of the trash talk: "Hey, you fucking chicken-hearted asshole, where the fuck are you? Have

75

you changed your pissy-shit little mind, you gutless wonder? Here I am sitting in this hot, humid, hellhole of a day room, sweating my ass off, waiting for you while you're home getting laid."

I shuddered thinking how the letter only got worse as it went on. How would I ever be able to explain that dumb letter to my mom? She was probably thinking that the army had changed me into some kind of a monster. I'd be ashamed to ask my girl what to do. Maybe I would call her. Better still, I'd write her and bring her up to date.

June 20, 1952

Dear Teenie Doll,

How is my girl?

Well, I start my training this coming Monday, and I expect it to be about the toughest three weeks I ever spent in this man's army. The only good part about it is that Frankie is in the same company as me, the lucky dog.

What a panic this place is. We have to get our heads shaved right down to the tops of our ears. It's also the rule to have the backs of our necks shaved every week, or it's a gig, so Frankie and I shaved each other to save the sixty cents. It really wasn't worth it in the long run. You should see the shape of our heads. His is square, and mine is round. What a joke. He's "Big Chief Little Brother with Square Head," and I'm "Small Chief Big Brother with Round Head." Ugh!

If you and Frank's girl, Maddie, could see us now you wouldn't recognize us.

How's the weather back home? You should be here. Why you poor girl you, you would melt away to nothing. The heat is unbearable. This is only the beginning of summer down here, and it's hit at least ninety-eight degrees every day since I've been here, but it gets cooler in the evenings.

I hear Rockaway is nice, but the water is freezing. I can't say that for the swimming holes down here. Frankie and I went into the water the other day, and it was scalding. (I'm joking.) It was really very warm though and not very refreshing.

Teenie, honey, I haven't the slightest idea when I'll be home, but I hope it's sometime soon.

What did Mary have? A boy! Congratulate Paddy for me.

I bet you finished school with flying colors like my brother, Richy. Just like true Donohues.

So long for now, Teenie, and I hope to see you soon.

Love,
Joe

I felt like I was Dr. Jekyll and Mr. Hyde when it came to letter writing. Maybe Frank was right. You were different people at different times, and your letters most definitely reflected that. I wondered if my mom would understand that.

CHAPTER 10

GEORGIA IN JUNE

Georgia in June was hotter than hell. Training began before dawn so we could get off of the field by noon. Frank fought the heat, and I fought myself. We had to be careful of gigs or demerits. Three gigs, and you flunked out of jump school.

The first week of jump school saw our First Student Regiment crammed into small, drab barracks that made it seem hotter on the inside than outside. Our day started before dawn with chow and a run in the dark. It was glorious to see the sun come up, but we came to dread it as the day wore on. The longer the day, the stronger the rays. Georgia was hot.

We double-timed everywhere we went. Once we stepped out of our barrack door or any door for that matter, we automatically broke into a run. The first order of business was a jog to the athletic field to do calisthenics. They were the same dirty dozen exercises that we performed in breaking the Third Army record in basic training at Fort Jackson. The difference here was that there were consequences for not doing something the way it was supposed to be done, the airborne way. This could easily result in a gig. You were allowed one gig the first week, two gigs the second week, and no gigs the third week. Three gigs, and you flunked out of jump school.

Frank worried me. He was not in the top physical condition that I was in. I had "Little Jimmy" Knox, my first sergeant in basic training at Fort Jackson, to thank for that. I made it my business to stay close to Frank. We were crammed into barracks that made it hotter. After our run and physical training exercises, which sometimes included hoisting a telephone pole from shoulder to shoulder with other trainees to show teamwork, we simulated jumping out of a plane. Body position was drilled into us through repetition. We actually had a model door of a C-47 to make the jumps look like the real thing.

"Get ready. Stand up. Hook up. Check equipment. Sound off equipment check. Shuffle, and stand in the door."

We practiced responding to those commands over and over again until we memorized, visualized, and performed them like trained dogs. The next thing was the small, two-foot platform from which we practiced our landing technique. This was crucial. We had to hit the ground using five points of our body. We hit and rolled on the sawdust-covered ground and then got back up on the platform and did it again. Front, back, left, or right, no matter which directional landing was called for, we had to hit the ground using the five points of bodily contact. For the rest of my life until the day I died, I'd know how to hit the ground and roll and make a five-point landing.

I liked the wind machine the best. It was neat. It was a change of pace and kind of fun. A fan as big as an airplane engine filled your chute full of air and dragged you along the ground. It took the place of what to expect after you parachuted from a plane and landed on solid earth. You would be flat on your back, looking up at the sky, thinking of the beautiful jump you had just made when you would start to move. You quickly remembered that your chute could catch drafts of wind and drag you backward along the ground. It was kind of like being in a rodeo and roping the steer, but now you had to tie him up before he got away from you.

It was the final performance after we were airborne. Dragged along the ground at twenty miles an hour or more, I reached back over my head and pulled the risers of my chute back over my face to my chest. In the same motion, I had to twist my body in such a way that it jerked me into an upright position and onto my feet. It was like a baseball runner sliding into a base and landing on his feet in an upright position. I then had to run like hell around the chute before it became inflated again and caught the center of the chute. All parachutes had a small opening in their centers with lines going across them called an apex. Once the apex was pulled down, the chute deflated. Using your arms like a weaver, you rolled the chute up in your arms and stuffed it into your AP bag as fast as you could. If done smartly, it could be an eye-popping performance.

The day got hotter toward noon. Tired and hungry and sweating from our workouts, we double-timed through a gauntlet of water sprays positioned on both sides of a pathway that led to a canopied water station. It was like running with your friends under the spray of an open Johnny Pump on a sweltering summer day in Manhattan.

We got soaked by the time we got under the tent. Barrels of drinking water laying in the street were lined up on both sides of the tent. On one side were kegs of cool water diluted with salt to replace the salt lost from sweating, and on the other side were kegs of clear, warm drinking water without salt. Most of us lined up in front of the cool water kegs. Frank was on the other side and waved me over. He didn't look too good. It was obvious he was overheated.

"Keep an eye out and pour water over my head, Joe, while I drink."

I took cups of warm water from the spigot and drank, and when no one was looking, I quickly poured it over his head.

"Don't stop, Joe, but don't get caught, man. Keep pouring," gasped Frank. "I'm dizzy."

Looking around, I dumped water over his head as fast as I could. I never saw Frank look so shaky. "Jesus, Frank, hold on. The day's over. We're going back now. We're almost there. We take it nice and easy on the way back. No gigs, okay? You'll be okay." I hoped that was true, not sure that I believed what I was saying. I sounded more believable than I felt.

On the jog back, he looked like a zombie. I kept up a constant chatter of encouragement, but he had his own mantra. He was like the little engine that could. He kept his own rhythm when his feet hit the ground. "I'm gonna make it. I'm gonna make it."

We double-timed our way back to the barrack, and our sergeant played with us and gave us a hard time. We weren't being enthusiastic enough when we were dismissed from formation, so we had to do it over several times. We were dying, and our sergeant knew. He wanted us to be energetic, so we had to fight ourselves and summon the enthusiasm.

We quickly dissolved into a tired, beat-up mob of has-beens. With bright, flushed faces and dark perspiration stains embedded in our sawdust-caked fatigues, we dragged our bodies up the barrack steps and headed straight for the showers. Without a word and without removing a stitch of clothing, we turned the faucets to cold and fully opened the showerheads. In ones and twos, tired bodies slid their backsides in slow motion down the drab green shower walls onto the wet concrete floor. Groans and curses mingled with the splash of water seeping into our sweat-soaked bodies. This scene became the ritual for the next two weeks of jump school.

Frank and I made friends with two guys in our barrack. Bobby Messic was a short, black-haired, milk-faced, seventeen-year-old Serbian from Ohio. He had such beautiful, rouge-stained, chubby cheeks that you wanted to pinch them every time you saw him except that he was a young bull. His parents were separated. He joined the army with his mother's permission. We called him "the Kid."

Johnny Cornacchio was a Jersey boy. A little taller than Bobby, he was a skinny eighteen-year-old with dark hair and a long Roman nose. We were tempted to call him Pinocchio, but we felt "Corny" was more natural. Corny and the Kid were regular army four-year volunteers like Mike and Squizzy. They all joined the army to go airborne.

Frank got in better shape by the end of week one. He did a scene that couldn't have been choreographed any better even in Hollywood. We came off the field at midday, dragging ass as usual. We walked at rout step at one point when Corny shouted, "Watch out! The Kid's going down."

Bobby was walking next to Frank when his knees started to wobble. The wobble turned into a buckle, and he started to go down. Like a drunken ballet dancer, the Kid pirouetted, and Frank caught him. As if on cue, a cadre's voice called out, "Pick up the step!" and then called the familiar, "Double-time march!" Under a torrid sun on a hot, dusty field in Georgia, sweat streaming into his eyes, Frank was double-timing in step with the Kid passed out in his arms. It was beautiful.

The next day, I screwed up royally. I didn't know what made me do it. I was in great physical condition, but I guess the temptation was too great. It was early morning. It was still dark out. All you could hear was the PT instructor counting by the numbers. It was early in the morning. I was only half awake. I didn't see any cadre close by, so I stayed down on a push-up and rested for a moment. I did it a couple of times and thought I had latched on to something when I felt a paratrooper boot on my ass holding me down and then exhorting me, "Push up, soldier! Push up! What? You can't push up, or you won't push up? What is it? All your buddies are pushing up, and you don't want to push up. You're tired? You don't want to be airborne? You don't want to be here? That's a gig. What's your name and serial number? Another gig, and you're out of here. Now squeeze out twenty good push-ups for me, or you get another gig and you're gone."

I hated myself for being lazy. I was mortified. Calisthenics were not where you should have gotten gigs. It was on tower and aircraft jumps where you got your gigs and flunked out of jump school. The instructor was pissed. He felt that I was trying to cheat my way through, and he wanted to make an example out of me. I don't know how I could have been so stupid. I told Frank about it during the break.

"A gig? Push-ups? What are you talking about? Push-ups are nothing for you. How could you do that?" he raged. "How could you fuck around like that and jeopardize our graduating together? How could you have done that?"

"I don't know. It was a dumb thing to do. I got caught, but don't worry. It won't happen again. I'm not getting any more gigs."

"Yeah, it won't happen again, because you're out of here if you get another gig. You understand? Joe, there is no next time."

"Look, goddamn it, I got a gig. Okay? I know that. I got tired. I got lazy. The heat got to me. Who knows? It won't happen again, I promise," I said, trying to calm Frank down and convince myself that everything was going to be okay.

My biggest worry now was that something might happen that I couldn't control. I wondered if I really wanted to be airborne. One more gig, and I was out. Forty percent of the trainees flunked out of the program in the second week of jump school, and I put myself in a position to be one of them. I was determined that it wouldn't be me. Week two wasn't called "torture week" for nothing. I could kick myself for putting myself in such a rut.

CHAPTER 11

TOWERS OF TORTURE

Looking down from the thirty-four-foot tower made me think of the first time I had jumped from a high-diving board. My thoughts were the same. The second week of jump school was all about finding out if you were afraid of heights. I was about to learn something about myself.

It was do or die week. We were in the hands of pros. The tower training group specialized in the proper procedures for jumping and landing. Corny, the Kid, Frank, myself, and a half dozen other soldiers stood on platforms four feet off of the ground. Straps crisscrossed through our legs and wrapped around our backs. Four risers extended to a flexible, circular, metal frame hanging from a crossbeam under the roof. It looked like the skeleton of an old-fashioned hoop skirt. Instructors on the ground would run us through paces and make certain that we performed the correct commands in steering our chute in the proper direction. Frank looked at me and silently mouthed, "No gigs." I shook my head and waited for the commands.

The megaphone barked, "Get ready. Heads down. Feet together. Go!"

I jumped up and out off of the platform and became suspended in midair. Like a swinging slab of meat, I was dead weight. Dangling, midair straps dug into my body and took a stranglehold on my crotch. I was in agony. I glanced at the other guys. Their faces were like mine. They were twisted in pain.

"Slip forward left" brought two dozen eager hands clutching the left riser and pulling sharply downward to provide slack for the straps biting into our unprotected jewels. The relief was instantaneous. This exercise was learned very quickly, proving again the power of pain as an excellent motivator for success. The next station, the thirty-four-foot tower, brought about the biggest number of gigs in jump school. It separated the jumpers from the non-jumpers.

I had been thirteen years old when I had walked out to the end of the high-diving board in Keansburgh, New Jersey. I looked down and quickly changed my mind about diving into the pool. I had been twelve feet up from the water, but it might as well have been twelve hundred feet. I could see right to the bottom of the pool. It was like I was on the Brooklyn Bridge, looking down into the East River. I turned around, and there was an older boy standing impatiently behind me. "Go ahead and jump."

"No, I'm getting off," I said, inching my way back off of the board.

"You can't go down. The ladder is full."

"I'm not diving off this board."

"Then jump. It's easy. There's nothing to it. Go ahead and jump."

I turned around and walked carefully to the end of the board and looked down. As I tried to summon the courage to jump, I felt the push and heard myself scream. I hit the water feetfirst and swam to the side of the pool. My heart was still in my mouth, but I had done it. I was thrilled at what had happened. I watched the other kids go off the big board with great satisfaction. I knew I was hooked. I hoisted myself out of the water and walked straight to the ladder. This time, I was determined to dive off of the high-diving board without being intimidated.

The thirty-four-foot tower was made of wooden beams. You could see daylight through them. There were four levels. The top deck was where you exited out of a simulated plane's door. There were handrails and a flight of open steps leading to each level. It reminded me of the four flights of stairs I had to climb to my apartment in Manhattan. I had lived on the top floor. Four stories up was a long way down to the sidewalk. The thought struck me that I was about to jump out of my window.

We went up the tower stairs by the numbers. I had to stop at each level and wait for the trainee ahead of me to move up. On my way up to the last level, two soldiers stood at attention, shouting at the top of their lungs, "I am yellow. I am chicken. I am yellow. I am chicken."

The words kept ringing in my ears as I went up the stairs. These guys refused to jump. They were gigged and being made into examples for the rest of us. If they refused to jump a second time, they would be washed out of the airborne.

Suddenly, I was on the high-diving board again. This time, nobody was going to push me off the board. I couldn't afford another gig. I had to jump. Two instructors helped me into a parachute harness. There was a lot of talking. "Pull this. Check that. How does it feel? Wait for instructions. Concentrate on your body positions. Head up. Push out. Palms on D ring. Feet together." There was a lot to remember.

They hooked me up to the outside cable. I stood in the door and peeked down. I was back on the goddamn diving board. Only this time, it was three times higher than the one in the pool had been. I heard the command, "Go!"

I leaped out, held my body position, and again experienced the thrill of the fall. I slid down on a cable and was stopped at the end by two trainees standing on a mound of turf. One was a private and the other a lieutenant colonel named Kenneth Pell, who would later become a regimental commander in the division I would be assigned to in Korea.

From a distance, it looked like the Coney Island "Parachute Jump." It was a 250-foot erector set made out of iron and the last barrier to "jump week" and becoming a paratrooper.

This time, I was harnessed to a real parachute. Four risers, two in front and two in back, were connected to an inflated silk canopy above my head. Slowly, I was hoisted up to the iron crossbeam on top of the tower. I held a piece of paper between my teeth and listened for directions. Just before I reached the top, I was directed to release the paper and check the direction of the wind. My biggest worry was that a sudden gust of wind would blow my chute toward the girders, which supported the crossbeams on top. I didn't want to crash into the Eiffel Tower and become a casualty before I ever touched the ground.

I looked at my chute as it moved slowly up to the top of the tower and under my hoop. I was 250 feet above the ground. I had a grand view of Fort Benning and the Georgia countryside. I waited anxiously for my turn to come. I swallowed hard as I went up, and my canopy quickly collapsed, hurling me down with breathtaking speed. It was like being on a roller coaster when your car slowly climbed to the top of the steeple chase, paused, and swooped down at break-neck speed, causing everyone to scream and keep their heads up.

In a flash my chute blossomed open and freed me from the tower. As I drifted down, I quickly pulled on the front risers, making sure that I would slip well away from the steel girders of the giant tower. The sound of a loudspeaker got my attention. I found myself following commands from the ground, getting ready to land using five points of bodily contact. I was amazed at the ease in which I manipulated the direction of my chute. I was in complete control, and I was enjoying myself.

It was Friday and my last jump of the day. Close to the ground, my chute began to oscillate, bringing me down sideways. I executed a backward parachute-landing fall, which wasn't my favorite landing position. I hit the ground hard, and when I got up to collapse my chute, I felt a twinge in my right foot. I jogged gingerly off the field because my ankle was really beginning to hurt. I passed an instructor who asked me if I was okay.

"I'm fine. Came down the wrong way," I said and made a show of walking it off, but my foot was throbbing. I could feel the ankle pushing against the inside of my boot. It was swollen, and it hurt.

"It's nothing," I assured him with a smile and jogged over to my group. I could feel the instructor's eyes boring into my back. What I didn't need now was to be yanked and put into another training cycle. I didn't want to miss graduating with Frank and the guys.

The day was done. My foot was killing me, but it was Friday. I knew I could make it back to my barrack without any help. I had the weekend to rest up for "jump week." I would have to use ice packs and Ace bandages. I planned to spend the weekend resting in the Airborne Gardens to get ready for Monday.

I hobbled to an outdoor table where the guys were sitting. The Airborne Gardens was much like a German beer garden back home. I half expected to hear the rousing music of a polka instead of Johnny Ray singing "Walking My Baby Back Home." At the table, the conversation was mostly about jump week.

"I was talking to some rangers, and they said it was easier to jump from the C-47s than the C-119s," said Squizzy in his quick, intense manner.

"Yeah. Why was that?" asked Mike in his soft voice, taking a slug from his beer. With his slow way of talking, he could have easily been taken for a Southern boy. Mike dated Squizzy's sister back home, and I think they were still seeing each other. Mike and Squizzy were practically brothers-in-law.

"With the prop blasts, you're not protected," continued Squizzy. "The C-47 engines are not as powerful, and they're on both sides of the cabin. On the C-119, the engines are bigger, and they have two cabins like a P-38, so you get it from both sides."

"So it's like *pow!* right in your face," I said, being dramatic and smacking my fist into my hand. I had my swollen foot up on the bench. It felt better elevated. I switched from boots to shoes because they were lighter with less pressure on my bandaged ankle. I moved sparingly.

"I don't know," said Corny. "I hear the C-119 can slow down to like 110 miles an hour. That should lessen the hit."

"Who cares?" said the Kid. "We don't have a choice anyway. We're jumping from the boxcar. No sense worrying about it. Let's have another round."

"What about choosing your chute?" I asked Mike.

"What about it?"

"It's easy," said Frank with an elfin grin. "You pick this chute, and you live. You pick that chute, and you die. Your fate is in your own hands."

"So what do you do?" asked Mike, flashing a wide smile. "Do you pray for divine guidance?"

"Well, the way I see it is that we have to pick two chutes, our main chute and our reserve chute, and we don't have much time. We'll be double-timing through a storage warehouse with mountains of packed chutes to choose from, so what do you do?" asked Frank, getting everyone's avid attention. "In that split second, how are you going to choose? What are you going to do?"

"Come on . . . what difference does it make?" said Mike, breaking the silence. "They're all the same, and they all open."

"Yeah," said Corny, "I'm going to grab the first chute I come to."

"What are you going to do?" asked Squizzy, looking at Frank.

"In the time that we have, I'm going to look for the newest, neatest packed chute there is and latch on to it. That's what I'm going to do."

Squizzy nodded. "I'm going to do the same thing," he said with a look of satisfaction on his face.

"You might want to do it differently," said Frank. "I'm only telling you what I'm going to do. I don't think all chutes are the same. I like new, and I like neat. I think a neatly packed chute shows that the rigger was careful and is a pro, and that's my kind of guy."

"I agree that a neat chute is important," I said, jumping in. "But I would go for old. I would look for the chute that looks broken in. One that's neat but old. The kind that falls open by just looking at it."

"Yeah," Corny laughed. "The chute that's bursting at the seams. The one that shows big bulges of silk sticking out of it. Me, I don't like ee, nee, me, nee, my, nee, mo. Whatever is in front of me, I take."

"Maybe we should compromise," said Mike soothingly after the laughter died down. "Maybe we should choose a new chute for our main parachute and an old-looking chute for our reserve."

Everyone paused for a moment. "I'll drink to that," said the Kid as he passed out beers.

"So is everybody ready for Monday?" asked Squizzy.

"My ankle is getting better beer by beer," I said and smiled. "I'm ready."

"Jump week should be easy as long as we don't look down," cracked Corny.

"We got through the towers. We'll get through jump week. Here's to Monday," said Mike simply.

"To Monday," came the response.

CHAPTER 12

AIRBORNE ALL THE WAY

How many people do you know jumped out of the first plane they ever flew in? I was twenty years old, and I volunteered for airborne training. Maybe it was a macho thing, and I needed to prove something to myself. Who knew? The one thing I was certain of was that I wanted to become a paratrooper and go airborne all the way.

"Are we going to jump today?" bellowed our training sergeant as he double-timed us to the warehouse where our chutes were stored.

"Yes, sir!" we shouted along with all the other boots.

"Without a chute?" he bellowed.

"No, sir!" we responded.

"Who are we?"

"Airborne!"

"All the way?" he asked.

"All the way!" we yelled in unison.

When we reached the warehouse, we kept on double-timing right through it, pausing in front of mountains of stacked parachutes. On the move, we had to grab a main chute and a reserve chute. The huge question was which one. There were hundreds of chutes to choose from. The same thought went through everyone's mind. It was like Russian roulette. Pick a chute and choose your fate.

Frank grabbed the newest and neatest chutes. He told me he was going to take the newest chutes. I told him that I was going to pick the well-used chutes. Our thinking was completely different, but we did agree that they had to be neatly packed. He figured new chutes were more reliable, and I thought the older ones were more dependable. Thank God we never found out which was the better theory.

Once outside, our instructors helped us into our harnesses and checked our main chutes for loose cords and showing silk. They pulled and tugged straps, impervious to our grunts and groans. I was very grateful despite their roughness. My mind was in a boxer's mode, concentrating more on the coming jump than the inspection of my chutes. I could feel hands going over the rip cord, making sure it was free in its pocket and that my reserve chute was properly hooked to the main strap. My instructor gave me the okay after he checked the chute packer's seal to make sure it hadn't been broken. I felt reassured after such a thorough inspection. I was all set and ready to go.

Walking was difficult. We were hunched over and uncomfortable from the tightened chute straps that dug into our groins. We needed to be physically lifted up by the helping hands of our instructors as we tried to climb up into the body of the C-119 boxcar. I was seated on the right side of the aircraft in the first stick. There were eight men to a stick and two sticks or sixteen men on each side of the plane.

It was cool being in an airplane. It was my first time, and I was excited. I wondered how it would feel when we took off and started to fly. I got butterflies in my stomach every time I thought about jumping out of the door of the plane when we got into the air. One at a time, I heard the engines cough, sputter, and turn over. The mighty roar sent tremors through my body. I could barely feel the plane begin to move. Slowly, we taxied to the runway, turned, and waited. Our engines roared, and we began to move and vibrate and pick up speed and lumber into the air. We were airborne.

I tried to sit back and relax. Streaks of sunlight leaked into the dark cabin. I peered across the aisle at the faces of the somber jumpers. Most were deep in thought, sitting almost trance-like in their bucket seats. Except for the hum of the engines and a few muted conversations, there was an air of quiet expectation in the cabin. I wondered how many guys had never been in a plane before. I wondered if they were having the same thoughts that I was having.

Abruptly, the jump master opened the side doors of the plane, and cool air and light flooded the cabin. As if on cue, the pilot maneuvered his way back from the cockpit to talk to the jump master, grinning and nodding his head as he passed us. He looked like he was enjoying our discomfort, and I wanted to wipe that grin from his face. At that moment, the trooper next to me gave me the elbow and pointed to the cockpit. My eyes almost popped out of my head. Two joysticks were moving by themselves in front of empty seats. No one was flying the plane. It was on automatic pilot. Thirty-two pairs of dumbfounded eyes glued themselves to the two men who were obviously enjoying our reaction. Now I really wanted to take the pilot out the door with me.

A red light blinked. All eyes shifted to the blinking light. This was it. I knew it was coming, yet the words sent a bolt of electricity right through me. "Get ready!" commanded the animated voice over the speaker. My body stiffened, and the adrenaline soared. "Stick one, stand up!" The first stick in the plane rose unsteadily to their feet. Eight bodies stood unevenly, holding their static line hooks to their chest. "Hook up!" brought the clicks of hooks connecting to the overhead guide wire. Safety pins were fumbled into their holes like threads into needles to secure the connection. "Sound off equipment check!" Each jumper in my stick shouted out the number of the man in front of him and tapped the back of his helmet so he would know that he had checked him out. I wasn't being completely honest. In rapid succession, the stick replied, "One okay, tap. Two okay, tap. Seven okay, tap." In seconds, they disappeared out the door.

My stick was next. Everything seemed to be going on fast forward. I barely checked out the man in front of me. I looked for loose silk from his chute and sounded off equipment check. The next command was to "shuffle and stand in the door!" I realized where the famous "airborne shuffle" had come from. We were so close together that the only way I could move with all my bulky equipment was to quickly shuffle my feet and try not to step on the boot heel of the man in front of me.

"Go!" became an electrified word. It made my heart pound faster as the man kept repeating that word as I moved toward the door. I looked ahead and saw a body standing in the door. He hesitated. It was like he was frozen in time. It was Gray, a buddy of mine from basic training. He was just standing there. *If he doesn't go, I don't go*, I thought to myself, and then he was gone.

I was next. My eyes widened, and the jump master looked at me and held up his hand. I stopped dead in my tracks, and he proceeded to get on his knees and peer out the door without a parachute on. A contorted face of squeezed flesh popped inside and motioned me to come forward. I stood there, not believing what I had just seen. He waved at me again, and I slid my static line forward, turned, and framed myself in the door. I remember the air hitting my face and looking out over the trees and thinking that it was a beautiful, sunny morning and feeling the slap on my backside and hearing the word, "Go!"

I reacted automatically. My exit was perfect. Just like in practice, my elbows were tucked rigidly into my sides, and my arms cradled the reserve chute with my palms across the D rings. My feet were together, and my head was down. My eyes were open, and in a blur of motion, the ground tilted and then turned over. I shut my eyes as I felt the blast of air from the plane's propeller. Like a yo-yo, the explosion of my chute's opening brought me to a sudden halt, sending my helmet over my eyes before hurling me back up in the opposite direction. When I recovered, I found myself alone in a silent world of slow motion. I looked up at my billowed canopy against a brilliant blue sky, and it was an awesome sight to see. Below me was a carpet of green with a few houses sprinkled about. It was like I had the world at my feet.

When I finally snapped out of my reverie, I felt comfortable enough to try out my chute and play with the risers. I tentatively climbed up my right riser because my chute was moving to my left. Lo and behold, I glided to my right. It was so easy. The more riser I pulled down, the deeper my descent. When I let up on the riser, the chute continued moving to my left. I tried my front risers, and I went swooping forward. I was having fun controlling the direction of my chute, and I felt great. I was enjoying myself until other chutes appeared, and I soon realized I wasn't alone. Like the holy pictures I got in church when I was a kid, the scene around me looked like a host of sun-washed angel wings descending from God's heaven to earth.

I looked for a clear spot on the ground void of collapsed parachutes. Megaphones squawked. It would be a left-landing fall. I tried to relax. I waited until I could see the treetop line, and I let myself go limp. I waited . . . and waited. "Now!" I shouted and thrust my hands up on my risers and pulled down to slow my descent, anticipating the touchdown of my boots. I knew landing was the toughest part of the jump. If you did it right, it was a piece of cake. If you did it wrong, it could be devastating. As soon as my boots hit the ground, I went into automatic. Without thinking about it, my body made the five points of contact. I hit the ground a bit hard and rolled. My chute collapsed, and I came to a pretty quick stop.

I lay on the newly plowed, turned-over turf of the landing zone and smiled, enjoying the moment. I did it. I just jumped out of a goddamn airplane. I quickly got to my knees and looked up at the planes overhead dropping their human cargo. It was a dramatic scene. The jumpers were violently shook back and forth like little rag dolls when they got hit with the air blasts from the propellers of the planes they jumped from and again when their chutes opened. I couldn't believe that I had been one of them just moments ago.

Thump! A body crashed down next to me. My smile turned to haste. *Thump!* Another body and another chute landed close by. I was being bombarded from above.

"Clear the deck, trooper," a metallic voice boomed from a megaphone. I knew it was aimed at me and quickly hit my release plate and wriggled out of my chute. Legs and bodies were falling down rapidly around me as I raced around to grab the vortex of my chute, and frantically rolled the parachute into my all-purpose bag. I realized I was in a danger zone. A guy could get clobbered and seriously hurt around here, I thought as I dodged troopers on the ground and joined up with those who were running off of the landing field toward our waiting trucks. I was wondering about the trauma our bodies were taking as we jumped out of airplanes and crashed to the ground when I fell flat on my face. I scrambled to my feet, lugged my all-purpose bag with my chute in it, and tripped again. I looked down at a stocking foot, and a boot ripped in half. My foot went right through the zipper part of my boot. In basic training, I had a shoemaker sew zippers into the side of a pair of my boots. I thought it was a cool thing to do because it saved me the trouble of having to unlace and lace my boots when I put them on and took them off. They also looked sharp.

It was just another example of the violent impacts your body took when you were exiting an airplane twelve hundred feet in the air. The propeller blast in combination with the opening shock of my chute was so powerful that it had ripped the boot almost in half. I shuddered to think what might have happened if the boot on my sore foot had been wrenched apart instead of the left. The additional strain would have probably knocked me out of jump week for sure. I would have joined the troopers who were seriously hurt in making their first jump. Colonel Pell, with whom I went through jump school and who later served in the same combat regiment with me, fractured a couple of ribs. Other guys suffered severe sprains, riser burns across their necks, broken bones, and concussions. I was amazed at the number of guys who got hurt yet managed to finish jump school despite their injuries.

My next two jumps were okay. My ankle held up fine. The fourth jump was problematic. It was a mass-exit jump of thirty-two men in four sticks of eight going out both doors at the same time. This was a simulated combat jump. On this flight, some guys across from me were joking and horsing around. I guess they were trying to stay loose, although in a sense, we were veteran jumpers by now. I smiled when they called me "horse face" because of the long look on my face. I exaggerated my words and moved my lips slowly so they could understand "fuck you!"

I went back to my solemn meditation. This was serious stuff. I was thinking about what I had to do. Even with three jumps under my belt, I was still uncomfortable jumping out of a plane. Once I was airborne, I was fine. It was getting out the door in the proper position that was most important to me. Right now, I didn't feel in a funny mood.

"Go!" brought the usual pandemonium and quick shuffling toward the door. The plane tilted forward slightly, which caused the man behind me to keep bumping into me. I was trying to keep my balance and stay some distance from the man in front me. It was impossible. It felt like I was going to carry the guy on my back and ride piggyback with the man in front of me. My exit was a hurried blur. The wind hit my face, and I dived rather than jumped. I braced for the opening shock. When it came, I looked up as usual to check my canopy.

My eyes looked in disbelief. *Goddamn it!* I thought. *A hole! I have a fucking hole in my chute.* Before I could figure out what to do, I found myself surrounded by falling parachutes and troopers frantically slipping and sliding their chutes to avoid midair collisions. I rapidly worked my risers to avoid getting tangled up with the other parachutes. In my mind, I heard the voice of my instructors: "If a hole is bigger than the size of your steel pot, then you had better be ready to pull your emergency chute."

Suddenly, my chute's canopy partially collapsed. I felt as though my stomach was in my mouth. My boots touched the bloated canopy of the jumper below me, and I freaked out. My adrenaline skyrocketed. With my legs sagging in the silk under me, I frantically pumped my legs up and down before my own chute collapsed, and then I hurriedly stepped off the ballooned canopy and sailed back out into open space. I floated down with my heart racing, not knowing what to expect next. Despite the lower jump height, I didn't seem to be getting to the ground any quicker, but everything around me seemed to be happening haphazardly and faster than usual.

I checked the hole in my chute again, hands pressed across the D ring on my reserve chute, ready to pull it if necessary, when I see this bug-eyed trooper swinging out of control and coming straight at me. I tensed, knowing we were going to hit. I brought my knees up as far as I could, and when we closed, I thrust my legs forward into his chest and pushed off with a sickening thud that knocked us clear of each other. I got a jolt of pain from my ankle; however, we didn't get tangled up, and I was grateful for that. I looked up quickly and saw that the hole in my chute had gotten bigger. I also realized it was too late to do anything about it, so I prepared myself to go into my landing position, hoping for the best.

None of the cadre on the ground called attention to my torn canopy, so I jogged gingerly off the field and climbed awkwardly into one of the waiting trucks on the other side of the field. I shakily lit a cigarette and slinked down on my seat. Guys were coming off of the field in dribs and drabs. Frank's head popped up, and he heaved himself aboard. His face was ashen, and he looked a bit shaken up.

"Over here," I said, sliding over to make room for him. He dropped his bag on the floor and threw himself down beside me.

"You look like you just saw a ghost," I said. "You okay?"

He dropped his head back and stretched out his legs. "You won't believe what just happened to me."

"What happened?"

"I'm not sure I believe it myself. I was being rushed out the door when the guy behind me stumbles and knocks into me just as I'm coming to the door. I go out the door, and I have a lousy exit. I barreled out headfirst, and over I go. When my chute opens, I'm upside down."

"You're what?" I asked incredulously.

"Joe, I'm fucking upside down. I'm coming down, and my left leg is over my head. Parachute cords are wrapped around the heel of my boot. I'm falling headfirst, and chutes are flying past, just missing me. My whole body is stretched out, and I'm playing Houdini, trying to get myself free. My fingers barely reached the cords, and I went into all sorts of wild contortions trying to slip the cords down off my boot."

"Holy shit," I said, surprised. I gave Frank a cigarette and lit it for him. "What did you do?"

"I prayed to the Virgin as I pried them off one by one. My chute is oscillating, and the ground is coming up fast. I managed to slip the last one off and get my chute upright just in time. I could have gotten killed. I almost died, Joe."

"It was the Blessed Mother. She took care of you."

"I know. I know. I owe her big time," said Frank, shaking his head in disbelief.

"Jeez, Frank," I said, smiling. "You almost bought it without going to Korea."

"It's not funny, Joe. Not funny at all," said Frank.

The last trooper to hop aboard was a lean, chalk-faced first lieutenant who groaned easing himself onto his seat. He was obviously in pain. He lit a cigarette and coughed as he inhaled his first puff. Through clenched teeth, he swore about the son of a bitch who kicked him in the chest at three hundred feet and almost killed him. I turned my head the other way, using Frank to shield my face from the angry lieutenant.

"My jump was shitty too. I'll tell you about it later," I said in a low voice as I slouched down in my seat.

The next day was our fifth and last jump before graduation. We simulated a mass combat jump in squad formation and had a mission to accomplish. We were loaded down with equipment. My cartridge belt was packed with ammo clips, a full canteen of water, and a bayonet. My M-1 rifle was broken down into three main parts and put into a GE bag strapped to my leg, along with our main and reserve chutes. Each flying boxcar carried four sticks of eight troopers. After we hit the ground from a thousand feet up, we had to bag our chutes, put our rifles together, find our squad leader, and rendezvous at a foot bridge just off of our landing zone with the other squads from our plane.

What a difference a day made. Without any major incidents, we finished our five jumps and got together at the Airborne Gardens to celebrate our graduation from jump school. Frank, the Kid, Squizzy, Mike, Corny, and I ended the day joyfully singing all the corny "Blood on the Risers" verses of the Airborne Anthem to the tune of "His Truth Is Marching On":

"Is everybody happy?" cried the sergeant looking up,
Our hero feebly answered, "Yes," and then they stood him up,
He leaped right out into the blast his static line unhooked,
He ain't gonna jump no more!

Glory, glory, what a helluva way to die.
Glory, glory, what a helluva way to die.
Glory, glory, what a helluva way to die.
He ain't gonna jump no more!

We were happy, tipsy, and airborne all the way.

CHAPTER 13

SIN CITY CELEBRATION

The First Student Regiment, Airborne Battalion, Company E, started jump school with 425 men. Three weeks later, 277 of us graduated and received our wings. It was time to party before we went home the next day. Phenix was the city to celebrate in. It was called Sin City, USA, and Frank and I learned why.

The Kid, Corny, Mike, and Squizzy went into Columbus to celebrate. Just across the Chattahoochee River in Alabama, the infamous Phenix City, also known as Sin City, was less than an hour away. Frank and I thought it would be more of a fun place to go.

We swaggered down the main drag, showing off our new airborne wings and spit-shined jump boots. The half-moon taps on our soles and heels drew a lot of attention. We paid extra for them because we thought the sound they made was the coolest of the cool. We passed honky-tonk bars with flashing lights and loud jukebox music. "The Wheel of Fortune" and "My Bleeding Heart" competed with Hank Williams and Southern Blues.

In the doorway of one bar, a smiling gal in a low-cut blouse stood with a drink in her hand and kept lifting her dress up in front of a floor fan to cool herself off.

Frank looked at me and grinned. "Let's have a drink here, Joe."

"Want to dance, soldier boys?" they asked, meeting us at the door and sliding their arms inside ours, and they sashayed us to a table near the fan.

The place was almost empty. In the back of the room, newly graduated paratroopers and their pickups were eating and drinking and laughing up a storm. Frank and I ordered some food and bottles of beer. Jackie and Tami were drinking bourbon. We were flirting and chatting in exaggerated, phony, Southern drawls and having a ball.

The service was great. The waiter kept coming over, and we kept ordering more drinks. I was feeling my beers after a while, and I could tell Frank was too. We were getting a little loud, but our girlfriends seemed just fine. I figured at the rate we were going, they would drink us under the table.

Tami was feeding the jukebox while Jackie was squeezing Frank to death on the dance floor. On an impulse, I picked up Tami's drink and smelled it. It didn't smell like bourbon. I took a sip, and it was tea. Frank and I were paying for bourbon, and they were drinking tea. We were being had. Indignantly, I hauled myself up and strode to the bar, wondering who this yokel bartender think we were. We were from New York City. Didn't he realize we had invented this scam?

I stood in front of the bartender and raised the glass in my hand.

"What can I get you, trooper?"

"You can get me bourbon when I order it," I said triumphantly, banging the glass on the bar. "I'm not paying for tea when I ordered bourbon."

"Luck a cheer, boy. Don't kick up a fuss, hear now?" said the burly bartender in a thick Southern accent. "You watch your manners now, hear?"

"I just want what I'm paying for," I said righteously. "I ordered bourbon, and I got tea. So tea is what I'm paying for."

"We don't do that here," sneered the barman, producing a Louisville slugger from under the bar. "You got bourbon. Tastes like tea to you maybe, but you got bourbon, boy," said the bartender, who laid the bat on the bar and leaned over to whisper conspiratorially in my ear. "Ah don't want no trouble. Don't wanta call the poe-lease."

I was taken back with the sudden threat of violence but caught myself and fired back. "Yeah, I want you to call the police. Go ahead and call them."

"What's going on?" asked Frank, coming over with Jackie from the dance floor. "What's all the commotion?"

"Your buddy's looking for trouble," said the bartender, motioning Jackie away.

I told Frank the story.

"We're not paying, and we're not staying," said Frank.

The bartender looked out the window and pumped the bat over his head a few times. "You fellas asked for them, but you don't know what you're asking."

Two light gray uniforms wearing wide brim Stetsons with .38 pistols strapped around mountainous bellies came through the door. They made our bartender friend look anemic.

The bartender turned toward Frank and me. "Y'all don't wanta mess with the poe-lease. By the time they call y'all MP fellas, you boys will need more than first aid."

"We got us some trouble here, Harold?" asked one of the gray uniforms with a chaw of tobacco bulging from the side of his jaw.

Frank and I were afraid to look at each other.

"It's up to these trooper boys," said Harold.

"Maybe they wanta to show us how many men they're equal to?" said the officer with the chaw in his cheek.

The beer haze cleared from my head after that remark. *Wonder where he heard that*, I thought.

"It's plain and simple. The bartender cheated us," Frank said, his voice taking on a hard edge as the troopers from the back of the room joined us.

"Can we be any help, sheriff?" drawled the tallest trooper in the group.

"Look, nobody wants any trouble," I said reassuringly, taking a five-dollar bill from my wallet and dropping it on the bar. "No problem. Right, Harold? Just a misunderstanding," I said, looking at the bartender.

There was a long pause before a hand reached out from behind. "No problem, just as long as you boys leave nice and quiet."

"Let's go, boys. You're finished here," said the tobacco-chewing sheriff.

"We're outta here," I said to Frank, putting my arm around his shoulder. "We're paratroopers, and we're going home tomorrow. This party is over."

CHAPTER 14

Home On Leave

The graduating airborne class of 1952 of Company E, Fort Benning, Georgia, dispersed to towns all over the country. Frank and I had three weeks before we had to report to Camp Stoneman in California. I never thought being home would be so stressful that Teen and I would break off our relationship and my mother would slap me across the face the night before I shipped out.

At Fort Benning after graduation, we waited in long lines outside of a field tent to receive our orders. All eyes were glued to the tent door. When a trooper came out you could tell by the look on his face whether he had gotten orders for the Far Eastern Command (FECOM) or somewhere else. All our guys received orders for FECOM. Mike and Squizzy were crushed by the news. They joined the army with a promise to be assigned an airborne outfit. The Kid and Corny were undecided.

In a huff, Mike and Squizzy headed to the office where assignment orders were cut. Frank and I went along for moral support. After they pleaded their case with little input from us, their orders for Korea were rescinded. They would wait at Fort Benning until new orders were issued for an airborne unit in the United States. To our surprise, Frank and I were offered the same deal. The one catch was that we would have to extend our service from two to four years. We wouldn't have to go to Korea. We would be stateside.

Frank and I turned the offer down. We could have stayed home in the National Guard and not been drafted at all. The truth was we wanted to go to Korea. The Kid and Corny didn't want to tempt fate, so we would all go to Korea together.

I was psyched. The top was down, and the radio was blaring country music. On the open road, the wind drowned our voices, and we had to scream to sing along with Hank Snow: "We're movin' on. We'll soon be gone." We were on leave and going home. Hallelujah!

For a little fun and adventure, we gambled on catching a free ride home in a military transport plane. One of our airborne instructors drove the four of us in his new Buick convertible from Fort Benning, Georgia, to Maxwell Air Force Base in Montgomery, Alabama. For ten bucks a piece plus the price of gas, we would get door-to-door service and a tour through the heartland of the South.

The ride was pleasant and uneventful except for the number of old, run-down, slave cabins that were still being inhabited by families. I had a better understanding of why Negroes wanted to move up North. Comparatively speaking, the tenements in Harlem offered better living conditions than the shacks I had seen along the roads.

Montgomery Air Force Base was huge. We found the MATS waiting room and signed up for the Midwest and the East Coast. Afternoon turned to dusk, and we got lucky. A plane was routed to Chicago and then to Ohio, and the Kid grabbed it. After midnight, it was our turn to be lucky. A plane landed for refueling en route to Boston. We grabbed it.

We giggled with excitement as we went up the mobile stairs into the dark, shadowy, twin-engine cargo plane. We strapped ourselves into web-belted bucket seats, tired and hungry and happier than hell. We would be in Boston in the morning, only hours from home.

The two pilots were characters. Dressed casually in flowered, short-sleeve shirts and summer slacks, they looked like they were flying to their country club for a quick round of golf. As a matter of fact, their golf bags were sitting in the bucket seats next to us. They were young officers in their late twenties and very friendly. They went through their emergency procedures, and when they pointed to the parachutes on board, they laughed and said that they didn't expect to use them on our flight. They told us they had never jumped from a plane. They were good guys. They even shared their coffee and steak sandwiches with us before we dozed off.

The next morning, we joined the early commute to Grand Central Station. I was amazed how many people worked in New York City. The ride from Boston had to be a good four hours. I assumed that they were mostly weekenders or vacationers.

"You guys have my summer number. I'd like you to come and stay over if you could. We'll have some fun before going to Korea. Rockaway is a great vacation place."

Corny and Frank nodded as we pulled into the station. "I'll call you, Joe, but don't count on me for staying over. I'll see how it goes with the family," said Corny, marveling at the cavernous, star-studded ceiling in Grand Central Station.

"I'm sure I can get away for a day or two. I'll look forward to it," said Frank.

The three of us shook hands and went our different ways. Corny was going by bus to Jersey. Frank was taking the Lexington Avenue subway uptown, and I was heading downtown to Penn Station and the Long Island Railroad.

I could feel the excitement well up inside me as my train pulled into my seaside station. I hurried to 107th Street and entered into a court of tiny gray bungalows. Identical wooden porches faced each other across a long cement walk. I was struck by how similar they were in size to the cabins I had passed the day before.

The taps on my boots were the only sounds I could hear in the courtyard. The bungalow porches were empty this Monday morning. I stopped in front of the tiny garden plot of overripe tomato plants my father so proudly nurtured. Through the screen door, I could see the frail image of my ninety-year-old grandmother in the kitchen.

"Up the stone throwers of Tipperary," I said through the door.

I heard my aunt Aggie's scream before I saw her. My grandmother and aunt surrounded me with joyful hugs and smiles. Everyone else was at the beach, so I turned around and walked quickly up the street to the ocean. I could feel my heart pounding as I hurried up the ramp to the boardwalk. A delicious gust of salty sea air hit my face, and I greedily sucked it into my lungs. This was what I missed most being away from home.

I shaded my eyes with my hands and slowly scanned the beach for the chair of the lifeguard. I found it immediately. The familiar green canopy with the faded yellow-and-white sunflowers stood out at a jaunty angle, staking claim to the weather-beaten Indian blanket beneath it. That umbrella and blanket were the same ones I remembered from when I was a kid. Some things never seemed to change.

The moment was interrupted with the piercing sounds of gonging bells from the belfry of St. Camillus Church. I froze along with everyone else. People stopped walking, and then, as if a giant wave was swelling up, the entire beach rose up as one. Bathers got up from their blankets and captain's chairs. Lifeguards stood at attention, and heads were bowed in prayer. The Angelus was recited three times a day in remembrance of the moment when the angel Gabriel appeared to the young girl Mary to announce to her that she was to become the Mother of God. It was a powerful show of faith by the Irish Catholics of Rockaway Park.

I waited for the two-minute ringing to stop before I moved down the boardwalk ramp onto the beach. My jump boots sunk deep into the soft, white-shelled sand, making it a cumbersome walk down to the water. I don't know who spotted who first, but my smiling, crying mother was the first to reach me and almost knocked me down in a bear hug. My father's wide grin showed cigar-stained teeth against a deep tan followed by my shy, six-year-old brother, whose birthday was today. We shook hands, and I could feel the tears welling up in my eyes.

I bent down, took a present from my satchel, and picked up the birthday boy. He tore it open and put the smallest overseas cap I could find on his head. It was a replica of the hat I was wearing with the blazing emblem of the parachute insignia on it. "This is for you, little trooper, and happy birthday!" If anyone had had a camera, this scene would have made a nice snapshot of the Donohue family together again.

The days went by quickly. Before I knew it, I was headed into the last weekend of my furlough. It seemed like I had just arrived home yesterday. Everything seemed to be coming in on me. Teen was still away. She and some friends from Hunter College had taken summer jobs as waitresses in the Borscht Belt in the Catskill Mountains. She had one day off a week and a strict schedule. She didn't drive and had no available means of transportation. She was far from home and would lose her job if she was late for work. Time was running out for us to see each other.

Frank said he would be able to come down to the bungalow for our last weekend on leave. The Kid and Corny couldn't make it to Rockaway, and that was understandable. Their families wanted their boys to be with them until the last possible moment. We had agreed at Boston station that we would meet at LaGuardia Airport for our trip to San Francisco. My cousin was the manager for United Airlines, and he had some problems pulling strings to book a flight for the four of us at the time we needed. There was a feeling that the fun time was over and that things were coming to a head. My father hadn't expected to pay upfront for plane reservations for four soldiers and wasn't sure just when he would be reimbursed. There was tension in the air.

Teen and I ended our relationship over the phone. The bar that I was calling from had a jukebox. At one point during a heated discussion, Frank tried to lighten things up. He played a romantic Tony Bennett song called "Because of You" as background music in the hopes that things might turn around. They didn't. I left the booth sad and relieved at the same time. It was hard to explain. I had mixed feelings. In a way, I had been set free by breaking up, but I also felt empty inside. I tried to convince myself that I had done the right thing. Now I could concentrate on going to Korea without distraction. I didn't have to worry about receiving a "Dear John" letter from my girlfriend. I had no girlfriend. All I had to do was get home in one piece. I told myself that everything would work out for the best.

"What are buddies for?" Frank said indignantly as he swooped the loose change off of the bar with his hand and stood up uncertainly.

"What are you doing?" I asked as he strode to the telephone booth.

"I'm calling Maddie. It's not right that she should wait for me. Joe, I don't like to think like this, but goddamn it, we may not be coming home." He paused for a pregnant moment and then ducked into the booth and started to dial. While he was waiting for his connection, he opened the door and poked his head out. "Play me some Tony Bennett on the jukebox, will ya, pal?"

The following afternoon, my aunt Mae, who was a Mother Superior and the principal of Saint Virgilius School in Broad Channel, and her sister, Kate, gave a going-away luncheon for me in the auditorium of the school. The students had decorated the hall in red, white, and blue bunting with a "God Be with You" sign in the background. The place was packed with the good sisters of St. Francis, relatives, and friends. I was glad to share the burden of the spotlight with my best friend.

Frank and I were dressed in pressed, class-A, summer, tan-colored uniforms with dark brown ties, shiny jump boots, and airborne overseas caps. We looked pretty spiffy. My parents and aunts escorted us around the tables, and the chitchat was warm and caring with lots of smiles and laughter. Frank knew my immediate family. There were some relatives and friends of relatives I didn't know either, but everyone was especially nice and made us feel at ease. My mom liked to tell our guests funny stories about Frank and me making our first jump out of an airplane. Eventually, she decided that it would be a good idea if we got up on stage and showed everyone what it was like. I couldn't believe she was telling the audience what we were going to do. Despite my embarrassment and protests, the applause from the tables drove us up to the stage. Frank was encouraged by the reception and led the way. I couldn't believe this was happening.

Frank played two roles, the jump master and the pilot of the aircraft. I was the scared rookie taking his first plane ride and getting ready to jump from it at twelve hundred feet before parachuting to the ground. It was a silly vaudevillian routine of clumsily mimicking the jump master's commands, showing fear, and displaying macho bravado in front of my fellow troopers. With some zealous flourish of buffoonery and slapstick comedy, the audience laughed, clapped hands, and seemed to enjoy themselves. We responded in kind by making complete fools of ourselves, clowning, laughing, and actually having some fun.

Later that night, Frank and I did the Rockaway Hop, which meant we went bar hopping and checked out the girls and danced. It was a typical summer's weekend crowd with lots of music and dancing. In McGuires, we bumped into two of my uncles and a cousin who had been at the farewell party that afternoon. By now they were in rare form, telling jokes and funny stories at the bar. Somehow, the subject got to Korea, and they started telling World War II stories.

My uncle Mike had been in the navy and made the famous "Murmansk Run" to Russia. It was a notorious sailing route for convoys bringing war supplies to Russia. They had to outrun German U-boats that clustered together to form deadly "wolf packs" and torpedoed many allied ships. Sailors referred to this mission as a suicide run. The bar was crowded, and a good number of people were tuned in to what was being said. At one suspenseful moment in the story, my uncle Frank, who was my uncle Mike's best friend, interrupted him, "You want to know what war is about? Take a look at this." Frank whirled around in his chair, slipped off his loafer, and brought his foot across his knee. He rolled down his sock to surprised oohs and ahs from onlookers who stared in horror at the gnarled foot. "A Kraut tiger tank at Bastogne . . . went right over it. I passed out after I tossed the grenade. I thought I lost my whole leg, but we stopped 'em."

Eyes popped and widened amidst groans and sympathetic sighs. I don't think we paid for a single drink the whole night after that story. On the way home, Frank told me how sorry he felt for my uncle Frank. "What a fucking experience. It must have been awful for the poor guy."

I hated to disillusion him, but I had to tell him the truth. "Don't feel sorry at all," I said. "My uncle Frank lost his foot hitchhiking on the back of a trolley car in the Bronx when he was twelve years old. He tells a great war story, but it's all bullshit. It was a jolly trolley, not a terrible tank."

Frank looked at me in disbelief. "Don't get me wrong," I said. "I know he suffered growing up. He had operations, rehab, a bad disfigurement, walked with a limp, and was classified 4-F in the draft while his pals went into service. It had to be rough for a competitive guy like my uncle. He was a star athlete in spite of half a foot. He played football and pitched for his Gompers High School baseball team when they won a city championship, but he was never one of those battling bastards of Bastogne."

There was a long silence before the chuckles turned to giggles, and the both of us had a good belly laugh on our walk home.

The next day, Frank came out of the water and passed a couple of girls wearing tight, form-fitting, Esther Williams, one-piece bathing suits, sitting on their beach blanket, playing loud music on their portable radio. From my captain's chair, I watched him stop and start a conversation with the girls. They talked and laughed, and a few moments later, Frank sat down on the blanket with them. There was no doubt about it. He was a natural with the ladies. The three of them looked over to me, smiled, and waved for me to join them. My mother and father gave me a rather curious look when I got up. I could only imagine what they were thinking.

Darlene had dark, short, wavy hair and wore heavy makeup. She liked to be called Dolly. Laurie was taller than Darlene or Dolly, with striking blue eyes and bleached hair tied up in a ponytail. We flirted, shared some loud laughs, and then went to the White House, which was a beach bar on the boardwalk facing the ocean. We killed the afternoon with more loud laughs mixed with storytelling, singing, and dancing to a busy jukebox. We had a good time and made a date for the next day, which was Sunday and the next to last day of our furlough. Monday evening, we left for Camp Stoneman, California, from LaGuardia Airport.

By lunchtime the next day, there was no sign of our dates. We figured it was a no-show. I read my book while Frank took a nap. It was late afternoon when my mom poked me. "Is that young woman waving at you?"

I looked over to the next blanket down from ours. "Hello, you big bum," mouthed Darlene, who was wearing a low-cut, revealing bathing suit. She took a deep drag on her cigarette and blew smoke in our direction. Laurie smiled and waved to us.

"Do you know them? Are they the same young women from yesterday?" my mother asked incredulously.

"Yes, Mrs. Donohue. They said they might see us on the beach," said Frank, gathering his clothes as he walked to their blanket. My father peered over his Agatha Christie paperback, not getting involved.

"We'll see you at six for dinner, okay, mom?" I said, getting up.

"Don't be late, honey. We might be having guests."

"Okay, mom. I won't be late.

"Have fun," I heard my father mumble from behind his book.

We hung out on the beach for the rest of the afternoon until it was almost six o'clock. I told the girls that I had to go back to the house to meet some relatives who were making a special visit before I went to Korea. Frank made some cockamamie excuse for coming with me when the truth was that he was hungry and didn't want to miss my mom's cooking. We made a date for seven o'clock to go out on the town.

My cousin Sonny and his new girlfriend, Alma, were already at the house, having whiskey sours and cheese snacks with my folks. They couldn't stay for dinner. It was a drop-in to say hello, good-bye, and good luck. Sonny was cool. He was a sergeant in the air force who was reactivated for the Berlin Airlift and still served in the reserves. I clued him in on our situation, and he enjoyed sharing our predicament with Alma.

Frank was in the outdoor shower, and I was talking to my cousin when I heard our names called out in the courtyard. "Joe! Where are you?"

Frank started singing, "Lover . . . when you're near me," and down the walk sashayed Lori and Darleen in their tight, wet bathing suits, looking like a couple of floozies.

"What are they doing here?" shrieked my mother. "Get them out of here!"

Frank came out of the shower in his robe and gave me, Sonny, and Alma a wry grin and called over to my mom. "Sorry, Mrs. Donohue, I'll take care of it. They're probably looking for me," and he hurried over to the girls. There was a loud, animated discussion. I excused myself from my guests and joined the conversation.

"Mom, Darlene and Lori are not staying, but they would like to take a shower, wash their hair, and change out of their bathing suits, if that's okay with you. Frank and I are going to meet them later at the Seaside Inn."

"I don't care where you meet them as long as it's not here."

"I'll get them out of here," my aunt Aggie said in a low, threatening tone.

"Stay out of this," my mother lashed back at Aggie.

I couldn't believe what was going on. "Okay, let's not get crazy," I said. "Everyone, please calm down."

"They are not to come into this house. Is that clear?"

"Yes, I hear you loud and clear. It will only be for a few minutes, and then they're gone."

The next half hour seemed a lifetime. Frank and I smiled and laughed a lot and tried to lighten things up. We even slipped the girls some money to hurry them along. Frank and I dressed quickly. We gulped our food, said good-bye to Sonny and Alma, and raced out of the house to the Seaside Inn. The chords of a guitar could be heard from down the street. Voices chimed in with the nasal cowboy singer as they lindy-hopped to "oh, listen to the rumble, the rattle and the roar . . . listen to the music . . . of the Wabash Cannonball."

The place was packed body-to-body. I poked Frank and pointed to Darlene and Lori laughing and chatting with guys at the bar. I looked at Frank and shouted in his ear as the medley went into "Detour . . . there's a muddy road ahead . . . detour . . . pay no mind to what it said."

"There go our dates and our money," I said sadly.

"Should have read," continued the song, "that detour sign."

Frank went ahead of me. We plowed our way through the crowd from the dance floor. I was expecting trouble; however, Frank nodded his head to the guys, and I smiled as if we were just coming back from the bathroom. We tried to act cool. "Sorry we're late, girls. How are we doing?" asked Frank.

"It's about time," said Lori. "These are the two mugs we've been waiting for," said Darlene, turning her back on the guys they were with. There was no fuss or bother, and I quickly ordered another round.

The evening got late and was too beautiful to spend bar hopping. Darlene and I left Frank and Lori on the dance floor of the Irish Circle so that we could walk along the beach. The moon was bright, and the air sultry. We ended up necking on the sand underneath the boardwalk and lost track of time. I woke Darlene. It was early in the morning. She was frantic about the time. She had to catch a bus to Brooklyn without Lori. She couldn't find her sandal. We looked for it but couldn't find it. She was afraid she'd miss the last bus home. She discovered she had left her house keys at home and realized that she was going to have to ring the bell and wake her parents. "I look like hell," she moaned. "And my father's going to kill me."

I didn't have the money for a cab from Rockaway to Brooklyn. Would I have taken her home to a father who was going to kill his daughter for staying out all night, drinking and sleeping on the beach with a soldier who was going to Korea in forty-eight hours?

We just made the last bus to Brooklyn. Darlene lived over a storefront in a three-story apartment whose vestibule door, without a key, could only be opened by ringing the bell. Darlene was nearly hysterical. We stood in the entrance to the store with our arms around each other. She wanted me to write to her. She kissed me. She cried. She wanted to be my girl. She loved me.

"I'm afraid to go upstairs. You have to come with me and talk to my parents."

"It was great fun, Darlene, but I can't just wake up your parents at five o'clock in the morning, a stranger, and try to explain what happened."

"You've got to," she begged.

"This is not the time to meet your parents, Darlene. I'm sorry. The evening is over. Tell them you missed the bus and you had to wait for a ride home."

I kissed her on the forehead and left. I was not going to try to explain to pissed-off parents what had happened to their daughter.

"Joe, come back here!"

I turned and waved. "I'll write," I said. "I have to go." I wasn't hanging around.

At the bus stop, I checked the schedule. The next bus wasn't due for another half hour. I sat down on the curb. It was getting light out. I put my head down on my knees. I was tired. It had been a long night.

"Joe, don't leave me. Please! I can't face them alone," kept ringing in my ears. It would be a long thirty minutes. I hoped the schedule was wrong and the bus would come earlier. I couldn't relax. I kept looking around expecting to see a crazed man waving a pipe in his hand and looking for that bastard Joe.

An hour later, I quickly stepped onto the porch of my bungalow. I reached for the door handle, and my mom was standing there in her bathrobe. "Oh, thank God you're home! I've been up all night worried sick," my mother cried. "What happened?"

"I'm okay, Mom," I said, opening the door. "I took Darlene home and—" *Whack!* She hit me right across the face. The blow froze me, and my cheeks burned as my mom stormed off into the bedroom and slammed the door shut.

I stood there, speechless, thinking. I was a twenty-year-old army paratrooper, away from home for six months and going to Korea, and I had gotten smacked for coming home late. It would have been laughable if my mother hadn't been so upset.

"I can't believe you took her home," said Frank, getting up from a cot in the foyer after witnessing the whole exchange.

"It's a long story, Frank. She missed her bus. She lost a shoe. She had no money. She left her keys at home. It's early in the morning, and she's afraid her old man is going to beat her. You get the picture. What was I supposed to do?"

"You should have stayed with us, but then you wouldn't have scored." Frank grinned and then continued, "Your mom's got a nice left hand."

"She hit me like I was a naughty little kid," I said.

"You were but don't worry. She'll get over it," Frank said, getting dressed. "I've got to get going, Joe. My folks are expecting me. I had a great time. It was a nice farewell."

"Thanks for coming. See you tomorrow night at LaGuardia.

"Corny and I will be there."

My cousin Joe Camming was a ticket manager for United Airlines. He insisted that he take care of the booking arrangements to California and drove my mom and dad and me to the airport. My dad would be reimbursed by my buddies for the money he laid out for the tickets. We had an eight o'clock flight and planned to meet at the United Airlines counter at around seven o'clock. By 7:15, there was no sign of my guys. By 7:30, I was getting anxious. At 7:45, there was still no sign of them. Passengers began boarding the plane. I was resigned to going to California alone. They were not going to make it. My mother was praying. My father was wondering about his money, and my cousin was upset. At ten minutes to eight, I saw two soldiers sprint across the airport lobby. "There they are!" I shouted.

My cousin bolted over to the check-in attendants. Corny and Frank had that exhilarated look in their eyes like they had just won their heat in a long-distance race. Guilty apologies, quick introductions, hellos, and good-byes were hastily made. My mom cried and kissed Corny, whom she had never met before, and asked God's blessing on Frank.

I shook hands with my dad, who was relieved everyone was here and had paid him for their tickets, though he was sad that I was leaving. My mom wrapped her arms around me. I could feel the tears on my face and hear only some of the words spilling out of her mouth: "Promise me you'll take care of yourself. Come back. Don't bring home a war bride. We'll love her just the same. Write often."

I smiled at the thought of Darlene. "Mom, I'm going to be okay, and I'm not bringing anyone except myself. Please don't worry. I'll be fine. You and Dad take care of yourselves. I'll be all right."

"Let's go," said my cousin. He ran up the boarding ramp, and we followed behind him. "Wait here," he said and ducked into the cabin.

"So what the fuck happened to you guys?"

Frank gave me a sheepish smile and then looked at Corny. "I gave our New Jersey buddy a quick tour of Times Square and the clubs on Stripper's Alley."

A stewardess and three passengers came off of the plane and passed us on the ramp. My cousin waved us up.

"I hope we didn't bump anybody," I said and shook my cousin's hand.

"You guys are a government priority," he said and smiled. "I'm glad your buddies made it. Have a nice flight to California and good luck in Korea. Kick some ass over there."

"Thanks again for everything," I said, and the three of us scrambled up the ramp into our plane. Who would have thought it, but it had been a hectic, tense, and sad furlough home. We were headed for Camp Stoneman, which was the entrance to the pipeline to Korea.

Army identification picture

Army recruit

Kitchen Police (KP duty) at Fort Jackson, South Carolina (1952)

"B" Battery, 45th FAB, basic training platoon at Fort Jackson, South Carolina (1952)

Basic training graduation day (1952)

PART 3—REPLACEMENTS

CHAPTER 15

AWOL #1: THE GREAT ESCAPE

It was a relief to be headed for California. The peace and quiet and boredom I looked forward to at Camp Stoneham turned into something more than I had expected. When Frank and I learned we were shipping out for Korea in the morning, we went "absent without leave," and I got caught.

Thick black eyebrows came together and formed an arch over soulful brown eyes. An ample Roman nose protruded over generous lips, which parted in an elfish grin. "You should have been with us, Joe. We had a blast," said Corny. "Didn't we, Frank?"

"Yeah, but it was just another day in New York. Sorry for being late, Joe, but I had to show the Jersey Boy Stripper's Alley," grinned Frank.

"You're right. I should have been with you guys instead of having to worry that you might miss our flight." As upset as I was, I liked Corny. He and Frank were my good buddies and fun to be with.

The long ride to California turned out to be a pleasant one, except for my duffle bag ending up in Oakland. At the airport in San Francisco, we had to wait around and kill time before the Kid's plane arrived, so I grabbed a cab and retrieved my bag. When he finally landed and came down the ramp, we gave him a big, loud "Airborne all the way!" and watched his chubby cheeks turn a crimson red. It was a quick reminder of how we had first started to call Bobby the Kid. Dressed in his summer uniform, he looked more like a Boy Scout than an army paratrooper headed for the war in Korea.

We had time before we had to report in and a lot of catching up to do, so we decided to have lunch in the airport lounge. A cute waitress took our order. "I know you're all twenty-one, even you," she said, smiled, and looked straight at the Kid.

"He's older than he looks."

"Yeah, I'm a lot older," said the Kid. He looked around conspiratorially and said in a low voice to our waitress, "Actually, I'm even younger than I look," which brought a big laugh from the waitress and from us.

I had forgotten that you had to be twenty-one to be served alcohol in California. In New York, the legal drinking age was eighteen. Frank and I had been drinking in the National Guard since we were seventeen, and of course, you were served beer on post, so we never gave it a second thought.

"Think about it, guys," said Corny, tongue in cheek. "We're not too young to die for our country, but we are too young to be served beers in California."

Camp Stoneham turned into a drag. One day blended into the other. From my top bunk, I could see the distant outline of the Sierra Mountains across fields of yellowed grass. Because the weather in California never changed, the scene from my window never changed. To make matters worse, every time I stepped outside, I was greeted with the strong, unpleasant smell of sagebrush, which fortunately didn't interfere with my appetite. After chow, we had another routine. We had to line up with our hands extended, fingers touching the fingers of the guys on both sides of us to pick up the proper distance, and walk around the barracks to police the area. I can still hear the sergeant's favorite refrain: "I want to see asses and elbows. It doesn't move. Pick it up."

I read a lot of Mickey Spillane pocketbooks while I was waiting for a formation to be called. This could occur at any time, and it kept us close to our barrack. When a formation was called, we dashed outside and lined up, hoping to hear our names called and receive our shipping orders for Japan. I became envious of those soldiers whose names were called. I would curse and mutter under my breath and troop back inside my barrack, climb up on my bunk, and continue reading my book. Looking out the window across the fields of yellow brush and the mountains in the distance only made matters worse. I began to understand what a prisoner must feel as he started to go stir crazy.

Those of us who were still waiting for orders were mostly kids who had recently completed one kind of vigorous training or another. We were young, bored, and primed for action. In other words, we were ready to explode. To release the pent-up energy, we ended the day with a pillow fight. The night was our delight. Like two football teams, we lined up each night for the charge of the light brigade. It was brutally simple. No rules. No penalties. Anyone who was able to touch the other end of the barrack wall was the victor for his side. Bodies slammed into each other, and pillows flailed mercilessly. It was sheer bedlam and joy. The spirited exuberance was a spectacle to behold and a great wonder that nobody got killed.

One evening just before chow, Frank and I were in a groove, lighting and ringing up free games on the pinball machine in the dayroom when two cadres came in and asked us our names. They told us that a hasty formation had been called twenty minutes ago and that we were on it along with Corny and the Kid. We were on the roster to ship out for Japan first thing in the morning. Frank and I were so hyped that we decided to skip chow and go into town and have a farewell dinner party. We had been saving a couple passes for such an occasion. The only drawback was that they were given to us by a couple of Hispanic soldiers who had already shipped out, so they were outdated. The word was that if we had money for a cab, we could get off base easily. All we had to do was flash the cards at the gate without them being closely inspected. If we took a bus, then we would need real passes, because the MPs boarded the bus and carefully checked out each pass.

"Nice and easy now," said Frank. "We flash our cards nonchalantly. Cabbie, when you go past the guardhouse at the exit, wave to the MP and slow down but don't stop," said Frank.

"You really eat this up," I said, smiling. "I hope it works."

"You've got to play the part, Joe. It's all showbiz. If we don't pull this off, we're in trouble, but it's not the end of the world. You know what I mean?"

"Yeah, I know what you're saying. What are they going to do? Send us to Korea?"

Frank looked at me, and we both laughed hilariously, thinking we were so funny.

"Okay, get ready. No smiles. Nod. Hold passes up. Keep going, cabbie. Yowie! Piece of cake," said Frank. We even received a salute as we passed through.

I thrust my head up to the driver's seat. "Cabbie, we want to go to a place that has good food and cheap prices and doesn't check soldiers for drinking age."

"I have place for you," said our Mexican cabdriver in a singsong voice. "*Peets . . . burg, Lee . . . tul Peets . . . burg. Food es bueno. Cost es bueno.*"

"Sounds *bueno* to me," I said in my best first-year-of-college Spanish.

The Barbary Coast looked like a decent restaurant. The patrons at the bar were friendly and bought us some beers. A couple of guys asked us a lot questions, which I thought was a bit much. When were we shipping out? Where were we going? What was our military specialty? I felt a bit uncomfortable talking about my service. Then suddenly, this guy who was holding his stomach staggered in from the street and collapsed onto the floor. He lay there, and nobody paid any attention to him. I could see blood on his shirt. Everybody shut up and just turned around. Nobody moved to help him. I was bug-eyed looking at the scene. He rolled over and struggled to his feet and made his way to the back of the restaurant, where he disappeared. I heard a siren. One of the waiters wiped up the floor and another came over to us. "Maybe MPs," he said. "If you want to leave, follow me."

Frank and I didn't need a second invitation. We followed the waiter to the back of the bar room where we had last seen the stabbed man. There was no one there. A door was unlocked for us, and it led to an alley. We thanked the waiter and took off.

After a few blocks, we came across a greasy spoon with a blinking neon sign announcing sizzling hot steaks and chops. We were starved. It was time to eat and get back to camp. "Can you believe that place?" asked Frank as we sat down at a scarred, beat-up table. "I felt like I was in a den of spies."

"I know what you mean," I said. "Remember in the last war how 'loose lips sink ships'?"

Frank laughed and said, "Of course I do. Maybe they were Commies. Who knows?

I wondered what happened to the guy who got stabbed.

A waiter came, and we ordered like it was our last meal. I had baked potatoes, a medium-rare steak, a salad, and Mexican beer. Frank had the same except he liked his stake rare and his beer American.

"There was no one there, and I didn't see any blood. It was like he disappeared into thin air."

"They were glad to see us go, Joe, and I was glad to leave," said Frank. "They didn't want a couple of GIs without passes and under the drinking age to be talking to the police and telling them what they saw."

"We would have all been up shit's creek. Maybe we should go back and thank the waiter," I said with a rueful smile. "I have to go to the john."

I came back a moment later. "This is a real classy place. Would you believe the bathrooms are under repair? I have to use the one in the restaurant across the street."

"Okay, but hurry back. We're going to get served soon."

I went outside to the bar across the street. The streetlights were few and far between and gave off little light. There was a darkened alley next to the restaurant, and as I passed it, I thought I saw movement, so I hurried my step. A deep voice came out of the darkness, "Military Police. Hold it right there, trooper."

"Oh, shit, MPs," I moaned and kept walking while I pulled my folded tie out from the epaulet on the shoulder of my khaki shirt and quickly tied a knot. I then yanked my overseas cap from under my belt and hastily placed on my head.

From behind, a flashlight caught me in its glare, and a voice boomed out, "Freeze, soldier!"

I stopped and turned around. Two MPs were in the alley. They had two soldiers against the wall, and they were checking their papers. One of the MPs walked toward me and waved me into the alley with his searchlight. "Over there, trooper," he ordered. "Put your hands against the wall and spread your feet wide."

"I don't understand. Is there a problem?" I asked as politely as I could.

"Lean against the wall and spread your legs, soldier," said the deep voice. A boot toe pushed the insides of my ankles farther apart. "You're out of uniform." Hands went up and down my legs. My rear end was patted, and a hand stopped on my wallet pocket.

"That's my wallet," I said. I took my hand off the wall and put it over my wallet pocket only to have my hand slapped away.

"Keep your fucking hand on the wall before it gets broken. I'll tell you when to move."

The contents of my wallet were checked.

"Turn around, Julio," the MP ordered with his flashlight on my open wallet.

"My name's not Julio," I said.

"It's not?" he said in mock surprise. "Well, that's not what it says here. Well now, I'll have to add stealing another soldier's pass and absent without leave to the charge of being out of uniform. Get into the jeep."

I squeezed in next to the other soldiers for the ride back to camp. I thought about Frank with all that food in front of him, waiting for me to come back. He'd think I had gotten mugged or murdered. He would look for me, knowing that something had happened. I hoped he had enough money to pay for the dinners. Otherwise the restaurant would call the MPs, and Frank would be checked out and arrested. I expected to see him brought in and really pissed off at me.

I had to take the laces out of my boots and give them to a tough-guy corporal who cross-examined and accused me of all sorts of things, which was a lot of garbage. I signed a simple statement as to what I had done, and then I finally got to go the bathroom. There was no place in the jail cell to lie down, so I sat and nodded the rest of the night. I couldn't sleep, and there was no talking. Several hours later, my cell door swung open, and three MPs carrying shotguns came in. They divided us into two columns and marched us to breakfast. We entered the mess hall with a guard in front of us and one on each side of the two columns. They held their weapons at port arms. Looking at us, you would have thought we were highly dangerous, maximum-security prisoners the way we were being treated. We passed soldiers already waiting for their food and went right by them to the front of the line. We were an obvious spectacle. Eyes knowingly gave us "bad dude" looks. Surprisingly, I found myself rather enjoying all the negative attention. There were some legitimate, bad-ass characters in the group I was in, and they looked menacing. The chow-line servers heaped food on our trays like this would be our last meal. Because I hadn't eaten dinner, I encouraged the large portions of eggs and bacon by holding out my tray and keeping it there until I was satisfied. I was getting firsthand treatment from the kitchen police. I wondered what my folks would say if they could see me now.

After chow, I marched out of step with a hint of a bad-ass swagger back to the Military Police Headquarters. I was given back my wallet and a copy of the statement I had signed and placed in a jeep with another soldier and brought to the officer of the day's office. The OD wasn't there yet, so I had to wait. The MPs had another stop and took off in the jeep with the other soldier. They said they would be back.

The receptionist showed me to a bench in another room. I sat down as she closed the door, thinking how badly I had screwed things up. Nobody knew where I was, and I was going to miss shipping out with my buddies later in the morning.

I was depressed. I was stuck here all by myself. I looked out the window. It was still dark, but daybreak was only an hour or so away. I don't know what made me do it; however, I tried raising the window, and it moved. My eyes almost popped out of my head. I pushed up some more, and the window opened. My mind screamed escape.

I stood up and tiptoed to the door. I heard nothing but the chatter of a typewriter. I stuffed my statement into my back pocket and went back to the bench. I slowly lifted the window, making as little noise as I could until I got it to the point where I snaked my body over the sill and let my boots hit the ground. I looked about, straightened up, and walked briskly to the back of the one-story office building and headed for the other side of camp. I knew my barracks were on the opposite side of the administration buildings. I wasn't sure exactly where or how far, but I was heading in the right direction. I saw an elevated red light in the distance and was sure it was the light from on top of the water tower near my barracks.

There was a movement on the street ahead of me, and I froze. My first thought was that they had discovered that I was missing and were looking for me. I turned and scooted across a lawn and ducked behind a building. They couldn't possibly know I was gone because I had just left. I had to calm down and concentrate on what I was doing. The commotion was people getting into a car that proceeded to go right by me and around the corner.

I came out and continued my power walk. The vision of being hunted by MPs with shotguns played in my head. I tried to dismiss the thought that they might shoot me. It was a crazy notion, but the idea wouldn't go away. I thought about going back. If I had gotten away without being noticed, I probably could go back and slip through the window, and nobody would be any wiser. Shit, I left the window open. I should have closed it. No, I couldn't. I couldn't reach it.

I walked. I trotted. I covered a lot of ground. There was no turning back now. I passed twin maintenance sheds that I recognized, and my heart did a double beat. How could I forget those sheds and the ditch surrounding them? The week before, I had pulled guard duty around those sheds and had nearly broken my neck. I was tired and had trouble keeping my eyes open when suddenly *bam!* I found myself rolling down the embankment and into the ditch. I leaped up, startled, thinking that somebody had jumped me, and then I realized that I had fallen asleep while I had been walking my post. I was embarrassed as hell having to explain to the corporal of the guard how I had gotten grass stains and dirt on my uniform. I told him I had fucked a snake in the grass, and he laughed and told me not to do it again.

As I jogged, I felt a surge of relief, knowing that I had made it. I smiled at the thought of the MPs reporting to the officer of the day that he had an AWOL prisoner from the replacement center waiting inside for him. The next street was mine. I could see someone leaning over the railing at the top of the stairway outside of my barrack. The figure waved to me, and I waved back excitedly. I broke into a run.

"Where the fuck have you been? I've been up all night waiting for you."

I frantically waved my hands for him to be quiet. I collapsed on the bottom step, sucking wind. "You son of a bitch. What happened?"

"Shhhh," I said and put one finger to my lips and waved my other hand like a baton. "For Christ's sake, be quiet," I gasped.

"Be quiet!" he boomed. "I should be quiet? I could hear the taps on your boots a mile away."

I leaped up the stairs two steps at a time. "The MPs ... they're after me. I just escaped from them," I blurted out. "I'm on the run."

At first, Frank looked at me in disbelief and then did another take. "Okay, okay, no sweat. You're okay. You're fine," he said, trying to calm me down. "I packed your gear. It's on your cot.

Change into your fatigues, and you're ready to go. The trucks are supposed to be here in an hour. We're *sayonara*, pal."

It was the longest sixty minutes of my life. I scanned the camp from the upstairs room of my barrack. I was looking for MPs in their jeeps, their shotguns at the ready, coming hell-bent to get me. I told Frank, Corny, and the Kid what had happened after I had left the restaurant to go to the bathroom. They were mesmerized by my story. When I finished, they just looked at me and shook their heads.

"All of the excitement and your escaping from Stoneham don't let you off the hook, Joe. You still owe me for your steak dinner, pal."

CHAPTER 16

ALOHA, HAWAII

I remembered Pearl Harbor. I was ten years old. My cousin Joan was eleven. We were with our mothers, visiting friends in Long Island. It was after dinner. We were clearing the table. The radio was on. We were listening to music when the program was interrupted by a news flash. Pearl Harbor in Hawaii had been bombed by Japanese airplanes. American ships had been bombed, and people had died. All of a sudden, we were at war. Our mothers cried, and we rushed home to Manhattan. Joan and I were scared out of our wits. We didn't know what war was or where Hawaii was. All we knew was that Japan was our enemy and that they wanted to take over our country. Ten years later, I was in Hawaii. Japan was our ally, and I was a soldier going to another war.

"Twenty minutes to paradise," said the old-time master sergeant to no one in particular. The plane started to bank, and I could see lights down below.

"Give me six dollars," Frank said, leaning over to look out the window.

"What for?" I asked with a surprised look.

"You owe me for the drinks, the steaks, and the tip from last night."

"You ate my steak and drank my beer, and I should pay you?"

"I didn't eat your streak. What I did do though was check every fucking restaurant and back alley in Pittsburg, California."

"Sure you did . . . after you finished eating my dinner."

"That's bullshit! I walked up and down every goddamn street, thinking I was going to find your dead ass in the gutter somewhere until an MP jeep spotted me. I must have looked lost because they drove straight toward me. I figured I was cooked. Here I am looking for you, and they find me. I had the urge to run, but in desperation, I took the bull by the horns and raised my hand like I was hailing a cab in New York."

"When was the last time you hailed a cab in New York?" I asked derisively.

"Just listen to my brilliance. I knew I was in proper uniform and walking steadily, so I decided to be bold. I walked right up to them and wished them good evening. I told them that I was looking for a buddy I had lost touch with about an hour ago and I was worried. I gave them the whole shebang. We ordered dinner. You went to the men's room and never came back. I told them I'd been looking for you ever since. 'Was he a paratrooper like you?' asked the MP behind the wheel. I nodded, and he told me that one of the MP jeeps picked up a trooper about then. 'Did he have a big red scar up his forehead?' one of them said. 'Yup. That's him,' I said. 'He's okay. They brought him in for being out of uniform and AWOL.' The other MP piped in and laughed like it was a big joke. 'He was also a little disorderly and carrying someone else's pass with a Spanish name on it,' the MP said. I almost choked but managed to smile and shake my head. 'What an asshole, and we're shipping out in the morning.' I was waiting for them to ask me for my pass. 'He'll be all right,' they said. 'He'll spend the night in the brig. We're going in. Would you like a ride?' I tried to act natural. 'Hope it's not an inconvenience for you guys.' 'Hop in!' they said."

Frank continued with his story, "All the way back to camp, I'm waiting for them to check me out. Instead, they talked about going to Korea or getting stationed in Japan. They dropped me off inside the gate, and I was starving from not eating dinner. I went straight to our barrack, hoping they had let you go. I laid all your equipment out on your bunk, hoping you would make it back on time. Now after all I've done for you, you're about to land in paradise and try to skunk me for the six bucks you owe me."

I was about to answer when the master sergeant pointed out the old lighthouse, Pearl Harbor, and Diamond Head as our plane banked over the green-blue water and white, pristine beaches of Hawaii. From the air, it looked majestic. Frank snapped away with his new toy, a cartridge-loaded, Japanese, miniature camera that he let me know cost him seven bucks. "Got some shots of the harbor and the crater," Frank said. "I only hope they come out."

Our plane finished its approach and bumped to a halt. We stepped off of the plane and were greeted with a huge ALOHA sign and lively island music. We were lined up in a single-file line and walked to a waiting entourage of grass-skirted, bare-bellied hula dancers. Banjos played, and barefoot dancers with flowers in their long black hair swayed their hips, smiled, and greeted us, "Aloha, Hawaii," as they placed a garland of flowers over each of our heads and around our necks. I learned that aloha in Hawaiian meant *love to you*, but it was a word that could be used as a greeting to mean *hello* or *good-bye*.

We went to an early dinner at a very fancy hotel not far from the airport. As a soldier, you didn't expect to eat on a patio overlooking Waikiki Beach. The military was seated wherever there was space. The four of us were assigned to a table where we introduced ourselves to a well-dressed, middle-aged doctor and his wife. They told us about themselves and were very friendly and attentive to us. We were a strange mix of khaki, cotton uniforms, linen jackets, and colorful silk dresses. The sun on the water, the soft, gentle breezes, the waiters in their white coats serving us food and drinks made for a fantasy moment. Yesterday, I was an AWOL fugitive escorted under armed guard to a mess hall on an army post, and today, I was an honored guest dining at a fine Waikiki Beach hotel.

The conversation got around to us. People asked what was it like jumping out of an airplane and where we were going next.

"We're going to Korea as replacements," said the Kid. "I just hope we all stay together. I'd feel better going into combat with my friends." He looked up at the couple with those innocent, baby blue eyes. "Better to fight with someone you know rather than with strangers," he said, looking too much like the face on the cover of a Gerber Baby food jar.

There was a pause in the conversation. Tears welled up in the eyes of the doctor's wife. She turned to me. "And you?"

"Yes, ma'am, we're all going to Korea," I said in a solemn tone.

There was a cry of anguish as she slammed her spoon on the table. "You're just babies," she cried and buried her face in her napkin and stormed off of the patio.

Her husband quickly stood up and apologized for disturbing our lunch. He mumbled something about a brother being killed in the last war and left the table. The Kid and I looked at each other, not sure what had happened, but we felt that whatever it was, it was our fault. The doctor and his wife never came back to the table.

We beat up on the Kid for giving sky soldiers a bad rap as baby-faced killers. Bobby Mesic, also known as the Kid, looked like a husky fourteen-year-old when in fact he was a solid seventeen and had gotten parental permission to join the army. I was twenty and looked seventeen. Corny was eighteen and looked eighteen, and Frank was twenty but looked much older. We teased the Kid and told him he was too cute and too young to die for his country. When all was said and done, the truth of the matter was that we were taken aback by what had happened at the table. I think it made us a little more aware of the seriousness of our journey.

After our fabulous dinner, we had to wait hours in the airport for our flight to Japan with a stop at Wake Island. We were told it would be a long delay. As day turned into night, bodies were strewn all over the airport. After some shopping and a careful count of our finances, we decided it was worth going into the airport lounge, which was livelier and more comfortable than the waiting areas. The cost of a beer in Hawaii was outrageously high. The word was out that Alaska and Hawaii were the worst posts in the army to be stationed because of the cost of living there. We shared bottles of beer, pouring them into glasses and nursing our drinks as long as possible.

One table was crowded with guys in colorful Hawaiian shirts, smoking cigars and sipping drinks. To our surprise, a waiter came over with a tray of beers. The guys at the table raised their drinks to us, and we reciprocated. Frank and I went over to the table and thanked them for the beers. The guys were navy pilots stationed at Pearl Harbor. They asked us where we were headed. We told them Japan and then Korea. They had just come back from R & R in Japan. They invited us to join them.

The table was very animated. The pilots were young officers and good talkers. We were privates and good listeners. They immediately took on the role of big brothers.

Thank goodness our money wasn't good at the table because we didn't have much left. They told us what they did to support the troops on the ground. They told us how they flew low to the ground, used napalm, and strafed enemy positions. They took out artillery, convoys, assault troops, and MiG fighters.

The four of us sat there, mesmerized. It was like listening to the older guys on the block proudly telling of their sexual exploits or the scrapes they had gotten into and who had done what in the fights. They were humorous. They were boastful, and they were serious. The two things that stuck with me were that communication between pilots and the soldiers on the ground was the key to success and that they were there to help us whenever we needed them.

Never in my wildest dreams would I have thought that ten years after the bombing of Pearl Harbor, I would be a twenty-year-old soldier sitting in an airport lounge in Hawaii, waiting for a flight to Japan, a former enemy, listening intently to the stories of combat pilots about a war I was about to become a part of. It was a day of acceptance for the four of us. We were now comrades, and at that moment, I felt a sense of pride as a replacement for the war in Korea. Our plane to Japan arrived after midnight. We had a long way to go with a stop over at Wake Island. As we got closer to our destination, Korea was not just a name anymore. I was impressed by the stories of the navy pilots. Like Hawaii, Korea was becoming a slow reality to me, but it wasn't going to be a paradise like Waikiki Beach.

CHAPTER 17

WAKE ISLAND

Wake Island was the first war movie I had seen as a
kid after Pearl Harbor had been bombed. William Bendix
was my hero. One Saturday afternoon, my pals and I saw
Brian Donlevy, Robert Preston, Macdonald Carey, and a
bunch of tough, fearless marines kill Japs trying to invade
the island. The only reason they surrendered was because
they were surrounded by the entire Japanese fleet and out of
ammunition.

After our air force friends said good-bye, we curled up on some
benches and grabbed a little shut-eye. When the announcement
came, it seemed like I had just shut my eyes. Frank and I joined
the scraggily bunch moving outside onto a darkened runway. A
light metallic-gray, two-engine military plane was sitting on the
tarmac rather majestically with a ground crew fidgeting around
her. We had our own private, unscheduled flight to the island of
my marine movie heroes before we got to Japan.

For hours, we flew over nothingness. It was an eerie feeling.
How insignificant we were. If the plane went down, we would
disappear from the earth completely, and it would seem like we
had never existed, so it was a grand moment when the cabin
buzzed with excitement hours later. A tiny morsel of an island
magnificently emerged in the middle of a vast, watery wilderness
highlighted by the morning sun.

We circled the crescent-shaped reef inundated by a shallow lagoon of light greenish blue water. It was a breathtaking view of stark simplicity. Frank, of course, was in his photographer's mode, snapping picture after picture until we landed on its airstrip.

The cabin door opened to a smothering blast of hot, humid air. We were on a sparse, desert isle. There were several hangars housing military transports and propeller-driven fighter planes, along with Quonset huts and a small motor pool of busy mechanics working on planes and military vehicles. Shade was at a premium. Wake Island was a pretty thirsty place. It looked more like a small private airport on a desolate Caribbean island rather than a strategic airbase in the Pacific Ocean, one halfway between the coasts of California and Japan.

We were led to a pinkish gray, one-story, cinder block building that served as a dining hall and a recreational lounge. Slow turning fans hung down from the ceiling. We sat on benches and ate from long wooden tables just like we would in any army mess hall on an army post. Officers sat at their own tables with a splattering of female officers and civilians. Noncommissioned officers huddled about in small groups. The food was good but nothing like the spread at Waikiki. The two things I liked were the pitchers of iced tea placed on each table and the fact that you could get refills any time you wanted them. On Wake Island, I discovered an unquenchable thirst.

After chow, the four of us went back to the terminal building and got some disappointing news. Our plane was in maintenance. We would be hanging around for a while. Frank and I wanted to do some exploring. We had seen the movie *Wake Island* as kids and were curious to see what it was like for the marines to be on the beach cut off and surrounded by the Japanese Navy. The Kid and Corny opted to go back to the recreation room, drink some iced tea, and stay cool.

We walked toward the beach and passed our plane sitting outside one of the hangars. Now we understood why our flight would be delayed. Naked without its engines, our plane looked like a bald shell of metal on a hot, sandy tarmac. Mechanics brandishing all kinds of tools and equipment were putting her together again.

"Who the hell wants to go back up in that?" I said.

"Yeah, maybe they won't be able to repair it, and we'll stay over until they get another plane."

"I don't see any hotels on the beach," I quipped.

"Look over there. Looks like something on the beach, and it's not a hotel," said Frank.

We got closer and got a real surprise.

"They're tanks," cried Frank.

I was so excited I tripped over a strand of barbed wire buried in the sand and kicked up a sun-bleached, frayed piece of webbing. I picked it up and was able to make out the faded letters US. It looked like it was from a first aid packet like the ones we used on our cartridge belts. My hands trembled. I was standing in front of the cannons of two destroyed Japanese tanks, holding some marine's first aid packet that he had worn during the fight for Wake Island. I tried to visualize what it might have been like on this exact spot in 1941.

The tanks were tiny like Frank's miniature camera. The gun barrels were intact but useless. They looked like 57-millimeter cannons, but that was a guess. I couldn't imagine how they managed to load, fire, and drive the tank at the same time.

"Go ahead and sit on the turret and hold up the first aid packet."

"You don't think this tank is booby trapped," I said and smiled, not sure if I was kidding.

"Nah, this is like a war memorial. Nothing to worry about," said Frank.

"You're right," I said skittishly. "There wouldn't be any land mines still laying around after all these years either."

"Will you knock it off and be still. Okay, got it."

I hopped off and handed him the pouch. Frank jumped up and put his boot dramatically up on the turret, looking as if he had just captured the tank. "Can you get the other tank in the picture as a backdrop?" he asked.

"The sight picture is so small I can get only get parts of you and the tank behind you. Hold it! That's good. Okay, General Patton, I got it. Let's get out of here. I'm dying of thirst."

We walked along the beach, and there was still a smattering of debris. "Imagine what it must have been like lying here helplessly, waiting for the Japanese assault. I'll bet those miniature tanks didn't look so miniature then," said Frank.

"I don't think the marines met them head-on. I think they were dug in off the beach and hit them when they came inland."

"How far inland could they go before they reached the other side of the island?"

"I think that was the point," I said. "The few hundred marines fought a delaying action and made them pay dearly for it. They were surrounded, and it was only a matter of time before they got wiped out, so they surrendered. They served their purpose. What would you have done? Would you have surrendered?"

"I don't know." Frank paused. "It depends on the situation at the time," he said thoughtfully. "What about you? Would you have surrendered?"

"I don't think so, but I can't be sure. Maybe I've seen too many war movies, but the thought of being captured and tortured or a firing squad is not for me."

"Me neither. I think I'd rather die fighting. Let's go back to our rebuilt plane."

Wake Island was a grim reminder of what we might have to face in Korea.

CHAPTER 18

GINZA GOOD-BYES

As a kid, I followed the war every day. When Doolittle bombed Tokyo, my friends and I were ecstatic. We were bringing the war to Japan and closer to victory. Ten years later, I was about to land in Japan and see Tokyo as a soldier. It was a weird feeling. I hoped that I could go shopping on the Ginza, Tokyo's Broadway, and have some fun before I shipped out to Korea.

It was evening when we landed in Asaka, a city just north of Tokyo. The first thing that struck me was the Japanese soldiers silhouetted against the glowing city lights of downtown Tokyo, soldiers surrounding the airport, armed with shotguns. It felt like they were prison guards and I was the prisoner. I would have felt better if Americans had been manning those posts. World War II had only ended seven years ago with Japan's surrender.

With my duffle bag balanced on my shoulder, I followed the guy ahead of me into a brightly lit waiting room. As I found a row of seats, my eyes nearly popped out of my head. A Japanese girl in a pleated gray skirt that reached down to her bobby socks and penny loafers was breast-feeding her baby in public. A soldier sitting next to her was casually reading a newspaper, his pistol holster inches from the baby's head. On the other side of the girl sat an old mama who was wrapped in a traditional, silk Japanese kimono and obi. I walked quickly through the terminal, trying

145

to take it all in without looking like an awed tourist. Outside, I noticed the night air was heavy and damp with a sweet fragrance to it.

"Nice smell," someone yelled out.

"Better than that meadow odor at Camp Stoneham," I agreed.

Japanese drivers waited by softly lit lanterns in front of their buses. They smiled and helped us with our duffel bags. On board, I had a seat to myself. Surprised, I sprawled out and made myself comfortable. I liked my first impressions of Japan. I heard it was supposed to be a good place to be stationed.

We drove in darkened silence. I looked over at Frank across the aisle, and he was zonked. Everyone was exhausted. Our bus drove through the motionless Japanese countryside at an easy speed. Our headlights pierced the fog, illuminating dense trees and creating craggy shadows on the road. Every so often, we would stop at a small hut on the side of the road. A Japanese policeman or soldier who was armed with a shotgun would come out, say something in a guttural tone, bow, and then wave us on. Sometimes we would slow down at a hut, and the guard would wave us through. There was a lot of security on the road, and it was all Japanese. *Where are the GIs?* I wondered.

Camp Drake was a replacement training center in Japan. It was our last stop in the pipeline to Korea. It was only miles from the Ginza. It was still being rebuilt from our saturation bombing during World War II.

At Drake, we had less than two weeks to get ready. Aside from running in the morning and doing physical training, I received booster shots (four in each arm), fatigues, underwear, socks, a sleeping bag, an inflatable rubber mattress, and a combat pack. I went through some serious field exercises, but the main focus was zeroing in on targets with my new weapon for combat. I spent two afternoons on the firing range with a brand new M-2 carbine that stunk from Cosmoline, the thick, dark grease that had covered the rifles in their wood packing cases. My carbine smelled for days, and so did I.

"Clean them up good and zero them in right. You're taking these babies with you, and they just might save your swinging ass," growled the ordinance chief, dramatically thrusting out a carbine. "Remember . . . this is your rifle, and this is your gun," he said, gleefully grabbing his crotch. "You want to take good care of both."

Frank grinned wickedly. "I know my rifle from my gun. I'm an expert with both."

We wiped the muck off of our carbines, lightly oiled them, and headed toward the range to draw our .30-caliber ammunition and our fifteen-round magazines. In the National Guard and in basic training, Frank qualified as an expert on the M-1 rifle. I was in the category below. I was a sharpshooter both in the Seventh Regiment and in basic training. Frank never wore glasses. I did for reading, but I never wore them on the range. I wanted to know how I would do without them.

The carbine was not my favorite rifle. It was too small and too light for my taste. It weighed six pounds and was accurate up to four hundred yards and used a smaller round of ammunition. In combat, it was not known for its dependability. The M-1 rifle, which weighed nine pounds and held an eight-round clip with semiautomatic fire, was accurate at a distance of seven hundred yards. They both fired .30-caliber ammunition, but the M-1 round was bigger and more powerful. Although the carbine held a fifteen-round clip and could be fired automatically, I felt more comfortable with the M-1 because I was more familiar with it from my days in the National Guard.

Part of our training at Drake was getting to know our enemy. An overview was given about the Korean people, its history with China and Japan, its geography and culture, and where the war zones were above the Thirty-Eighth Parallel from the Yellow Sea to the Sea of Japan. We were shown captured Korean, Russian, and Chinese weapons and their camouflage and concealment techniques. We were told about the Geneva Convention and how to act if captured by the enemy. We were warned about the clap and shown films about trench foot and frostbite. That same night, a sergeant came into our barrack and scared the crap out of us. He cited all kinds of statistics about being captured, missing in action, and dying from battle wounds.

"You don't want to be a burden on your folks. Bad enough you didn't make it. The least you can do is pay for your own funeral and have a little something leftover for your loved ones."

Frank and I each took out a ten-thousand-dollar policy naming our parents as benefactors. We never told them. We didn't want to worry them. We figured it would be a nice surprise for them. It would be a little something extra from their loving sons. The idea was corny as hell, but the sergeant's sell was good. The reality of war had caught up with us.

Our weekend pass at Camp Drake would be our last one before we went to Korea. We visited Yokohama and Tokyo, which were still ravaged from the bombing raids of World War II. Mt. Fuji with its snowcapped peak rose majestically into the sky and was a constant reminder of Japan's serene beauty.

Our target was the Ginza, but we made sure we shopped at the fabulous Tokyo PX. Rumor had it that you could find anything and everything there not sold in the States and at a cheaper price. I sent home silk pajamas and a kimono for my mom and a smoking jacket for my dad. (When I got home, I learned that they never wore them because they were too small.) For myself, I bought one of those zippered, silk jackets with a red-and-yellow, fire-eating dragon on the front and "Korea" spelled in large letters on the back followed by the words "When I die, I'll go to heaven, because Saint Peter knows I already spent my time in hell." (I never wore the jacket either, and it wasn't too small for me.)

Our last day was spent on the Ginza. We ended up in a light-studded bar called "the Wild West." It had cowgirl waitresses, cowboy music, and Western-style food. After dinner, we sang "Don't Fence Me In" along with a Japanese trio strumming guitars in their boots and Stetsons when hoots and beer glasses flew across the room. A table of rowdy soldiers shouted insults at the singers and imitated their Western twangs. Corny got pissed off and went over to them and asked them to cool it. The Kid, Frank, and I quickly followed, and the soldiers erupted on their feet, yelling and cursing. Chairs got pushed over, drinks spilled and glasses broken. Shoves turned into swings that were interrupted by someone saying, "Need a hand, Yank?" And then a blur of Aussie soldiers joined the fray.

People were jumped and pinned down to the floor. A five-foot cowboy with glasses, a flowered shirt, and a string tie materialized out of nowhere with two Japanese policeman. He waved his arms and gesticulated wildly, bowing to the policemen as he talked. The policemen, their faces stoic, watched the paralyzing struggle on the floor. The GIs on the bottom were calling us "Nip lovers." "Nothing but fuckin' Nip lovers," they said.

The Japanese policemen were like statues, occasionally grunting and nodding to the manager. They didn't get physically involved, which was probably a good thing. The glass throwers were restrained by fellow soldiers who got them cooled off and moved their asses out of there before they ended up in the brig. The relieved manager signaled his cowgirls to come and clean up, and the cowboy trio started singing and clapping to the tune "Deep in the Heart of Texas."

The four Australians joined us, and the manager gratefully brought us a bottle of sake. The bottle multiplied as the night went on. By the end of the evening, we were talking like Aussies, and they were talking like Yanks. We wore their wide-brimmed, side-up bush hats, and they wore our airborne caps. We sang along with the cowboys until they went into "the Streets of Laredo," and Corny became indignant. "They shouldn't be smiling. Laredo is a very sad and serious ballad."

The Kid banged his hand on the table. "Listen up, everybody. You guys realize . . . that Corny, this trooper sitting right there, is the only cowboy from New Jersey. He knows—and I shit you not—every cowboy song ever written. Corny, why don't you go up there and show those guys how to do it?"

Corny swayed up to the podium. The music faltered and then stopped. The Japanese trio was not sure what was happening. They looked like they were ready to beat another hasty retreat, but Corny smiled and waved his arms and sweet-talked them into staying. Seconds later, he turned around, and in a low, melancholic voice, he began to sing a cappella. After several lines, the guitars tentatively backed him up.

"Ah spied a young cowboy all dressed in white linen—" The place quieted down.

It was captivatingly sad but nicely done. The Japanese trio smiled and bowed and gratefully applauded the cowboy form New Jersey. We, of course, went berserk. It was a fun good-bye to the Ginza and a fitting farewell to friends both old and new. It would be the last time the four of us would be together again.

CHAPTER 19

SEPARATION BLUES

When I roughhoused as a kid, my mother would warn me, "Out of fun comes crying." I don't remember who threw the first punch. I was kidding around, but Frank didn't have to throw me down a goddamn flight of stairs the night before we shipped out for Korea and went our separate ways. That was the really unexpected blow.

The two gymnasium-sized floors were covered with wall-to-wall soldiers, their gear splayed across iron bunk beds, waiting for a ship to take them to Korea.

On the second day of this frenetic scene, Frank and I got picked for a guard detail. A tall, bespectacled, no-nonsense sergeant read off a short list of names and duty hours. Frank and I were on different two-hour shifts. I would relieve him at his post at nine o'clock in the evening, when I would begin my shift. The sergeant carefully walked our group through the various posts we would be responsible for, showing us where each fire alarm was located. At the end of the tour, he gave us our instructions. It started off with a dire warning: "This will be one of the most dangerous guard duties you will ever pull. Look around you. There's a lot of movement and a lot of smoking. People get careless. Accidents happen, so stay alert. Now listen up. At all times, guards must wear the red plastic helmet liner with the words 'Fire Guard' stenciled across the front in white lettering. For sanitary reasons, it is recommended that you wear your fatigue cap with the brim tucked up under the liner. To be properly relieved from duty, you must check in with the guard you are replacing, ask for any specific instructions, and then take the red helmet liner and place it on your head. Then and only then will you be properly relieved from your post. Any questions?" he asked.

I looked at my watch. It was time to go. I got up from my bunk. I would have to look for Frank. I spotted him walking up the stairs on the ground floor.

"Well, now don't you look cute in your little red fire helmet?"

"Hey, Joe, right on time," said Frank, taking off his helmet liner.

"Whoa, not so fast, fellah," I said as I checked my watch. "Still got . . . two minutes and five seconds to go," I said with exaggerated seriousness.

"Not by my watch," he said. "It's time."

"Excuse me! I have just enough time for a quick smoke. I'll walk with you and keep you company. I'll even count off the seconds as I'm smoking," I said, lighting up.

Frank looked at me like I had two heads. "Don't fuck around, Joe. I'm tired."

"Hold your water. I'll be finished in . . . one minute and fifty-six seconds. Fifty-five seconds . . . fifty-four seconds . . . see how fast time goes by. You'll just have to be patient."

"Don't be a ballbuster," said Frank, taking the helmet off his head and holding it out to me.

I stepped back on the steps and away from Frank. "You are out of uniform, soldier," I said in a feigned shock voice, reprimanding him for not properly carrying out his orders and pompously reminding him that he was not properly walking his post in a military manner and that he was not relieved from duty until I accepted the red helmet and placed it on my head. I blew a cloud of smoke into the air.

Frank gave me a resigned smile. "Let's go, asshole. It's time," he said, trying to put the helmet on my head.

I ducked and knocked it away, backing down the stairs. I checked my watch. "Twenty-two seconds, trooper, and please show a little respect and some discipline here," I said mockingly as I backed away slowly, but Frank was having none of it. He kept coming down toward me, and he wasn't smiling anymore. I started to giggle. "What specific instructions do you have for me, soldier?" I asked.

Frank had fire in his eyes as he leaped down the stairs and grabbed at my shirt, which turned me around with such force that I stumbled backward and fell down onto the landing. There was a brief moment of silence and stunned realization about what had just happened. I got up slowly, gasped for air, and dove wildly up the stairs, falling, stumbling, and swinging with rage. Tears burned my eyes as I collided with Frank and brought both of us down hard. We lay their squirming. Frank was trying to pin me, and I was trying to hit him, simultaneously cursing and sucking wind.

Hands and arms and shouts of "break it up!" and "knock it off!" got us off each other.

Frank and I sat on the stairs. "You guys okay?" asked a voice.

We both nodded. "Yeah, we're good. Fooling around," said Frank, forcing a smile.

"You okay?" I shook my head, but I was really pissed. "Why'd you do that? You didn't have to do that."

"I don't know. I lost my temper, okay? You shouldn't have fucked around like that," he said.

"Yeah, and you can't take a little fun," I said as I picked the red helmet up off the stairs, slammed it down over my fatigue cap, and walked angrily away.

The next thing I knew, I was being poked awake. Frank's face was over me.

"Joe, I'm shipping out. I got my orders. I'm leaving now."

"What about me?" I asked, bolting upright in the bunk.

153

"Your name didn't come up. It wasn't called," he said with sadness in his voice." I was hoping I'd be able to wake you and tell you we were going together, but it didn't happen."

"Damn it! Goddamn it! You're going without me?"

"I'll have my mom give my mailing address to your mom," said Frank.

I got slowly up from my bunk. "Yeah, I'll do the same," I mumbled in disbelief.

"We'll be fine, just fine," said Frank, tears welling up in his eyes. "We'll be okay."

"Yeah, we'll come home together," I said and nodded. "Who knows? Maybe we'll end up in the same outfit. You never know. In the army, anything can happen," I said without much conviction. "We could meet on a chow line somewhere like in jump school," I said with false enthusiasm.

"We will, old pal. Everything will work out."

"You're right," I said, hearing my voice crack.

"Shoot straight, partner, and take care of yourself," he said.

I nodded and said, "Sorry about last night. You were right. I was being an asshole."

"Hey, what's a few punches between pals," he smiled as he walked away.

I was still feeling sorry for myself when my name was called the next day.

CHAPTER 20

THE CROSSING

When Frank and I left Camp Drake, Corny and the Kid were still there. The four of us had been together since jump school. We were no longer the four musketeers. I always had a feeling that maybe they never went to Korea. They were both regular army volunteers, whereas Frank and I were draftees. They could have been reassigned to one of the occupation outfits in Japan. Anyway, I was sad going to Korea without my buddies despite the nice send-off we got at Yokahama.

As I waited for transportation to take me to the Port of Yokahama, a group of air force replacements came into Camp Drake. I was surprised to meet two old neighborhood friends, Bobby Wascik and Red Murphy, who had lived on my block. The army never ceased to amaze me. I kept meeting guys I knew from Manhattan in basic training, jump school, and now Japan. In many ways, the army was like a small neighborhood unto itself.

The drive to Yokahama was a short one. I trudged up the gangplank of our troopship in fresh fatigues and combat gear but without the new carbine that I had zeroed in at Drake. In its place, I had brought a used M-1 rifle like the one I had had in basic training.

The salty sea air smelled delicious as usual. It was one of those beautiful, late, sunny afternoons that made you feel like doing something special. It was a picture-perfect day for a cruise to anywhere but Korea. People gathered on the dock to see us off. More than a few soldiers were looking for family, friends, or a familiar face. An air force band busily attended to the tuning of their instruments. Crowded bodies were foreshadowed by roofless walls that jutted up from behind the pier like tombstones in a cemetery. Leftover rubble from the bombing raids of the last war was an obvious reminder of still being in a war-torn zone.

Below deck, everything suddenly changed. The air was stale, and the lighting was poor. Five bunk beds, one on top of the other, were coupled with another five bunk beds and stretched along the hold of the ship. The bunks were so close together that if you rolled over, you ended up in the bunk of the guy sleeping next to you. That was a real problem. Nobody wanted the top bunk because every time you climbed up or down, you disturbed your buddies in their bunks, so you became a nuisance. If you rolled over away from your buddy, you could fall out of your rack and hit the concrete deck below.

Back up on deck, sunlight reflected off of the brass instruments as the band played a medley of tunes. When the blast from the boat's stacks blew, it shook the hell out of everybody. We were grateful that the crossing would be a short one. I couldn't wait to get back up on deck. Glorious sunshine reflected off the brass instruments as the band played a medley of tunes. White leggings, helmets, and crossed straps glistened against summer air force jackets. People waved, which provided a festive air to our parting. I found myself waving back, even though I didn't know anyone. The blast from the boat's stacks shook the hell out of me, and it took an instant before I realized that our ship had slipped gently away from the dock. The band was in the midst of the "Saint Louis Blues March." In my head, the naughty version played, "Saint Louis . . . woman . . . she had a yen . . . for men. She never went to bed without her fountain pen."

I listened and watched as the dock grew smaller and smaller. From a distance, I could see the band march briskly off the dock and disappear into the mulling crowd.

They're probably going back to their nice, clean dining hall for dinner served by cute Japanese waitresses, I thought. *Or maybe to a restaurant in Yokahama and listen to some jazz with their girlfriends.*

I stayed up on deck and felt the gentle breeze wash over me as I watched the dock slowly disappear behind the wake from our ship. Guys behind me were already lining up for chow. I was in no rush. I guess I was feeling a little sorry for myself. I thought about those air force guys on the dock and the wisdom of joining the service for four years of soft duty in Japan as opposed to being drafted for only two years and doing hard duty in Korea.

We ate standing up. A Fred Astaire and Ginger Rogers movie was the film for the evening. The Pacific was usually a calm ocean, but when the small swells grew into big ones, everyone turned green at the same time. I heaved over the side, and not everyone took the wind into consideration or made it to the railing in time. The guys below deck had problems getting to the johns on time. Suddenly, things turned ugly. We became a ship of putrid smells and vomiting soldiers skidding on slimy, slippery decks. Amid all this chaos, a chain bar holding open a hatch cover gave way and came down on top of a soldier's head, sending him to sick bay in serious condition. For us, he became the first and maybe the luckiest casualty of the war without ever getting to Korea.

The next day was unbelievably sunny and calm. It was hard to believe what had taken place the day before. As we passed through Sasebo, a huge US Naval base at the southern end of Japan, warships flying the flags of our NATO allies were in their berths alongside American ships. There was everything from submarines to destroyers to tugboats.

A British aircraft carrier cruised by our ship. It seemed tiny compared to American aircraft carriers. I toured the *USS Enterprise* when it was docked in New York harbor at the end of World War II, and the thing that impressed me most was its size. The deck of the *Enterprise* looked a mile long and hovered over the water like a towering skyscraper. Up to that time, I had imagined that all aircraft carriers were pretty much the same size.

I was not unhappy at the sight of a floating air strip brimming with fighter planes. It was a nice feeling, knowing they would be on your side in the war.

"Look, Korea! Over there." There was a commotion on deck as everyone scrambled to look. People craned their necks to see a distant, hazy island.

"That's not Korea," said a soldier, bobbing his head up and down like an ostrich. "We just left Sasebo."

"You're right," said another voice. "It's probably another Japanese island."

One of the crew chirped in from behind, "That's Tsushima. The last island we'll see crossing the Strait of Korea. Pusan is on the other side."

CHAPTER 21

PUSAN EXPRESS

Pusan is the largest port city in Korea. In the summer of 1950, American and South Korean soldiers had been driven by the North Korean Army down the Korean Peninsula to the Port of Pusan. With their backs to the sea, General Walton Walker gave his famous command, "Stand or die."

As I stood on the dock at Inchon, I tried to imagine the thousands of troops in this port holding off overwhelming NKA infantry. Thank God for General MacArthur. His landing at Inchon put the Communists in a vise. From Inchon in the north to Pusan in the south, we had the enemy caught in the middle. Now I was waiting for a train to take me north to my new outfit, the Fortieth Infantry Division in Chunchon.

Clouds of dust kicked up from the truck traffic going up and down to the wharf. Pusan was a busy port city. It was the largest in Korea. I wore a new cartridge belt, steel helmet, and backpack. Everything about me was new except my M-1 rifle. I slung my duffle bag up into the troop carrier. Helpful hands hoisted me up, and I fell into a seat where I pulled out the miniature camera that I had bought at the Super PX in Tokyo.

The short ride to the Pusan train station was my introduction to Korea. Round, emotionless faces in drab, loose-fitting, shapeless garments turned to look at us. It was obvious that soldiers riding in trucks and going through their town was nothing new to them.

Some women and children held out hands, hoping for cigarettes or chocolate bars to be thrown to them.

The men looked particularly old. I supposed the younger ones were in military service. The papa-sans interested me the most. Some of them looked absolutely ancient. I took pictures of wrinkled faces and gnarled, bony fingers clutching long-stemmed clay pipes. There was cigarette smoke puffed from wispy beards and toothless mouths. Many of the old papa-sans squatted in pajama-like clothing on the side of the road and stared. I would have loved to have known their thoughts. The Koreans I saw were a sad-looking lot compared to their Japanese cousins 120 miles away across the Korea Strait.

Our convoy came to a halt in front of a patched-up, wooden platform supported by boarded-up windows, cracked ceramic walls, and a slanted roof of red tiles and corrugated tin. A gray, bloated boiler with a front bumper that looked like an old man's pointed beard sat on rusted train tracks in front of the station. Three oversized wheels with a connecting bar guarded the engine on each side. The Pusan Express reminded me of my first train set as a child, except it wasn't black, it wasn't shiny, and it didn't have a big silver key on its side to wind up and make it move.

A water tower that was balanced on precarious wooden stilts with a dangling long chain poured water into the belly of the beast. Hissing sounds of steam rose up into the air. I ducked my head, entered the train, and found myself in a miniature box of a car. My helmet barely missed hitting the roof of the car. At five feet nine and a half inches tall, I was a giant among men. Gratefully, we stored our gear in overhead racks. Ammunition and boxed lunches were stacked at the two ends of the car.

Carved initials, scratches, and graffiti decorated the hard wooden slats that were shaped to form to the contour of an elf. I had to chuckle at one that confidently proclaimed, "Killroy Was Not Here!"

Two people sat uncomfortably across from one another. There was plenty of conversation going on, even though everyone kept sliding down off their slippery seats.

Phil was a small kid from a small town in Vermont. He was never away from home before. I couldn't knock him because New Jersey was the only state I had ever visited. He was very friendly and homesick, and he loved to talk.

"Now look at that beautiful view," he said. "This time of the year with the sun shining on the mountains reminds me of the coming football season. I love football. I played wide receiver in high school. I wasn't tall. I didn't have long arms, but I was shifty and quick and could change direction on you real fast and be past you before you knew it. My brother plays fullback on the team, and I bet he's practicing right now. He's a little bigger than me but strong as a bull. We say he plays bull . . . baaaaaaack."

Our slow-moving train screeched to a halt. The suddenness thrust us off of our seats and into each other. Several sergeants with carbines ran alongside of the stopped train. There was a bevy of áctivity with shouting and whistles being blown. Something was happening. Everyone in our car strained to see what was going on. After several minutes of being motionless, the Pusan Express lurched forward, and we began to move again at a snail's pace.

Our tall, lanky, train sergeant made his way to the middle of the car. "Listen up! Our engineer thought he heard what sounded like shots being fired. He could be right. He could be wrong. The train checks out. No sign of anything being wrong. Everything looks okay, but just in case, every man gets one clip of ammo. The clip goes in your pocket, not your weapon. I repeat . . . the clip is not to be loaded into your rifle. When we get to Seoul, I collect the clips. Understood?"

Phil smiled at me. "I think the sergeant is more afraid of us than the infiltrators."

I returned the smile, but I didn't think it was funny. The ride wasn't peaceful anymore. Rumors raced through the car. We had been fired upon by snipers. Infiltrators were in the area. We might be attacked.

Our train sergeant made his way down the aisle. "Everything's under control. There's no sweat. Relax and enjoy the ride. Nobody's ever been killed on the Pusan Express," he mocked. "Look at the beautiful mountains of Korea surrounded by lush, shit-filled rice paddies, dusty, curvy roads, and clap-carrying *moose-a-may*," he chortled. "You'll be seeing all of them. Remember now, I get back a clip of ammo from every man in this car when we get to Seoul."

I tried shutting my eyes, but it was impossible to relax. Too much was going on. I slid down my seat and looked out the window. Taegu, Taejon, Chonju, and Wonju were familiar-sounding towns from earlier battles in the war. I closed my eyes and wondered if I had just witnessed my first taste of combat without even knowing it.

CHAPTER 22

ROAD TO CHUNCHON

How could you tell a North Korean from a South Korean? It was not a gag line. The answer was you couldn't. In Korea, your enemy could be in front of you. He could be behind you or even among you. He could be anywhere.

We got off of the Pusan Express at the Yong Dung Po train station without our clips of ammo. It was almost deserted except for us. We sat down on our duffle bags and waited. It was overcast and looked like rain. I heard the faint sounds of thunder and caught distant flashes of lights in the sky. "Looks like rain," I said to no one in particular.

"It's not rain. Those are fifty-fives and outgoing," said our train sergeant.

That remark got everyone's attention. The next several minutes were spent in hard listening, low murmurs, and quiet contemplation. Stillness settled around us. Everyone perked up, thankful to hear the moan of engines. They arrived in a cloud of dust and grinding gears.

Hi ho, Silver! I thought.

"Okay, let's move it," barked a relieved sergeant, suddenly alive and full of energy.

Our names were called, and we climbed aboard, filling the benches on both sides of the trucks. The rear gate came up. It was closed and secured, and we were on our way to the most

God-awful, uncomfortable ride in my life. It was like riding a bull in a rodeo. You held on to your seat for dear life. It was much like swinging and swaying with Sammy Kaye and bumping and grinding with Carmen Miranda. There was plenty of bitching and wisecracking, but there was nothing you could do about potholes and rutted roads and a lousy suspension system. The Pusan Express had been a joy ride compared to this.

I was in an open truck and a perfect target for snipers. My only hope was they would have trouble hitting a constantly moving and swerving target.

My eyes were glued to the countryside, not knowing what to expect. As we headed east, our small convoy rolled through a number of tiny hamlets. They seemed to just appear out of nowhere. To me, they all looked alike—a few shanties, scattered chickens, a mangy dog or two, young girls lugging babies, women and children doing chores, old men squatting on their haunches staring at us. They all seemed the same.

There was an obvious lack of young men. The few I saw wore an assortment of army uniforms and Korean clothing, which could mean anything. I supposed most of the missing men were in the military, but then again, maybe they weren't. Maybe they had gone over to the other side. I couldn't help thinking of an army pamphlet I had read that said the average life expectancy for a Korean man was forty years of age. From what I was seeing, I wasn't so sure that was correct.

A young Korean woman in her late teens standing in the doorway of one of the shanties rested a half-naked baby on her hip. Her long, shiny, black hair fell down to her waist. A bright red blouse was tucked halfway into a tight, dark blue skirt that fell just below her knees and showed off a nice pair of legs. She wore no shoes, no stockings, and no makeup. She had on thick red lipstick that matched her blouse. She looked like a Korean version of Jane Russell in the movie *Outlaw*, and her appearance had brought cheers, whistles, and shouts in English, Japanese, and Korean *pidgin* from the guys on the trucks.

"Hey, sweetie!" a GI yelled, "Marry me. I'm all yours!"

"Chop, chop, my *chimpo*, honey girl!" chimed in another voice.

"*Bero, bero, ichi bon, baby-san!*"

The young woman looked away. As far as she was concerned, we were just truck noise. She never reacted. She ignored us completely.

"So what do you think?" asked the old sergeant, rocking along next to me, his voice rising above the din of the truck engines

"She was beautiful," I said.

"Yeah, they should all look like that."

I nodded my head in agreement.

"After a while, they all start looking good to you. When that happens, they'll send you off to Japan on R & R, which means rest and recuperation, but everybody calls it rape and rampage. It's a good deal. It gets you back to civilization for a little while. I've been stationed in Japan since the war ended. They needed ordnance people, so here I am, but I'm getting too old for this. It's time for me to hang it up," he said with resignation. "This is my third war. It's time to go."

I smiled, not sure I had heard him right.

The old soldier continued, "I've been in since '18. I was a big kid at fourteen. Told them I was seventeen. My mother was dead, and the old man didn't care, so I joined up."

"You were in World War I?" I asked incredulously.

"Yup, I was in the big one," he said with pride.

"Unbelievable," I said.

"Think we're all dead or in wheelchairs?"

"No, but I was in the National Guard. My regiment lost a lot of men in World War I. We got decimated on the Hindenburg Line. Every locker in my company had the name of a soldier killed in that battle. It seemed like ancient history to me."

"Well, I could have been one of those names, and here I am sitting next to you going to war."

I just shook my head. I couldn't believe I was going into combat with a veteran from the World War I who was older than my father. I felt like I was in the twilight zone.

Halfway to Chunchon, we passed a hamlet and got a whiff of a terrible odor. Fingers squeezed noses, and breaths were held. It was our first encounter with the smell of a rice paddy. Heads turned, and faces squinted. The stink was awful. Suddenly, there's an explosion, and our truck swerved to a skidding, thumping halt. Everybody froze for an endless moment before bodies went diving onto the floor and over the back of the truck. I ended up shaking in a ditch on the side of the road. My rifle was useless because I had no ammo. Breathlessly, I looked around, but nothing was happening.

"It's a blowout!" someone yelled.

Sweet words brought thankful relief and embarrassed smiles. I walked nonchalantly back to the truck. Drivers from the other vehicles came over, and they had a big powwow. The flat could be fixed, but something had to be banged out. It might take a while. It was getting dark, and it was decided to disperse the men among the other trucks. Our driver and his sidekick would stay with the vehicle and repair the damage.

Our train sergeant pointed to Phil and me. "You and you, stay."

I nodded, but I couldn't believe what I had just heard. Two green replacements were going to stay behind while my World War I veteran and the other guys from our truck climbed onto the other vehicles and went on their merry way.

"Couldn't we all kind of just hang around and leave together?" I mumbled to Phil.

Phil and I were given a bandoleer of M-1 clips that we divided between us. The corporal riding shotgun had a carbine and a walkie-talkie.

"Don't sweat it. We're in friendly country, and Chunchon's a *skosh* away. But you never know. Just to be sure, one man in back and one man in front. Okay, let's go."

"Can you believe this?" I said to Phil.

"The corporal said no sweat," Phil said and grinned.

Across the road from us was one of those Asian arches that looked like the pie symbol we had used in geometry class with

Brother Anthony. On both sides were short, stone walls. I could make out small huts and the lush green field of a rice paddy. Our driver and the corporal worked with their backs to the farm. They faced us as the farmers worked in the field.

The road was pretty empty. Phil and I locked and loaded our M-1s and watched the people working across the road. We were in the middle of nowhere. The sky was growing darker, and it definitely looked like rain.

Our driver and the corporal were grunting and growling. I could see people looking out at us from inside the entrance to the compound. They were curious but went about their work. A small group of Korean farmers talked and gestured toward us. They look excited like they were arguing. Other Koreans joined them. They looked angry.

"The Koreans are coming out," I said.

Our driver and the corporal turned around.

"Put 'em in your sights," said our driver.

Phil readied his rifle, and so did I.

"Keep your safeties on," warned the corporal. "It's probably nothing. Stay cool."

My heart was beating like an Indian tom-tom. It was getting dark and tough to see.

The Koreans reached the archway and turned off behind the wall. Now we couldn't see at all.

I slipped the safety off my M-1 automatically. I was ready to fire if they came over the wall. I could feel droplets of sweat rolling down my cheeks. I knew I was being watched. I could feel it, but nothing happened.

"It's okay. They're farmers. Keep your eyes open and tell us what you see," said the corporal.

"There's a whole bunch of kids looking at us," said Phil.

I scampered down toward Phil's end of the truck. "Yeah, I see them," I said.

"If they come out, don't let them near the truck," said our driver excitedly.

"We're almost out of here."

"They're standing under the archway," I said, putting the safety back on inside my trigger guard, hoping nobody noticed, and cradling my rifle in my arms.

"A few more minutes," said our driver. "I'm almost done."

A young woman came toward the entrance. She balanced a tall bucket on her head. She looked directly in front of her. Her head never moved. She walked tall and straight like a zombie in a scary B-movie flick. She was dressed in a spotless, white, Korean, high-waist smock. Her black hair was tied behind her head in a bun. Brown, almond eyes looked passively out from a moon-round face. I brought my rifle up into position.

"A woman is coming out," said Phil nervously.

The corporal turned around quickly. "Not a bad-looking *moose-a-may*. She's okay."

"Finished," said our driver. "Let's bug out of here . . . fast."

Those were the sweetest words I had ever heard. For my first day in Korea, I had experienced two incidents of uncertainty. First, I had been armed for self-protection against infiltrators, and then I had been disarmed for protection against myself. It was all quite confusing, but in Korea, you could never be quite sure who or where your enemy might be.

CHAPTER 23

YORKVILLE REUNION

The rest of the ride to division headquarters was short and uneventful. When I reached my assigned company, I was in for a big surprise. I met guys from my Yorkville neighborhood in Manhattan. It was like homecoming week in college, except that I was the one coming to Korea and they were the ones going home.

At division headquarters, Phil and I were both assigned to the 224th Infantry Regiment of Fortieth Division. Our new outfit had been in a reserve blocking position for only a few weeks. They had trained at Camp Cooke in California and had come to Korea together as a complete unit. Now after they had served at Kumwah and guarding prisoners in Koje-do and Cheju-do, the men were ready to rotate home. What they needed were replacements.

I was put into a heavy weapons company. Phil went into a rifle company. We were both in the Third Battalion. I was in Mike Company, and Phil was in King Company. Our division commander was General Joseph P. Cleland. I suspected his name was Joseph Patrick, the same as mine, and it made me think that I had something in common with my commanding officer.

The Fortieth Division was made up of the 160th and the 223rd Infantry Regiments. Our regimental commander was Colonel Hugh Harris. We were in IX Corps under Major General

Willard Wyman, which was part of the Eight Army in Korea under General Van Fleet, a famous leader in World War II.

After we spent the day at division headquarters, we set off early the next evening in a three-truck convoy filled with green replacements, lurching uphill and looking for our respective assigned units. The drivers were having difficulty finding where they were supposed to drop us off. I chatted with one driver back in Chunchon who had just been assigned to the motor pool. In civilian life, he had never driven a jeep or truck in his life. I assumed that a lot of these guys were not only new drivers but new to Korea as well. They took their drivers' education course over here.

The darker it grew, the slower the pace and the quieter it got inside the trucks. Partially black-painted headlights barely illuminated the road. Soldiers with flashlights appeared periodically along the route and identified themselves by outfits. Names were called. Bodies jumped out of the trucks. At one such point, Phil's outfit was identified, and his name was called. We shook hands and wished each other good luck. Farther up the road, we stopped again.

Somebody asked, "Anybody going to M Company?"

"Yo!"

Four or five of us responded at the same time. We worked our way to the rear of the truck. There were hasty pats on the back and encouragements from the guys still on the truck. I climbed down, helped by unseen hands. Flashlights that were aimed at the ground flicked on and off.

A roster board was illuminated by a shadowy figure. "Fall in over here," he ordered.

It was pitch black outside. I walked up to the light.

"Name and serial number?" asked the soldier.

My little group responded as truck gears worked to climb the hill with the last of their cargo. Satisfied that we were all in the right place, we were told to follow the bobbing and darting white lights up steps crudely cut into the side of the hill. A thick, hemp rope was stretched out alongside the stairs and could be used to hold on to for support. There was no talking. Only the belabored breathing of replacements lugging their gear uphill could be heard.

At the top of the stairs, the ground flattened out a bit, and I could see dim lights up ahead.

As I got closer, I could see the outlines of squad tents. Our arrival was noted quickly. As I passed by, I heard people inside yell, "Replacements! Damn, we got replacements."

The tents became a beehive of activity and voices. "We got raw meat. Man, oh, man, my ticket home."

Everybody wanted to see the new replacements. Voices cried out, "Anybody from California? How about Pennsylvania? What about Georgia? Any New Yorkers?" somebody asked.

"Yeah, New York!" I shouted.

"Where 'bouts?" came the quick words.

"Manhattan!" I shouted. "Yorkville!" I yelled, keeping up the pace behind the two flashlights in front of me. We stopped at a sparsely lit tent, and a flapped canvas door was pulled open. I ducked through and looked up.

"Donohue," a mustached face of a skinny sergeant said, "Welcome to Mike Company. I'm Sergeant Lewis." He extended his hand and seemed really glad to see me. "This will be your bunk."

Outside, voices were yelling, "Where's the replacement from Yorkville?"

"In here!" I shouted.

I had to step back from getting knocked over. Three or four soldiers in different modes of undress, which meant they had probably dropped everything to see the new replacement, burst into my tent like a bunch of excited kids visiting Santa Claus for the first time.

"Hey, I know you, man," said the grinning soldier in the white T-shirt.

"Yeah, I'm Joe Donohue. We played baseball together on the Eagles. You're Roy Curly. You hung out on Eighty-Third Street, the block I live on."

171

"Yeah, I remember," he said, smiling. "I live around the corner from you."

I turned to a tall, lanky fellow whom I recognized from grammar school. "You're Paul Schenelly. You were a couple of years ahead of me at St. Stephen's."

"Senelly," he said, "That's right."

"You're not Hungarian anymore," I said, deadpanned.

"He's been Senelly since Camp Cooke," said the blond soldier. "I'm Bill Sptizer. You can call me Spitz. I'm from Seventy-Eighth Street. I lived around the corner from St. Monica's. I played ball with the Jets. We used to play you guys all the time."

"And we won!" I said.

Spitz smiled. "Not all the time."

"You did when I was pitching," said Roy.

"They call you Hoop, Roy, Curly, or Otts Man?" I asked, looking at Roy Curly.

"That depends. Yeah, Roy will do, but the guys I came over with from the neighborhood call me Hoop. So you remember Otts Man? I haven't heard that one in a long time," he said, evidently pleased that I had remembered all his names.

"You know Charlie Edsel?" asked Roy.

"Yeah, he and his brother, George, lived around the corner from me on Eighty-Fourth Street, near where you lived."

"They lived on East End."

"He went out with Carol Beckman, a real pretty girl. Her sister, Joan, was in my class in St. Stephen's."

"He's here with Billy Carroll. Yeah, man, we were all drafted from Yorkville together. Went to Camp Cooke for basic and then to Korea."

"I never expected this," I said. "I'm so glad to see you guys."

Everybody started talking at once and laughing and asking questions about the old neighborhood. I couldn't talk fast enough. These guys were really glad to see me. I never felt so welcomed anywhere in all my life. I told them about Frank and how he would have loved to have been here. It was like a reunion.

"This is going to be great. Being together in the same outfit—who could ask for anything more?" I said.

There was a long pause. Everybody looked at me funny. There were quizzical looks on their faces. Roy looked at me, and in a very somber tone, he said, "Hey, man, we're going home."

CHAPTER 24

DRAGON GUN

Unfortunately, the 75-millimeter, recoilless rifle got as good as it gave. It could hit the tail off of a monkey at five hundred yards. When I fired the weapon, flames shot out from both the front and back of the barrel. The dragon in all its fury was dramatic to behold. The only problem was that it gave my position away. By the third shot, it became a shoot-and-scoot mission. Joe Chink had us zeroed in.

The older guys from my neighborhood took me under their wing. They had been drafted the year before me and were ready to go home. They introduced me to everyone. They told me what formations to make and which ones to ignore. They clued me in on everything and covered for me on certain situations like drinking beer in between tents when I should have been in some boring work detail. We rapped about the neighborhood, and I heard all their war stories, which always quickened my pulse.

On the day of my interview with the company commander, also known as "the ole man," my neighborhood pals stood in line with me outside the company command post. They gave me the scoop on the platoon leaders inside, namely who were the good guys and who were not.

They had me primed for the mortar platoon. The 80-millimeters and the 60s were okay, because they were usually in unexposed firing positions. They pushed me to try to get into the 4.2 mortars because they were the biggest and best and farthest from the line. They drilled into me that it was all about getting as far as you could from the Main Line of Resistance (MLR).

The machine gun platoon was good, but the platoon sergeant was young, tough, and a drinker. In addition, you might have had to pull outpost duty. The last thing I was told was to keep away from the 75-RR platoon. It was the pits. It was primarily an antitank weapon, and you didn't want to face down a tank. It was also too loud, too flashy, and the first thing the gooks went for.

I was next up. The wood-crate tent door with the plastic window opened abruptly, and a smiling private stepped out and bellowed, "I got me the mortar platoon."

"Next man," a voice cried out from inside the tent.

I stepped smartly inside and saluted my company commander. The "ole man" was not so old. He was a second lieutenant of medium height in his mid to late twenties, slender, with a close crew cut, and he beckoned me to take a seat. I was told that he was ROTC, a former platoon leader and a veteran of Kumwah Valley, the last battle for Papa-San Mountain. He was very intent, low-key, and all business. His piercing eyes looked straight through you. He introduced me to the platoon lieutenants and their first sergeants, whose names I forgot almost immediately. The two I remembered included the tall, lanky, balding, blond lieutenant from West Point, one with a long German last name, and the first sergeant from the machine gun platoon who looked about the same age as the old man but more intimidating. The sergeant's name was West, and he had both a reputation and an easy name to remember. His face was even more memorable. Thin, stringy, dark hair covered a sickly, milk-white face. A sharp nose was underlined with a wispy mustache the color of his hair. High cheekbones encapsulated sunken, sleep-deprived eyes. The word was that when he drank, he was a real pain in the ass. When he was sober, he was the best. He was cool in combat and looked after his men. Loyalty was the key.

He asked me a few questions about machine guns but seemed impressed with the fact that I was a college student and an Irish kid from New York. I got the feeling I was being sized up six ways to Sunday. To his right sat the West Point 75-RR platoon leader, and next to him was a real old-timer warrant officer (from World Wars I and II). His name was Kelly. He was a legend in the company who took care of the rookies. Holding a white, spotted puppy in his lap, he was both gentle and probing in his questioning.

Strangely enough, Lieutenant Gotshall's opening statement was, "So you knew Curly and Spitzer in New York?"

"Yes, sir, I did."

"Was Curly really a bookie?"

"I don't know if he was an actual bookie, but I do know he took bets on games. That was common with a lot of guys from the neighborhood. They would take and make a few bucks, probably dropping off some bets to the local bookie. They would get a commission of sorts."

"I'm sure he was booking bets here in the company," said Lieutenant Gotshall with a crooked smile.

"I'm sure of it," said West, showing teeth whiter than his skin.

"We had this softball game back in regimental reserve," said the company commander. "There was heavy betting on the game. Curly and his buddies were playing in the game, and there were players from New York, your neighborhood, on both teams. You know where I'm going with this?"

"I couldn't really say," I said with a straight face, my mind creating a scenario with my Yorkville buddies having fun and making some money at the same time.

There was a long pause with rueful smiles in the tent.

"Joe," asked Lieutenant Gotshall, "what is your experience with heavy weapons?"

I gave my background as a rifleman in the National Guard with no real heavy weapons training at all until my basic training at Fort Jackson. I told them of my extensive training on all types of machine guns and mortars.

"Have you ever fired the 75 recoilless rifle?"

"Never," I said with a perfectly straight face.

"You never fired the 75mm during basic training in heavy weapons?" asked the West Point lieutenant.

"I saw a demonstration, and I did fire a subcaliber device that was hooked up to the weapon," I said, "but I never fired a real round because they were so expensive."

All three veterans looked at each other and then looked at me.

My company commander leaned forward. "Talk to me about this subcaliber device, Joe."

At this moment, I knew that I should have kept my big mouth shut.

"Do you have any questions for me?" asked the company commander.

"No," I said, shaking my head glumly. Somehow, I sensed that I had blown it.

"Joe," said the West Point lieutenant, "the 75mm recoilless rifle is the best direct-fire support weapon we have in our company. Every rifle company on the line looks to it for its accuracy and its effectiveness against tanks, bunkers, troops, you name it. The Chinese revere the weapon. They have their own 76s, which they use to great effect. They call it the dragon gun because it can kill both ways by spitting fire out at both ends of its barrel."

"Very interesting," I said halfheartedly.

"One more question," said the old warrant officer, warding off the affections of his mongrel dog, Mike, the company mascot.

"Yes?" I asked, trying to maintain a stiff upper lip.

"Were you ever a bookie or a runner?"

"No, never," I said, trying my best to smile along with the rest of my interviewers.

"Well, Joe, if I was a betting man, I would bet on you. I think you would make a fine gunner in the Recoil Platoon."

"Thank you, sir," I said appreciatively. In my mind, all I could think of was that I was in the fucking 75s. I had been assigned to the fucking "dragon gun."

CHAPTER 25

YON-CHON BIRTHDAY

I crawled up and down hills, waded across streams, sloshed through rice paddies, tracked moving targets, gauged distances, simulated loading and firing my 75-millimeter recoilless rifle until exhausted. I never knew for sure where I was in Korea. I always seemed to be in no-man's-land. On the night of my birthday, someone said that we were near a place called Yon-chon but spelled Yeoncheon. It was like Chunchon was sometimes spelled Chuncheon. Most Korean places seemed to have more than one spelling.

On my twentieth birthday, friends from the Manhattan District Attorney's Office, where had I worked as a clerk in the complaint bureau, met me for a drink in a bar in Chinatown.

One of the guys in our party had just gotten out of the US Marine Corps. He had been with the first marine division in Korea. After a few drinks, he began telling us unbelievable stories of what it was like fighting Chinese soldiers in the retreat from the Chosin Reservoir. I sat there, spellbound, never thinking in my wildest imagination that I would spend my twenty-first birthday in Korea on a hill in a place called Yon-chon.

I received my training from the few corporals and sergeants still around from the Kumwha Campaign. They were my instructors. They were veterans known as "short-timers" because they only had a few weeks left before they would go home.

They were highly motivated to make sure that we were ready for combat. They depended on us to replace them. Few would be going with us. They didn't want us to screw up. They wanted to go home on time and in one piece.

I had mixed feelings. I was happy that Hoop and Spitz and the neighborhood guys who had trained in Camp Cooke and fought as a unit would be rotated home together, but I was sad that they were leaving me.

I smiled at the thought of all those guys on the same boat. I could see them planning their own homecoming party in one of the neighborhood bars. It would probably be the Old Stream, which was a popular hangout. What a blast that would be. I only wished that I could be with them.

I was being trained as a gunner because the old gunners were close to rotating home. We ran the same drill all day. I lugged a three-legged, iron tripod that was used for thirty- and fifty-caliber machines guns and the 75-millimeter recoilless rifle on my back. Each of my arms held a leg of the tripod while the third leg hung down over my back. The tripod was heavy and cumbersome. Every time a fire mission was called by our trainers, I would run ahead of the squad, heave the right leg of the tripod high off of my right shoulder, and twist it to the left so that the tripod leg hanging down over my backside twirled forward and sank solidly into the ground. Our gun crew ran after me and lowered the bottom part of the rifle bore into the tripod's belly hole and inserted the bolt pin to fasten the weapon to the tripod. Ammo bearers then formed a protective arc, acting as riflemen on both sides of the weapon.

We tried to be quick and smooth setting up the weapon, but the weariness of the exercise made it difficult to achieve. I couldn't count the times I clocked myself in the back of my helmet because I didn't lift the right leg of my tripod high enough over my head. At 140 pounds, it wasn't easy.

One night after I had trained all day, I sat next to my weapon on the ridge of a hill overlooking a gully. The moon was bright enough to give me a number of spots to sketch as targets. My section sergeant was a short-timer. He helped me with my compass and the rifle's eight-power scope to measure distances between targets. I drew a range map for my position. When I finished, I sat behind my weapon, thinking about going up as a replacement, a possible gunner, and a squad leader. I didn't know what to expect or how I would react. There were guys with more seniority in our squad, but they didn't seem to be bothered by that. Three guys in our undermanned squad had seen some action. Pop, my gunner, was a thirty-something, World War II veteran but an alky. He had been busted from sergeant so many times he was never quite sure of his rank. He was frail, thin, and balding, with wispy blond hair and a blotchy, milk-white complexion. He liked to bitch and moan all the time. He wore a shit-eating grin on his face that made me think that there was something that I was not privy to, and he was probably right. I was glad he was a short-timer because I didn't trust him. Lord knew what he thought of me as an assistant gunner. The sooner he left for home, the sooner I'd make gunner.

Three skinny Koreans always hung out together. They spoke number huckin' one to number huckin' ten *pidgin* English. They smiled and nodded their heads a lot. A Californian Mexican was a veteran of a few months and a private first-class who knew the 75-millimeter rifle pretty well. I could learn something from him. His name was Martinez. He was soft-spoken and shy, with a slender build and a neatly trimmed mustache that looked good against his olive skin. He was very friendly. Another friendly veteran in our squad was a tall, slow, lumbering, black soldier from the South, with soulful eyes and a constant pained look on his face. He didn't talk much but did his job well. I liked him.

As a recoilless rifle squad, we were an odd mix of young, old, inexperienced, experienced, black, white, educated, uneducated, Mexican, American, English—and non-English-speaking South Koreans who didn't know each other at all. Not exactly what I was expecting for a group of soldiers about to go into combat together. At first, I felt a bit uncomfortable that I'd been made assistant gunner with help from combat veterans in the crew. I quickly got used to it though. My time with the National Guard, a year of college, the goddamn subclaiber device in basic training, my neighborhood guys, and basic communication skills all played a part in my being groomed for the job.

"Hey, Joe," whispered my section sergeant. "We'll be moving soon. Don't forget to name and date your target map, 30 September."

"Okay," I said with a jolt, suddenly realizing that it was my birthday.

"Hey, today's my birthday," I said in a low voice.

The soldier in front of me turned around. "Happy birthday," he said.

"Thanks," I said.

Next to me, Pop asked, "It's your birthday?"

"Yeah," I replied.

"Well, happy birthday Joe."

I couldn't believe I was having a birthday celebration with guys I could barely see and hardly knew on a hill at night in a place called Yon-chon in Korea. I was twenty-one.

CHAPTER 26

BLOCKING AREA
OCTOBER 2, 1952

DEAR MOM AND DAD

I wrote a lot of letters home and to Frank, and I received a lot of letters in return. When I needed something special, I would write my folks, and they would send me a care package.

Dear Mom, Dad, and Ricky,

Hope you are all feeling fine.

What a surprise yesterday. I received five letters, two from the Conroys dated September 12th, and three from you dated 10, 11, and 19th of September. It has just caught up with me. I hope it's the last of the back mail. In your letter, you asked me quite a few questions. Here are my answers:

No. 1. Dad's package with the watch, medals, and socks was given to me September 25th.

No. 2. I am in a heavy weapons company in a regular infantry division. The paratroopers in Korea are also regular army except when they pull back in reserve. They make pay jumps to receive $50 a month, but they do not receive $45 foxhole pay when they are on line. They cannot draw two hazardous duty pay. Therefore, we are receiving the same pay as they and we aren't even jumping. I'm still airborne though (qualified jumper)!

182

No. 3. I still haven't received my birthday package. (Note date on letterhead.)

No. 4. There is mail call every day even when we are on line.

No. 5. In a previous letter, I stated the articles I needed most.

No. 6. I met Bobby Wassick about a dozen times in Camp Stoneham, California, but I haven't met him in Japan or Korea yet.

No. 7. Please don't send me any money unless I ask for it. You see, we either use occupation money Yen or Wan. US currency is forbidden. Boy, you should see me. They made me an assistant gunner, and I wear a .45 pistol on one hip and a Bowie knife on the other. I look like Daniel Boone.

Say, "champ," what do you eat for breakfast? For the few times I went bowling in California, my highest score was about 169. Of course, I'm not saying what my other games were. I hope your team does better that the Giants. Ha, ha. My Dodgers are going all the way this time. I just heard this minute the Brooks beat the Yanks. That's two in a row, kid, only two more. We had a review tonight in our battle clothes (fatigues), and we all had on blue silk scarves. Our outfit is almost up to strength now. Believe it or not, I can't wait to go up front. We get four points a month then. Now I'm only making two points. The quicker I get out of the volcano.

Well, I'll be seeing you all. I figure in either late August or the beginning of September.

Your Loving Son,
Joseph

PS: My next letter will be to Ricky, the little stinker.

PART 4--COMBAT SOLDIERS

CHAPTER 27

CHUNCHON BLOCKING POSITION
OCTOBER 1952

GOING ON LINE

I turned in my M-1 rifle for a carbine and a colt .45 sidearm. I sharpened my trench knife and applied a light coat of oil to everything metal. My weapons had been test-fired, cleaned, and inspected. My sixty-pound backpack, flak jacket, burlap-covered steel pot, and cartridge belt were standing by. I was going on line as a replacement and an assistant 75 recoilless rifle gunner with butterflies in my stomach, but I was ready to go.

Mike Company loaded up on trucks and headed northeast. Several hours later, we came to a huge field. Pup tents dotted the assembly position. Orders were shouted. Men jumped off trucks and lined up to be taken to their bivouac area. Two shelter halves were made for a two-man tent. Conversation and sudden outbursts of laughter lasted late into the night. Trucks kept coming and going, unloading their human cargo.

"Hey, where's headquarters, company?" someone yelled.

"Look over there!" I shouted in reply.

"Anybody know where there the medics are?"

"Yeah, playing cards in their tent," remarked a wise-ass comedian.

It was organized chaos. Everybody seemed to be looking for somebody.

Pop passed out early. This was fine with me. Excitement and nervous energy must have taken its toll on me because I slept like a rock. I know this for a fact because when I woke up in the morning, I almost had a heart attack. Looming over me was the barrel end of a 90-millimeter cannon from a Patton, M-46 tank.

With his sly grin, Pop told me that at just past midnight, the tank company came in with searchlights glaring and engines clanking and woke him up. He said that I never moved. The tankers couldn't believe that I was still asleep. At first, they thought I was faking it, but they soon realized that I wasn't fooling around. It became a challenge for them not to disturb me. Pop said that one of the tankers tested me, going nose-to-nose, and I never budged. On the way back from chow, one of the tankers laughingly told me that he wished that I could have seen the look on my face when I woke up in front of the treads of a Pershing tank. From what he told me, bets had been placed on my waking up or not.

We marched out of the assembly area and passed our regimental band playing Sousa's "Colonel Bogey's March." It was jaunty and uplifting until we passed a battery of artillery firing their cannons, which brought me back to reality really quick. Our column came to a sudden halt, and everyone bunched up in confusion. I could see a couple of jeeps tilted down off the side of the road. Several more were parked under trees, with sound equipment and microphones surrounding them. We were waved off the road onto an open field. Our platoon leader signaled a break, and the smoking lamp was lit.

In between the jeeps, there was a cluster of big brass officers. Screeching loudspeakers came to life. Their humming and shrill whistling got everyone's attention. A colonel with a microphone urged order. "Okay, settle down. Settle down," he repeated until a hush fell over the field. "Good afternoon, men!"

A thunderous response flowed across the field, "Good afternoon, sir!"

Colonel Hugh Harris, the commander of our regiment, welcomed my namesake, General Joseph P. Cleland, the commanding officer of the Fortieth Infantry Division. We were originally a California

National Guard outfit referred to as the Sunburst Division because our patch was a bright, fiery, golden, pointed sun contrasted against a royal blue backdrop. It reminded one of the Nationalist Chinese flag.

General Cleland, also known as "Jumping Joe," jumped up on a jeep to make certain everyone could see him. He applauded the regiments for their accomplishments in combat. He reiterated the importance of the sector of the Kansas Line, which we would be defending, and its strategic importance in the war against the North Koreans and Chinese. He graphically described what would happen if the Communists broke through our positions, retook the capitol, Seoul, and drove south to Pusan.

We were replacing the Wolfhounds of the Twenty-Fifth Infantry Division's Twenty-Seventh Infantry Regiment. They were high up in the Taebaek Mountains on farthest eastern part of North Korea, just above the Thirty-Eighth Parallel. Our division would be dug in from Heartbreak Ridge on our left flank to Bloody Ridge and the Punchbowl on our right flank. The enemy would test us, but we would meet the test and defeat them because we were the best. We were the fighting Fortieth, "the Ball of Fire." He wished us good hunting, and then he saluted us. Two thousand troops stood and returned the salute.

Colonel Harris, our regimental commander, leaped up on the jeep's engine, saluted the general, and took the microphone. He picked up the tempo. He told us about how well trained we were, how he believed in us. He reminded us of the great job we did handling the Chinese uprising in the prison camps at Cheju-do and Koje-do. We were the best. We were the Galahad Regiment.

"Remember Kumhwa?" he shouted. "When the 224th takes a hill, by God, that hill is taken. It's ours. And by God, we are going to take hills!"

Our regiment leaped to its feet, cheering, yelling, and swearing to kick ass. It was like a pep rally. We were psyched. We were like football players coming onto the field to play the big game. We practically ran off of the field onto the waiting columns of trucks. We were raring to go.

193

Although we were only several miles from the front, we drove for hours in diversionary routes to mislead the enemy about our actual destination. By late afternoon, we were chugging uphill, tilting from side to side, passing other trucks packed with soldiers, coming down from the Main Line of Resistance (MLR). They were one happy, boisterous, bunch of GIs.

Grungy soldiers with tired faces grinned and waved to us. When the trucks crawled by us, we could sometimes reach out and touch them. At those moments, we were like two moving escalators going in opposite directions. There was hand slapping and taunts.

"You'll be sorry. Throw us your girl's telephone number. You won't need it anymore."

At one point, there was a huge roar like a crowd at a ball game when something exciting would happen on the field. Something was happening between the troops in the trucks just ahead of us. Moments later, a soldier in our truck suddenly leaped up and snared what looked to be a soccer ball thrown from a truck wobbling by us. There were squeals of revulsion and laughter as the yellowed skull with protruding jaw and hollowed eyes was juggled about. I went along and smiled like everyone else, but I was glad when it was tossed back to the next open truck that passed us.

I was still wondering about the skeletal head of the enemy soldier as we continued our circuitous, torturous route until our asses ached and the words "piss call" became a beautiful sound. Hundreds of us slowly unlimbered off the trucks, bent in agony, and straggled to the side of the road. We fumbled to find ourselves with moans of relief as arched sprays of instant joy poured down the mountain wall. It was a sight to see and an unbelievably happy moment.

Back on the trucks, it was nice to watch the sun set, but when darkness fell, the convoy became an accordion of fluttering little lightening bugs, blinking their way up twisting, curving hills that had only one side of the road. The invisible cliff on the other side made our ride a hairy one. When we reached our destination, we disembarked, relieved to have our feet back on the ground.

With a bright moon and flashlights, Mike Company was formed up into our regular platoons. The march became more difficult once we moved off of the road and tried to keep together by squads and follow the dark figures of our platoon sergeant and his Korean guide. Their flashlights pointed to rocks on the ground. I had to concentrate on where I was going. I was both walking and climbing as I followed the flashlights and tried to keep up with the others without stumbling. Going uphill with a full pack was a strain. For a moment, I was startled by the firing of a machine gun. It didn't sound that far off. It was ahead of us, somewhere on our left. I started to perspire. Sweat was rolling down my forehead. Cursing and swearing and the thud of equipment being thrown to the ground broke the silence of the night.

"Keep it quiet back there!" The loud whisper came from Sergeant Brawley, who brought us to a stop. "I don't want to hear a sound. Do you hear me?" he said, facing us in the dark. "I know it's hard, but keep it down."

Brawley was a no-nonsense guy from the neighborhood I hadn't known. He was competent and low-key, and I liked him right away. He was a veteran and a short-timer who did his job well.

"For Christ's sake, squad leaders, keep your men quiet and watch where you're walking."

We started up again, and before long, we were stumbling along to the cries of our own voices.

"Shut up! Quiet, goddamn it! Knock it off," were the hushed, constant reminders from all of us.

I kicked ponchos, sidestepped mess kits, and was appalled at what was being dropped along the way. I grew up where you kept things forever. You never threw anything away. The last straw was to see Pop shirk his pack off his back and throw it down.

"Fuck this, man. I ain't carrying this shit anymore."

"What are you doing?" I asked in horror. "You can't do that. You're going to need all that stuff."

Pop sounded beat, almost apologetic. "I just can't carry it anymore, Joe, and I won't."

There was no anguish or emotion. It was a plain statement of fact from a beaten man. I felt sorry for the old reprobate. Maybe I was being played for a sucker, but at that moment, I truly believed him. I simply picked up his rucksack and slung it over my shoulder.

"Leave it, Joe. I'll get another one."

Our Korean guide kept getting confused in the dark. Every time we stopped and thought we were there, we would end up backtracking or going in another direction. The extra weight I was carrying became very uncomfortable. As we neared the top of the hill, I could see the tracer rounds from the machine gun I had heard earlier. The glowing tracers appeared suddenly and formed an arc of dotted lines, which would disappear into the night followed by a rush of low sound. A sinister silence fell on us once the firing ceased.

When I finally reached the crest of the hill, I was greeted with a landscape bathed in a grayish blue light from distant searchlights that cast shadows on the rocks, bushes, and bare-bone trees in front of us. It was worthy of a spooky Hollywood set. My imagination could easily accommodate North Koreans, Chinese, Frankenstein, or the Wolfman coming out of the hazy, broken light and lurching at us in a ferocious assault.

It was a noteworthy introduction to a lit battlefield. A few days on line taught me the meaning of darkness. Without a moon, you were totally blind. You relied on your hearing when it came to what might be in front of you, and your mind played mayhem with your imagination, which made evenings very unpleasant.

On cloud-filled nights, antiaircraft searchlight batteries were set up on hills behind our MLR. They would bounce their powerful beams off of low clouds and illuminate the battlefield. To me, they were like beacons of light sent from heaven. These were relatively peaceful nights.

Our Korean guide stopped, and we halted. There was a flurry of activity as the advance party from our company made contact with Sergeant Brawley. In all the confusion, Pop was happy at least. He got his rucksack back. Moments later, names were whispered.

"Donohue, Martinez, follow me."

The trench was around five feet deep and ten feet wide.

The flashlight bounced off of the trench floor, and we followed along, passing gun bunkers every hundred feet or so. Nobody seemed to be around. It was very quiet and dark except for the garish blue glow out in front of the trenches in no-man's-land. Brawley stopped in front of the dark entrance to a sandbagged bunker.

"You guys will sack out in here. Our 75 platoon will be manning machine guns until we get more replacements. In the meantime, you'll be reporting to Sergeant West."

I shook my head in disbelief. All of my intense training on the dragon gun, and I end up going on line as a machine gunner. What would Hoop and Spitz say to that?

CHAPTER 28

FIRST SIGHTING

I stared across no-man's-land on the east slope of Heartbreak Ridge overlooking Satae-ri Valley with its steep, rocky, and rolling hills. I searched the barely visible hilltops for an unseen enemy in the dark of night. I wondered if he was doing the same with me. I had my answer sooner than I had expected. A faint light appeared out of the fading darkness. It moved slowly in front of me as if it were on a track of some sort. I was stunned and stared at it as it bobbed and weaved and shimmered and shook. My enemy knew I was watching him, and he was taunting me.

Sergeant Brawley nudged me awake with a flashlight in my face. I slid off of the stretched, interlaced, black communication wire that served as my mattress and felt for my cartridge belt, rifle, and helmet, which hung from nails jutting from wood beams of the sleeping bunker. I followed Brawley down the trench. It was near dawn but still dark.

"Betty!" a low voice called out. Sergeant Brawley came to an abrupt halt and responded "Boop!"

"That's the password for today," Brawley said as he pulled a shelter, which served as a door to a gun bunker, aside. Sergeant West and a soldier from the machine platoon were huddled over a .50-caliber machine gun. Heads nodded, and mumbled words were exchanged.

Sergeant Brawley told me that Wes, as our machine gun platoon's sergeant was often called, would be my mentor until we received more replacements to cover the undermanned machine gun positions. I nodded, pleased to know that Sergeant West was a respected combat veteran.

The .50-caliber machine gun sat on top of a platform of sandbags several feet off of the ground, with its barrel sticking out of an opening about four feet wide and three feet high, which gave the person manning it a commanding view of the ridgetops in front of us. Sandbags and logs afforded protection from incoming rounds. Grenades, bandoleers of ammo clips, and spare gun barrels hung from under the roof of the bunker. A gray power phone was hooked up next to the machine where a pair of field glasses was draped over a spike protruding from the sandbag wall. A piece of cardboard was wedged into the log beam over the aperture of the .50-caliber gun. Penciled dashes connected to enemy positions that were circled and labeled. The numbers of yards to the targets were printed boldly above the dashes.

I was briefed by Sergeant Brawley. Our MLR was Heartbreak Hill. It ran east to west. No-man's-land was the valley below called Satae-ri. Our 160th Regiment was to our west over by Sandbag Castle. To my dismay, I learned that our outpost shared the ridgeline with the North Koreans and was only yards apart. Separation was mounds of sandbags built to provide the high ground for whoever occupied it. Bloody Ridge was to my front and a little to the left. Our 223rd Regiment was on our right just outside of the Punchbowl sector of the line. After that was the Taebaek Mountains and then the Sea of Japan, and after that, I think there was the good old US of A.

I don't think I had more than a half hour on the .50-caliber machine gun in basic training so I was grateful for Sergeant West's quick review. Handling the .50-caliber brought back the enormous power of the weapon. The rounds were twice the size of my M-1 rifle. They could penetrate armor. They could shoot down planes.

"Betty! Boop!" came the muffled reply as Sergeant West pushed through the shelter's door.

"The Twenty-Seventh Regiment is off the hill. Their rear guard is gone. This place is all ours."

"Sergeant," I cried. "Look straight ahead and to the left."

I pulled back the bolt on the fifty and let it slide home. The ring of metal on a quiet night was startling. I forgot how much noise it made. The back of West's arm shoved me back.

"Don't fire!" he said and grabbed the binoculars off of the bunker wall.

A yellow light swayed just below the ridgeline and then stayed still. It looked as though someone might be carrying a lantern of some sort. The light went out, and our phone rang. I handed it to West just as the light came back on. It started to move slowly across from us.

Boom, boom, boom . . . boom, boom, boom came the cadenced pounding of a .50-caliber somewhere to our right followed by a lighter rapping of a .30-caliber machine gun.

West whistled into the power phone. "CP, CP . . . Mike 51," he whispered. He repeated "CP, CP . . . Mike 51. Shall we fire?"

I was fascinated by the amber light. It would dance and then stop. It would wobble, bounce, and be still.

"Cease fire!" West called into the phone. "Cease fire right now, goddamn it. All weapons, hold your fire."

The two guns that were firing stopped. "Okay . . . will do. Over and out," said West as he handed me the phone.

"Calls are coming into the command post from all over the hill. Everyone's to hold their fire. Artillery's been notified, and if needed, they'll throw some rounds on it."

"It's a setup," said Wes. "We fire, and we give our gun positions away. Then they plot us in and knock the shit out of us when they're ready to attack us."

Looking through his binoculars, Wes said, "There's a couple of gooks jiggling a light on a wire out there, saying, 'Here we are, Joe. Where are you?'"

"I wouldn't tell them," I said, trying to be funny.

"It makes no difference, Joe. They know who we are and where we are."

"Come on," I said disbelievingly.

"I'm dead serious. Did you hear what happened earlier this evening?"

"No, what happened?"

"When the 160th went on line, they got a broadcast from loudspeakers saluting the Fortieth Division as the Mad Dogs of Koji-do. That was our last duty in the prison camps of Koji-do and Cheji-do. That light we saw was a greeting from the North Koreans. They were welcoming us on board, Joe."

CHAPTER 29

CLOSE CALL

I couldn't get the moving light and the fact that it was a baited trap for us to give away our positions so we could be targeted and killed out of my mind. It was a great lesson for me to be on my toes. Sandbag Castle was not very far down the trench from me, and I was concerned about that. I was alone in a gun bunker with a weapon I wasn't that familiar with. I had never been in combat before, and I wondered if the North Koreans knew that. To say I was a bit apprehensive would be an understatement. I was scared shitless.

Replacements had been coming in, but there were none for me. I was still alone. I kept myself busy by stacking ammo cans and cleaning my .50-caliber. I used my field glasses to see if I could spot the enemy positions marked on my gun bunker's target map.

It was late in the day. I was still fussing around my bunker, making sure everything was in order. All of a sudden, I was jolted by a heavy thud on my bunker roof. I froze. Thump! Thump! Footsteps! Somebody was on my bunker roof. *Good God . . . gooks!* I thought. I ran to the entrance of my bunker and peered out. There was no one there. A sudden blur leaped across my bunker roof to the other side of the trench. I yanked out my .45-caliber, and pressed against the sandbag entrance, I shouted,

202

"Halt! Who—" as a body landed on the trench floor. I pulled the trigger. *Click!*

"Jesus Christ!" spilled out in a frantic scream followed by "What the fuck?"

A soldier was sprawled on his back in front of me. He looked up wide-eyed in disbelief.

I looked down in horror at the unshaven face of a frightened GI with unsightly dirty-blond bristles of hair sticking out of his jowly red cheeks. Like an endangered species of porcupine, he looked ready to strike. I leaned against the outside of the bunker, my heart pounding wildly, and thrust my .45 into its holster.

"Man, I'm sorry. I'm sorry."

For the longest moment, we just looked at each other.

"What the fuck were you trying to do?" he said, using the butt of his condom-covered rifle barrel to ease himself up off of the ground.

There was an awkward silence. The answer was obvious. He got up slowly, brushing off his rifle and straightening the two bandoleers of ammo that crisscrossed his chest. I picked up his helmet and the pieces of toilet tissue that had fallen from it and handed them to him. A slow, canary-swallowing grin spread across his face.

"Francis Leahy, like in the coach of Notre Dame, but I'm from Boston," he said, firmly holding out his hand.

"Joe Donohue from New York City," I said sheepishly.

Leahy looked like a leprechaun. He was short with a friendly face and mischievous eyes. He was a rifleman doing *scoshi* time, which meant that he was doing short time and close to going home.

"What the hell were you doing on the roof of my gun bunker?" I asked.

Leahy looked at me with a smile that showed big, spaced, yellowed teeth.

"I came up the reverse slope and cut across some bunker roofs to get to my platoon. It's done all the time. You'd better get used to it."

"You're crazy, man. You must make a nice target up there."

"That's why I was in such a hurry," he said and laughed.

"Why didn't you answer me when I challenged you?"

"I was in midair when I heard the challenge and click. What could I do? You scared the shit out of me."

I shook my head, still not believing what had just happened.

"God, that was a close call," I said, sliding my pistol back into my holster.

"Yeah and I'm outta here in more than a *skosh*. It was almost sooner than that. Thank God for watching over cocky, dumb Irishmen, especially those who take shortcuts and those who fire unloaded pistols."

"Amen," I whispered.

CHAPTER 30

JUST DON'T LEAVE ME

In the wee hours of the morning on my fourth day on Heartbreak Ridge, we were hit by a battalion of the North Korean People's Army. I was alone with my gun, and my phone was dead. I didn't know what was happening. I was worried about being overrun. I was afraid of being left behind, and worst of all, I was afraid of being captured.

We were mostly new replacements relieving the battle-weary soldiers of the Twenty-Fifth Infantry Division. I was visited by my company commander, who had assigned me to the 75-millimeter rifle platoon.

"Donohue, we're spread out thin, and I need every gun bunker covered, so I still need you on a .50 to cover this sector of the line," said Lieutenant Gotshall, who was far from old despite his nickname. He was a lean, fresh-faced, twenty-four-year-old ROTC graduate from the Midwest with a flattop. He was four years older than I was.

"As soon as I get a replacement, I'll send him up to you, but it might be a while. Sergeant Brawly is still your platoon sergeant, but he'll be working with Sergeant West of the machine gun platoon. The 75-millimeter platoon will be manning machine guns. Your call name is 'Upper Seventy-Five.' Sergeant Brawley will show you to your new bunker."

The first thing that struck me about my new "home" was that I had to pass a tank hidden behind a wall of rocks to get to my bunker below it. The second thing was that my new gun position was much bigger than the one I had just left. This was more like a cave gouged out of a mountain. Wood pieces from artillery ammo crates were hammered together to serve as a door. The entrance curved around a wall of sandbags where two stretcher-like bunk beds hung one above the other. Another wall separated the sleeping quarters from the gun position. On the other wall, hand grenades and machine gun barrels were strung above a five-foot-wide, rectangular aperture. A rolled-up shelter was tied with commo wire for use as a makeshift shade. Sitting majestically on a platform of sandbags, an air-cooled .50-caliber machine gun pointed out at the broken landscape of no-man's-land leading across the valley floor and up into the enemy lines. Stacked cans of belted ammunition lay neatly on the dirt floor surrounding the platform. A gray phone was hooked onto the wall next to the weapon. It was my fourth day on line and my second gun position. This time, I had a tank sitting practically on top of me. The M-46 looked like a proud hen sitting on its nest. Up close, a canvas tarp that was draped over its turret broke up the tank's silhouette. Its long, 99-millimeter cannon peaked over a wall of sandbags resting some sixty to seventy feet above my machine gun bunker.

The evening routine was a half hour check-in call from our command post, and I looked forward to it. It broke the monotony of sitting alone in the dark, peering out of my bunker window. Different gun positions called in their reports. We could all hear each other on the phone at the same time. The 75-RR and machine gun platoons were mixed into each other. I had been with M Company for several weeks, so I was talking mostly to guys I had never met before. I found myself imagining faces to fit the voices I heard over the phone.

Hands in my pockets and a blanket folded over my knees, I leaned back against the sandbagged wall of the gun bunker next to the phone and looked at the starry blackness outside and listened to the silence of the night. As I concentrated on the murky outlines of trees and rocks, my eyes and ears played tricks on me. I swore tree trunks moved, and I heard voices. A quick look away and then a return to the mover would find it back where it had been before. I would have bet money I had seen movement and I had heard noises. It was so real that I had to fight the urge to call the CP at times. I soon discovered that I wasn't the only one hearing and imagining things.

"Psst . . . psst, CP? CP? This is Mighty Mike One . . . Mighty Mike One," came the whispered voice.

"Mighty Mike One, this is CP."

"Keep hearing tapping sounds. Right front. Close. Maybe fifty yards out."

"Mighty-Mike One, I read you. Hold your fire. Keep alert while I do a position check."

Voices crackled over the phone. "Mighty Mike Two, okay . . . Mighty Mike Three, all quiet. Mighty Mike Four, nothing to report. Lower Seventy-Five, okay. Upper Seventy-Five, I think it's the wind," I said. "I keep hearing a sound like a branch hitting metal. Whatever it is, it's making the same dull noise."

On line, you had to be careful that you didn't call in too many false alarms. It didn't look good. Guys would think you were skittish. You could become suspect and lose the trust of your buddies, and that wasn't good. Nobody wanted to be in a combat zone with nervous nellies. It was bad for morale. I had a lot of work in front of me to get used to my new gun position and feel comfortable.

When the explosion came, it took me a few seconds to realize what had occurred. It happened suddenly and without warning. The second blast was different. Debris peppered the outside of the bunker. A sandbag split open, throwing a puff of dust into the air. The field phone rang and confirmed what I was experiencing. We were being attacked.

I pulled back the handle on my .50-caliber machine gun. Tracers were crisscrossing the black sky. Flares started to pop. Light and shadows illuminated the terrain in front of me. I peered outside. I didn't see anything. Nothing moved. Another explosion landed, and my bunker shook like hell. Two more explosions came close together. It suddenly dawned on me that when the tank fired its 90-millimeter canon, it caused my bunker to shake. I couldn't be sure if the rounds were coming in or going out.

There was a cacophony of sounds in front of me. The heavy *whumps* of mortar or artillery rounds mixed with the *rat-a-tat-tat* stuttering of heavy machine guns. The echo was a giveaway. I knew rounds were headed our way. The mountains gave us a warning of what was coming.

My bunker phone rang. "Upper Seventy-Five? Upper Seventy-Five? Joe, where are you?" demanded the voice on the phone.

"CP! Upper Seventy-Five," I shouted above the din.

"It's West. We've got company. How are you doing?"

"Okay, I guess."

"Do you see anything?"

"No, nothing. Only parachute flares and shadows when they hit the ground."

"Okay. Load up. Hold your fire. Stay on the intercom. If you see anything, give a holler."

I see muzzle flashes in front of me from the hills and the valley floor. The flashes reminded me of matches lit in the upper and lower decks of Madison Square Garden during a hockey game. A burst of light would appear and then go out, first in one place and then in another. Long dashes of tracer rounds passed over my bunker. I flinched and looked in awe. I had never been fired at before. Now tracer rounds came at me. They looked huge. It finally occurred to me through a blinding flash of the obvious that the machine gun rounds were meant for the tank above me. I knew it because I hadn't fired my weapon. I didn't think the enemy knew I was there.

I heard banging sounds and shrill noises coming from directly in front of me. Rapid-fire explosions shook the shit out of my bunker, and I dropped to the floor and reached for the phone.

"CP, CP, Upper Seventy-Five here. CP? CP, this is Upper Seventy-Five. CP!"

Shit! Fuck! The goddamn phone is dead.

The valley floor came alive. I saw small clusters of flickering lights that looked like fireflies on a summer's night.

"West, can you hear me? I see lights and hear banging noises!" I screamed into the phone. West! *Shit!* I thought. *Now I'm really alone.*

I didn't know what was happening, but as if on cue, everything erupted. I was aware of M-1 rifles and carbines being fired from our trenches and the sounds of burp guns and grenades being thrown. Things were getting closer. More flares popped in the early morning darkness. I was mesmerized by the fireworks, but I was still looking for targets to fire at. I kept thinking about the words of my drill sergeant in basic training: "In World War II, fewer than half the men in a battle fired their weapons. That meant they only used 50 percent of their firepower."

Maybe I shouldn't be holding my fire, I thought. *Maybe I should fire at the muzzle flashes.* The tankers above me were firing their 90-millimeter canon plus their .50-caliber machine guns. *Do they see something I don't see? Are there targets of opportunity that I'm missing?* I decided to cover my sector of fire from stake to stake, whether I saw something or not. I pulled back on the operating rod and let her slam home. I started with my left firing stake and tentatively pressed my thumbs down on the trigger bar. The deep, bass sound of my .50-caliber joined the babble of battle. A surge of power and exhilaration went through me. I had to fight the urge to fire more rapidly. I had to calm down. I had to keep firing in small bursts of three. When I hit my right stake, I began to traverse the other way.

The noise level dropped, and darkness covered the front. There was a long pause in the action, and I heard what sounded like whistles. I strained to listen, and then I heard drums banging. Then I heard horns, bugle blasts, and yelling. What the hell was going on? Flares and rounds began again. I fired in the direction of the sounds. I watched the incendiary rounds from our .30-caliber machine guns and joined in a macabre orchestra of musical death. Then there was an abrupt halt. My gun had jammed.

"Oh, fuck! Sweet Jesus, help me." I yank up the feeder cover. My hands swiftly roamed and explored the feed belt of the gun in the blackness of my bunker.

"Help me, dear God," I said. "Help me!" All the while, I kept envisioning gooks spilling into the trenches. My hands, which groped the innards of the gun, were doing things as if they belonged to someone else. They trembled and fumbled with the belted rounds that fed into the weapon. I swore they were being guided by an unseen force because I didn't know what the hell I was doing. I pulled the bolt, and it came back freely. I let it slam forward in jubilation. "Thank you, dear God," became my chant as I fired the weapon.

I heard shouting coming from the bunker door behind me. I whirled around and lunged for my carbine.

"Who's in there?"

"It's me!" I shouted, relieved that the question was in English and thinking who the hell this person thought it was. "It's Joe Donohue, Upper Seventy-Five!" I yelled above the commotion of battle.

"Okay, don't shoot! Hold your fire."

I pushed the flimsy door open and saw two figures hunched down in the trench. One of the figures stood up. "Everything okay?"

"Yeah, I guess so. My phone's dead, and I'm firing at whatever I see. What's happening?"

Both guys rushed past me toward my gun aperture and quickly fired their carbines from both sides of the .50-caliber. "You're okay here. One of our gun positions called in and said that a bunker took a hit from gook grenades."

"Wasn't me."

"Looking good," they said and ran by me and out the door.

"Whoa. Wait. Wait!" I shouted, running after them. "My phone is out. I don't know what the hell is going on, and I need help. I'm all alone."

"The CP knows your situation. We'll tell the tankers and the other bunkers. Stay on your weapon."

"What's your name?" I asked.

A tall, lanky guy with a big toothy grin answered, "George Reimer, Whitestone, Queens."

"I knew you were from New York. Joe Donohue, Yorkville," I said and smiled, relieved that somebody knew my situation and hopefully wouldn't forget a fellow New Yorker. My biggest fear up to now was being overrun and no one knowing about it.

Minutes later, above the din, I heard, "Joe! Joe! It's Reimer."

I stopped firing and rushed to the back of the bunker. George and his buddy dragged the motionless body of a soldier down the trench. "Everything's *dai-jo-be*. Trenches are secure. Hang in there. The tankers know your situation," said Reimer.

"Hey, look," I said in a pleading tone, "whatever happens . . . just don't leave me."

CHAPTER 31

WE'D BETTER FIX BAYONETS

Every soldier quickly learned the rules of combat. The first several days were critical to a soldier's survival. It was no guarantee, but every day on line improved your chances of not making a stupid mistake and getting yourself killed. I was grateful for the fact that I could have made a stupid mistake and gotten us all killed.

Sergeant West was very emphatic. "Pedro, you help Joe on the .50 until we get one for you. Listen to him, and you'll be all right."

I could only guess how Pedro felt. I was a draftee, a private E-2 in the army less than a year and a few days on the front line, and he was my assistant gunner. I went over the weapon with him. I explained the routine. I told him who was who and what was in front of us and gave him the information that I had pretty much memorized from Sergeant West.

Corporal Pedro Colon, my assistant gunner, had been stationed in Germany as an office clerk. He had been born in Puerto Rico. He joined the army with the intent of being a twenty-year man and retiring from service with a good pension. Because he was regular army, he volunteered for Korea to advance his career. He'd been in the army seven years. I could see that he wanted to impress upon me that I was just a kid compared to him. In his accented English, he kept telling me how important his job was in Germany and how he had it made there with all the *frauleins*. It was obvious that Pedro had a problem dealing with the difference in our ages and rank.

Colon wanted me to know that he was a professional soldier. He had joined the service after World War II. He did occupation duty in Germany. He was bored as an office clerk. He wanted to see some action. Going to Korea, especially in a line outfit, was a sure way to get promoted, so he had volunteered for Korea. My first thought was that he had fucked up in Germany and had been sent to Korea.

"So come on, Pedro. What did you do?

"What do you mean?"

"Nobody volunteers for Korea. What happened?"

A hurt look showed on his face. "No, it was nothing like that," he said, shaking his head. "I volunteered, man."

I gave him a snide look and smiled. "Yeah, so did I."

If Pedro had any doubts about liking me before, he didn't have them anymore.

A gold-rimmed frame wrapped itself around thick, Coke-bottle glasses. When light reflected off of the lens, his magnified eyes took on the look of a startled deer, which could be both humorous and unsettling at the same moment. White teeth peeked out through a Caesar Romero mustache. By all appearances, he was a mild-mannered, soft-spoken, young Puerto Rican in his late twenties who looked more at home behind a desk than a rifle.

I pulled the first shift, and Colon went to sleep. It had been a long day for him. The trek from division to regiment to battalion to company to being put in a gun bunker with a stranger could take its toll on any replacement. Heck, I was a raw recruit myself. I was having a hard time getting adjusted to my new surroundings. I could understand where he was coming from. I found it hard to believe that the peaceful valleys and mountains in front of me were part of the battlefield.

Sunlight played off of frozen peaks and ridges and displayed magnificent shades of gold, purple, red, and blue. The broken forms of splintered trees and dangling limbs took on a grotesque silhouette of bizarre shapes and shadows. I was amazed when this serene, twisted, beautiful, landscape in front of me was disturbed by the sudden chatter of a machine gun and its reverberating echo or the small puffs of smoke from exploding mortar and artillery rounds, which would leave their ugly scars in the snowy landscape. After the intrusion, the silent, scenic beauty of the mountains and valleys would return in a somewhat different form to become the new reality of the moment. It was an eerie feeling that was always difficult to describe.

Colon took the second shift. Everything was copacetic.

I was shaken awake in the dark for the next watch. "Everything is good all over, Joe. The tankers come by and say hello. They bring coffee. It has to be heated. I think I go back to sleep. Okay?"

"No sweat, Pedro."

I didn't mind cold coffee because I wasn't a coffee drinker and I couldn't really tell a bad cup of coffee from a good one. I used to get a lot of ribbing from the guys in the National Guard and basic training because I thought army coffee was just fine. Anyway, I always enjoyed a cigarette more with something to drink.

I sat down next to the .50, holding an Old Gold cigarette down between my legs. I bent my head down below the open aperture in front of the gun every time I wanted a drag. When I came back up, I took a mouthful of the coffee, which I still thought tasted pretty good.

Check-ins every half hour broke up the monotony. A chilly night turned into a chillier early morning. It started with artillery fire. I could see the explosions out in front of me. I was mesmerized. I just watched them until the phone hissed and announced an attack alert. I went to Colon and shook him awake.

"I think we're getting hit, Pedro. Let's go," I said.

Rounds started coming in faster. I thought they were mortars. Machine guns started firing off to the left of us. Pedro came up to the gun.

"What's happening?" he asked.

"I don't know. We're getting hit. We're being attacked. The phone's open."

The explosion brought both of us to the floor of the bunker.

"That was close," said Pedro in a calm voice.

It was too close. In an instant, it hit me. I recognized what it was. I jumped to my feet, cursing the goddamn tankers. "The fucking tankers," I could hear myself yelling. I looked around and realized that Pedro was still on his knees.

"Get up, man. It's the tank upstairs," I said, pleased that I could recognize their 90-millimeter rounds as outgoing and not incoming.

Suddenly, there were rapid explosions in front of us, and it was a no-brainer. They were incoming. More machine guns were firing now. Flares shot up in front of us. Shrill whistles, clanging drums, bugles, and yelling became part of the assault. The distinct *burrup, burrup* of Chinese burp guns was close. I could feel jolts of energy surging through my body. Fear could do wonders to the brain.

"Let's lock and load."

Pedro looked at me with his bulging eyes as if he didn't understand me.

"Get the ammo cans. Move it, man!"

"Cover your sectors! Cover your sectors!" was shouted from the phone's mouthpiece.

I fixed on flashes and used them to cover a zone. I could only see instances of movement and lots of shadows from falling flares. I worked the barrel slowly from left stake to right stake. I felt more comfortable. This time, I had a live phone, an assistant gunner, and cans of ammo stacked up neatly and waiting for me. Pedro was slow-moving, as if he was in a daze, but he hung in there. This was his baptism by fire, and he was doing fine. The fighting was louder and more intense than my first fight had been. More rounds were being fired by both sides. I naturally accepted the tank upstairs shaking the shit out of us, but I didn't like the fact that he was drawing a lot of fire in our direction. The gooks were throwing a lot of stuff at us. Geysers of dirt were being

Joseph Donohue

thrown up in front of us, and I could hear the whiz and thud of shrapnel hitting our bunker. Then as quickly as the action started, it ended, as if both sides decided at the same time to stop fighting. Sporadic fire could be heard at intervals, growing dimmer and fading away.

"Cease fire!" was repeated over and over again on the intercom, and the words could be heard up and down the trenches. The smell of machine gun shells, gunpowder, burning burlap, and smoldering wood hung in the air, overwhelming the senses.

The two of us sat quietly against behind the gun platform, too tired to move. Pedro turned his head toward me, and in a whisper, he asked, "What do we do now?"

My heart was still racing. I looked at him in silence. It was a good question. I thought hard for a long moment. Pedro looked at me, waiting for an answer. I felt I had to say something. After all, I was the combat veteran. All I could think of was our squad tactics that we had learned in basic training and Sergeant Knox's stern admonition, "When an attack is stopped, you counterattack."

I looked at Pedro straight in the eye and solemnly said, "We'd better fix bayonets."

The gold-rimmed glasses slipped down his nose. That zany look was etched in his horror-filled eyes. Pedro got up and lurched against the bunker wall. He hadn't quite made it. Pedro had pissed his pants.

I slipped the trench knife from my scabbard and said earnestly, "We're going to have to go out after them."

The sound phone whistled, and I picked it up. "Mike 51, stand down. Casualty report?" asked Sergeant West.

"Negative," I said and sighed in relief and silently thanked God that someone hadn't sounded a rebel yell or blown a goddamn whistle, because two green and inexperienced replacements would have looked pretty silly and very dead charging over the top alone.

216

CHAPTER 32

A LETTER FROM FRANK

It was always great hearing from Frank. He was a morale booster. He was my closest friend and neighbor on line. We shared information and experienced the realities of combat. It was good feeling connected and looking forward to going home together.

Hi, Ol' Buddy,

How are you doing? Win any medals lately? I hope you're keeping your powder dry.

I'm okay. I'm in Fox Company, Second Battalion, 179th Regiment, Forty-Fifth Infantry Division. I've been up on line since October, around the same time as you, I guess. I'm up in the Punchbowl area. We're to the right of the Fortieth. Maybe we'll hook up here somewhere. Wouldn't that be great?

It's not too bad up here now, although my first day, we caught harassing fire, and that same night, we had a fire mission. I was on a 60-mortar with a guy from the south Bronx. Would you believe I'm stuck with another Irishman? You'd like him. His name is Tim Sullivan. He's a good mortar man. We threw out over a thousand rounds, including six misfires and a changed tube. We did okay. We held our own except for two guys who shot themselves in the foot, and I'm not trying to be funny. Tim and I were ready to shoot them again along with the rest of our company.

217

Three days later, I went out on an ambush patrol. Our lieutenant looked right at me when he asked for volunteers, and I hate to admit it, but I volunteered. My brother would kill me if he knew. Back home, he told me that there were two things I should always remember: never volunteer for anything and never underestimate your enemy.

We didn't go too far. We set up near one of our outposts. It was dusk when we went out. We could hear the loudspeakers. Someone said they heard them welcoming Fox Company patrol. Anyway, they did play Tony Martin singing "There's No Tomorrow."

We lay out for near nine hours without making a sound. We didn't move. My nose was running, and I was afraid to wipe it. I kept my eyes and ears open. The only sound was from our radioman. Every half hour, I would hear, "CP, CP, this is Fox Company patrol. Negative. Over." That was the only thing I heard. At 2400 hours, our lieutenant spread the word for us to pull back, and when I got up, I couldn't feel my feet. I had pins and needles and couldn't walk. My feet went to sleep. They were numb. When I got back to my bathroom-sized bunker, Timmy had some hot coffee waiting for me on our rinky-dink, handmade stove. He's a good man. I'm lucky. I drank half the canteen cup and collapsed into my rack.

One more story before I sign off. I was on guard one night with a guy named "Poochie." I never did get his last name. We're hearing noises over and over again coming up from the barbed wire. I whispered to him that I was going to throw a grenade down there, and he nodded okay. I pulled the pin and held it, listening. The fuse is supposed to be good for seven seconds when you release it, but I was a bit nervous and let it go after three seconds and ducked. "Bam," the damn thing exploded almost immediately. I'm lying there, thinking, "So much for basic training." If I was going by the book, I wouldn't be writing you this letter now.

My family's fine. I hope yours is too. Write me soon.

Whatever happened to "the Kid" and "Corny?"

Frank

CHAPTER 33

CHEERS FOR SANDBAG CASTLE

Sandbag Castle was a castle made out of sandbags. On cloudy nights, huge antiaircraft searchlight batteries positioned on bluffs from the rear would bathe the castle in eerie light. The castle marked the dividing line between us and the North Koreans on the MLR. It was built to create an outpost that commanded the high ground for both sides. Whoever occupied it posed a threat of attack into the other's trench positions. It was a visible symbol of power and control.

My range card showed gook trench junctions and possible gun emplacements. Distances went from several hundred yards in front of us to just several feet on the left of our trench line toward Sandbag Castle. Our Division's 160th Regiment was on our left. A bastard regimental combat team was on our right flank, and our 224th Regiment was in the middle of the line called the Kumsong Sector. Our 223rd Regiment was in reserve. Our platoon was mixed in with King and Love Company. I tacked my hand-drawn map above our gun bunker. It also showed prominent forward peaks in front of us, including Bloody Ridge, Snake Pit, Able and Baker Hills.

Sandbag Castle was nothing more than sandbags stacked on top of each other, but it was a very strategic fortification for both sides. Whoever commanded the castle occupied the high ground and could fire down into the trenches of their enemy so it was constantly being fought over. It was like the kid's game of "Capture the Flag," except this was no game. It was our most dangerous threat. We were very vulnerable. A concerted attack might overrun us and breach our line, with the possibility of the NKPA spilling down into Seoul and again invading the capital of South Korea. It was easier for the North Koreans to attack us from the castle than it was for them to try to come across the valley and up into our lines. It was the same for us, except there was no North Korean capital to capture.

On some nights, eerily bathed in blue-white light from our powerful airplane searchlights situated on mountaintops to our rear, you could see a small flag flying on top of the castle. There was no doubt about who was "king of the mountain."

On one particular night, the lights came on, but there was no flag to be seen on top of the castle. Everybody wondered what had happened to it. There hadn't been any big battle or firefight, but there was no flag either, American or Korean. As usual, rumors flew of an imminent attack.

A few nights later, the lights came on again, and Sandbag Castle was illuminated again without her flag. *Whew, whew, whew!* came the whistling whisper of the bunker phone.

"Watch for movement on our side of the castle. Stay alert and hold your fire." Field glasses from every bunker had to be trained on the castle.

An enemy machine gun opened up with slow bursts of fire, and then it was joined by another one. I scoured the castle for action. Rounds exploded on the far side of the castle. Artillery fired from behind us. A machine gun opened up on our side, and then the lights went out on the castle.

I could see flashes from enemy gun positions. Our intercom came to life again. "Hold your fire! Cease fire!"

Suddenly, the whole line was blanketed in darkness. There was dead silence. Something was brewing. Our guys were locked and loaded. Our .50 was ready. Minutes went by. There were occasional bursts of enemy fire but nothing sustained. I wondered who had opened up on our side. Those guys would be in for it. We waited a good while more, not knowing what was happening. Everybody was tense, manning their weapons.

The lights came on as suddenly as they went out. A deep roar floated up and down the trenches followed by yelling and cheering. "Old glory" was back. Voices could be heard on the intercom, singing burp gun boogie: "Ol' Joe Chink cumin' down the trench, with a burp gun boogie sticking out his ass. We're movin' on. We'll soon be gone!"

It was a hell of a temptation not to fire your weapon because it was such a great moment. Sandbag Castle was ours once again.

CHAPTER 34

BLISTERING COLD

Arctic winds blew down from Manchuria into Korea, plunging the temperatures on our hill to near thirty degrees below zero. The first snowfall in the Taebaek Mountains blanketed the MLR into a frontline of white-covered trenches and gun bunkers. We dug in for the winter. Frostbite became our newest enemy.

To keep warm, you had to dress in layers. I started with long johns, which were form-fitted underwear that covered my body from neck to ankle. From the waist up, I wore a fatigue shirt under an olive army sweater, a scarf, a flak jacket, and a parka with a rabbit-fur-trimmed hood. I tucked a field hat with ear flaps under my helmet liner and steel helmet. Sometimes I would be fortunate enough to have hand warmers brought back from R & R in Japan. They were like warm, metal, cigarette lighters. I'd slip them inside my mittens or leather gloves, and they would keep my hands toasty warm. Below the belt, two pairs of wool socks covered my feet, which were tucked inside a pair of oversized, rubber galoshes, which we called "Mickey Mouse boots." They were nice and warm, but the problem with them was if I had to walk any distance at all, my feet would start to sweat and freeze up, so I switched back to dry combat boots, which were not as warm but more comfortable. A pair of field pants covered my fatigue pants. On top of all this, it was standard operating procedure to wear your cartridge belt and pistol and carry your rifle with you at all times.

Keeping the supply road open behind us became a daily challenge for the engineers. We needed the road open for food, ammo, medical supplies, and other provisions. We did have a homemade tram set up from the road up to the first-aid station, but it had limited use and was dependent upon the deuce and a half trucks having use of the supply road. One means of transport that didn't rely on wheels was the Korean Service Corps. The KSC was made up of *papa-sans* who were too old for military service. They were paid peasant wages to hump supplies up the mountain on their backs. We called them choggies and were never quite sure if they were friends or foes. They had no standard uniform. They were bundled in soiled, brown, quilted jackets and wore flapped caps and canvas high-top sneakers just like the North Koreans. They were a common sight on the hill, and even though you were glad to see them, you kept a wary eye out for them. There were persistent rumors that they sometimes gave our positions away to the NKs, who would then zero in on us with mortars and artillery rounds.

Going to the crapper was a real chore, because it was a cumbersome routine. The layered clothing had to be removed piece by piece. Not only that, but the shitter was built out in the open on the reverse side of the slope facing the supply road. You had a box seat to what was coming and going, and the travelers could watch everything that you were doing. It was real theater. It wasn't like the enclosed outhouse that the officers used, which offered some privacy and shelter from the elements but cut them off from their fellow comrades in arms.

One snowy morning, I made my way down to the enlisted men's shitter, slipping and sliding in my Mickey Mouse boots until I reached my humble, communal commode. It consisted of a three-foot, square, wooden box with a circle cut out in the middle of it. On this particular day, the wind was blowing in gusts, and I had to brush the snow off of the lid. I used my trench knife to chip away at the thin layer of ice surrounding my crevasse. Satisfied with my chopping and cleaning, I unbuckled my cartridge belt and took off my parka but kept the hood draped over my helmet.

I dropped my two pairs of trousers, found the opening in the back of my long johns, and proceeded to lower myself slowly into position. You tried to anticipate making contact, but the initial shock of ass on ice was always a shocker. You never got used to it. Once past that, you became a seamless tent of covered clothing waiting for relief.

What never ceased to amaze me was the naturalness of it all. Aside from their bitching and complaining, soldiers adjusted to their outrageous predicaments with a sense of aplomb. Here I was sitting outside in the middle of a snowstorm, taking a crap with a scarf covering my face and a hood over my head, only my eyes peering out, waving to my buddies as they passed me on the hill.

"Mornin', Joe."

"Mornin', Marty."

Others would pass by from time to time. "Hey, Joe, enjoyin' yourself?"

"Yeah, I'm doin' okay, Mule."

"Need a line up there, Joe?" yelled Meeks, our communications man, smiling as he plodded along below me.

"No, I need you to come up here and keep me company," I yelled back, and then I froze.

Several feet down in front of me, the tail end of a shell protruded out of the snow. I got up and yelled down to the next person I saw.

"I've got a live one up here!" I shouted as I pulled on my clothes. The figure just waved back. I shouted again and again before I realized that he was one of our KATUSAs (Korean Attachment United States Army).

"*E-dee-wha, e-dee-wah!*" I yelled, waving him to me. I wanted him to get a GI. I didn't want to leave the commode so I could stop anyone walking toward the danger zone. I found a stick and stuck it in the ground and topped it with toilet paper to mark the spot.

The KATUSA kept nodding his head and replying in Korean. I didn't know what he was saying, but he sounded like he understood, because he took off down the hill. A few minutes later, he returned with a GI and handed me packets of toilet paper, smiling. After an explanation and a few laughs, the situation was resolved.

Once a day back in battalion, they would try to cook a meal and send it up to us. In the snow and cold, that wasn't always possible. After a few days of greasy combat rations, a hot meal looked like a gourmet meal. I thanked my father for the food packages he sent me twice a month. Jell-O, crackers, canned fruit, soups, tea bags, and cookies were my comfort food. They were a good backup in place of a hot meal.

Later in the day on my way back to my bunker, I was told that choggies brought up chow to Love Hill, which was pretty close to my gun position. If I hurried, I might catch a hot meal. I scooted up the trench but got there late. They were cleaning up. There was no hot water and no clean trays. The freezing temperatures glued the remnants of the meal to the plastic tray. I guess I was pretty hungry because I picked through the used trays, trying to find one that was fairly decent. I took some small pieces of toilet paper, which I now had plenty of from inside my helmet liner, and tried to wipe away the grime from the tray. The choggies tipped the metal chow bins to fill my tray, and I encouraged them to fill it to the brim, disregarding the separated compartments. I wanted to cover the guck still sticking to the tray so I could just skim off the top portion of food from the tray. It had stopped snowing; however, the sky was overcast, and it was getting dark. I had to eat fast. I looked at the red, greasy sauce covering thick, cheese-covered noodles, and I wasn't sure I could eat it. It wasn't very inviting, and it was bitter cold. I had to think about it. I was standing in a foot of snow, freezing my ass off. Was it worth it? *Maybe I should just turn around and go back down the trench to my bunker and grab some of my comfort food and forget it.*

I went for it. I lifted my left arm up and put my right hand under my armpit and pulled the wool glove off and stuffed it in my jacket pocket. I started to shove the food into my mouth. The pain started gradually, and then the tips of my fingers began to burn. I ate faster, and the pain became greater. I put the tray down and breathed hot air on my fingertips and saw in disbelief tiny white spots. They looked like blisters. Frostbite! I quickly put my glove back on and squeezed my right hand under my armpit to protect it from the blistering cold. I couldn't wait to get to my gun bunker and put my numb hands over our charcoal-lit ammo can for warmth. If this was what the cold in Korea was going to be like, we were in for one hell of a winter.

CHAPTER 35

DEE-JACK-A-MOE'S CHERRIES

It was an unwritten law. If you received a package from home, especially a food package, it was to be opened immediately and shared with your buddies. Nobody had an argument with that.

It was right before Christmas. We had gotten a new replacement. His name was DiGiacomo. Immediately, everybody called him "Dee-jack-a-moe." Sometimes it was Dee, because it was easier to say than the real Italian pronunciation of "Dee-gee-ah-como." "No K in the Italian," said Dee.

Dee-jack-a-moe was a piece of work. He was a corporal and a paratrooper from the Eleventh Airborne Division in Fort Campbell, Kentucky, who had reenlisted in the regular army to volunteer for Korea. He was middle height and husky with thick, bushy eyebrows arched over long, upturned eyelashes. Big, sad, puppy-dog eyes seemed to be either mocking you or pleading with you to pet him. At first, you felt sorry for him until you realized that he was a bit of an actor. When you thought he was about to whimper and you wanted to console him, you would be taken aback by a sudden, twinkling, impish smile that seemed to say, "Gotcha!"

We suspected all volunteers. If you could get it out of them, they all had a story to tell. For some, it was a way of avoiding a court-martial and doing jail time. More often than not, it was a clash with superiors that had gotten them into trouble, and they

227

found themselves volunteering for Korea afterward. For a few, it was a way of getting out of a Section 8 and ending up in the loony bin. Then there were guys who were always on sick call, screwing up, or gung-ho assholes (which could have possibly included me). It wasn't uncommon for a career, twenty-year, regular-army man looking for a battlefield promotion and a better retirement pension to volunteer for Korea. This was totally understandable. Of course, the honest-to-goodness patriot who wanted to go to war to fight his country's enemies was admired and appreciated. My biggest fear was getting a replacement that had once been somebody else's problem and was now yours. In Korea, you quickly realized how much your life depended on trusting the guy next to you.

The phone hissed in our snow-covered bunker. "Upper Seventy-Five," I answered.

"Mail's coming," said the voice in our command post.

"Hot damn!" I whooped. "Mail's on the way."

Moments later, a soft voice outside our bunker announced, "Mail call. Donohue and Dee-jack-a-moe have packages."

"Bring it in, Ed. What are you waiting for?" I asked.

Ed was a volunteer replacement. He was a nice guy. He was an ex-heavy weapons man like us, but he had one little problem. On line, he was so nervous of the Chinese attacking him that he wouldn't or couldn't go to sleep. No matter what time of the day or night, he could be seen by his machine gun, looking out across no-man's-land. He wouldn't move or eat and hardly talked.

He was carried off of the hill on a stretcher to our medical unit back at battalion. We heard that he refused to be sent back to division headquarters. When we saw him again, he was our company mailman. Every day, he would drive his jeep up on our service road to deliver and pick up the mail. We thought it was his way of making amends for his behavior on line.

"We thought you might need some help opening your packages," snickered Reimer and Mason, two wise-guy New Yorkers from our 75-millimeter rifle platoon. They were soon joined by Olson and Rock, two good buddies from our machine gun platoon.

Dee-jack-a-moe grabbed his package first and ripped it partly open. With a sly smile, he said, "It's from my mom. We're going to have a merry, merry, little Christmas."

He looked at me. "How about you?" he asked.

I looked at my box and knew right away. "It's from my folks."

"Well, what are you waiting for? Open it up, Joe," said Olson impatiently.

I slit open the box. Neatly packed underwear, candles, flashlight batteries, a couple of Agatha Christie pocketbooks and boxes of Jell-O, and crumbled, colored cookies didn't generate much excitement, although hands did grab for the cookie crumbs with appreciative smiles. Luckily, Dee-jack-a-moe gave out with a hoot and a holler, and all eyes reverted back to him. I was grateful because I suddenly realized that the Christmas-colored cookies were the stale, moldy, crumbs from the carved-out loaf of bread from which the neck of a pint of Four Roses protruded. I didn't have the heart to spoil their fun. My present would be enjoyed another time.

"This is straight from heaven," intoned Dee-jack-a-moe, holding his package against his ear and shaking it gently over and over again as he looked at each of us with a knowing smirk. We couldn't see what was in the crumpled package, but he had our rapt attention.

"This is a gift from the god of war to us," he announced solemnly as a diabolical smile spread across his face.

"Okay, okay, so what have you got? Get on with it, man," said Rock impatiently in his low, quiet voice.

Dee-jack-a-moe held up his hand. He was not to be rushed. He savored the moment. He built up the drama. He was not to be denied. With great flair, he cut the tan, hairy cord from around the package and slid his trench knife across its cardboard seam. He tore open the flaps and removed the thick, corrugated packing from within the box. His hands disappeared inside and hurriedly explored its contents and then abruptly stopped. Everybody tensed. He carefully lifted two objects shaped liked chalices and wrapped in tissue reverently over his head.

"What have I got? Observe please."

Our gaze followed the objects as he peeled off the wrapping and rapidly intoned, "Gentlemen, what you see before you are the eighth and ninth wonders of the world. Two quart-sized jars of pure joy have been lovingly prepared by my mother and packed with the largest and finest brandy-soaked maraschino cherries money can buy. Observe their dark red, swollen bellies jammed hungrily against one another, ready to burst."

Dee-jack-a-moe held one of the jars up to the Coleman lantern hanging from a bunker beam, and with an admiring eye, he slowly turned it around for all to see. Satisfied that he had our attention, he said plain and simple, "Gentlemen, they must be set free immediately."

With an exaggerated effort and appropriate grunt, he twisted off the top of the jar, which opened with a pop. "Now I will demonstrate the proper procedure for consumption. First, in order to free these plump little babies from their cramped quarters, you must gently pull them up by their stems, making sure the stems do not become separated from the cherry. Before this intricate maneuver is attempted, gentlemen, you must put yourself in the 'ready position' so that drops are not carelessly wasted."

Dee-jack-a-moe bent his head back and opened his mouth. Using his tongue as a net, he positioned it directly under the freed cherry and slowly lowered the glistening, smooth fruit into his mouth to a round of approving ahs and pats on the back. Like a priest giving out Holy Communion, Dee-jack-a-moe proceeded to wish each of us a merry Christmas and a happy new year. Biting into the marinated cherries bloated with juice and soaked in brandy brought a sudden rush of warmth into the welcomed bellies of bodies living and surviving in below-zero weather.

It was a moment of instant gratification. I turned to Dee-jack-a-moe and said, "Those were the most delicious cherries I have ever tasted in my entire life."

Dee-jack-a-moe grinned with delight. "Your mom's Christmas cookies were fantastic too."

CHAPTER 36

BLOOD IN THE SNOW

"Let it snow. Let it snow. Let it snow," kept going through my head. The weather really was frightful, and the fire in our bunker was far from delightful. We used whatever we had for fuel. For me, charcoal was the worst. The fumes went up my nose and into my mouth. I never ate charcoal-cooked food again. It made me gag. In the winter on the hill, one of the foods I liked best was Jell-O. It didn't have to be heated. You mixed the flavored powder with water, threw in a can of fruit salad if you had one, and *bingo!* you had a quick, tasty meal.

I poured water from a jerry can into a cookie pan I had saved from one of my care packages from home. I ran out of fruit salad, so I just emptied two Jell-O boxes of strawberry powder into it, stirred it around, and brought it outside my bunker. I placed the whole kit and caboodle on top of a snow-covered sandbag.

I started back to my hooch when Kim Pan Soo rushed up to me all excited. "Dee-jack-a-moe, Dee-jack-a-moe, *tak-son mashida*," he growled, making little gestures with his tongue, sticking it out of the side of his mouth and whirling his index finger in circles next to his temple.

"*Ee-dee-wah, Joe-san*," he cried, waving me after him.

I followed Kim up and over the trench and down the rear slope of our hill. We moved awkwardly in deep snow through some brush and over a stream. Moon and Choi, who were from

231

another gun crew, were bouncing up and down on a fallen tree branch, trying to break it for kindling for their bunker's stove. They pointed down below them. Dee-jack-a-moe was bareheaded, his helmet in the snow. He struggled to get himself up the hill. Commo wire was wrapped around his waist and shoulder and tied to a fallen limb. He looked like he was swimming in the snow. He roared and swore and laughed as he tried to climb back up the hill, pulling the firewood behind him. The Koreans watched silently, occasionally grunting words among themselves. You didn't have to know the language to know what they were saying. Dee-jack-a-moe was drunk as a skunk.

I locked hands with the Koreans, and we formed a human chain down to Dee-jack-a-moe. When I reached him, I grabbed his arm, but he shook me off with a shout and a wild-eyed grin and offered me his canteen. I slipped and skidded on my butt and landed next to him. He looked surprised. His ears and nose were cherry red, and his mustache was covered with snow. He leaned into me with a goofy look on his face and winked.

"That was a great landing, sky soldier. You came down right next to me."

"Here, let me help you out of your rig," I said and cut the commo wire that was wrapped around him with my trench knife.

"I don't need no fucking help," he said, swinging and swaying like a punch-drunk fighter. Dee-jack-a-moe slipped farther down the hill.

We grabbed him under his arms and by his parka's hood, and slipping and sliding all the way, we dragged him backward up the hill to the cheers of Dee Jack-a-moe, who was enjoying himself and urging us on like a couple of huskies.

We got him up the hill minus the tree limb. Now we had to get him down into the trench and to our sleeping bunker without being seen or at least without being too obvious. Dee-jack-a-moe didn't make it easy for us. The trench was only a few feet wide, so we bounced clumsily from side to side. Dee-jack-a-moe was mumbling and singing to himself. "For God's sake, keep it down," I hissed, vapor misting from my mouth. In the snow, Dee-jack-a-moe seemed like he weighed a ton.

"Wow! Hold up a moment," ordered Dee-jack-a-moe, and with his Santa Claus smile, he patted the canteen on his belt. "Let's have a drink. Whadevayasay, old sky soldier buddy? Airborne all the way?"

"Jesus, Dee-jack-a-moe, you get busted, and your old trooper's ass is gonna get court-martialed."

"Whada they gonna do?" he bellowed, looking at me, blurry-eyed. "Send me to Korea?"

It took all of us to get him into his top bunk. Dee-jack-a-moe then leaned his head over. "Don't wake me for dinner, gentlemen," he announced haughtily before he passed out.

Later that night in my bunker, the sound of explosions snapped my eyes open. I waited, holding my breath. For a brief moment, I hoped that I was dreaming. The distinctive burp sound of Russian guns was loud and clear. I laid there, tucked warmly in my sleeping bag, and tried to wish the noise away. The phone rang. I didn't want to answer it. I wanted to say in my sack, roll over, and go back to sleep. The soft glow of a Coleman lantern helped me find the ringing field phone.

"A-tack-kee! A-tack-kee!" said Kim from our gun bunker. "Everything *dai-joe-be*."

"I'll be right there, Kim," I said. *Dai-joe-be* meant that everything was okay for now. I quickly slipped into my boots, grabbed my parka, helmet, cartridge belt, and rifle, turned to Dee-jack-a-moe's bunk, and slapped it.

"We're getting hit. Let's go, man. Move it!"

There was no response.

"Get the fuck up, man!" I screamed.

The deep, slow booms of artillery brought Dee-jack-a-moe's head up from his sleeping bag. He stared at me blankly as I strapped on my pistol belt. "Move your ass! We're getting hit."

Dee-jack-a-moe gazed at me uncertainly and then dropped back on his bunk. "Wait 'til they're in the trenches," he groaned.

"Fuck you, Dee-jack-a-moe." I grabbed my carbine and put out the Coleman lantern, plunging the bunker into darkness. Outside was an orchestra of sound and flashing lights. The Mule and Pak were on our .50-caliber. Moon and Choi were on a .50 next to ours, so I squeezed into a crevice of the trench wall between our two gun positions. In effect, I became a rifleman covering both guns and the trench line. I slammed a clip into my carbine and peered above the embankment. I strained my eyes to follow the fingers of our ridge, which sloped down in front of us a couple hundred yards to the valley floor. The whole line was alive with gunfire. I could see muzzle flashes down below. They looked like fireflies. They would glitter for a split second and then get swallowed up by the darkness. They would suddenly appear in a different spot and disappear once again. There was no way of getting a fix on the glimmers of light and returning accurate fire. My biggest worries were lights multiplying and growing bigger. The bigger the light, the closer the enemy was. I fired where I saw the closest lights. Pitch-black darkness provided cover for both sides. Nobody knew for sure what damage they caused on the other side.

Mortar rounds exploded in front of our gun bunker, but they were too far away to be effective. The Mule kept firing in short bursts. The fireflies seemed to have spread out, but they also seemed closer now. A couple of rounds came in pretty close. I didn't like being out in the open. I felt naked without a roof over my head. I pressed against the side of the trench, waiting for the next round to come in. I decided that if the mortars got any closer, I would make for the cover of our gun bunker whether it was crowded or not.

Longer bursts from our .50-caliber made me wonder if the Mule and Pak were seeing something that I was not seeing. The burp sounds of the guns seemed closer. I popped up and fired at flashes. The tempo increased. I heard rebel yells as the whole line seemed to be firing at the same time. I leaped up and fired at sounds, sights, shadows and flashes and then dropped down into the trench. I wasn't sure what was happening except that the action had increased. A mortar round exploded without warning, sending dirt and debris over my head. I bunched up into a ball and yelled to the Mule and Kim, "I'm coming in! I'm coming in!" I waited, but there was no answer. I yelled again, "I'm coming in!" There was still no answer. They couldn't hear me. I hesitated. I didn't want to spook them. I didn't want to go dashing into the gun bunker and get blown away. I lay there, trying to get up the nerve to take a chance and go for it. Another close round made my decision for me. I took off, yelling at the top of my lungs, "It's me! It's Joe! It's me!"

I landed on a mound of shell casings that covered the bunker floor. The smell of expended rounds, which I didn't mind, hung in the air. The Mule and Kim never turned around. I picked up the phone on the second whistle. The noise level went down dramatically around us.

"Cease fire!" I screamed, patting the Mule on the shoulder. "Cease fire!"

The Mule and Kim turned around, and I gave them a thumbs-up. Those words were always beautiful to say or hear. Dave grinned and immediately lit up a butt while Kim cleared the weapon, wiped it down, and busied himself as if we had just finished a firing exercise.

The firefight couldn't have lasted more than twenty minutes, but it seemed to go on forever. All I wanted to do was go back to my sleeping bunker and crash like Dee-jack-a-mo. That son of a bitch had slept through the whole thing. I would deal with him later. First, I just wanted to hit the rack for a few hours before I pulled the next watch.

"Joe, Joe, wake up. We gotta problem," said Mule. "Come on. Wake up."

"Yeah, they're in the trenches, man," said Dee-jack-a-moe, sticking his face into mine.

"What? What's the matter?" I asked, waking up with a start.

"Infiltrators! That's what. For Christ's sake, get up, Joe."

"What? Where?" I asked, leaping out of bed.

"Come on, man. Move your ass," demanded Dee-jack-a-moe, running out of the sleeping bunker.

I stumbled along, pulling on my boots and jacket and grabbing my pistol belt.

"Goddamn son of a bitch," wailed the Mule. "Looky here."

Dee-jack-a-moe was already bent over with his gloved hand pointing to the ground and following a zigzag trail of red splotches in the snow. "Blood," he said solemnly.

"Wasn't that where you were in the trench?" asked the Mule.

"Yeah, around here," I agreed.

"Looks like ya got somebody, Joe," said Mule, shaking his head deliberately.

My reaction was one of shock and horror. "Can't be," I said in disbelief.

"No doubt about it," said Dee-jack-a-moe, straightening up. "And he came through here," he said, looking at me accusingly.

"What the fuck do you know, Dee-jack-a-moe? Yeah, he came through while you were shit-faced sleeping," I snarled.

"Ya must have missed 'em, Joe," said the Mule with a scowl on his face.

"I didn't miss anybody because there was no one there," I said.

"Just because you didn't see anyone doesn't mean there was no one there," said Dee-jack-a-moe with a smirk on his face.

"Fuck you, Dee-jack-a-moe!" I yelled. "You wanted them in the trenches, remember?" I said. "What's the CP doing about this?" I demanded.

"Didn't call the CP," said Dee-jack-a-moe.

"Whadayamean you didn't call the CP?"

"Wouldn't look good," said the Mule.

"It's your ass, Joe. If anybody finds out you let them through—" said Dee-jack-a-moe, pausing long and not finishing his words.

"We'll cover for ya, Joe," said the Mule, putting his arm around my shoulder. "We're all in this together."

"He can't get far," chimed in Dee-jack-a-moe, pulling back the bolt from his carbine. "We'll get him."

I looked form the Mule to Dee-jack-a-moe. "You guys are crazy," I fumed. I walked quickly toward the phone. "I'm calling this in right now."

The Mule jumped in front of me, and Dee-jack-a-moe grabbed my shoulder. "Now hold on, Joe. Not so fast," they said, smiling.

I roughly pulled away and lost my footing, which caused the three of us to tumble down on top of each other. The Mule and Dee-jack-a-moe were howling with laughter as they pinned me to the floor of the trench.

"What the fuck are you doing? What's going on?" I cried as I wrestled and thrashed about under a tangle of arms and legs. "What's so funny?"

"We ate yer Jell-O," roared the Mule.

"We ate your strawberry Jell-O and tried to replace it by making some more, but we spilled it in the snow by mistake," said Dee-jack-a-moe, enjoying himself thoroughly.

"Dee-jack-a-moe thought it looked like blood in the snow. Thought we'd have some fun," said the Mule, coughing, laughing, and grinning from ear to ear. "So we made up a story. We had ya goin' pretty good, Joe."

CHAPTER 37

SATAE-RI VALLEY, HEARTBREAK RIDGE
DECEMBER 25, 1952

BARBED WIRE CHRISTMAS

Loudspeakers were used at night by both sides to speak to one another. We jokingly referred to our broadcaster as "the Whistler" because he would pierce the evening darkness with a slow, solemn, eerie tune to get the attention of his listeners. Their side often played music along with their propaganda, so we called theirs "the Disc Jockey." Tonight was something special. It was Christmas Eve. We weren't quite sure what to expect.

The Disc Jockey started off his program a little different than usual. He played Bing Crosby's "I'll Be Home for Christmas" and "White Christmas." He wished that we could have been home for Christmas instead of being in a country where we didn't belong. He lamented that we were alone and far from our families who missed us so much. Only if we surrendered to the peace-loving Chinese People's Volunteer Army would we be warmly welcomed and sent safely home to our loved ones.

Everyone enjoyed the Disc Jockey except Ackerson, our new man. He was personally going to kill the son of a bitch. "Ah know they're cumin' and ahn waitin' for them," said Ackerson, giving me an assuring shake of the head. "They'll get a Christmas they'll never forget."

238

"Look, Ack," I said. "They're not stupid. They know you're here waiting for them, and they're staying put, so good night." I smiled. "I'm hitting the sack."

Moments later, I was startled awake by the sound of our machine gun and Ackerson's yelling, "Come on, you gook bastards. Come and get it." I stumbled out of my rack and dove up next to him.

"Where? Where?"

"Back of them tree stumps over on the left in front of the barbed wire."

I saw the stumps and waited.

"See 'em?"

"No. Where? I don't see anything."

"They're right on top of us, goddamn it. Call the CP!" hissed Ackerson as he began to fire.

"There's nothing there!" I shouted. "Hold your fire."

"Are you crazy? No way, man."

I grabbed Ackerson's arm, but he violently pulled away and kept firing.

The phone rang, and I picked it up. "Ackerson's firing and seeing things. I need your help up here now," I demanded.

Lyle Olson, a big, blond machine gunner from Nebraska, and Sergeant West, our platoon leader, rushed into the bunker as Ackerson and I got in each other's face. They separated us, and we went outside and climbed up on the bunker roof to get a better view of what Ackerson was firing at.

"They were sneaking up right over there and there just in front of the barbed wire behind those tree trunks," said Ackerson knowingly.

"Where are they now?" asked Olson in a low, calm voice.

"They're out there. Don't you see them?"

"He keeps seeing stumps move," I said. "He won't let me sleep. He doesn't like to be alone on the gun at night. I keep telling him not to stare at those stumps. You look at them long enough, and your eyes start to play tricks on you. You have to look away for a moment and then go back to your target. He

239

won't listen. He'd rather call in an attack, open fire, and scare the hell out of everybody."

Ackerson glared at me. "You callin' me a liar, Donohue?"

"I'm calling you crazy," I shot back, and with that, Ackerson rushed at me. We tumbled down on top of the trench and into a pile of C-rations at the bottom of the hill before Lyle and West jumped down to pull us back up.

"Now hold it, goddamn it. We're all a bit jumpy tonight. Ackerson, I want you to go with Lyle back to his bunker." West looked at me. "If the ole man okays it, I'm going to take a few men and check along the wire of our sector. I think that would help calm the men. I'd like you to come."

The cat had gotten my tongue. I didn't want to go patrolling along the perimeter of our company's positions on Christmas Eve. West was a good platoon leader. He was well respected by the men, including me. He was a straight shooter. He told it like it was. There was even a story that he had traded blunt words with a general and had gotten away with it. There was another side to West that wasn't so hot. If he thought you were a good soldier, then he liked you. If not, then he would rag you without mercy. West had gotten a "Dear John" letter from his wife. He went on R & R in Japan and shacked up with a nurse whom he later learned went to school with his wife back in Pennsylvania. After that—and I saw it myself—he was known as a drinker who was fiercely loyal to his men and sometimes took unnecessary risks in combat.

I broke the silence with a nod. "Okay! I'll go," I said despite knowing that in the army, you never volunteered for anything.

"If it's a go, command post at 2200 hours. Anderson or Dee-jack-a-moe will man your bunker."

It was a go. There were four of us.

"We do a simple recon, nothing more. The night's clear. Good visibility. We take our time. Nice and quiet. We spread out five yards apart. We do a diamond formation. Joe on the left. Meeks with the radio on the right at the base of the slope. I'll take point. George takes up the rear. We go along the barbed wire from our CP gate to Mike 50's gate. No mines to worry about. One bandoleer and two grenades each man. Password is snowman. Challenge is snow. Response is man. Should be a quiet, thirty-minute cakewalk. No sweat. Any questions?"

We stopped at each gate entrance, each of which opened into no-man's-land. It was a long thirty minutes. It felt more like an hour. One by one, we squatted down whenever West came to a stop. I could barely see. It was dark, cold, and quiet. At one point, machine gun tracers arched over the MLR, but we weren't the targets. A carbine opened up somewhere, and a couple of grenades exploded, which brought us to a long halt. The firing was accompanied by flares going up ahead of us near where I thought my gun bunker might be. Instantly, Ackerson's maniacal face flashed in front of me, and I had the craziest thought of Ackerson seeing us as gooks and firing at us. Crazy thoughts for a crazy situation, but it spooked me just the same.

West sidled over to Meeks. I didn't recognize the gate in front of my gun position. Everything looks different from the other end of the hill and at night. West motioned for George and me to go through the gate. West and Meeks followed quickly behind us. I made my way up to my gun bunker and heaved a sigh of relief.

West asked for a report. Nobody saw or heard anything. Everything was copacetic.

"What happened with the firing back there?" I asked.

"Somebody thought they saw something, but who knows?" said West. "The important thing is we did our own little recon and everything was negative. I'll get on the horn and send the word that everything's *Joe Toe*. That should help calm things down. Get some shut-eye. Good show."

Christmas morning was cold, clear, and bright. Mule brought some pancakes up from the service road, and he draped over his canteen cup to keep them warm. He was smiling and bubbling with news. "I got two Christmas stories for you, Joe. You'll die when you hear them," he said, grinning from ear to ear. "At daybreak this morning, an ambush patrol found Christmas cards and ribbons from the People's Republic of China hanging on our barbed wire."

At first, I thought he was kidding, but he wasn't. I eventually read the cards, which urged us to surrender so we could live and be with our loved ones for next Christmas. I don't know how I looked, but I was in total shock, too stunned to speak.

"My second story is even better," crowed the Mule. The cooks down on the service road said that the dinks freed a GI prisoner over by our 160th and they had the poor fellow cross over to no-man's-land dressed in red long johns and carrying a white sack filled with cookies and candies. They let him go as a Christmas present to us. God's truth, that's what I heard."

The Mule was right. I never expected, especially after last night's patrol, that I would be reading greeting cards left on barbed wire by Chinese soldiers wishing me a merry Christmas.

CHAPTER 38

TURKEY SHOOT NEW YEAR

**At exactly twenty-four hundred hours, every United
Nations soldier on the front line in Korea fired his weapon
and shouted Happy New Year to the People's Army of North
Korea and their Communist Chinese comrades. Nineteen
fifty-three began with a bang, rumors, and plenty of changes.
I got my 75-millimeter rifle back. Dee-jack-a-moe was made
a section sergeant for two of the four recoilless rifle squads in
our platoon, and there was talk of our division coming off of
the line.**

I kneeled next to my 75mm. I checked my watch impatiently.
Anticipation was building. Everyone's weapon was at the ready.
The phone rang, and I lunged for it. I listened and nodded.
The countdown started. "Ten . . . nine . . . eight—load her
up, Mule—three . . . two . . . one . . . *bingo! Happy new year
everybody!"*

Tracers crisscrossed the sky and ricocheted off the tops and
sides of mountains. From our battalion rear came the whispering
sounds of artillery shells overhead that crashed with great
booming explosions. Our tankers joined us in the clanking of
tubes with our mortars as high-explosive antitank shells, Willy
Peter rounds, rockets, and projectiles swished out of barrels into
enemy positions. Like the Fourth of July, exploding geysers of
flame, burning shrapnel, and brilliant showers of shimmering

shards of white-hot phosphorous floated to the ground. For one crazy, mad minute, pandemonium filled the sky as every weapon on line opened up in celebration of the coming new year.

Cries of "cease fire" were followed momentarily by the boisterous and uneven singing of "*Auld Lang Synge*." It was corny but great fun and a great morale booster for the troops.

Our intercom voice announced hot coffee and doughnuts up where our tank was dug in. I took the Mule's canteen and my own and hustled up the trench. I was not disappointed. The icing-covered doughnuts were fresh, and the coffee hot. In my hurry to get back down to my bunker, I slipped in the snow and fell on my ass, spilling half of the hot coffee on myself. I made it up to the Mule by breaking out what was left of the Four Roses my father had sent to me for Christmas. I poured whiskey into our canteens, so we toasted each other with coffee royals. We got back our 75s. We were no longer attached to the platoon manning machine guns. We toasted to each other's health and our new section sergeant, Dee-jack-a-moe. Being a corporal already didn't hurt him.

Things were starting to happen. There were rumblings that the Fifth Regimental Combat Team (RCT) was coming up to replace our 223rd Regiment, which was covering us on our right flank near the Punchbowl area. If that was true, then we were certainly next to be relieved. The effect rumors had on us, whether they were true or not, always amazed me. The thought of suddenly coming off of the line was hard to believe, but we allowed ourselves the luxury of thinking about it. Everyone became energized with anticipation. We just knew it was going to happen.

Sure enough, the Fifth Regimental Combat Team came up on line next to us. We were fired up with excitement, but there was a downside. Replacement regiments, no matter how good their reputations, would be quickly tested for weak spots in their line. Unfortunately, we would be involved.

"We're going on 100 percent alert," said Lieutenant DeBrun, our platoon leader. "Aside from the fact that we connect with

Fifth RCT, intelligence has it from a captured gook prisoner that our 75-RR, along with the tank's 90mm are going to be specially targeted. Probably a stealth raid at night."

I frowned skeptically. "Are you putting me on, Lieutenant?"

"This is no joke. We'll have a detail of riflemen with automatic weapons to give us extra support. We're taking it seriously. The dinks saw a lot of firepower from you guys on New Year's Eve. Whatever happens, we've got to be ready."

I felt chilled at the thought of being singled out as a personal target by the dinks.

"You're gonna get a delivery of some ammo crates marked 'canister.' They're special rounds for a special purpose."

"How so?" I asked.

"They're like buckshot. They might even be outlawed by the Geneva Convention, but one round can spray a fifty-yard area and break up an assault. If we need them, we'll use them, so keep them handy. This is a 100 percent alert. At 1600 hours, everybody is up until first light. Start a guard schedule now. Your gun crew can grab a few hours before the alert. All the 75s will be in their primary positions. The tankers will pull off a few yards from their positions on top of the ridge and stay in defilade in a wait-and-see mode. Any questions?" asked the lieutenant.

The first shift went on alert. It was a foggy, damp evening. We assumed it would be a sneak attack by night. It was just our luck that the weather prevented the use of our searchlights from lighting up the battlefield. The stand-down came in increments. At 0400, our gun crew was put on 75 percent alert, but no one could sleep. At 0600, we were on 50 percent alert, with everyone wide awake. By daylight, nothing had happened, so the alert was called off, and everyone breathed a sigh of relief. Now everyone was exhausted. It was especially tough for those who had to man our gun position while everyone else hit the sack. The alert brought home to us the danger of the 75-RR being a prime target for the gooks. The New Year was shaping up to be a bit more ominous than I had expected.

245

CHAPTER 39

ANOTHER LETTER FROM FRANK

I enjoyed hearing from Frank. His letters always put a smile on my face. I couldn't wait to write him and tell him my story of my patrol and the Christmas cards left on our barbed wire by the Chinese People's Volunteer Army.

Happy New Year, Kemo Sabe,

How are you doing? I'm doing pretty good. I'm in reserve. It's fucking heaven. I just received your letter. I'm going to write you today, I promise. I hear you guys are catching a lot of shit. Hang in there. It can't be long now before you go into reserve. You're due. Our divisions seem to be following each other around. I hear that we'll be moving up mosh-skosh.

I just got back from Chunchon. I was sent to NCO school. I don't know why, but they're always sending me to school. I came out second in my graduating class. They're going to make me a sergeant. I guess they finally found out that I'm a natural leader of men. They want to send me to OCS and make me into a lifer. They've got to be kidding.

We bribed a couple of Korean guards on our way back and sneaked some moose on post. They looked the other way when we got some food out of the mess hall to pay them for a little yoe-nay, boom, boom! What a way to fight a war.

Just before we came off line, my lieutenant invited me out on patrol again. This time, I told him, "Thanks but no thanks." So what happens? At 0100, a call comes in that our patrol came in the wrong way and wandered into a mine field. One of our guys was badly wounded. George Underwood, a buddy of mine from St. Louis, was with me when the news came in. He said he thought he knew where they were, so I said, "Let's go."

We headed up the trench to the patrol's jump-off point. It was a beautiful night. A bright half-moon bounced off the snow and lit our way. We met up with Pollack and Red, two guys from our company who just sent a couple of men to the aide station to get some litters. The patrol was just on the next finger to our left. When the litter bearers came back, we went out the gate and along a beaten path to a fork and then had to traverse in virgin snow a foot deep. We made a single set of tracks, Indian-style.

I spotted the patrol above us on the side of a hill. There was a body in the snow just below them. They were frozen in their tracks. They were afraid to move. We headed up the hill as fast as we could, heaving our stretchers out in front of us, hitting the snow, expecting at any minute to be blown to hell. The lieutenant waved at us and then motioned us to stop when we reached the body. It was one of our KATUSAs. His name was Chun-Lee. He was dead.

Our platoon leader was a pretty gutsy guy. He came down to us slowly, leading the way. His men fell in behind him. They must have been scared shitless. Two soldiers were carrying and dragging a moaning, crying soldier from my platoon. He was a young kid from Michigan. His name was Chuck. On the way down, he kept telling us how cold he was. We stopped to pour blood out of the litter and throw a couple of blankets over him. He kept pleading with us not to step on another mine. Carrying him, I switched with Pollack and slipped backward down off the trail. I lay there with my heart in my mouth.

Everybody stopped and stood there looking down at me. I lay there, afraid to move. Red and the lieutenant bent over and gave me their hands. I held my breath and scrambled up in three giant steps.

When we got back, the lieutenant thanked me and told me that he liked having me on patrol with him. I told him it was my pleasure. I lied. Be good and stay out of trouble.

Frank

CHAPTER 40

SMOKE GETS IN YOUR EYES

It was around dawn. I had been watching globs of thick gray fog floating over the snow-covered ground when muted flashes caught my eye. Sudden spouts of smoke would momentarily blow the fog away, and dark pockmarks would appear in the snow only to disappear again through the soupy, thick haze. The intercom sounded, "Everybody up. Hold your fire and wait on me!"

Gook artillery was laying down a screen of smoke that mixed in nicely with the dense fog. This was the first daylight action I had seen in Korea. This was also the first time that our four squad of the 75-RR platoon had been at full strength. Clark, McChesney, Kim, Yang, the Mule, and the rest of our guys stumbled into the trench and took up their places. This was something we practiced endlessly. Each man had a position to cover and a job to do. They stretched out along the trench line from the gun bunker to our ammo shed. They did everything from hauling shells to guarding our flanks and rears. There was always the special danger of someone running down the trench in the heat of battle and getting caught in the rear blast of our seventy-five.

The Mule and I anxiously waited for our orders. After a couple of hundred feet, the finger of the ridge we were sitting on disappeared down into the valley floor. The point where it disappeared was my primary target, so I zeroed in on it. I could hit that spot without seeing it, because it was already marked with a stake.

Our range card had its exact range and elevation. It was a fixed target, because if the Chinks popped up there, they would be right on top of us. It wasn't a very good field of fire for us.

The second closest target we zeroed in on was an old network of abandoned Chink trenches, tunnels, and bunkers that were filled with barbed wire and mines. It was several hundred yards off to our left, and we had a good view of it. Other targets were less threatening and farther away from our gun position.

Fifty- and .30-caliber machine guns opened fire and were quickly answered by Chinese Maxim heavy machine guns and mortar rounds that threw more covering smoke on the ground on our side of the line. A machine gunner on our left had interlocking fire with a machine gun on our right, creating a crisscross pattern of burning tracers out in front of our bunker. The machine gunner on our left was screaming and heehawing at the top of his lungs, "Yeah, ya fuckers! This is from West 'By God' Virginia! Hear me? West 'By God' Virginia."

In the midst of the excitement, the overhead artillery shells landed close in front of us. The Mule and I looked at each in amazement. We could hear them coming from behind us and watched as the explosions threw off fluttering gels of white phosphorous that stuck to the bushes and tree limbs right smack in front of us.

Frantic voices joined mine, complaining that the incoming rounds were from our own artillery, which our CP denied, and we heard a chorus of screaming curses and swearing ranging from "bullshit" to "up your ass incoming." We assumed it was a screwup because the firing didn't stop right away.

I heard voices over the intercom say, "They're breaking. They're breaking. They're going into the old Chink trenches."

"Upper Seventy-Five. Fire mission," announced the voice from the intercom. The noise around us was deafening. Lieutenant DeBrun's voice was steady above the din. "One round canister, intersection of Chink trenches in your sector. Let's see what these babies can do." Immediately, my assistant gunner and I stuffed rifle patches into our ears as I opened the breech and he shoved the projectile home. He tapped me on my helmet, and I slammed the breech closed and brought the barrel to bear on our prearranged target.

"Fire in the hole!" I yelled, and guys around me repeated it.

The recoilless spit flames out of both its front and rear without movement, except for the fog, which swirled vehemently from the buckshot being thrown into it. As for the 75-RR, there was no kick and no recoil, only the deafening noise of a shell being slowly lobbed into the old Chink trenches. I flung open the breech for another round to be loaded and waited. I got antsy waiting, especially in the midst of an attack. Our tankers now joined in the close bombardment, and I nervously wondered if our artillery rounds were short on purpose. The fighting was close.

I could hear sporadic voices over the intercom from our riflemen. "They're pulling back. They got wounded. I can see them. See over there. Some went down. They're jumping out of the trenches. Let's go get 'em!"

The fog and smoke were good cover for them. They had to break out of those mined positions while the visibility was still poor and in their favor. They knew we were close enough to come after them. There was sporadic firing along our lines. Everyone was looking for movement in the direction of the trenches.

"Fire at will," replied DeBrun.

We had stacked twenty-pound 75-RR rounds in the ammo shed, because everything was piled neatly according to type—high-explosive shells to be used against infantry, antitank rounds to be used against armor, smoke as markers and for setting up screens, white phosphorous for burning, and our new canister missiles for scattering fire. The canisters from our 75s were incredible. It was like somebody rapidly waving cigar smoke away with his hand. Smoke and fog jumped quickly apart, exposing weird shapes and forms and gaping holes in which to peer through and look for moving targets. After several rounds,

DeBrun's voice came quickly over the intercom, "Cease fire! Cease fire 75s. All 75s, cease fire."

The cackle of a carbine broke the short silence of the cease-fire. Over the intercom came, "Get you! Yeah, I get you, you gook bastard. Now I got you. Huh! Huh! Huh! Got you! Got you! Huh! Huh! Huh!" I could hear Kahuii's voice over the intercom. He was in Mason's third squad 75mm recoilless rifle gun crew.

"Upper Seventy-Five, Upper Seventy-Five, what the hell is going on up there?" growled Lieutenant DeBrun on the intercom.

"Reimer, our 75mm gunner, answered, "Sounds like somebody got themselves a gook."

Later, we learned that a gook soldier either got confused in the fog and had gotten turned around the wrong way after the assault or was trying to surrender to our forces. In any case, he had wandered into Lower Seventy-Five's position and gotten himself "banana clip" dead by Henry Kahuii, an assistant gunner from Hawaii who had emptied his entire carbine into the enemy soldier.

Our company commander, Captain Roberts, was furious at the lost opportunity of getting a POW. Kahuii never admitted that he had blown a chance to capture a Chink soldier and earn an extra five days of R & R in Japan. He claimed that smoke had gotten in his eyes and that in the fog, he had thought he had been firing at Chinks who were attacking his gun bunker.

CHAPTER 41

COMING OFF THE LINE

The call from the CP was music to my ears. "Get your cotton-picking ass down here on the double. We got some Thunderbird boys who want to move into your digs."

It was so unexpected. I just never thought that Frank's Forty-Fifth Division would be relieving my Fortieth Division! I was so excited that I flew down the hill half-expecting Frank to be waiting for me in our command bunker.

In the cold, damp, chill of predawn, Mike Company evacuated Heartbreak Ridge. Loaded down with heavy equipment, we came off of the line, bitching and moaning only as happy warriors could be with the knowledge that we were going to the safety and comfort of a rear-echelon training area.

Sleeping in a warm bed with hot food and clean clothes seemed like a fantasy. I was so excited that I had been fully packed and ready to go for hours. At 0100 hours, nothing happened. I waited. By 0200 hours, nothing happened. By 0300 hours, I was nodding and dozing and thinking the worst. At 0400, the phones came alive. "Mount up! No talking. No sound. We move silently. Squad leaders, line up your squads. This is it. Quiet as you go."

Figures emerged from bunkers and squeezed through trenches filled with jostling bodies. My fourth squad was next.

"Whatever happens, keep an eye out for each other and fucking stay together," I said. "Okay, let's do it."

We came off of the hill as quietly as we could, smiling silently as we met familiar faces. Bent over and carrying fully loaded backpacks, we took turns carrying our 75-millimeter recoilless rifle. I had the tripod slung over my shoulder with the rest of the squad taking turns and helping out. We trudged downhill and joined the snaking line of dark figures slithering arduously down the winding mountain road.

About twenty minutes into our withdrawal, we halted and were told to take a break. We hadn't gotten very far. I could still make out the trench line on top of Heartbreak. Nevertheless, it was a relief to throw down our heavy loads, plop down, and take ten, even though there was no smoking and no talking.

I expected to move shortly. I looked at my watch. Ten minutes became thirty minutes, and still, we waited. I closed my eyes and opened them again when a wet flake landed on my nose, and then another hit my face. It was snowing.

In just seconds, it was snowing heavily. I slid the folded poncho off of the back of my cartridge belt, removed my helmet, and pushed my head through the opening. As if on cue, every soldier in the 224th Regiment had hidden themselves underneath their ponchos as the big, fat flakes fell silently and lazily on top of them. The slithering serpent had come to a halt. Tucked inside our covered shields, we sat with our backs against our packs and waited.

Finally, words were passed down the line. "On your feet. Let's move out."

Half asleep, I struggled to get my squad up, stamping, brushing, and shaking off snow. Contorted figures poked up out of the snow. It never ceased to amaze me how combat infantrymen were able to sleep anywhere at any time and under any conditions. My watch showed 0630. It was snowing lightly now.

I checked out my squad. They got up, breaking their snow-sculptured molds, stamping their feet, and pumping their arms. We were stiff, wet, and cold as we saddled up to move out. It was a perfectly miserable way to start the day.

"It won't be long now," I said cheerfully. "We got a hot meal waiting for us, and the smoking lamp is lit, so keep it down and stay together."

Loaded down with heavy backpacks and equipment on a snow-covered road and wearing Mickey Mouse boots was asking for trouble. The bottoms of our rubber shoes packed the snow down, making it slippery for the guys behind us. I remembered how hard it was hiking the straight-up hill of Heartbreak at night in nice weather. I expected it would be even tougher going downhill during the day in bad weather. The sliding and falling started almost immediately.

Every few steps, someone would go into a skid. Carrying our weapons denied us the full use of our arms in keeping our balance. If we tilted forward, the packs on our backs drove us face-first into the snow. If we tilted backward, we landed on our rumps. The sad part was that it was impossible to get up without a helping hand, which only made matters worse. The surprised look of realization that one had when he was losing balance and control made for hysterical laughter. Soldiers became unwilling dancers in a comic ballet of flailing arms and skipping legs that resulted in a chain reaction of pirouetting bodies crashing into the snow-covered ground.

What wasn't funny was when somebody slid helplessly off the road and down an embankment. Often when this happened, anyone trying to halt the skid put themselves in danger of losing his own balance and being swept along with the other person. When this happened, a chain gang would be formed to bring the men up. Needless to say, there was always the unspoken fear of possible mines.

To make a bad situation more palatable, there were contests and bets on who could take the most steps before falling. Cheers and arguments were now mixed with wisecracks and obscenities. In spite of the torturous trek coming off of Heartbreak, spirits were high. I think most of us thought of it as sledding merrily into reserve.

The morning became brighter, and it stopped snowing. The service road became more level. There was much less falling and hurt. Our pace quickened, and we made better time. We came around a bend in the road and then came to an abrupt halt, bunching up and banging into each other, which brought the usual comments.

The word spread quickly, "Trucks! The trucks are here!" We couldn't see them, but that didn't stop the nods of approval, smiles, and pats on the back from the immediate good news.

Outside of their trucks, drivers shouted instructions. There was a piss call before we stored our heavy equipment and rucksacks on the back of one truck and gratefully scrambled aboard another. I had to squeeze in between Reimer, Mason, Meeks, and other squad members. We were packed in like sardines. I smiled to myself, grateful to be sitting with my buddies going to a rear base. Everyone seemed to light up their crushed, damp, Red Cross cigarettes at the same time, enjoying the moment.

The trucks moved cautiously along the snow-packed road. There was much bumping and rolling from side to side. The midmorning sun was bright and I managed to doze even though the temperature was well below freezing. No longer marching, I cooled off. The sun gave little warmth. We were soon freezing our asses off as we rode in an open truck with damp fatigues and dried sweat that had turned into chills. By late morning, there was a mass of forms huddled together in a grim grip of silence on the floor of the truck, trying to stay warm from pure body heat. There was no joking about queers or fags, only shivering and uncomfortable grunts from the bumpy ride.

"Last stop!" was music to our ears.

We untangled ourselves from our cramped positions and slowly straightened up. I jumped along with others off of the rear of the truck onto the snow-covered ground. The pain was instantaneous. Shock waves vibrated up from my boots as my stiff legs buckled helplessly beneath me. Wails of hurt echoed in the freezing cold as guys fell to the ground, hobbled up and down, and stomped their feet fighting off cramps and numbness, trying to get feeling back into their limbs.

Once the blood started circulating through our bodies again, I got my guys into a ragged formation. We grabbed our gear and left the 75s in the trucks for later. Everything was waiting for us. We were assigned tents and lined up for chow. Everybody was exhausted but not too tired to eat. It didn't bother us that the breakfast eggs couldn't be broken because they were frozen solid. We thought it was hilarious. We didn't care. This was the start of a vacation for us. We were on a prepared retreat. The coffee was sizzling. There was crisp bacon and real milk and butter to go with the pancakes. On a full stomach, my squad and I went into our warm tent with a belching stove and crawled into our sleeping bags for a long-deserved sleep. Much to the organization and understanding of our service company, Mike Company of the 1224th Infantry Regiment pretty much slept the day away in warm tents, safety, and with filled bellies. No one in my platoon stirred after breakfast. Everyone was exhausted. I don't think anyone wanted anything more than just sleep. At that moment, we were in heaven. We were off the fucking line.

CHAPTER 42

HENRY KAHUII FROM HAWAII

I should have remembered what the train sergeant had said on the ride up from Pusan, which was as far south behind enemy lines as you could get. When he had passed out clips of ammo because of the threat from infiltrators, he had said, "Nowhere in Korea is safe. The enemy can be anyone, anywhere, so never, ever let your guard down."

After evening chow, we were left alone. I walked back to my tent and talked the night away. At dawn the next morning, I was awakened to a bugle call and the hustle and bustle of camp life. My body was still achy and stiff from coming off of Heartbreak the day before. I wasn't complaining. I chuckled gleefully, thinking of the falling snow and the slipping and sliding and tumbling off of that goddamn hill.

The shouts to morning chow were music to my ears. It was a lively affair. There was laughing, storytelling, and lots of backslapping. The loudest outbursts came from the guys who knew each other only as names and voices over the intercom. It was hard to explain the feeling of talking to strangers whose voices you knew so well as buddies on the phone. Names now had faces. In my mind's eye, most of these guys looked nothing like the guy I had pictured over the phone. It was a weird sensation, trying to accept the image you had formed in your head with the stranger standing next to you.

Coming back from chow, I took in my surroundings as if seeing them for the first time. My sleeping quarters was a gray, heavy-canvas squad tent that housed two nine-man crews plus a few other men from our platoon. Standard army folding cots were lined up on both sides of the tent opposite each other. They were separated by an aisle that led to the front and back entrances of the tent. The front door was a canvas flap with a see-through plastic widow. Just inside the front entrance, the first thing you encountered was an imposing, three-and-a-half-foot, iron, potbelly stove with a long funnel leading up and out of the hole in the slanted roof of the tent.

After breakfast we had a shakedown inspection listing all the articles of clothing and equipment we had, didn't have, and needed to have. On it was a list of dos and don'ts while in reserve. During the inspection, all our weapons were duly recorded and ammunition collected. We had weapons but no ammunition. It made me feel absolutely naked. I would miss the comforting feeling of having my loaded Colt .45 tucked into my belt underneath my sleeping bag for the past three months.

After a real meat-and-potato dinner, not the canned, soggy, lumpy stuff from your C-rations box, it was nice to come back to a warm, lighted sleeping area. It was still bitterly cold outside, and light snow covered the ground. Seeing the sparks scurrying out from my tent's roof and disappearing into the night air was a welcome sight. It was like coming home to a luxury hotel.

When I stepped through the flapped door, I went straight to the stove and warmed my hands. Life was good. In reserve, I had cooked meals, no worry about fire missions or being attacked, and a red-hot potbelly stove giving off lots of heat—what more could I ask for?

Squatting in a small circle to my right, Pak, Kim, and Choi were animatedly chatting with some KATUSAs from another platoon. There was gesturing and interruptions followed by howls of laughter. It was evident that they were swapping war stories and enjoying themselves. I smiled and nodded to them as

I passed by. "*Choh-sum-nee-dah! A, ne! A, ne!* Hey, *ichi-bon* Joe, Number huckin' one," came the happy replies.

I was reading one of the many Agatha Christie mystery novels my father had sent me when Henry Kahuii burst through the tent entrance like a raging bull. His two-hundred-pound body swayed from side to side as he swigged from a bottle of what looked like whiskey. He was evidently celebrating his first night in reserve. He lost his balance and lunged forward, just missing the hot stove and landing on the floor. I didn't know if he was laughing or crying, but I did know that he was smashed. He was muttering gibberish, sprawled out on the tent floor.

The suddenness of his arrival caused a pause in the chatter from the KATUSAs. Kahuii was now shouting or singing something. I could never understand Henry very well when he was sober. For the most part, he grunted in a deep, growling voice with some Hawaiian words mixed in. Annoyed, I got up and went over to him. "Come on, Henry. Give us a break. It's sack time."

I struggled to get him up on his feet. At one point, he gave a King Kong roar and broke away, whirling through the entrance doorway. The Koreans and I looked at each other and shook our heads, and then we went back to what we were doing. I hadn't been sleeping very long when I was awakened by screaming, cursing, and angry shouting.

"Shut the fuck up, you gook assholes! Get out of my tent. Get the fuck out of here!" bellowed Kahuii, lurching forward menacingly. The only light in the tent came from a dimmed Coleman and the glowing stove, which cast Kahuii's squat, gyrating shadow against the canvas wall. He looked fierce. Wild-eyed, he was staggering, jerking his head back and forth with quick gulps from a no-name bottle of rotgut whiskey.

A few voices from beds were shouting, "Aw, come on! Knock it off."

It was bedlam, a bad scene. The Koreans became indignant and shouted back angrily in their staccato, guttural language. Henry launched himself toward them. Everyone backed off but little Choi. He stood his ground. I don't know if he was being defiant or if he froze. He was a sweetheart of a kid, but he had a cool toughness to him.

It happened quickly. Kahuii thrust his fist forward, and Choi went down. I leaped out of my cot and jumped in between them. "Back off, Kahuii," I rasped and helped Choi to his feet. Dazed, he looked at me and gave me a bloody smile. One front tooth of a beautiful smile was gone.

I screamed in Kahuii's face. "Look at what you did! Look at his face, you stupid fuck. You knocked his tooth out. What the fuck's the matter with you?" I said, trying to stop the bleeding. A few of the men got up and came over. Stupefied, Henry stood there and then stormed outside. The Koreans brought Choi outside to the medics.

I went back to my bunk so angry that I was shaking. I was trying to calm down when Henry came back inside, muttering under his breath and blabbering something about why he had done what he had done. I got up and went over to talk to him. He shrugged his shoulders in a conversation he was having with himself. Then he went silent, turned around slowly with a queer expression on his face, and gave me a strange look.

"Joe Chink," he whispered as he pulled a trench knife from his scabbard. "Joe Chink," he said louder and walked toward me with the bottle in one hand and a knife in the other. "Joe Chink."

I didn't know if he was kidding me or serious. "Don't bullshit me, Henry. It's Joe Donohue and not Joe Chink, and you're in big fucking trouble. Deep *kimchi*, Henry, and your ass is mud."

Henry kept coming, very slowly, with his knife held low in the attack position.

"Stop fucking around," I said as boldly as I could. As I looked at the crazy leer on Henry's face, I thought that maybe Henry didn't actually know what he was doing.

"Okay, take it easy. Calm down," I heard myself say in a surprisingly soothing and steady voice. "It's me. Joe Donohue. Hollywood Joe, okay?" I said, hoping he would recognize the nickname some of the guys had given me for telling and acting out stories. It didn't work. Henry kept coming. He went into a crouch position and backed me up the aisle to my bunk with my ass against the wood frame of the tent.

"You Joe Chink," he grumbled.

I was ready to panic. My .45 was hanging off the wood beam over my bunk with an empty clip in its handle. It was within easy reach. I thought of making a quick grab and bluffing him and then hammering that son of a bitch to death. I also thought he may not have been drunk enough that he didn't remember that we had all turned in our ammo. I could almost feel the blade of the trench knife going into my stomach as soon as I moved. I thought that I was going to die right here in my sleeping tent . . . on vacation in reserve in Korea.

It happened fast. A zip from a sleeping bag in the corner of the tent, and a soldier leaped up and went out the rear of the tent. Kahuii turned his head, and the Korean in the sleeping bag next to mine jumped up. I shoved Kahuii, and the two of us along with a couple of more soldiers leaped over cots and went out the front entrance. There was snow on the ground. It was freezing out. In our stockings, we're yelling, "Help, help, corporal of the guard!"

As we hobbled up the street, we were joined by more soldiers. Heads poked out of tents, wondering what the hell was going on. Our cries were heard by a slight figure running toward us. As he got closer, I could see him looking at us hopping up and down in socks and our long johns. I waved to the guard and told him what had happened. "One of our men is crazy drunk and has a trench knife. He's dangerous. He almost killed me," I said. The baby-faced guard just nodded. We were a lynch mob now, led by a helmeted kid with an M-1 rifle running down a dark company street on the bank of the Inje River in Korea.

Outside the tent, we could see Kahuii's shadow lurching over the potbelly stove, stabbing the red-hot pipe and howling, "I'll kill you, Joe Chink. I'll kill you all."

We got to the entrance of my tent and could see that crazed leer on his face. The smell of alcohol and his own burned flesh was mixed with screams of, "I'll kill you, you motherfuckers! Come and get it!"

Our teenage leader rushed through the tent door, and Kahuii shouted, "Joe Chink!"

Those were the last words I remember from Kahuii. The kid was good. He never hesitated. The child sentry went right at Kahuii with his M-1 rifle at port arms. He was army-manual perfect. A vertical butt stroke caught Henry in the stomach and doubled him over. The rifle stock came up into Kahuii's face followed by a gang tackle that brought all of us crashing to the floor. Despite being drunk, burned, bruised, and bleeding, it took all of us to pin him to the ground. The jeep came, and Kahuii was shackled, sobbing and cursing.

Why did Kahuii crack up? I think a couple of things happened. It was just a couple of days ago that he had emptied a carbine into a Chink soldier who had wandered right up to his bunker and scared the hell out of him. Another was the story that the gooks had penetrated the Fifth Regimental Combat Team's sector after we had left Heartbreak and that the 223rd Regiment would be going back up. Rumor was that our outfit might be next. Henry likely had dealt with these two things, and they took their toll on him.

The next day, I was on a work detail with Mason, a gunner from the third squad who gave me the elbow. "Look who's coming behind you."

Kahuii, his hands bandaged and manacled, was being led under armed guard to a military police jeep. He spotted me and gave me a sheepish grin. As he walked by, his puffy, gorilla face broke into a naughty-boy smile. With his head bowed and in his deep, guttural voice he growled, "Hey, Joe, I heard I tried to kill you the other night. No hard feelings, man."

Here was this Section 8 psycho apologizing to me, and I didn't know how to react. "Hey, no problem, Henry," I replied. "Think nothing of it."

I couldn't believe what had just happened. The nonchalant way Kahuii and I had reacted with each other was unreal. Here, this guy had tried to kill me, and I shucked it off as if nothing of importance had happened. I thought back to my ride on the Pusan

Express and the words of our train sergeant had told us. Nowhere in Korea was safe. I never thought that being in a peaceful, secluded, rear-echelon, reserve area in Korea was dangerous. I was wrong. Here, the enemy was one of our own.

CHAPTER 43

INJE RIVER RESERVE

The Inje River reserve area wasn't that far from our old battle positions on Heartbreak. We were several miles south on the bank of a very narrow river with low-lying hills and scrubby-looking people living in them. Reserve was lots of training, soldiering, and teamwork. We expanded our camp site. We built things. We beautified our area. We had live entertainment from our own outfit and the USO from the States. It was all in preparation for going back on line as a rested and efficient fighting unit, but first, you had to survive being in reserve.

The first order of business in reserve was "beautification of the area." In army jargon, this meant you had to make the place look as clean, neat, and attractive as possible. To do this, we crossed the Inje river and cut down young trees for wood in order to build fences, huts, benches, and a platform for presentations and entertainment.

The Korean government got paid for each tree we felled, so our count had to be accurate. I had never chopped down a tree or handled an axe. All the country boys became teachers. They wanted to show me how to do it right. They got a kick out of my uncertain and awkward swing. I was a good student though and eventually got the hang of it. I enjoyed the work. It was a great learning experience for a city kid like me.

The fun part was getting the trees across the frozen Inje River. We set up three-man races. The contest was to see how fast a team could slide their saplings across the frozen river to the other side after the trees were cut down. It was like coming off of Heartbreak all over again. With all the pushing came sliding and falling as we tried to hop on the skinny logs. We were like bobsled teams in the Olympics. It was a lot of fun.

I was simply amazed at the creativity and ingenuity of the guys in our outfit. Logs were cut and whittled and chopped to fit into one another like giant tinker toys. There were additions, modifications, and expansions to our mess halls, shower stalls, latrines, barbershops, and mail rooms. Beautification of the area was as much a part of our day as physical training, tactical problems, and the firing and cleaning of weapons.

A platform was built with a sound system and floodlights for a "hootenanny night." I remember I learned to like wailing country and Western music in basic training in South Carolina and jump school in Georgia. Our regiment gathered on the parade ground after chow for a hillbilly jamboree. I never saw so many guitars, banjos, harmonicas, washboards, and other instruments appear out of nowhere. These guys were good. I heard that there were some big-name players back in civilian life performing that day. The players and audience were so in tune, and there was enough singing and roaring and hootin' and hollerin' that you could hear us all the way to Pusan.

We got a beer ration in reserve, something like a couple of 3.5 beers a day. Someone came up with the bright idea that we'd have a contest where the winner would take all. Each platoon put up a week's ration of beer as the prize to be won for the best platoon in the company's weekly inspection. Every platoon cleaned everything in sight from men to uniforms to weapons. Thanks to my airborne training, my squad became the model for the others. Not only were boots spit shined and rifle bores shining, I had the brass buckles on our web belts polished and glistening and covered with handkerchiefs until the inspection. The KATUSAs in our squad first thought we were joking, but when they saw how serious everyone was, they quickly got with it. Needless to say, our platoon won the inspection and the beer prize.

Captain Roberts, our company commander, came and congratulated our platoon. He was a ruggedly handsome, World War II commander who was not only rotating home but retiring from military service as well. He gave us an impromptu farewell speech, introducing Captain Munges, our new company commander, and Lieutenant Olsen, our new platoon leader and a former high school math teacher from Ohio.

During the course of our celebrating, Evans, Reimer, Dee-jack-a-moe, the Mule, Mason, Martinez, Tucker, Pak, Kim, Choi, Van Sycle, McChesney, and all the other guys in our platoon invited their friends from other platoons, so it became one, big, open, beer racket. The beer didn't last very long, but everybody had a good time. So much for inspections and winning beer contests, I thought.

A few days later around midnight, the camp was startled out of bed by the sound of machine gun fire. Everyone ran from their tents with empty carbines, M-1s, and pistols, thinking it was some sort of training exercise, only to see the evening sky covered with the long trails of live tracer bullets flying overhead. There was shouting, running, and total confusion as we ran toward the ammo dump until we realized that we weren't being fired upon.

It wasn't until the next day that we learned that the rounds being fired over our heads toward the main supply road had come from the hills behind us. The story was an attempted robbery had been made on a convoy of trucks carrying Korean money up to the front line. The KATUSAs got paid in their own currency, and we got paid in federal printed "script," which reminded me of Monopoly's funny money. I vowed to myself that as long as I was in Korea, I would never be without ammunition again.

MPs normally patrolled up in the hills. Because the shooting had come from the hills, combat patrolling became part of our training ritual. I knew guys in my platoon would sneak away up in the hills for sex and booze. It was a gamble. If you got caught, you got busted and confined to quarters. Now I was going through a hovel of huts, seeing the way poor, mountain people lived. I didn't like it. To me, it was a hostile environment of suspicious, primitive people who dressed shabbily and lived in squalid conditions and were desperately trying to survive.

One sunny day on our way down from the hill people, our platoon walked on the frozen Inje River to hook up with our battalion convoy on the other side of the river. The sun was warm for March. We walked in squad formation. Smack in the middle of the river, our steps started making crackling sounds. A hundred yards from shore, our steps made crunching noises. Our new platoon leader, Lieutenant Olsen, halted us. We stopped and looked at each other, thinking the same scary thought. Would the ice hold our weight, or were we about to become a disaster? I was glad I wasn't carrying the 75mm on this patrol. Olsen spread us out to distribute the weight of our squads. The sounds continued but seemed less ominous. It was hard to tell for sure. I know I was fighting the onset of panic. The urge to run was powerful. Everybody was now walking as lightly as they could. We weren't exactly tiptoeing, but each step was more carefully made, looking and listening for fault lines in the ice.

We were one relieved platoon when we got to the other side of the river. Lieutenant Olsen's decision to spread the men out had been a good one. He made a positive impression with the men. I was happy to see the vehicles waiting for us. I climbed into a jeep, grateful for the ride and relieved to be on land.

Along the route of the convoy, the hill people from across the river blew whistles, banged gongs, and waved to us. At one point, we stopped, and startling news spread along the convoy of trucks and jeeps. "Stalin's dead. Joe Stalin died of a stroke. It was a brain hemorrhage. The leader of Communist Russia died in his sleep."

I wrote a letter to Frank, who was on line up in the Punchbowl area. I told him we'd be breaking camp soon. I wondered if after the death of Joe Stalin, the war might end suddenly, sending us home sooner than we had expected. I told him my outfit was going to a place called "Little Pittsburgh" for more training before we went back on line. I told him how "Little Pittsburgh" had gotten its name. The smoke pouring out of the potbelly stoves in our tents during the winter looked like the smoke-belching steel mills of Pittsburgh. At least that was the story that had been told to me. In warm weather, they called the place Wondang-ni. I didn't know why for sure. In any event, I was heading up his way. Maybe we'd bump into each other.

I signed off, "Your Pistol-Packing Papa, Joe."

CHAPTER 44

FRANK AND ME AT MUNDUNG-NI

**Little Pittsburgh was a tough training area not far
from a place referred to as Mundung-ni, which was west of
Heartbreak Ridge and a prelude to the real thing. The day
before we were to break camp and move up to an assembly
area below the Punchbowl, I got the surprise of my life. It
came at the end of the day, but it could have been the end of
the line for me.**

We arrived on St. Patrick's Day, but it was no party. Little
Pittsburgh was not like the reserve area on the Inje River. It was
more like a holding area and the last chance to get ourselves
combat-ready. Every morning, besides physical-training exercises,
we ran our butts off. We went through squad- and platoon-size
tactical drills, humped up and down hills, and practiced firing our
carbines, pistols, and our 75-millimeter recoilless rifles. This was
serious stuff. Everybody got with it.

George Reimer, Chuck Mason, Dave "the Mule" Anderson,
and I were the four PFCs and gunner squad leaders in our platoon.
Dee-jack-a-moe was already a corporal, so he was made acting
section leader for the third and fourth squad guns. Our squads
were mostly KATUSAs.

My Korean gun crew of Pak, Kim, Choi and Yang were good
soldiers who knew the weapon and performed well. We were to
leave Little Pittsburg tomorrow and do a twenty-mile hike to an

assembly area near the Punchbowl. The march was to show the top brass that we were in good shape, tough, and ready for action, which we were, but what we really hoped for was that the peace talks at Panmunjom would end the war right now.

I came off the field early, leaving Elias, my assistant gunner, to oversee the cleaning and wrapping of the 75-RR. It was chow time, so I had the whole squad tent to myself. I decided to clean my .45 while I was waiting for the guys to come back.

I was just about finished cleaning my pistol when I glanced up and saw a figure with steel pot and rifle coming across the parade ground. In the distance, I couldn't make out who it was, but there was something familiar in the way the soldier walked.

I went back to my pistol. I pushed the spring back under the barrel with my thumb and locked it into place. I pulled back on the housing, slid the safety latch up, and looked through the barrel. As I slipped the safety catch off and let the housing jump forward, I clicked the trigger and shoved the empty pistol into my holster. I caught a glimpse of the figure from the parade ground coming through the rear of the tent. The bent-over helmet and rifle straightened up with a booming, "At ease soldier!" and a broad smile.

I was stunned for a moment, and then my legs shot me upright. I stood there in disbelief.

"Frankeee! Frankeee Babe! What the hell are you doing here? Where did you come from?" I asked as we shook hands and pounded each other into a bear hug.

"I was here earlier, but you were in the field, so I went back to 120th Medics to see my buddy, Tim Sullivan. I told you about him in a letter. So how're you doing? Let me look at you."

"I'm doing fine. Shit, man," I said, "you're a sight for sore eyes. I can't believe you're here."

"When I got your letter, I knew exactly where you were going. This was my regimental rear before my outfit moved up to the Punchbowl," he said, pointing in that direction.

"So what are you doing here?"

Frank laughed and said, "I went AWOL to see an old buddy of mine."

"Are you nuts?" I screeched. "They'll court-martial you if they catch you."

"No sweat. I got a good buddy, Stu Levy, who's covering for me. We just got back from R & R, and they told us that Tim was in the hospital. I figured since I just got back, nobody would miss me for a few more hours."

"I hope so. Do they still shoot deserters?" I smiled.

"Not to worry. My mortar squad knows where I am. I want you to meet Tim. He's in the 120th Medics right down the road from here."

"What happened to your buddy?"

Frank looked at me seriously, holding my attention, and then he beamingly smiled, "He's getting circumcised for sanitary reasons. Can you believe that shit? I'm thinking of doing the same thing. It's a good deal. A lot of guys are doing it. You catch a break from the action. You get a *sukoshi* R & R and maybe a little ass too. At least he won't be getting shot at. Shit, he'll have a warm bed, clean sheets, a nice pillow, a shower, hot food, and clean clothes."

"Okay, okay, you sold me," I said, holding up my hands, "but I'm already circumcised. Now I want you to meet some of my buddies."

We walked over to the mess hall, talking a mile a minute. "Hey, you guys, I want you to meet my long lost brother," I said as my opening line before I introduced Frank as my best friend. Frank was in his glory being in the limelight. I knew he'd love that, and I was as excited as a kid for Frank to meet the guys.

"This is Rock, a middleweight from Philadelphia. Lyle's family owns a farm in Nebraska that's bigger than Manhattan, and Chuck here is a wise guy from the west side. George's uncle owns that gas station we always go to on our way to Rockaway. I wrote you about how I first met George. The Mule next to George is from Missouri, and Yang wants to move to Japan with his family. In front of him is Dee-jack-a-moe, a jumper like us who likes cherries." I went on and on with the introductions.

After chow, Frank and I walked to the main gate. I said with a pained smile, "Here we go again, Frank. We're going AWOL just like in California."

"Yeah, just act natural, pal," Frank smiled, and we roared with laughter. Smiling and chatting away, we purposefully strode through the wooden gate without a problem.

It was still light out as we headed down the long, narrow road and fantasized about being home for the summer and going to the beach in Rockaway. We turned right, and the painted red cross of the 120th was easy to see. We found Tim trying to read a *Stars and Stripes* newspaper in a poorly lit room. He was sitting on a cot, and his baby face showed a look of surprise to see Frank walk in with a stranger. There was pain etched in his Irish face as he held out his hand to shake. I already felt that I knew Tim. He could easily be one of the tribe from Irishtown in Rockaway.

"I heard a lot about you from this guy. Glad to meet you, Joe," said Tim with a quick smile. So what took you guys so long? I thought you were coming right back, Frank."

"Joe wanted me to meet some of his buddies," said Frank defensively and then looked at me accusingly. "It was his fault," he said with a mock smile on his face.

"It was my fault," I said with a smile. "It's nice to meet you, Tim. Frank's always mentioning you in his letters, and now I know you're real. How are you doing?"

"I'm hurting, and I'm bleeding a lot. Look at this," said Tim, turning over the blankets and showing a blood-splattered apron under which was a blood-soaked wrapping over his penis.

"You need a fresh bandage."

"I know," said Tim, but I like the way it looks, like I'm the real deal. Now I know why they do this at birth . . . so you don't remember anything. Anyway, I made sure I had my R & R first before I had this operation," said Tim, looking pleased with himself. "Okay, enough about me. How was Japan?" he said, turning to Frank.

"I've got to sit down for this," said Frank, sliding over a chair.

"Here we go," I said, knowing we were in for a good story.

"I'm still not circumcised," said Frank, "and looking at you, I know I'll never do it now."

"If it gets any worse up there, you will," said Tim knowingly. "They're throwing a lot of shit at us. You'll see soon enough, Joe. It's a bitch up there."

"What am I supposed to do?" I said hopelessly. "I'm already circumcised." They both laughed.

"Okay, are you ready for this?" said Frank emphatically. "So I get pulled off of the line. I'm dirty and tired, and I need a shave. I get back to division and get rid of my pistol and rifle and draw $500 in won, which I turn into yen."

"That's a lot of money," said Tim.

"Look, we only live once," said Frank, and then hesitating, he dramatically looked at both of us and continued, "Or . . . do we?"

"Come on. Get on with the story," I said anxiously.

"The next day, I'm on a Globe-master four-engine job headed for Japan. When the plane lands and taxies to a stop, the front ramp is lowered, and a sergeant greets us, 'Gentlemen, this way please.'"

Tim giggled and said, "Come off it. Sergeants don't talk like that."

"This one did. I swear it. He wasn't a veteran, of course, and knew who he was dealing with. Anyway, after the 'all you can eat' steaks and ice cream, I shower, shit, and shave and get into class A's. I happen to look up on the bulletin board and see this card pinned to it, 'the Happy Heaven Hotel.' I turned to this guy named Temple from Easy Company and said, 'That's for me, a happy hotel.' Temple looks at me and says, 'Then what are we waiting for?' There were taxis waiting for us outside. It was so crowded it was like being on the floor of the New York Stock Exchange, where I used to work. An MP had to escort us through a crowd of pimps and prostitutes to a line of taxi cabs. Our cabby knew the hotel just outside of Tokyo. If you ever get to Tokyo, Joe, this is the place to be," said Frank, looking at me.

"Not everyone gets to go to Tokyo on R & R. You lucked out," said Tim.

"I know, but the *baby-sans* wanted me there, and I just couldn't disappoint them, so when I got to the hotel, I ordered three martinis. I told the bartender to back them up and that we needed some women. He calls for a hostess, and she brings the drinks and the two of us into a waiting room. They send in five women at a time. Temple and I are sitting there, sipping our drinks and looking them over. He's a little anxious, so he picks one right away. I was in no hurry. I took my time and enjoyed my martini."

"Since when did you start drinking martinis?" I asked disbelievingly.

"Whadaya mean?" said Frank indignantly. "Don't you guys know what a good martini tastes like?"

"Frank, we're beer drinkers, remember? Maybe we had a shot of rye once in a while, but martinis?"

"I'm a bourbon man myself," said Tim, "but go ahead with your story."

"I'm trying to," said Frank. "It's not easy with all these interruptions. Now where was I? Oh, yeah, so I see one little gal who looks a bit nervous. She had a nice figure with a great set of jugs. She wasn't beautiful. She was average- to good-looking. I gave her an approving look, and I pointed to her. She looked at me shyly and came over and sat on my knee. Her name was Matsuko, and she turned out to be a wonderful lady."

Frank paused, and I softly started singing in an alto voice the *pidgin* version of "China Nights," which was the number one song in Korea for GIs. "*Shina No Yoru*" became "She ain't got no yo-yo," and Tim chimed in perfectly with "She ain't got no yo-yo." And smiling, we finished the words in perfect harmony.

"To make a long story short, she was terrific. Every day, she scalded me with the hottest Japanese bath I could stand. Then she would dry me and rub me down gently, if you know what I mean, and then she would walk on my back and massage me. She even washed my underwear and socks. For breakfast, she had a whiskey sour waiting for me out on our balcony, and we ate looking out on Mount Fuji. It was beautiful living. In the afternoon we went sightseeing and shopping, and I bought her dresses and clothes. We would come back to the hotel. And she would undress me, and we would make love. We would play American records and dance, and sometimes we would invite other couples in and have a party. We had dinner at a different club each night. I can't believe how fast the week went by. The last night was sad. She was sorry to see me go. We really had something. I told her I would never forget her, and I gave her whatever money I had left."

"*You what?*" was the simultaneous shout from Tim and me.

Frank looked startled at our response and then smiled, grasping the soapy, operatic ending to his expensive, short-lived romance.

"Well, Monsieur Butterfly Boy, at least you can laugh at yourself," I said, shaking my head sadly from side to side.

"That's not the end of the story," said Frank, sitting up straight in his chair, smiling in amusement. "I get back to camp, and there's a delay in my return flight. I've got a twenty-four-hour extension and no money. Temple's got enough yen for one last *sayo-nara, ichi-ban, boom-boom* brothel in Tokyo. It was a bit seedy, but we were beating the system and were feeling pretty good about it. One more night in paradise. We take a taxi back to camp, and Temple can't come up with enough money to pay the driver. I couldn't help him 'cause I had empty pockets. Our driver goes from nice to nuts. He gets out of the cab, and he's bowing and cursing at us at the same time. He doesn't know whether he should shit or go blind. An MP comes over, and he starts bowing and howling at him. The MP was a nice guy. I know that's hard to believe, but he really was okay. He asks us if we have anything at all to barter with. I have my combat infantry badge, airborne wings, and a sterling silver ID bracelet I got at high school graduation. The MP spoke pretty good Japanese-English *pidgin* and strongly suggested to the driver to take my valuable treasure. I threw in my good dress wings to close the deal. Right now, there's a cab driver in Tokyo tooling around with a pair of wings on his shirt and a Hungarian name scrolled on his bracelet, identifying him as Frank J. Milisits. So much for leaving my mark on Japan."

Tim was uncomfortable. He kept sitting up and then sitting down and then getting up again. He would do a little walking, bent over like an old man. He was embarrassed when some of the walking wounded would go by and glance at him. He wouldn't make eye contact with them. Sometimes he would just let his bathrobe part enough to see his bloody bandages and hope nobody would come over to try to comfort him and ask questions. It was good the ward was poorly lit, and it was an evacuation station. The wounded were in and out, most going to Japan for further treatment. He hadn't really spoken with anyone, so nobody knew exactly why he had been operated on. They assumed he had been wounded in the groin, and Tim did nothing to dispel that notion.

Frank and I played our roles as caring, visiting buddies. We had to talk in very low, hushed tones and be careful not to look like we were enjoying ourselves. A couple of times, Tim couldn't help himself. With tears in his eyes, he would bite down hard on his blanket to cover a laugh. The downside was that in trying hard not to laugh, he would stretch the stitches in his penis, which was really painful and resulted in a coughing moan that brought looks of silent understanding and empathy. It was embarrassing.

Lights out was a relief. It also meant that it was time for me to leave. I said good night to Tim. Frank decided that he would stay overnight and sleep in one of the empty cots rather than try to hitch his way up to the front at night.

"How the hell am I going to get back? It's pitch-black out there."

"It's not far, Joe. Don't sweat it, man."

"I should be over there somewhere," I said, pointing.

"Yep, just take it slow. Backtrack and follow the main supply road. Your road to your camp goes right into it," said Frank, reassuring me.

277

"I know. I know, but there were a few roads that went into the MSR. I'm sure I'll find it when I come to it," I said with false confidence.

"Look!" said Frank. "There's a vehicle turning into your road. I'm sure that's it. That's about the right distance. It's less than five minutes away."

"I know. I see it. That's it. That's my camp. It's black as shit, but I'll be okay."

Frank turned toward me. "Hey, we're almost there. Three more fucking months, and we're out of here. Don't get fucking killed on me," Frank implored.

"And you don't be an asshole hero. Remember what your brother said about outdoing him?"

"We're going home together, Joe. I can feel it. I know it."

"Okay, let's do it then," I said, shaking his hand.

"I'll try to catch you on the road tomorrow," said Frank, giving me his standard bear hug. I walked down the ramp outside the MASH unit to the supply road.

"Hey, trooper!" called Frank.

I knew the routine, although I could barely make Frank out. I returned our silly, exaggerated airborne salute, letting my open hand come slowly down to my side like a parachute descending in air. I knew we were both smiling at that one.

It was darker than dark. Nothing moved. The night was dead. I could hardly see the road. I knew I just had to backtrack from where I had started, but at night, everything seemed different. Nothing looked the same. I started walking briskly in the direction I had come from, hoping I would get my bearings as I went along. I hadn't walked very far when the silence of the night was shattered by a loud voice.

"*Chung-jee!*"

I slowed down, not sure what was happening, but I kept on walking until I heard the sliding rod of metal slamming on metal, which brought me to an abrupt halt.

"*Chung-jee! Ahn-yo!*"

A chill shot up the back of my neck. I froze. I knew I was being challenged; however, I didn't know for sure what was being said, and I didn't know the password for the evening. I couldn't see the voice coming out of the darkness. I could only imagine that a rifle was pointed at me. A Korean soldier was pulling guard duty. Was he nervous, or was this routine? I couldn't be sure. I wasn't sure what to do. I tried not to act scared or come across as a threat. I made a conscious effort to act calm and a little bit annoyed.

"GI, Fortieth Division," I said as forcefully as I could. "It's okay. *Dai-joe-bee, cho-sum-nee-dah*, number-one GI, okay?" and I resumed walking at a brisk pace, bracing myself for the sound of gunfire. I could imagine what was going through the Korean guard's mind. He had to be as nervous as I was. I was trying to intimidate him. I was betting that he would back down, and at the same time, I was scared shitless that I would be shot at.

I heard what sounded like *ah-ma-tay*, and I started thinking of my high school Latin. *Amo, Amas, Amat.* I snapped out of it with "*Cho-tah-mah-tay*, okay? *Cho-sum-nee-dah, go-men-a-sigh!*" In both Korean and Japanese, I think I said, "Take it easy, okay? Good-bye." I wasn't sure what I was saying. I was just blurting out words that I hoped would convince the KATUSA guard that I was a GI.

I winced as I took my first few steps and tried not to break into a run. By the third and fourth steps, I was more than just walking. I was quick-stepping, almost double-timing. I couldn't get away quick enough. What happened if this guy started shooting? Did I shoot back then? He probably couldn't see me that well in the dark. He could pump off a clip in a second and just cover an area. I could jump off the side of the road. I might have to fire my .45 pistol if he comes after me. What a crazy fucking situation to be in. I could end up getting killed in a rear-echelon reserve area, waiting to go into combat. What a gruesome joke on me.

I kept walking rapidly, and there was absolute silence except for my heavy breathing and my boots hitting the ground. Nothing happened. There was no shouting or shooting—nothing. And then suddenly, low, bouncing lights appeared in the distance in front of me. They were trucks.

I ducked down beside the main road until the lights made a right onto another road to my left. They were heading for my compound. I was sure of it. I got up off the side of the road and jogged in a crouch behind the last truck. The small convoy halted before the barbed wire gate. Flashlights wobbled as they checked trip tickets. I was panting, anxiously wondering how I was going to get into camp without being seen.

I didn't know the password. I didn't have a pass or permission to leave the area. People could have been looking for me right now to go over the orders for tomorrow's march. All this was racing through my head when I saw my chance. The gate swung open, and the first truck went through. As the second truck was halted, I took off on the side of the road until I was even with the truck. I lifted my head to see that the guards had their backs to me and scampered back up on the road. I ducked my head below the beams of light from the stopped trucks and made a quick right turn inside the blacked-out compound and bumped into a piss tube and stumbled.

Voices called out, "Who's there?" and then flashlight beams hit me as I stood there in the spotlight with one hand on my fly and one hand shielding my eyes.

"Will you horny fuckers kill that light and get off on somebody else?" I yelled.

The flashlights were redirected with obscenities, and I breathed a sigh of relief. I had made it. I was all shook up, but I had made it. I thought about how easy it had been to leave an army base and how tough it had been to get back in. I could have bought it back there, and Frank and Sully, who were probably less than a thousand yards away, were completely unaware of what the fuck I had just gone through. I would never forget Frank and me at Mundung-ni.

CHAPTER 45

GOING BACK UP

I was excited. I was scared. I remembered what it was like the first time. Now I was a veteran with twenty-two points. I knew most of the guys in my company. I knew it could get messy. I needed fourteen more points to be rotated off of the line. Four more months, and hopefully, I would be going home with Frank. I was anxious to get on with it.

We were on the road at sunup. We were to hike to an assembly area twenty miles away just behind the Punchbowl, where Frank's Forty-Fifth Division was deployed.

I marched at ease with a full combat pack. Our 75mm recoilless rifles, along with our other heavy weapons, were loaded onto trucks. I passed the 120th MASH unit, which wasn't more than a few city blocks away. I thought I recognized the spot where I had been challenged last night. The guard, whom I never saw, was still only a voice. There was no one around the ramp I had come down last night. It was empty. If the guard was where I thought he was, then he couldn't have been more than a hundred feet away from me.

As I marched by in route step, I looked at the outside stairs and checked both sides of the road, hoping to see Frank. I kept looking for him for the first couple of miles, thinking that I might see him along the road, but he was nowhere around that I could see.

I marched at ease and at a fair pace. We made good time. We reached the assembly area around noon. We lounged on the ground, chatted, and waited for the trucks to bring us our lunch. Out of nowhere, a Bell helicopter, the type used for evacuating wounded, hovered above us. We watched it as it slowly descended onto the field. The chopper with the white star on its side kicked up a storm of dust as it daintily touched its wheels to the ground and landed. We surrounded the ship as its rotors stopped spinning.

A shock of white hair emerged from the helicopter before it was covered with a cap that had two stars. Another general and a colonel with a white-handled pistol strapped in his holster joined him. Names were mumbled and whispered. One was General Cleland, the commander of our Fortieth Division, but I didn't know what he looked like.

"Where are you from, soldier? What do you do?" and other opening remarks were asked of the soldiers surrounding the officers. The surprise visit was a bit showy and intimidating. At one point, the white-haired general addressed the group, booming, "How are we feeling, men?" The response was unexpectedly weak and mixed. "Can't hear you!" shouted the general.

"Okay! Good!" yelled the men.

A single voice replied loudly, "Tired."

"But not too tired to fight," answered the general quickly, looking out at the men around him in triumph, waiting expectantly for the proper reply.

There was an awkward silence.

"Yeah, I'm too tired to fight," was followed by smiles and guffaws from the ranks.

The general was a little taken aback.

"You mean to tell me that after a twenty-mile march, if a Chinese machine gun opened up on you, let's say from that ridge over there and your life was on the line, as tired as you are, you wouldn't fight?" asked the general sarcastically.

"Ah don't know, sir. Ahm just all tuckered out," came the high-pitched, Southern drawl of finality from a thin soldier with metal corporal stripes pinned to the upturned brim of his field cap.

It was a bizarre moment. This lone soldier was either trying to be funny or a wise ass engaged in a supposedly honest, straight-talking dialogue with a general. I wasn't sure. There were nervous smiles, shocked faces, including mine, mixed in with the uneasy shifting of bodies and sniggling from the troops. The generals and their aides, including our own officers, were aghast. If looks could have killed, we would have been one dead group of soldiers.

"Well, others would fight!" roared the general in exasperation, weaving his entourage through the crowd to greet other troops.

Of course, there was no way we wouldn't fight. After all, we were going on line to fight. Whether we marched twenty miles or not was beside the point. Everybody knew that. What was surprising was the blunt exchange between a corporal and a general. It was so totally unexpected.

I thought about that moment often. Was it a gutsy corporal talking for all of us? Was it the talk of a scared soldier who was at his wits' end and about to lose it before going back on line? The corporal touched feelings that were bottled up inside us all. This time, we would be going back up as short-timers. This meant that we had only a few months to go before we were rotated home. This time, we also would know the soldiers who got wounded or killed. The endless truce talks at Panmunjom were frustrating. Everyone was disappointed. We had just come from a well-deserved rest in a pleasant reserve area. There was a touch of spring in the air. The front line was just over the mountains in front of us. That was a fact. It was hard to get your head into it. Reality was setting in. Everybody was uptight. Ready or not, we were going back into combat.

CHAPTER 46

ON LINE A SECOND TIME

I was a part of a small detachment of squad leaders selected to act as a forward element for our company. Our mission was to set up a temporary command post for our platoon and secure the area until the main body of troops came up in the morning. It was the darkest, longest, loneliest, nerve-wracking night of my life.

I was pleased to have been chosen by our company exec to attend a briefing held by Captain Monges, our new company commander whose name we immediately pronounced Mungus as in "fungus." I felt very important. I was directly involved in our company's plan of operation for going on line. Lyle Olsen, Rock, Young, George Reimer, Mase, the Mule, and a couple of other squad leaders formed a part of a small forward element that was to relieve a skeleton crew from the Fifth Regimental Combat Team. The 223rd Regiment from our division would relieve the Sixty-First ROK Regiment of the Twentieth ROK Division on our right flank. Frank's Forty-Fifth Division would be to our left. The 160th Regiment from our Fortieth Division would be in corps reserve. We would be spread out along the Minnesota Line in the Punchbowl area.

I removed all identifying insignias from my uniform and covered my helmet with burlap to hide the markings on it. I slipped into a full combat pack with carbine and pistol clips bulging in their pouches. A last-minute top-off of my canteen, and I boarded our truck convoy. Although the shortest route between two points was a straight line, we chose the scenic route and a circuitous ride to the Punchbowl. Forget about escaping detection. Everybody knew we were being watched, but it was standard operating procedure (SOP) for new troop movements and deployments to try to deceive the enemy.

When we finally reached our destination, it was late in the afternoon. A half-dozen soldiers sitting along the side of the road quickly stood up to greet us and escort us up the dugout steps to our new mountain positions. They looked like only front soldiers could look. They looked tired. The picture that came to mind was city construction workers coming off the job after a hard day's work in the sun. We, on the other hand, were well rested and clean-shaven, wearing fresh fatigues with shined boots.

I smiled as we passed a large wooden sign sticking out of the ground.

"It ain't no joke," someone upfront said. The black painted words read, "The Rats on This Hill Are So Goddamn Big That You Can Saddle Them Up and Ride Them Down to Chow."

It was eerie walking along the trench line. There was no sign of life. Shadows played off of the gunless bunkers, which were spaced at least one hundred feet apart and added to the sense of abandonment to the area. I was shown to a bunker that had been used by a 75-RR crew before. It had a cave next to it that could be used for ammo and equipment storage. There was also a new hole in the ground being dug for a new gun position that would take up some of the space between the gun bunkers along the trench.

There was a tank position well off to the right and above us. It wasn't right on top of us like back on Heartbreak, but it was still close enough to be a force. It made sense to put the 90- and the 75-millimeter cannons close together because they packed a hell of a punch. On the other hand, they were primary targets for the Chinese, who had an excellent reputation as fine mortar-men. There was also a sizable sleeping bunker behind the gun position about thirty yards down the reverse slope with enough bunks to sleep six men.

The trenches were bare. We were bunkers apart from each other. Long stretches of the line were covered by a few unseen carbines and pistols. We had bunker communications and access to artillery fire, but somehow, that didn't seem very comforting. Our mission was straightforward. We were to hold these sector positions until the main body of troops came up in the morning. It sounded simple enough until I was actually doing it. Then the dangerousness of the situation hit me.

I ate my cold combat rations as I sketched in my notepad what I saw in front of me. What immediately bothered me was the position I was covering. The ground sloped slightly downward for about one hundred yards before it suddenly disappeared. What was so worrisome about that was that if I ever saw the Communist Chinese Forces, they would be right on top of me, with direct supporting fire from their mountain positions directly behind them. It was a nightmare scenario.

Tonight, I would be pulling an all-night guard without relief and with only my phone to keep me company. It would prove to be an interesting experience. Right now, the sun was going down, and it would soon be dark.

When evening came, there was a total blackout. I was in a void. I put my hand in front of my face and couldn't see it. In short increments, I would bring my trigger finger toward my nose and say, "Now," when I expected to touch it. In the beginning, it wasn't all that easy.

When the moon came out, it was beautiful. It illuminated the battlefield and made me feel more comfortable. I could see again. It was really a good companion. As the night wore on and the moon moved overhead toward the enemy's mountaintop, I tried to keep it from reaching there. I found that by blinking each eye individually, I could pop the moon up and down and keep it from disappearing for a few moments longer. As if on cue, when it finally did go down and darkness enveloped me again, the snow flurries began to fall, and my imagination caught fire.

In my mind's eye, I envisioned hordes of Chinese patiently working their way across the Punchbowl floor and snaking their way up the hill in front of me. I wouldn't see them unless they stepped on a mine or tripped a flare, and then it would be too late.

They would already be on top of me. The chilling snow made everything even more uncomfortable. Fortunately, it was a distraction, which made me extra alert. As much as I peered into the darkness, I couldn't see a thing. I strained my ears to pick up sounds, which only made me think of the worse-case scenario. The next twelve hours would be long and difficult before our guys made it up here in the morning. So much for leadership, I thought.

CHAPTER 47

PUNCHBOWL WELCOME

We were meticulous in removing all identifying insignias from our uniforms and helmets. We took a tourist route to the Punchbowl to deceive our enemy about where we were really going. Two days after we got there, duds from an artillery barrage had our outfit's name painted on them. At the time, I was sitting on our trench wall and writing a letter when a shell from the barrage brought me diving onto the ground. In the fall, my pen slipped on the letter, and without giving it much thought, I sent it home with an apology for what had happened, which caused my family to freak out.

Our two-gun sections were now at full strength. Our four-gun crews were together manning recoilless rifles instead of machine gunners, which we only did on special occasions. In reserve, we trained exclusively on the recoilless rifle and had gotten to know each other even better than before. Three of the squad leader gunners, namely George Reimer, Chuck Mason, and me, were from New York City. Dave "the Mule" Anderson, our fourth gunner, was from Missouri. The New Yorkers had over twenty points, which put us on the short-timer's list for the thirty-six points to rotate home. Although it wasn't the main topic of conversation, everyone knew that there would be casualties. Fighting had intensified all along the MLR since the last time we

288

had been on line. I just prayed to God that we would all rotate home safe and sound.

I was sitting on top of the trench wall with my back against a sandbag, writing a letter to my folks. I had a lot of exciting news to write about. I couldn't wait to tell them about Frank's unexpected visit, my making corporal, and going back on line. I was becoming a short-timer. I was getting closer to rotating home. I figured it would be sometime in July. This was going to be a long letter, and I hoped I could fit it all in because I was running out of writing paper.

April, 14, 1953

Dear Mom and Dad,

How are you doing? I'm fine. Three more months, and I'm home. You'll never guess who I met. I'm alone in my tent, lying across my cot, waiting for my squad to come in off of the field, and I see this figure walking across the—

Wheeeeeee . . . boom!

I rolled off the top of the trench and hit the ground, causing my pen to scribble across the page of the letter I was writing to my folks. I was about twenty feet from the nearest bunker. Like a screeching car jamming on its brakes and crashing, another round fell on the outside of the trench wall near where I was sitting. My heart pounding, I scrambled to my feet with the letter in my hand and threw myself at the half-opened door.

I slid past Reimer, who gave me his toothy, Teddy Roosevelt grin. "*Oso-o-ship-shio*, Joe," he said, kneeling behind the open door. I stayed on my belly, waiting for the next round.

"There are other guys out there!" I said, hurriedly moving next to George, who was behind the half-open door.

"I see one of them," he said.

We peered cautiously out of the bunker door and heard the sputtering whistle of another round and slammed the door shut, burying our faces into the hard bunker floor. Stones and shrapnel hit the hoochie.

"Oh, shit!" I said.

"That one was in the trench," said George.

We cracked opened the door to see the face of a frightened deer on a soldier who had charged straight at us.

"Come on, man. Move. Move!" we shouted, expecting another round at any moment.

"Open up!" screamed the soldier as his body hurled itself through the half-opened door, which we immediately slammed shut behind him.

"Are you okay?" we asked.

The soldier was a new man from upstate New York who gasped the word "okay" as he fought to catch his breath.

"I thought for sure you had it," said George, smiling.

I could never understand why we all smiled after a fright like that. It had to be an involuntary, nervous reaction over which you had little control. I witnessed close-call smiles all the time in close-combat situations. It was a common occurrence.

After the barrage ended, I found myself down to my last sheet of writing paper. I apologized to my folks for the soiled, ink-scratched letter and told them what had happened in what I thought was a very humorous way. They didn't think it was funny. A couple of weeks later, my dad sent me a letter chastising me for upsetting my mother. I realized I had done a foolish thing and was very careful not to write anything like that again. My dad gave me his work address at the post office if I felt I had to write such letters in the future. I never used it. From then on out, all my letters home were as cheerful as I could make them.

A bomb fragment was found with the 224 numerals of our regiment on it, and the next day, the Army of the People's Republic of China officially welcomed our division to the Punchbowl over a blaring, screeching loudspeaker.

CHAPTER 48

PINNED DOWN

The phone whistled. "We've got company. Stay alert. Chink patrol in the valley." It was broad daylight. Gooks usually only attacked at night. I was covering for Rock on his .30-caliber, water-cooled machine gun while he was away from his bunker. I could hear the echo of Chink machine guns firing across from their side of the Punchbowl.

The phone hissed again, "Targets of opportunity!"

I didn't see anything. I checked Rock's target map when machine gun rounds suddenly kicked up dirt in front of the bunker. I hit the deck with the phone to my ear and my back against the wall under the .30-caliber. Rounds came right through the bunker aperture. One hit the water can, which was connected to the machine gun and which sent a mixture of antifreeze and water spilling over me.

The phone spoke again. "Return fire! Targets of opportunity! *YOYO!*"

"I can't put my head up. Goddamn it! I'm pinned down."

The Chinese were cave diggers and tunnel builders. During the day, I would see shovels of sand flying over the trenches. They dug into the depths of the mountain as opposed to us, who dug trenches and bunkers on the tops of the ridges. Thankfully, we had a tremendous advantage. I never had to worry about napalm and bombing runs the way the Chinks did. Thank God Americans controlled the air. On top of that, the Chinks had to worry about our 75mm recoilless rifles, our 90mm cannons, and our artillery and mortar barrages.

Enemy patrols were very active at night. They kept us on our toes. Often, with the help of our big searchlights, I would see them moving down and out of their trenches and then losing themselves in the craggy hills before they disappeared into the dark valley below, where they would go on patrol.

Our patrols went out mostly at night. Though they rotated by platoons, there was a huge strain put on our riflemen and the gun crews who covered them. Often my crew along with the other three squads pulled 75 to 100 percent alerts. This meant guys stayed up into the morning hours. Scheduling guard shifts became a bitch. To give an example, I came off alert with half my squad and got everyone into a sleeping bunker except myself. All the bunks were filled with exhausted soldiers, some from other squads and platoons. I needed a place to crash. I was tired and cranky and didn't care where it was that I racked out as long as it was inside somewhere. I could always sleep on the bunker floor, but that would be the last resort.

I went back outside to our gun bunker and got on the horn and asked around, hoping to find an empty bed.

"I got one, Joe," said Rock in his soft, low, whispery voice.

"Oh, you're my man," I said happily. "Put it on hold. I'll be right there."

Rock's bunker was a combination sleeping and gun bunker. It was close to my gun bunker and a good stone's throw away from my sleeping bunker. I dragged myself along the trench and squatted outside of Rock's bunker.

I whistled softly. "Rock, it's Joe!"

A shelter was pulled back, and with his dark complexion, brush mustache, and gleaming white teeth, Rock offered a welcoming smile. "Hey, Joe, come on in," said Rock warmly, patting me on the back and letting the curtain fall close.

"Hey, man, I really appreciate this," I said. "I had visions of sleeping on the ground, wrapped up in a blanket."

"I got a bunk. It's not much, but it has a sleeping bag and a blanket. It's Chu's rack. He's in a MASH unit."

"What happened?" I asked, leaning against the aperture wall.

"He caught shrapnel yesterday. Got it up the ass, but they said he'd be back soon."

"I hadn't heard, but that's bullshit," I said. "That really pisses me off. They should put him on light duty and keep him in the rear somewhere. That goes for anyone who gets wounded. They served their time and shouldn't have to come back up. Let somebody else take his place. Send up a replacement for God's sake. You mean to tell me they don't have anybody else," I said, my blood starting to boil.

"That's not the army way, Joe. You know that," said Rock in his calm tone. "They just patch 'em up and send 'em up. Hell, I'm shorthanded on my .30-caliber, and I want to fix up my gun bunker now, not next month."

"What's wrong with it?"

"It's not deep enough, and the window is too wide. I must make a nice target for Joe Chink. I've tried picks and shovels, and it's a waste of time. I'm digging into solid mountain rock. It's got to be blown out. The engineers and the Pioneer Platoon are too busy. They want me to choke my motor. What do they know? I know what I need, and I need it now," said Rock, smiling and slapping me on my shoulder. "How's with you?" he asked.

"I'm tired with all these fucking alerts. This is the second time that I've had a gun bunker practically sitting on top of a tank. We're such a big fat target, and we keep getting reports that the Chinks are coming to get us. That's what last night's 100 percent alert was all about."

"Ole Joe is a pretty good shot," said Rock appreciatively. "That's why I want to do this gun bunker over now."

"You gotta be careful," I said. "We're working on a new gun bunker. The hole is already dug out, and still, we're drawing fire. The Chinks spot our movement and the newly turned soil and mark us as a target," I grumbled.

"Come on, Joe. We'll whine and moan later," said Rock, leading me past his water-cooled .30-caliber. We crouched low as we stepped down the sandbagged steps into a three-man sleeping bunker. "Chu's bunk is on top. There's a sleeping bag and a blanket up there."

"Hey, man, I really appreciate this," I said.

"No problem. Sleep tight, Joe."

I removed my cartridge belt and folded my field jacket to use as a pillow and thought I was going to puke. The smell of garlic and stale sweat smacked me in the face. Chu evidently liked to eat his *kimchi* in his sleeping bag, which was a soiled, shiny black. The blanket underneath it was caked in dry mud.

I took off my boots and hoisted myself up, careful not to wake the body underneath me. I rolled the sleeping bag up into a ball and threw it off to the side. I lay down in my field pants and sweater with the blanket over me and my field jacket as a pillow and conked out. As uncomfortable as it was, I evidently fell into a deep and fitful sleep, because I remember a couple of times during the night, somebody putting a blanket over me. I awoke with a start. Rock was shaking me, but I forgot where I was for a moment.

"Time to get up, Joe. Did you get some sleep?"

"Yeah, fine."

"You had a rough night, man. I had to come in off the gun a couple of times to quiet you down."

"No shit? Sorry, man."

"You gave me something to do. Broke the monotony," he said. "Probably scared the hell out of Joe Chink," he snickered.

"Sorry about that. Thanks again, Rock."

"No problem. Can you do me a favor, Joe?"

"Sure, what's up?"

"I need to go over to the Pioneer platoon. I know some of the guys, and they said they could get me some dynamite caps and fuses for my bunker. I shouldn't be long. Maybe an hour tops," he said. "Can you hold the fort for me until I come back?"

"Yeah, let me check in with my crew first to make sure they know where I am."

No sooner had Rock and his assistant gunner left when the echoes sounded. The phone came alive with voices, "Enemy patrol, enemy patrol spotted in the valley!"

When the tempo picked up and rounds landed nearby, I began to understand Rock's concern about the depth of his gun bunker and the size of its open window. I suddenly felt very visible and vulnerable.

A round hit the side of the aperture, sending me to my knees. I turned my back and leaned against the sandbags under the aperture, and with my right hand, I grabbed the phone. Another splash of rounds came pouring into the gun bunker, puncturing the water can next to the machine gun, splashing antifreeze off of the top of my helmet and down the back of my neck.

"Targets of opportunity! Short bursts! What can you see?" asked the voice over the phone. A line of machine gun bullets ripped the top of the sandbag wall behind the gun like a high-speed typewriter. I couldn't see what was happening, so I raised my hand above my head and used my thumb to pull the trigger and fire down the hill. I was crowing curses and swearing as I tried to get out of the way. I explained what was happening into the handset. I heard guffaws from the CP and realized what I was describing must have seemed comical to them. Suddenly, I wanted to get obscene. I wanted to scream at them. I wanted them to haul their safe, sorry asses up here and keep me company. Sitting on the bunker floor pinned down with rounds flying over your head was not a funny event.

CHAPTER 49

STRETCHER BEARERS!

Shouts of "stretcher bearers" brought GIs on the run. It was electrifying. Casualties needed to be carried off of the mountain. Either soldiers were wounded in action (WIA) and in need of swift medical attention, or they were killed in action (KIA) and in need of grave registrations. Being a stretcher bearer could be a dangerous job.

I hustled up the hill from my gun emplacement when I heard that lunch was being brought up to the hill next to us. On my way back from chow, I got caught up in a duel. Streams of tracers from a Chinese heavy machine gun were coming in on the tank that was positioned above my gun bunker. I was no more than fifty yards from it and found that I had a bird's eye view of what was happening.

Armor-piercing rounds exploded like bursting sparks around the tank. They made popping sounds like a string of M-80 firecrackers. The tankers returned fire with their 90-millimeter cannons, which made for great drama. In spite of this great show, I hated being out in the open when rounds were coming in. Timing and pure luck was everything. At the first hint of a lull in the firing between the tank and the maxim, I took off. I ran behind the tank and jumped down into the trench toward my bunker when I heard shouts of "stretcher bearers."

Soldiers stumbled toward me and yelled, "Casualties! Casualties! We got wounded!" A medic ran alongside of four GIs who managed a stretcher through the narrow trench. Trailers jogged behind for relief. I fell in line with them.

"Switch," panted a carrier. I squeezed next to the runner so I could take one of the handles like a baton in a relay race while the carrier was still running; however, it was awkward and clumsy. We had four carriers, a wounded soldier, a medic running beside the stretcher, and four trailers following the trench's winding path uphill and downhill. A sudden change in direction shifted weight and instantaneously brought an aching jolt to my arms and legs. My hands started to burn. I happened to be wearing my jump boots with the taps on the soles and heels, which made the going more difficult. My combat boots had a rip in them, and I was waiting for another pair to be sent up to me from our company rear. We kept banging against the side of the trench, jarring the poor, wounded soldier who kept screaming, "I'm blind! I'm blind! I can't see! I can't see!"

Blood was pouring from his nose, ears, and head. His eyes and his face were covered with dirt and black powder burns. The medic had a blood-soaked compress over his forehead and eyes, and he kept saying, "You'll be okay. You'll be okay. We got an ambulance waiting. We're almost there."

All the while, the soldier was writhing in the stretcher and sobbing. "My wife, my baby, I'll never see then again. I'm blind! I'm blind. I can't see."

Slipping and sliding and cursing under my breath, I joined the chorus of grunted words, "Hold on, soldier. You'll be okay. Hold on," but I didn't really believe them. I thought he was going to die. I just wanted him to stop screaming. The sheer terror and panic in his voice was too horrible to listen to.

I kept switching from bearer to trailer. I was on the handle and sucking wind when we reached the ambulance, which had somehow made it up from the supply road and was waiting for us on the end of the hill line. It was a blessed relief to put the stretcher down. No sooner had I straightened up when the drivers waved their arms wildly, "Pick up the stretcher, goddamn it. Move it. Move it. Slide it on and get the fuck out of here. We're taking fire from snipers. Get the hell out of here!"

With a surge of adrenaline, I heaved the stretcher up onto a slide track and fell to the ground on legs of jelly. The medic jumped on board, and the drivers shrieked at us to get the hell out of there. And then they took off.

As our crew tried to catch its breath, we heard the zings of rounds going over us. One round thumped into the ground, and someone gasped, "Hooch." An old, gook, busted-up, lean-to-type bunker lay halfway down the hill, and we made a mad dash toward it.

Gasping for air, I tumbled into the destroyed, gook bunker along with everybody else. I was sweating, and my lungs seemed like they were on fire. I lay there, spread-eagle and breathing hard, but I felt protected. Cigarettes were lighted, and canteen tops were twisted open to wet down dried throats. As tired as I was, I felt good. I was glad to have been part of a team of stretcher bearers that had gotten the wounded soldier into an ambulance and on his way to a MASH unit for treatment.

"I wondered if the gooks had their old positions zeroed in," I said with a straight face, which brought a sudden silence and stillness inside the half-open hooch.

"Fucking Donohue," said one of the stretcher bearers with a snicker. "Only you would think of something like that."

Without a word, we got up slowly and quietly, as if not to draw anyone's attention to us, and quickly scooted back to our gun bunkers.

CHAPTER 50

"ROCK'S DEAD"

I don't know why some guys were called by their last name like West, Mason, or Dee-jack-a-moe while others were called by their first name like Lyle and George instead of Olsen or Reimer. I could see nicknames through association like Mule, Fungus, Tiny, Wall Street, Hoop, Hollywood, or Quick Draw, but no one ever called him Arthur. He was Rock. He was the real thing. He was rock solid. It could easily have been a nickname because it fit him so well. It was my saddest day in Korea when I heard the words, "Rock's dead." To this day, I can still hear those words, "Rock's dead."

The hot meal came up late in the afternoon. I went down to the service road with a bunch of guys to find that it was a good one. I loved chicken. It was my favorite food after steak. It was less expensive so it was served more often on line, which was fine with me.

I had gotten my tray filled with food and my canteen cup of warm coffee when a jeep pulled up behind me. A general and a colonel got out to shouts of "attention!"

It was an awkward moment. I stood there with my arms full, and the general came right up to me and smiled. I think he was the same general I had seen back in the assembly area before I had come on line. I remembered the colonel. He wore the same

299

black helmet and prominent, pearl-handled pistol strapped to his waist. I made an effort to straighten up a bit for the general.

"Chow looks good, corporal. What do we have today?"

"Chicken, sir," I said.

"Looks good," he said, touching my chicken with the back of his hand. "And it's warm too."

I was taken aback. What nerve! He actually had touched my food. Then he said, "What do you think would happen if an artillery round came in right now on this very road, corporal?"

I looked around at the men who were bunched up on line, anxious to get their hot chow and bring something back up to their buddies on the hill.

"Pretty messy, sir," I replied.

"I think so too," he said. "Spread them out, colonel," he ordered.

"Three-yard intervals!" bellowed the colonel. "Let's go, men. You should know better than this. Come on now, spread it out!"

I sat down on the road to eat. I made sure that I chose a spot not too close to the other guys who were eating. Too bad the general hadn't stayed longer. He might have seen something interesting. Two stretchers were brought down the hill and placed next to each other on the side of the supply road. An army blanket had been strapped around the tops of the stretchers, leaving bare feet exposed with dog tags wrapped around toes. The buzz was immediate. "What happened? Who got hit? Who died?"

Lyle scurried over to me, his face twisted. He looked at me and shook his head slowly from side to side.

"What's up?" I asked.

"Joe, Rock's dead."

It was like getting punched in the stomach. The breath went out of me. Everything stopped. I stared at Lyle.

"What happened?" I asked.

"A mortar round," said Lyle.

"When, where?" I asked incredulously. "How did it happen?" I couldn't believe what I just heard.

The words kept repeating themselves in my head. Rock's dead. Rock's dead.

I put my tray down and walked over to the stretchers. I squatted and read the toe tags. Both bodies were covered up, but in my head, I could see Rock's face under the blanket. I could see him with his eyes closed as if he were sleeping. I could barely recall the other soldier. I think he was a KATUSA from another platoon.

I looked down at the stretcher. The blanket was bloodied. I couldn't believe I was looking down at Rock's body. I mumbled the words, "Jesus, Mary, and Joseph be with him," and said other prayers for both of them. I was just saying words. I went back to where I had left my tray to finish my meal. I kept staring over at the stretcher as I ate. I remember hating myself. Here I was eating my goddamn chicken, and my good buddy was lying dead only feet away from me. What the fuck was wrong with me?

An explosion on the top of the hill bolted me upright. As black smoke puffed upward, our chow line and crew scattered for cover. "Clear the road! Back to your positions!" brought bodies racing in different directions.

I don't know why, but I decided not to use the dug-out trench stairs leading up the hill. I scampered up the hill instead, thinking it was the shortest and quickest way back to my bunker. Halfway up, more rounds exploded on the hill, and I threw myself facedown into the ground. I suddenly realized that I was caught out in the open. I felt naked without cover. This was the second time this had happened on the Punchbowl, and I felt stupid and vulnerable. I peeked up to see where I would run to next when I saw one of our young bunker boys from the command post screaming and running awkwardly down the hill. "Wall Street" was usually a brash, funny, smart-talking, Korean kid who was now a frightened little boy crying and dragging himself along with sheer terror in his eyes. As he passed me, I could see blue watery veins in his bare, split-open leg, which was grotesquely turned the wrong way.

Seeing this gave me a jolt of energy that got me moving. With butterflies in my stomach, I hopped up the hill like a frightened jackrabbit running as fast as I could. The trench never looked so good. I jumped into it and looked for the closest bunker I could find to take cover in. I had completely forgotten about Rock until I heard the cry, "Stretcher bearers!"

The words came rushing back again, "Rock's dead."

CHAPTER 51

RAPE AND RAMPAGE

They called it R & R. It stood for rest and recuperation. GI Joes jokingly referred to it as rape and rampage. Every soldier in Korea got to go to Japan for a five-day vacation. Travel expenses were paid for by Uncle Sam. Families that could afford it made arrangements to meet their loved ones there. Guys got engaged. Some even got married. Besides going home when you got your thirty-six points, soldiers looked forward to going on R & R. It was good for morale. For some, it meant even more. It might be the first and only time they would get laid before they were killed in action. They wanted *baby-san* love. They wanted to hear, "I love you, Joe."

When my R & R turn came, I was more than ready. I was still reeling from Rock's death. Every time I looked out of my gun bunker, I was reminded of what had happened. The explosion from the mortar round had blown a piece of Rock's uniform out onto a bare tree limb in front of my gun bunker. It wrapped itself around a splintered branch and just hung there. It became a permanent fixture of my everyday world. It was impossible to avoid. I would sit in front of my aperture and stare at it. As much as I looked away, I couldn't help but come back to it. It was a gruesome reminder of my tragic little world on the front line.

When the word came up to me, it was like a release from prison. McCrawford, a North Carolina boy from the mortar platoon and airborne like me, came bursting into my gun bunker, stuttering from excitement.

"Donohue, we're going to Japan! We're going to Osaka on R & R, boy, you and me. Grab your gear. We're leaven heah." Mac was smiling and pumping his fist in the air like he had just knocked out Joe Louis. "Here we come, Japan! *Baby-sans* beware! Mac and Joe are coming to town!"

I was so ready for Japan. I felt like I was going to levitate and take off on my own. In less than an hour, Mac was down on the service road, waiting for me in a jeep. Outside my command post, Dee-jack-a-moe and Reiner were waving and yelling to us, "*Tak-son onas. Tak-son baby-sans. Tak-son boom boom.* Have fun, guys."

We were like a couple of giddy kids on the last day of school. I was psyched. The jeep brought us back to battalion, where we hopped onto a truck and headed toward Chunchon. We snaked along curving roads, stopping and picking up soldiers from different parts of the line. The farther back we went, the more we picked up from our company, battalion, regiment, and finally division rears. Now we had a convoy going into Seoul.

Mac and I and the other front-liners stood out like sore thumbs. We were more animated, and they were more nonchalant. Our uniforms were put together, and theirs were fresh and proper. Shiny metal shone through the scraped black paint of my helmet. Dried crusts of mud spotted the veterans' boots and outfits. I wore a dirty, heavy wool, drab shirt over an army sweater tucked into mud-crusted fatigue pants. My underwear was weeks old, but my socks were pretty good. They were only a few days old. Dry socks were priority laundry because they prevented trench foot. Mac and I had our scuffed jump boots, which were no longer shiny clean. I was starting a mustache that looked scrawny and didn't help my appearance any. Mac and I were definitely curiosities. I felt like shouting, "What do you want? We just came out of our rat holes a couple of hours ago."

Entering the outskirts of Seoul was not a pretty sight. We passed a sprinkling of deserted rice paddies and thatched huts. It seemed that all that was left were splintered telephone poles and the crumbled outer walls of the city. Seoul, the capital of South Korea with millions of people, was the largest city in Korea, and I saw very few people on our trip in. The devastation was worse than in Pusan. Rubble was everywhere. Even the buildings still standing were damaged in one way or another. It was like looking at the destruction of the German city of Dresden in World War II. The devastation was unbelievable.

Our trucks came to a stop in front of a beat-up railroad terminal. An old sergeant and a young corporal were waiting for us. We jumped down from the trucks as our names were called to line up. After roll call and a visit to a stinking men's room, we went out into the late afternoon sun and sat down on the train station's stairs and waited.

Across the street was an old, beat-up church. It had a white cross perched above a slated roof. It looked like it might have been abandoned when a tall, lanky, American or European minister came up the street toward us out of nowhere. He had a subdued elegance about him. Dressed in a light gray suit with a shiny black vest, he wore a brown-collared shirt and a light tan Panama hat surrounded by a colorful band. What looked like a prayer book was tucked under his arm, and as he came up the steps, he tipped his hat and smiled and wished us a good day, which brought several of us to our feet, nodding and returning his greeting. It seemed like such a natural thing to do. I had been in a military setting for so long that it was like a jolt of culture shock to see a civilian going about his normal business in the city where he lived.

The old sarge with the long line of hash marks down his sleeve told us in an almost gentlemanly manner to line up for chow. We shuffled into a vestibule that led to a cavernous hall bustling with activity. It had been set up as a combination mess hall and dining room.

It was like my first experience as a kid in a fancy restaurant. There were sparkling white table cloths covering dozens of round tables. Linen napkins and place settings with glasses of water and a little vase of real flowers were set on each table. Korean girls in freshly starched uniforms greeted us with smiles and graciously took our orders. Excitement was growing. The hall was abuzz and getting loud with laughter.

"Didn't I tell you, Joe?" said Mac, poking me with his elbow and smiling from ear to ear. "Just smell that cooking. That's real food, man, and it's just the beginning. I got us the address of a hotel in Osaka with the reputation for having the prettiest women anywhere. We're going to have a ball, man."

I wasn't only smiling. I had a kind of moronic giggle that kept erupting out of me. "You were right, Mac," I said, bending over conspiratorially. "Imagine what Japan is going to be like. You'd better give me that million-dollar address in case we get separated."

Waitresses in spotless white aprons scurried about. Everyone seemed to order the same thing. Steak, potatoes, and rolls with real butter were followed by coffee, apple pie, and ice cream. The food tasted almost foreign to me. I had forgotten what it was like to eat American dishes. When one of the waitresses smiled and bowed and asked me if I would like some more, I lost it. I choked. My eyes filled with tears, and my throat tightened, so I just nodded and mouthed the word "yes." The simple question and smallest token of courtesy overwhelmed me. In eight months, I had become so completely immersed in another role in another world that I had become a stranger to my old world. I had forgotten what it was like to be treated so nicely.

Mac and I landed in Osaka, raring to go. We were transported to an R & R center where we stripped off our fatigues and underwear. This was a little embarrassing because our last change had been over two weeks ago. We got powdered down for lice. Our peckers were checked for VDs. We showered and shaved before we hit the sack in new underwear. I flopped luxuriously on a cot with clean sheets and pillows. Everything was so luxurious I had trouble sleeping for the big day.

Early the next morning, we got class-A uniforms and passes. I exchanged thirty-six thousand yen for a hundred dollars and kept a fifty-dollar traveler's check in my wallet. Mac and I used condoms to blouse our pants over our shined jump boots, pinned our silver airborne wings under our blue combat infantryman badge on the left breast pocket, and looked very sharp. In all the confusion and excitement of processing, we got separated, but I had the address in Osaka where we were to meet.

I stood on a long taxi line of soldiers anxious to get started. Mac had a good half-hour start on me. When I got to the front of the line, I stepped out the door with my traveling bag, and I was assaulted by an unruly mob of Korean kids yelling, shrieking, waving, and screaming through the fence surrounding our compound. "Here, GI, over here. *Ichi-bon baby-san. Ichi-bon.* Young sister, you like. Good time girl, *chop chop chimpo*, you like. *Su-ko-shi, o-ka-neh*, cheap, you like. Another Korean boy yelled, "Here, GI! Over here! You like number one, long time, short time, good time."

Two MPs quickly came to my aid and escorted me down a long path leading to the closed, wire-fence gate. "When the gate is opened, don't stop. We'll walk you straight ahead to a line of waiting cabs. Get ready."

The MPs cleared the way while they rushed me through the waiting mob to a cab. I hopped in and slammed the door shut as the cab lurched forward with a flying fury, throwing me back on the seat. "Train to Osaka."

"Ah, so! Okay, Osaka."

I thought New York cabdrivers were dangerous. This guy was crazy. He drove like a madman. He pulled into the train station with a quick brake that catapulted me out of my seat. He graciously opened my door, smiled, and bowed happily several times after I gave him his tip.

I had the address of the place where I was to meet Mac and showed it to my cabbie, who pointed to where I should go to buy my ticket. All that I knew was that the place was in downtown Osaka. I know I looked like a lost tourist because a couple of tough-looking kids sidled up to me and started giving me a hard sell about going with them to meet their pretty sisters for a good time. One kid grabbed my arm, and I pulled away from him. "No!" I said adamantly. They became more demanding, pleading with me, "You no sorry. My sister is *ichi-ban*. Number one! You come with me."

"Hey! Fuck off!" I barked. "No sister, no *baby-san*, no *o-na*."

I was getting a little edgy. A small, middle-aged man with black, bushy eyebrows, wearing a long black topcoat that reached down to his knees and a beat-up gray fedora pulled down over his eyes, came charging out of nowhere. I pulled back in surprise. A distorted, angry face gave a contorted hiss and three swift kicks in the direction of the kids. It scared the hell out of them and me as well. He turned to me and bowed. He came toward me with short, quick steps and produced a wallet with a badge in it. With staccato, broken English and Japanese, he bowed and grunted what I made out as an apology for the street urchins' behavior. It took me a moment to realize that this stern, scowling man was a plainclothes policeman. Relieved, I showed him the address I was looking for, and he helped me purchase a ticket for the train to downtown Osaka.

"*A-ri-ga-toh, domo a-ri-ga-toh*," I said and smiled gratefully and then bowed my head again.

A squint of the eyes and a half smile barely made it through his hard face. "*Sy-o-nara* and good luck, *soldier-san*."

I boarded the train, feeling good, and for the first time in my life, I knew what it was like to be tall. I mean, really tall. At five-foot-ten, I was looking down on everyone. The train ride wasn't so different from a ride on the subway in New York City. I held on to a leather strap and nobody made eye contact. I was the only American soldier in the car, and I knew everybody else knew it too.

At my stop I hailed a cab and another kamikaze cabbie took me to my hotel, which was nothing more than an ordinary-looking apartment building in the middle of a plain-looking side street in Osaka. I walked up the steps to the front door, checked the address again to make sure I was in the right place, and rang the bell. A small, gray-haired *mama-san* welcomed me into the vestibule with a garish smile of gold and silver and gestured for me to remove my boots. I wanted to make sure I was in the right place and asked if Mac was there without much success. I quickly checked the assortment of shoes lined up outside the door and was relieved to see Mac's shiny, cordovan jump boots standing tall above the others. I pulled off my boots and placed them next to Mac's and followed the *mama-san* down a carpeted hallway. Before I reached the end of the hall, a shrieking young woman came running down the hall and jumped up and straddled me, giving me a big kiss and a hug. Dumbfounded, I stood there with a squealing *baby-san* in my arms and Mac's laughing voice. "She's mine, Joe. Go get your own, boy."

Wrapped in a flame-spouting dragon emblazoned on a multicolored, silk kimono and clutching a tall drink in his hand, Mac beamed, "Joe, meet Yuki, and Yuki, meet Joe. Now get yourself a little woman and come upstairs and join the rest of us. Come on, man. Move it."

Mama-san brought me into a room with several comfortable chairs. She offered me a seat and tea and said, "You pick . . . you like." She then bowed low and left the room.

Moments later, the door opened, and in stepped a slim, rather tall, well-dressed woman in her mid-to-late twenties who quietly closed the door on a long line of ladies in waiting. I thought she was one of *mama-san's* staff because most of the girls I saw coming into the hotel were in their late teens and looked like bobbysoxers. She, on the other hand, was dressed in a gray skirt, black ballerina slippers, and a white silk blouse. She sat down, and I thought she was a business woman acting as a liaison helping me to negotiate a deal. I was taken aback when she told me in pretty good English, "Hello, my name is Miko."

"Hi, my name is Joe."

"Like GI Joe," she said and smiled.

"Yep, like GI Joe."

"My name is Miko," she said again and smiled. "Miko Dai-na-moto like in dynamite. I am dynamite, Joe. I'm number one *ichi-bon*. You like. I show you dynamite good time. I love you very hard. You see. You like very much."

She had my number. She sizes me up and pitches me right. She tells me that she doesn't work here. She looks for special people to give them a special time. She looks for number one GI to take home to her *mama-san* and family. No dark soldiers. No riff raff soldiers. She promised very special place, big tea house, not very far away. "Five days, sixteen thousand yen. Food and drink extra. I take *ichi-bon* place, *ichi-bon* time, lots a love, lots a fun. You like."

I figured I could handle the forty-five dollars for the week. Neither Miko nor I could persuade Mac and his girl to come with us. Mac was in love. His *baby-san* worked and stayed in the hotel. He didn't want to leave her. She didn't want to leave the hotel. Miko and I left the hotel with her sister and her soldier. All the *baby-sans* in Japan seemed to be each other's sister.

We found a cab waiting at the door. Getting out of Osaka was hair-raising. Our Japanese driver was the same as the others. He was *yakimoki* crazy behind the wheel. As exhausted as I was, he kept me on the edge of my seat. Miko and her sister laughed, telling me everything was *dai-jo-be*. At one point, brakes screeched, and it felt as though our cab may have bumped another. Our driver leaped out of his seat and confronted the other driver. Face-to-face, a strange ritual took place. Harsh-sounding words followed by grunts and bows took place like long lost brothers who unexpectedly met on the road. Without warning, the ritual ended with both drivers going back into their cabs and driving off as if nothing had happened. The other soldier and I looked at each other and shrugged.

The country house was beautiful. It looked like it sat on stilts coming out of the ground. Round, greenish stones led to the entrance stairs, which separated the shrubs and flowers on both sides of it. Two wraparound porches smelling of cedar stood over each other. We were met at the entrance by a house boy and a *mama-san* dressed in a traditional Japanese kimono and holding a baby. Our sister *baby-sans* squealed and showered the baby with coos and kisses. Miko introduced everybody, and the other soldier and I were seated on a bench where our boots were removed. Wood-framed wall panels of rice paper slid open, and I walked into a lobby of exotic scents. Miko led me up a curved staircase to another porch, and we stopped at one of the panels and went inside. She helped me into a kimono and sandals and disappeared only to come back dressed in a colorful, flowery kimono, carrying a tray of food and tiny cups of warm sake with a cold bottle of Nippon beer.

I was starving and exhausted. I finished the beer first, but I knew I wouldn't last very long. My body was being drained of energy. I forced my eyes to stay open. My head was nodding. Thirty hours ago, I had been on a hill in the Punchbowl. Now I was having sandwiches and sake with Miko, and I could hardly keep my head up; however, it was too early to go to bed. The sound of a female vocalist came floating up the stairs: "Fly the ocean in a silver plane. See the jungle when it's wet with rain. Just remember when you're home again, you belong to me."

Applause and shrill, piercing laughter followed the next record.

"There's a shanty in the town, on a little plot of ground, and the green—"

Somebody's having fun, I thought, closing my eyes. I barely remembered getting onto the mattress on the floor. I do remember crawling under the sheets and blanket and the luxurious feeling of my head hitting the plush, rolled pillow.

Early in the evening, I awoke to laughter. Through heavy-lidded eyes, I saw Miko and two of her sisters sitting on floor pillows under an amber-colored lantern. I didn't know how long had passed when I was awakened a second time by the light of a handheld candle and the giggling faces of two young women and the words of "*boy-san* paratrooper" and others. Miko then appeared and angrily shushed them away.

I awoke a third time to low, soft murmurs. Only this time, the room was steeped in total darkness, Miko straddling me and rocking slowly back and forth. Through the darkness, I heard myself groan and looked up to the smiling face of Miko above me. Her eyes closed, and her head tilted upward as her small, delicate body slowly came down to meet me.

"Hello, Joe."

"Hello, Miko."

"I love you, Joe."

"I love you too, Miko."

I had four more days left of R & R.

CHAPTER 52

POOR OLD CHOGGIES

R & R was over. I got back to my gun bunker, and part of Rock's torn uniform was still twisted around the tree limb in front of me. Nothing seemed to have changed. The smell of rotting bodies being uncovered by the melted snow was new. It was the job of the Korean Service Corp to bring them in whenever possible. The KSC was made up of South Korean men who were too old for military service and who worked for us as laborers. They humped hills in all kinds of weather. They carried food, wood, water, and other supplies on their backs up to the front line. They were a poor, ragged-looking lot that were often accused of being spies for the NKA. They were just hard workers trying to make a living, and we didn't always treat them well; however, I don't know what we would have done without them.

I wasn't feeling too hot during the flight back from R & R. The fact that former General Ike Eisenhower had flown in the same plane that I had been on didn't help my air sickness any. It was a short, bumpy, low-altitude ride to Kimpo during overcast weather. I wondered if it was an omen, coming back to Korea and feeling as miserable as I did.

The next morning, I watched two choggies from my gun bunker haul a body in. The choggies looked like two weary hunters who had to haul the carcass of their prey far from the kill site to their camp. A decomposed body of a Chinese soldier was tied to a tree sapling like a dead deer. Commo wire was used to tie wrists to one end of the pole and ankles to the other end. The choggies rested for a moment by rolling the poles off of their shoulders and dropping their burden onto the ground near my bunker. I offered cigarettes and a light, and they took them, nodding appreciatively.

Buckteeth protruded from an open mouth. A smooth, waxen, blackened face peered out of a dirt-covered bundle of clothes. Matted hair stuck out of his oversized canvas cap. The earflaps from his hat were spread out on the ground like two giant moose ears. A .50-caliber round protruded through the ankle of one of his muddy sneakers. It was a sight that made Miko and Osaka feel light years away.

In looks and dress, the two choggies were almost indistinguishable from the guy they were carrying in from the field. They were the Korean version of New York bowery bums sitting silently, smoking, and staring off into space. You could never be sure of them. There were persistent rumors and stories that some of them were spies and infiltrators. Whenever something unexplainable happened, they were the first ones that came to mind. A tossed grenade down a bunker stovepipe, the disappearance of a GI from his listening post, the discovery of a dead body inside our lines, or whatever unexpected horror took place, they would often be looked at with suspicion and treated with disdain.

After the choggies brought the corpse down to the service, I was surprised to see some GIs with a small group of choggies to the left of my bunker, walking out toward no-man's-land. I didn't recognize any of the soldiers. I thought it might be a work detail of some sort. It was strange, because not only were they exposing themselves to possible enemy gun fire but they were heading into an unclear mine area as well. It just didn't look right. The soldiers lagged behind, motioning the service unit forward. Some of the choggies hesitated and turned around. Several soldiers unslung their rifles, slid the bolts back, pointed their weapons at the laborers, and yelled at them to keep moving. The choggies froze in their tracks. I couldn't believe what I was seeing. For several seconds, there was a standoff until geysers of snow and dirt exploded in front of the Koreans. The Koreans dropped what they were carrying and ran back toward the GIs. A round fell in between the GIs and the Korean laborers, which brought both groups scrambling back toward the trench line. I saw several of the service corps workers go down. They were helped up by their own men running behind them. Everybody got back into the trenches and found cover. It was a strange scene. A half hour later, I was in my sleeping bunker, fooling around and doing a standup comedy routine, overdramatizing a story about riding in a New York subway. The guys in my squad got a kick out of hearing stories about New York City. In the middle of my performance, Lyle Olsen swooped in and sat on an empty bunk. His blond hair set off his blue eyes and flushed face. It was plain to see that he was angry. Lyle was a pleasant farm boy from Nebraska, with a droll sense of humor that masked an inner toughness and a more serious side of his personality. He was a no-nonsense, straight-shooter when it came to his squad and very popular with his men. Now he was agitated and plain pissed off. As he swore through clenched teeth, he kept shaking his head from side to side and throwing his trench knife hard into the ground.

"Goddamn assholes wouldn't listen up. Almost got everyone killed," said Lyle, pounding his trench knife harder into the dirt floor.

"What happened? Were you with those guys outside?"

"I was passing by and told them they were heading for trouble, but they paid no mind to me. They were riflemen who came up with the choggies and seemed to know what they were doing."

"I was watching from my gun bunker. I didn't know what was going on, but it didn't look right."

"Well, the way I got it was that the choggies brought their loads up and dropped them off. Then they were told that they had a pickup to make and were led out into the suspected mine field. Well, you saw what happened then."

"Yeah, I saw what happened. I don't feel comfortable around choggies, and I don't know that I trust them that well. But I sure as hell wouldn't use those poor bastards to clear a suspected mine field. That's bullshit," I said.

"I know what you're saying, Joe, but some guys don't feel that way. They figure it's their country we're fighting for and half of those choggies are infiltrators anyway, so what's wrong in letting them take a little walk and help us out a bit? Maybe there's nothing out there. If it's clean, then they helped us clear a path. If it's not, then they died for their country. Better them than us is the way they look at it."

"It's a shame," I said. "I bet half those *papa-sans* would switch places with our young KATUSAs in a minute and fight for their country if they could. Where the hell would we be without those poor, old choggies and the jobs they do for us?"

CHAPTER 53

GRIM REALITY

R & R was a distant memory. I was back in the trenches. No warmth, no lights, no bathrooms, none of the comforts of Japan. I was back to C-rations, hungry rats, circling crows, incoming rounds, gook attacks, battlefield casualties, and more deaths. Osaka was a fantasy, a dream. I was back on line. I was back to griping, dying, grieving, and guilt. I was back to grim reality.

Our 75-RR platoon fell into a good deal. We would be manning a new gun position several hundred yards behind where we were now. It was located on a ridge that commanded the high ground and could cover our company sector in case it was ever overrun. It was close to the line but not on the line. It was isolated and safe. From there, you could look down and see the other 75-RR squads and actually wave to them. It was an envious position.

Our new platoon leader, Lieutenant Olsen, no relation to Lyle Olson, my machine gun buddy, said he would try to give each squad a turn at the new position, even if it was for a short time. It was like a *su-ko-shi* R & R. It became a must-have for the gun crews.

Before I went on R & R, my gun crew was next in line to man the new gun position. We were supposed to exchange with the third squad gun crew. When I came back from my R & R in Osaka, my gun crew still hadn't moved. My guys started to bitch. I kept asking Dee-jack-a-moe when we were going to make the switch. He kept telling me, "Any day now." My squad was pissed off, and Dee was on our shit list. We hardly ever saw him anymore. Since he had become section leader, he had turned into a no-show, a bunker hunker. He never came up the hill from the CP to check us out. If he wanted anything, he called us on the horn, or we went down to him. My guys felt cheated. They felt they should have been up in that position by now. Since Rock's death, nobody thought that it was always the other guy who got killed. We were all a bit jumpy.

I had been getting god-awful earaches since our last fire mission, so I called the CP and got permission to go to a MASH unit in battalion rear for the pain. When I arrived, I was surprised to meet Kim Pan Soo, a KATUSA from our platoon who was now a doctor's orderly. I didn't know he had been reassigned. We were glad to see each other again. Kim haltingly introduced me to the doctor who examined me and told me that I had a ruptured eardrum. He gave me drops and earplugs and told me to avoid loud noises, at which point I thanked him for his excellent advice. He never ordered me home.

I hitched a ride back and stopped off at our company headquarters before I went back up the hill. I got the same kind of reception that I had gotten from Kim. Guys greeted me warmly and couldn't talk fast enough. They wanted to know everything at once, ranging from how their buddies were to what it was like on line. They brought me into the mess tent for a sandwich and fruit juice. They heard the fire fights and saw the casualties being brought down for transportation to the rear. The sounds of battle only fed their imagination. Anxiety was high. They had a different view of the war.

The mess sergeant wrapped a sizeable, salt-covered steak for me. I never realized what empathy and a little guilt could do for a frontline soldier. I thanked him profusely and reported back to the CP and told them what the doctor had ordered. After the smiles and wisecracks, Dee turned to me and told me that he could get his hands on a *hibatchi* and cook up the steak for me and find a little something to wash it down with.

"Sounds good to me," I said. "Then we can talk about the new counterattack position for my squad."

"Sure," said Dee-jack-a-moe.

I went back up the hill to my gun position and waited for the call, which never came. I called back down first thing the next day.

"Can't do it tonight, Joe," said Dee-jack-a-moe.

"Why not?" I asked.

"Too much is happening. I'll let you know when."

The next night, Dee-jack-a-moe couldn't do it either. The following day, the timing was not right. I know I was being stalled, so I went down to the CP.

"Hey, Joe, what's up, trooper?" asked Dee.

"I came for my steak," I said.

"Oh yeah, yeah," he said. "Look, something came up, man. I'm sorry," said Dee, standing in the bunker door.

"Whadayamean?" I gushed.

"Let's keep it down, Joe. The old man came up, and I thought it would be a good way to help you out with your squad, so I cooked the steak up for him and the new lieutenant. He's going to do it," said Dee-jack-a-moe, closing the bunker door halfway behind him and keeping me outside.

"When?" I asked.

"When he's ready," said Dee-jack-a-moe with an annoyed look. "I don't know, but soon."

"You're fucking with me," I said. "You're full of shit." I could feel my face redden.

"Hold on!"

"Fuck you, Dee-jack-a-moe."

"Hey, take it easy man."

"Bullshit," I said. "First you eat my steak, and then you bullshit me about switching gun crews. You're so full of shit."

"Don't be such a fucking crybaby, Donohue," Dee shot back. "Your turn will come, okay? Keep your fucking shirt on."

"When, when will it come? When it's time to move off of the line or be carried off," I said, putting my face into Dee-jack-a-moe's face.

"Are you scared, Donohue?"

"Scared? Look who's talking about being scared!" I screamed. "You're afraid to go out of your bunker and take a piss," I said in a high, squeaking voice that sprayed saliva into his face.

"Hold it! Hold it right there," said Lieutenant Olsen as he stepped out from behind Dee-jack-a-moe in the CP. "Now, what's going on here?"

Shaking, I went through the whole story with Lieutenant Olsen.

"Go back to your position, Donohue. I'll call you after I speak to the captain."

"I appreciate that, sir," I said, looking at Dee-jack-a-moe, who had the balls to nod his head in agreement, as if he and the lieutenant had decided on this course of action together.

I saluted the lieutenant and left. I felt pretty good about myself. I knew Dee-jack-a-moe hadn't done anything. He didn't want to make waves with our new platoon leader, Lieutenant Olsen, and our new company commander, Captain Monges. They were both experiencing combat for the first time and didn't need any extra pressure. As an acting platoon sergeant, Dee-jack-a-moe wasn't looking out for us. He decided not to make waves. He went political. He decided to kiss ass with the brass.

Dee-jack-a-moe kept us working on an old and dangerous project. Our section of 75s were building a new bunker on an old site, but we weren't doing it fast enough. Dee-jack-a-moe was getting heat from within the command post. Captain Monges wanted the bunker built yesterday. Our new commander was becoming unpopular with the platoon because he was showing some of the traits of Dee-jack-a-moe. Not being visible, showing false bravado, and having a loud mouth will capture the attention of the troops.

Our third and fourth squads took turns digging, hauling rocks, and filling sandbags. It was a lousy detail. The gun bunker had been started by the outfit we had relieved. The hole was already dug. It was about five feet deep and a dozen or so feet long and maybe ten feet wide with strands of loose commo wire strung across the front of the hole as guides for laying down sandbags. The downside to the new bunker was that it drew fire from the Chinese who could see that something was happening. Even if we worked at night, the newly turned soil was spotted the next day. It was hard to conceal what we were doing. Everybody bitched and found reasons why they couldn't work on it, including me. The more Dee-jack-a-moe pushed us, the more excuses we had for finding more urgent things to do. This lousy detail was another reason to switch with the gun position behind us as soon as we could.

Tucker, Martinez, Van Syckle, Mule and I were working on the bunker one day. Van Syckle worked inside the hole, and Martinez, Tuck, Mule, and I worked outside. Like silent killers, mortars gave no warning. Once in a blue moon, if the wind was blowing just the right way, you might be able to hear the ping and whoosh of mortar rounds leaving their tube. This day, we heard nothing. They landed with a whump and a cloud of smoke. The weird thing about mortars was that you saw the burst before you heard it, which was what made them so frightening. You could see your own death coming and never knew what hit you.

The first crunch froze me. I threw myself down, burying my face in the ground. Luckily, the rounds landed to the left of us below the trench line. The Chinks had the range. Everybody had to find cover before the enemy fired and blanketed the area. I lifted my head up and saw Van's polka-dot eyes bulging out at me from under his steel helmet, his nose just above the rim of our quarry.

"Let's go!" I screamed. and leaped up, making a dash for Vanny's head. A dozen strides later, I dove through the strands of wire, taking Van Syckle and Martinez with me to the bottom of the hole. We got up in time to see the petrified look on Tuck's face and watch him come barreling at us and hurl himself down into the pit. We helped him up, and the four of us popped our heads up and looked for Anderson. The Mule was still out there, hugging the ground. We ducked back down into the hole as the explosions hit. In quick succession, we leaped up and peered over the edge of the hole and started screaming for him to come in. A slow-moving Anderson got to his feet. He crouched down low and weaved his way toward us. We scattered as the Mule came crashing down on us. We lay in a tangled heap at the bottom of the abyss, our heads cradled in our arms, afraid to move.

"Sons of bitches!" sputtered the Mule. "Goddamn sons of bitches!"

We unwound slowly and looked at each other in surprise. No one was hurt. We cursed and giggled in relief as we checked each other out.

"Whoo-ha. Whoo-dee. Whoodee-ha," squealed Tuck happily in his high voice.

"If only you could have seen your faces," gasped Van Syckle, who had witnessed it all. "Three scared-shitless assholes sprinting like frightened deer and diving through, under, and over that goddamn commo wire, and it never moved. So help me God, it never moved."

I played the scenes over in my head. I tried to picture three bodies diving into the hole without disturbing any of the stretched wire around it and then plummeting down a five-foot drop onto hard ground without getting hurt. The realization of what had happened was unbelievable. At the end, smiles turned into bent-over, belly-holding laughter.

Nice things happened the next day too. We got the word to switch guns with the third squad. Evidently, the bitching had paid off. Finally, it was our turn to go into the coveted counterattack position up on the ridge behind us for a little relaxation. I showed Mason and his assistant gunner our fire sector and range card. Then my gun crew followed Mase to the ridge behind us, and he gave us the rundown on our new position.

"Mase, watch out for Dee-jack-a-moe. He's hiding on line and making himself scarce, but he'll rant and rave about having to finish the new 75mm gun bunker. He's hot to trot over that. The Chinks have it zeroed, and the CP wants it finished ASAP. Good luck, man."

My squad loved their new digs. As soon as we got settled in, we waved down to our buddies in the third squad. The next day, I checked my notebook and had a memo that read, "Turn mountain sleeping bags in for summer ones tomorrow, without covers." I smiled at the memo. In combat, things could go from the high excitement of combat to the boring chores of everyday, commonplace living.

From inside our sleeping bunker, I was checking off sleeping bags when the intercom rang.

"Miker 4," I answered.

"Joe?" a low voice asked.

"Yeah, it's me, Dee," I said, waiting for some bullshit to be laid on me.

"Miker 3 bought it."

After a pause, I said, "Say again?"

"Third squad got hit."

"Fuck, no!"

The look on my face and tone of voice must have told it all. All eyes in our sleeping bunker turned toward me. I kept shaking my head in disbelief. I repeated the message.

"Mason is dead. So is his assistant gunner and St. Claire, a rifleman from Love Company. Two KATUSAs were wounded. A mortar round came right in on them."

I hung up the phone. I was dumbfounded. "We have to go back *chop chop*," I said.

A thick, sad, sorry silence engulfed us all. It was difficult to fathom what had just happened. We all went into ourselves. The reality of it was so hard to believe. Mason had been from New York, my hometown. We hadn't known each other in Manhattan. He had lived across town from me on the west side. We had come into the company together. We had been short-timers. We had talked about going home together. Now three of our buddies were dead, and three had been wounded in the twenty-four hours since we had switched guns. All the petty arguments, raging anger, bitching, and griping to get to this plush assignment ended in grief and remorse. No one said the obvious, but everyone thought it. It could easily have been us.

CHAPTER 54

Rat Attack

The joke going around was to be nice to rats because they could be our dead relatives. Somebody heard that in India, Hindus believed that rats were incarnations of their ancestors, so it was a sin to hurt or scare them. They revered them. In Korea, we hated them. They weren't our ancestors. We chased and killed them whenever possible.

It had been raining for days. Although it pretty much stopped, there was still a damp chill in our water-soaked bunker. I checked my watch. Five minutes to go. Damn! I didn't want to go outside. I didn't want to go out there. As damp as it was, I'd rather have stayed inside the bunker and submerged myself in the warmth of my goose-down, cozy sleeping bag. I looked at my watch again. The face glowed from inside the shell of my sleeping bag. The minute hand had to be out of whack. It was moving way too fast. I stared at it as hard as I could, as if staring would slow it down. It had to be out of control racing around like that. I had no choice. I had to get up and get moving.

Reluctantly, I undid the zipper of my bag, sat up slowly, wiggled my stocking feet into my boots, took the .45 pistol from my belt, and put it in its holster. A flick of my Zippo lighter, and I lit up a smoke from my metal-covered pack of Old Gold and instantly tasted the apple honey in it. Whether sent from home or gotten from a USO carton, butts on the hill always seemed to be soggy and limp. Even in dry weather, the tobacco was soft and loose. I was a Brooklyn Dodger baseball fan, and Old Gold cigarettes, one of their sponsors, made me think of the broadcast voice of Red Barber, baseball, and home.

Now it was time to snap out of it and get going. It wasn't fair to be late. Everybody bitched about going out to the gun bunker. I scaled the guard duty down to thirty minutes. It made it more bearable to be out there, but it cost us less sleeping time.

I was relieving Elias on the 75mm. The word challenge was "Atlantic." The response was "Pacific." I rolled the rubber band off my poncho, which was folded neatly over the rear of my belt. I removed my steel pot and slipped my head through the face opening and replaced my helmet. I hustled outside and paused to fasten my pistol belt around my waist. It was a full moon. Somebody was coming down the trench on the run. The sound of pounding boots got louder, and my first thought was that it was Elias coming back to make sure somebody was coming to relieve him. I was ready to chew ass. As bad as it was, you don't leave your post. The noise was almost on top of me, but I couldn't see anyone until they made the turn in the trench. I grabbed under my poncho for my .45 and braced my back against the trench wall. "Halt!" I challenged. "Atlantic!"

There was no response. I went into a crouched position and suddenly jumped up when I saw dark, shadowy, squirrel-like figures racing toward me.

"Jesus!" I hissed as they scrambled past me. "Goddamn big fuckers."

I scooted up the trench toward my gun bunker, cursing to myself, thinking that I had actually halted rats. I got the shivers just thinking about them. There must have been three or four of them. *Big as cats*, I thought, shaking my head.

The sound of metal on metal was like an explosion. I hurried along and saw Elias standing tall in the trench behind the 75mm recoilless rifle with an iron firing stake in his hand. Suddenly, he hopped backward and then took a quick step forward, swinging the iron stake like a baseball bat. Whack . . . thump . . . and then boing as the sound of iron hitting iron rang in the air.

"Little fuckers," Elias called out in a loud whisper that was followed by the unseen, muffled cries, "Quiet, goddamn it! Knock it off! Shut the fuck up!"

"Fuck you too, man," Elias sang back at the faceless soldiers in his soft, singsong Mexican accent.

"Shhh," I hissed. "Be quiet!"

Elias whipped around. "Oh, Joe, am I glad to see you, man. *Muchas gracias, amigo*. What happened, man? You're late."

"I just halted a pack of rats that wouldn't halt, and I'm not late," I replied indignantly. "And what the fuck do you think you're doing making so much noise?"

"The fucking rats are all over the gun bunker, man."

"Come on. You've got to suck it up, man. You're making so much noise you never heard me. If I was an infiltrator, you would be dead right now."

"You're right, man. I couldn't help it. I'd rather face the Chinks any day than rats. The LP out front is hearing something. Everybody's jittery. Here, take this, Joe," said Elias, handing me the iron stake. "You'll need it for our little friends, or they'll be all over you. Good luck, *amigo*," said Elias, beating a hasty retreat down the trench.

I took a deep breath and ducked into the gun bunker. I knelt down on a couple of sandbags piled up on top of each other and looked out of the opening facing no-man's-land. The moon lit up the outside, but it was dark and quiet inside. Everything was dead still. I could sense them, but I couldn't see them. I sat back with the iron firing stake lying across my lap. I knew they would be coming. I had visions of them creeping up on me, so I kept jerking my body and waving my arms to scare anything that was there. I thought I heard movement, but I wasn't sure. It was hard keeping my eyes straight ahead. I kept looking uncomfortably around me.

I checked my watch. The second hand hit the twelve. Twenty-six minutes to go. Now I knew why Elias thought I was late. Every minute was like an hour. I felt a light touch on my back, and I sprung to my feet, swinging the stake around me and hitting the end of the barrel of the 75mm with a loud *ping!*

"Shut up, asshole!" a whispered voice shouted out.

"Fuckers, dirty little fuckers," I screeched under my breath as I pulled the poncho hood up over my helmet and tied its strings tightly under my chin. *I'm not doing any better than Elias*, I thought. My face was now framed and sealed, and my body tented. I thrust my arms out with assorted grunts and hissing noises like a spasmodic samurai. I figured movement was my best defense. It would scare them away. I looked at my watch. Twenty-two minutes to go in this hellhole, and I needed a smoke. I needed a friend. I didn't know why cigarettes were always such good companions, but they were. I wouldn't be able to move around as much, but they would give me some comfort.

I undid my neck strings and lifted my poncho over my nose with my mouth inside. I found my cigarettes and lighter and leaned away from the bunker aperture, my back against the wall. I lit up, cupping smoke in my hand when *thump!* Jesus, something had tapped me on the helmet, and I leaped up, hitting my head on the low bunker roof, which brought my poncho strings sliding down my nose, knocking sparks on my chin and the lighted ash of my cigarette onto my field jacket.

"Oh, shit! Ouch," I yelped, dancing around slapping myself until I had put it out.

A chorus of "Who the fuck is that?" and other creative comments filled the night air from surrounding foxholes and bunkers. The field phone whistled, and I pulled it off of the wall.

"Upper Seventy-Five," I whispered heavily.

"Dee-jack-a-moe, CP, how's it going up there?"

"I think we're having a rat attack. People are sure as hell making a lot of noise up here scaring away rats." I said in an annoyed voice.

"We'll check it out. We don't want to telegraph our positions and invite mail call from ole Joe. Over and out," said the CP.

I knew I should have been more honest with my report, and I also knew that I couldn't stay in the bunker any longer, so I went outside into the trench behind my seventy-five, where I could be more mobile in scaring my little ancestors away.

CHAPTER 55

THE WITCH DOCTOR

**He was a funny kid who took his job seriously. For the
frontline soldier, he was their Johnny-on-the-Spot angel who
gave them first aid when they got hit. He was a short, skinny
kid from Harlem. When he laughed, which was as often
as I smiled, which was a lot, a gold front tooth sparkled in
the middle of pearly teeth. Often, he was the first step of a
wounded soldier's ticket home. The stenciled letters on his
black helmet spelled the words "Witch Doctor."**

I woke up to a gorgeous, warm, sunny morning that seemed
quieter and calmer than usual. I don't know why, but I thought
it was a Sunday. Maybe spring was in the air, and I knew that I
would be going home in a matter of weeks. At any rate, I was
feeling perky and wanted to be outside on this beautiful day.

I thought it might be nice to do a little gun cleaning and
sunbathing at the same time, so I went to our ammo bunker and
pulled out one of our light .30-caliber machine guns. I carried
the weapon and my shelter to a fairly level spot on the reverse
slope of our hill, pretty close to the supply road. I had a good
view of the road going down the hill and the woods behind it. I
took off my fatigue shirt and put my back to the sun. I kept my
fatigue cap on but removed my helmet. I broke down the weapon,
laying its parts neatly side-by-side on my canvas shelter. I began
by ramrodding the barrel and then applying light oil to it and the

330

other parts of the machine gun. My relaxation was disrupted by the puff and noise of an exploding artillery shell that had landed in the woods far across the road. I didn't rush, but I put my shirt and helmet back on. When another round landed significantly closer, I was motivated to move more quickly. I jumped up and pulled the four ends of the shelter together like one big diaper, jumbling all the parts together. When I heard a round land behind me, I panicked and ran. Instead of going back up the hill to my bunker, I headed downhill toward the supply road. I looked for the nearest shelter I could find while I struggled with my heavy load. I hobbled along. I wasn't quite sure what happened next. A round landed close behind me, and either my boot had caught a root or I had tripped on a rock or I had been lifted up by the blast, because the next thing I knew, I was flying through the air. It felt something like the air vibrations from the propeller blast of a flying boxcar. I lost everything as I tumbled down the hill and rolled into old, discarded, broken strands of barbed wire lying across the bottom of the embankment.

I don't think I lost consciousness. If I did, I don't remember it. I do remember lying there, stunned like someone had rattled my brain. I couldn't think straight. I remember the explosions. I knew I had been thrown down the hill. I could see blood on my hands. I couldn't see my whole body, but when I moved my fingers and other parts of my body, there was no sharp pain. I knew I was cut up because drops of blood dripped down my face. In spite of everything, I thought maybe I was okay. I became aware of more explosions, but they seemed far away.

I just lay there. I knew if I moved suddenly, I could hurt myself. I turned my head to its side and thankfully saw some soldiers running down the hill toward me. One soldier was way ahead of the others, leaping down the hill as graceful as a gazelle.

"Don't move. Don't talk," said the GI. "Gonna get you out of there." He smiled. A gold tooth greeted me with "Witch Doctor" stenciled across his helmet.

Hands and rifles appeared, suddenly freeing me from the tangled strands of wire. A compress was thrust across my forehead. "Where does it hurt?"

I couldn't be sure. I was helped up. Hunched over in a crouch, I walked gingerly with support, stamped my feet, twisted my body, shook my arms, and moved my shoulders back and forth. I was banged-up and sore but not in agony.

"I'm okay." I said warily. My head, hands, and arms bled but not profusely. I was stiff and sore but not in any real pain. "I'm okay. Just shaken up a bit," I said.

"Can you walk? Do you want a stretcher?"

"No, no, I can walk. Where's my shelter?" I asked suddenly.

The rhyming Burma Shave signs along the roads in Korea, which warned about the costs of lost weapons, went through my head. "I've got to find my shelter," I pleaded.

"Don't worry about that now. First, we're going to the aid station and get you cleaned up." The Witch Doctor smiled his wonderful smile. "You do a nice swan dive. We saw the artillery shells coming in, and then we saw this soldier, who looked like he was shot out of a canon, go flying down the hill and rolling into the wire. You a lucky dude, man. Probably write you up for a Purple Heart."

"What? Are you serious?"

"We've done it before. You're a casualty of war, man."

"No way," I said. "My mother would have a heart attack if she got a letter saying that her son was wounded in battle. She would become the real casualty and besides, the guys in my outfit would rib the shit out of me. Thanks but no thanks, and thanks for coming down for me. Rounds were still coming in. You didn't have to do that," I said, smiling and shaking his hand.

"That's my job, man. You're all finished here. Cleaned up and almost as good as new," said the Witch Doctor, smiling and flashing his beautiful gold tooth at me.

I later found all the parts of my light, air-cooled, .30-caliber machine gun.

CHAPTER 56

LUCK OF THE DRAW

Coming around a bend in the trench, Mule and Reimer were talking. We almost knocked into each other. I stopped. We slapped leather. It was a quick draw. I won. I was the fastest gunslinger of the day. I wondered sometimes how much life depended on the luck of the draw. George and Anderson were distracted. Alcanter, a replacement assigned to my squad, requested a transfer to a rifle company because "that was where the action was." He died while on patrol. He could have played the cards he had been dealt and stayed with me. Would it have made a difference?

"Tonight, my bunker, 2400 hours, on the QT, a surprise," said Reimer.

"A reward for my quick draw," I kidded.

"No questions. Just be there."

At midnight, I banged on George's hoochie door.

"Who's there?"

"It's Joe, Hollywood Joe," I said.

"What's the password?"

"Fuck!" I shouted.

The door flew open.

"You!" a voice replied.

George stood there with a panatela jutting out of his huge mountain of teeth and thrust a beer into my hands. I was

333

dumbfounded. Clouds of billowy, gray-white cigar smoke surrounded him. I could make out Vanny and Coleman puffing away with beers in their hands and Ole Tuck with a wad bulging out of his cheek.

George put his arm around me. "My brother is a genius. The guys back in company had choggies bring it up yesterday and surprised the hell out of me."

Reimer's brother was a Korean War veteran. George told me that his brother had met a girl on R & R with whom he had fallen in love, and when he got discharged from the service, he had returned to Japan and married her. Now he was selling American cars in Tokyo and speaking pretty good Japanese. He was a sharp salesman who knew all the angles and had good connections with the top brass from selling cars to them in Tokyo. He had been in close touch with George since George had gotten his orders for FECOM (Far Eastern Command), which included Korea.

"Everything in scrip," said George. "A buck a hundred. Spades double. If you go down in spades, it's double-double."

"Okay. Dealer stays out, and I need your intercom to tell my crew where I am."

"Hey, Hollywood, this is a private party!" yelled Van Syckle, calling me by my sometimes nickname.

"Yeah, no more invitations. Pinochle players only," bellowed Coleman.

"Thanks to my brother and his wife," said George in agreement. "You can take your calls from here."

"No signals. Anyone caught cheating gets shot between the eyes," said Ole Tuck with his crazy grin.

"Agreed?" asked George with a straight face.

Everyone chimed in agreement, but Ole Tuck got me to pause. He was more animated than the rest of us were. Central Casting would pick him first to play a crazed psychopathic killer in one of their movies.

"I deal," said Coleman.

I listened to the check-ins on the half-hour. Everything was quiet outside. Inside, the cards couldn't be dealt soon enough after a game was won or lost. It was two against one at the end.

I put my cards in order, and my heart skipped a beat. I tried to keep cool as I spread my cards, which showed a spade flush with all of the aces, the jack of diamonds, and two clubs, one of them a king. I closed my cards nonchalantly and listened to the distant thunder of artillery. I thought, *A four-hundred-spade hand. Maybe more if I can do a little finessing.*

I opened the bid. "Three hundred spades," I said.

All eyes zeroed in on me.

"Four hundred hearts," said George, puffing on his cigar.

"Are you kidding me?"

"Nope, four hundred, sweethearts," he said smugly.

I smirked, looking at him in disbelief.

An artillery round came in fairly close as I blurted out, "Four-fifty spades."

The intercom came alive with chatter from the gun bunkers.

Everybody passed and started to get up. "I got it in spades. I threw down my hand, showing my meld and the tricks that I would take.

"Bullshit," said George, turning over the cards, showing how they would stop me.

The next explosion hit, and everybody headed for the bunker door.

"You don't make it, Hollywood," shouted Coleman. "You lose a club trick. Maybe two, and you go down."

"You gotta pay up!" leered Tuck.

"No way," I said as I rushed toward the door. I pushed it open and took a step outside. George grabbed my cartridge belt from behind, which brought me back.

"Don't be in such a rush. Let's—" Wham!

A piece of shrapnel the size of a softball, red-hot and burning, had embedded itself into the sandbag next to where my head had been. I stood there as the others froze with me. I looked in awe at this jagged piece of smoldering iron that would have taken my head off. I looked at George. No words had to be spoken. I took a deep breath and bolted toward my gun bunker as fast as my legs would take me.

Days later, we eventually played out the hand, and I did lose. I went down-double in spades, which was disgraceful for me. I sent the plays of the game home to my dad, who belonged to a pinochle club and was an excellent player. Weeks later, he sent back the play-by-play, and the key trick I should have taken to win the game. Even with the luck of the draw, I played the cards that were dealt to me wrong. I had made one costly mistake at the end of the game and lost, but it could have ended a lot worse if it hadn't been for George delaying me at the door of his bunker. That would have been my second costly mistake. Only it would have been an ill-fated and an unfortunate ending to the evening. In combat, as in life, it really does come down to the luck of the draw.

CHAPTER 57

Frank's Last Letter

I was always glad to hear from Frank, especially now that we were close to our thirty-six points and eligible to rotate home. The question was when. Our dream was always of going to Korea together and coming home safe and sound on the same ship together. We were closer to that reality now.

Happy Fourth of July, Pal,

I got great news, and I got shitty news. I hope you're sitting down for this one. Squizzy is dead. He got killed in a night jump at Fort Campbell. The good news is that I'm rotating Kemo Sabe, which means that you're rotating too, if you haven't gotten the word already. Ain't life a bitch? I feel terrible. What a nice kid. I still can't get over it.

I got a letter that Mike and Squizzy were on maneuvers and Squizzy's stick landed in water and he drowned along with two other troopers. I guess the wind had something to do with it. They probably got caught up in their risers. Do you remember the cadre at Benning telling us stories about night jumps and how a road and river can look the same and if you don't figure it out, you're in deep shit? All the things that you had to do were mind-boggling. Get rid of your helmet, hit your release, catch your risers under your armpits, check the direction of the wind,

337

and let go just as you hit the water. While you're under the water, you were to swim in the opposite direction to your chute. I often wondered about the guys who couldn't swim. I'm glad we didn't have to do any of that stuff. Mike was devastated. They were such good friends. A lot of the guys from the Seventh Regiment went to the funeral. It was a tough one, poor Squizzy.

It makes you think. We might have been with them after the big hassle we had at Benning getting those reassignments. I guess we made the right decision. Here we are you and me, fighting a war in Korea and going home together. What a twist of fate.

Sully rotated home in May, and that son of a gun never said good-bye to me. He says to me that he's going down to the CP and that he would be right back. The next thing I see is Tim in the back of a deuce and a half with a couple of other guys, driving down the main supply route, going to the rear. Stu followed a couple of days later.

Right after that, my company commander asked me if I would be interested in working with technical liaison officers back at battalion, and I said yes before I even knew what it was. Now I'm working with technical liaison officers who interrogate South Koreans who infiltrate into North Korea across the Mundung-ni Valley. Have I got some great stories to tell you!

Would you believe that my orders for rotation came on the Fourth of July? I get called down to headquarters, and my lieutenant tells me that I'm going home. A truck is coming up in the morning to take me to Chunchon and that I should be ready by 0800 hours. I couldn't speak. The lieutenant shakes my hand and then pulls out a quarter bottle of scotch, and we drink to my going home. I thanked him and told him that I would like to buy what's left of the bottle for the guys in my hooch. "Here," he says, "Keep it. It's my present to you."

The guys in my bunker all congratulate me, and we finish the scotch. One guy named Cozy Cole, who's a real hustler, produces a five-gallon water can of his own brew. It's a two-week-old concoction of yeast, juice, raisins, sugar, water, and God knows

*what. We called up the chaplain's assistant, who had an accordion
and played songs for us. We all got pretty stupid.*

*You've heard me talk about George Underwood. He's an old
mortar man and buddy of mine from Fox Company. He's back
here with me. The guy's a technical genius and funny too. On
the sly, he's rigged up a system like a rocket launcher that can
go on the top of his bunker. We all go outside, and the accordion
is playing while George loads up one of those new 3.5 mortar
shells, and he hooks it up with a truck battery in some way.*

*"This is for you, Frank," he says and turns to the accordion
player and says, "Okay, on the count of three, 'He's Movin On.'
Ready? Well one . . . two . . . and one, two, three, play it!"*

*'Old Joe Chink comin down the pass, playin the burp gun
boogie on the colonel's ass. He's movin' on . . . he'll soon be
gone—"*

*George touched the two exposed terminal wires together and
whoosh! The goddamn shell went wobbling into the air and over
enemy lines. God's honest truth. It was a hell of a send-off.*

*I can't wait, Joe. We should be going back on the same boat.
Stay loose.*

Meet you in Inchon.

Frank

CHAPTER 58

FEAR OF DYING

I was shaken awake. Reimer beamed down at me. "My brother pulled it off. I'm going home. He wrote to General Gaither. Told him he was a Korean War veteran living in Tokyo and would like to see his kid brother before he rotated home. I'm gone. Jeep's waiting. You're next, man. Take care. Catch you in Rockaway. *Sayonara*, Joe."

I felt like I had just gotten the wind knocked out of me. I couldn't move. I just lay there in my sleeping bag. I was glad for George and sad for myself. We had come into the company at the same time, and I had assumed that we would go home together. I was wrong! Enough for assumptions, I was still here, and he was gone. How come? Why was that? Was it because someone was able to pull strings? There were always exceptions to the rule. There was the right way and the army way. It just wasn't fair. We were dealing with life and death here. Every second counted.

Right now there were a lot of short-timers in the outfit, so we would need a lot of replacements. I had never really thought about it before, but now that it affected me, I thought about it all the time. I wondered how it worked at company headquarters. What was the process? One replacement came in, and five guys were waiting for him to replace them. How did it work? How did they figure who went and who stayed? Did they count the exact day, hour, and minute that you came into the company? Was how much time you had spent on line important? How many firefights you had been in? Patrols you had been on? I was a short-timer, so it was important for me to know these things. Every extra moment on the front line could be your last moment in life.

I had been chomping at the bit. I had been in harm's way too long. I was obsessed with going home. After Mike and Squizzy had gotten their orders changed from going to Korea to going stateside, bad things seemed to pile up. Squizzy had died in a night jump at Fort Bragg. Rock had gotten killed from a mortar. Rumor had it that he had died from exploding dynamite caps while he had been working on his bunker. After we had switched gun positions with the third squad, Mase and Shev had been mortally wounded along with St. Claire, a rifleman who had happened by. Weeks earlier, switching from my squad to a rifle company, Alcantar had stepped on a mine. He had died on a stretcher outside my bunker while medics had tried to save him. I kept his M-1 rifle. I needed it for comfort. It was my favorite weapon, and I felt more protected with it than my carbine or pistol. I had already come to the realization that it wasn't always the next guy who got killed or wounded. It could just be that I didn't make it off of this damn hill alive.

I got a call from our CP. I should come down and get two new replacements for our gun section. None of them were replacements for me. They were nice kids. They were big, fresh-faced, eager, and lost. I led them up the trench to our gun bunker. I said hello to guys we passed by. The replacements said nothing. They took everything in and stared at me like I was some sort of curiosity. They were quietly checking me out while trying to understand their new environment. They were looking for information.

I wasn't sure how upbeat and positive I could be. Peace talks between the UN and Communist leaders had started up again. This was a positive, but the fighting on line had gotten worse. We were being bombarded regularly with Chink 76s, artillery, heavy mortars, and machine gun fire. Our F-86s put on a dazzling show for us with daily air strikes dropping napalm and strafing enemy positions. Both sides tried to inflict heavy casualties on each other. We were the bargaining chips in the negotiations at Panmunjom. How could I tell these replacements that they had come here at the worst possible time?

I stopped by our 75-RR bunker and introduced Elias and Martinez. I went into my spiel: "My name's Donohue, and I am the leader of the fourth squad, second section of 75mm recoilless rifles. Welcome to the Mighty Mike Company and the Dragon Gun Platoon," I said and smiled. "We are the rifleman's best heavy weapon and at their beck and call. We got it when they need it. We have four rifle crews divided up into two sections of two squads each. I don't know where you will end up because we're receiving more replacements each day," I said. I smiled, knowing that one of them would eventually be for me and I could get the hell out of there. I was tired of this bullshit.

"Follow me," I said and brought them up to the sleeping bunker to meet our KATUSAs and give them a quick orientation. We huddled around a makeshift table of old ammo crates. I went through the drill of providing routine information and fielding questions from them in return.

Before I finished, incoming rounds of artillery landed fairly close. All eyes went to me. I acted as if it was no sweat, but incoming rounds always brought a jolt of adrenalin. After all, you were being targeted for death. Somebody was trying to kill you.

I tried to be cool, explaining what was happening. I got on the horn to hear our guns reports. "Gun positions along with outposts and listening posts report negative movement," I said. "Not to worry. It's not an assault. It's probably an artillery barrage. It's afternoon. Chinks are night fighters. We don't sweat it. We're on standby alert."

The tempo picked up, and rounds came in close enough to have shrapnel spray the bunker. When it became more intense, I told them to pick a spot and hit the deck.

I grabbed the phone and threw myself on a bottom bunk. I pressed into the sandbag wall and listened on the horn. We were getting rocked. The bunker shook, and I started to repeat to myself, "Protect me, dear God. Protect me, dear God." In desperation, I asked God for a sign that I would make it. I never prayed so hard for anything in my whole life.

Suddenly, I smelled ocean air. It was unmistakable. It was the fresh, salty sea air of Rockaway. It was real.

Dee-jack-a-moe yelled my name. "Get into the trenches, now!"

I hung up the phone. "We're going outside. Lock and load."

"I need clips," cried one of the replacements. "Me too," said another.

I quickly grabbed an unopened ammo can of .30-caliber rounds from under a rack and broke the lid with my trench knife. I was mesmerized. My hands fumbled and shook as if they belonged to someone else.

"Let me try," said one of the replacements, using his bayonet to pry open the can. Hands greedily scooped up rounds, and clips were quickly slammed home into rifles.

"Okay, safeties on. Let's go!" I said and went outside.

"I'll man the phone," I said to Elias. I was embarrassed by what had happened in the sleeping bunker. I shook my head from side to side. What must those poor, green replacements be thinking?

The barrage lifted. I cradled Gil's M-1 rifle reassuringly in my arms and leaned back against the bunker wall, scanning the terrain in front of the aperture. I felt better. I was more relaxed. I smelled the ocean in Rockaway. I had my sign. I was going to see George this summer in Rockaway after all.

CHAPTER 59

HEARTBREAK AND JOY

I started the month of July with great expectations. This was the month when I would be going home. Unfortunately, the Fortieth Division left the Punchbowl and went back to Heartbreak Ridge, making me uncertain as to when I would be going home. The month became a roller-coaster ride. My emotions went from the comic to the pathetic, from the absurd to the euphoric, from heartbreak to joy.

I was caught completely off guard. Orders came down for us to saddle up and get ready to move out. The whole line jumped into action. Rumors sprung up, and in a sudden frenzy of activities, they fed upon themselves. First, I heard that we were hooking up with the Forty-Fifth Division to spearhead a big offensive into North Korea that would break the stalemate at Panmunjom. Another rumor had us going back to Kumwha in the Iron Triangle area. The story that seemed most likely was that we would relieve our Division's 160th Regiment at Koje-do and guard war prisoners. You could pick your rumor. They were all bad. I never heard a good one like we were going home, so we thought that might be a good rumor to start, but nobody believed that one.

Two days later, it happened. We were visited by an advanced party of the Twentieth ROK Division from the Kumwha-Kumsong sector in the Iron Triangle. It looked like we were switching

344

places. Just my luck, here I was, a short-timer waiting for my rotation orders, and we're moving to another part of the front. Now they'd never find me.

The day before, I had received a bubbly letter from Frank. He was going home. He was sure that when I had received this letter, I would be going home too. He was all excited. We'd meet in Inchon and go home together.

I hoped Frank was right. I wanted to believe him, but I had my doubts. It was not just me who was making the move but my whole regiment. My regiment was being relieved by the Twentieth Republic of Korea Division, which could foul up my rotation home. I'd probably get an extension of duty. The next letter I received from Frank would probably be from New York while I was part of an invasion force to God knows where.

Waiting was the hard part. My squad was packed and ready to go. I got a call from the CP. Advanced units of the Twentieth ROK Army were here. There were some South Korean soldiers on the supply road with a truck of supplies. "Go down and give them a hand and show them to their bunkers," I was told. I sent Elias down to them with our KATUSAs.

Minutes later, I got a call from Elias. "Hey, Jose, they got a load of shit in their wagon. Live grenades are bouncing around on packs and belts. Open gasoline, ammo cans, and half-eaten food are mixed in together. Nobody wants to touch it, man. Come take a look."

I went down to the road. Our KATUSAs, Pak, Ahn, Yang, and Choi were arguing with the South Korean soldiers.

"No good, Joe. Number ten," said Yang, the elder statesman for our KATUSAs. "Bang, bang, have yes, no good" said Yang. "Number huckin' ten!"

"Tell them I will give them tape." I made a wrapping motion with my fist and pointed to the grenade pins. "We help them unload after that. Otherwise it's no-no," I said, shaking my head.

A lean, bare-headed, effeminate Korean officer in neatly pressed fatigues with a bright red scarf around his neck emerged from a roadside bunker. Smoking a cigarette, he stood motionless and looked at us without any expression. His eyes squinted as if he was sizing up the situation. He bellowed something in a harsh tone, and a young boy ran out of the bunker and hurried over to us. He spoke to one of the Korean soldiers, and they both went back to the officer, who stood with his palm up and dragged on his cigarette. He screamed at them and then suddenly hauled off and cracked one of the soldiers across the face and lashed into a diatribe that sent the boy back into the bunker and the humiliated ROK soldier back to us. He started jabbering ferociously to Wang, who turned calmly to me and shook his head.

The officer gave me a defiant look and put out his cigarette, and without a word, he returned to his bunker. I brought the ROKs up to our positions without their wagon of supplies. I moved our 75mm and its ammunition to the service road with our other weapons and equipment and boarded our troop transports and waited as usual.

What an arrogant bastard, I thought. That haughty son of a bitch was insulted that our KATUSAs kicked up a fuss, and I supported them. He never said a word to me. I felt like I was being slapped in the face. Maybe I was being too sensitive or too edgy, but I didn't need that kind of an incident to end my day. I was so pissed that I would have loved to punch that pompous asshole in the mouth and wipe that smirk off of his face.

The word spread through the trucks before anyone told us anything official. We were relieving the Forty-Fifth Infantry Division. My spirits zoomed. I was relieving Frank. He was just over on our left flank. We weren't moving far. Maybe I wouldn't get lost after all. We were going back to Heartbreak Ridge and Sandbag Castle. It was like déjà vu all over again. Not only was I relieving Frank's regiment, but I was returning to the area where I had first gone on line and received my baptism by fire. It was like coming around full circle. To me, it was a good omen.

The bad part was that my new gun position was next to an exposed part of the line called "Skyline Drive." When you crossed it, you had to duck down low and run like hell so you wouldn't be silhouetted against the skyline. At this spot, the Chinese held the high ground from across the valley. They sniped, used their 76s, 82s, and fired their maxims at us. It was a real danger zone. You avoided it at all costs.

I didn't go out into the trenches any more than I had to. If a hot meal made its way up the hill, I didn't leave my bunker. Everybody respected the fact that I had thirty-six points. I had a wood ammo box nailed to the sandbag wall of my sleeping bunker filled with C-rations and cans of food from home.

Someone yelled, "Chow's coming up, spaghetti and meatballs!"

In a flash, I was hungry. It was my favorite army meal. How could I resist chopped meat with noodles of spaghetti floating in a thick, greasy red sauce? I put on my battered steel pot, grabbed my canteen cup and all-purpose knife from Japan, which housed a foldout fork and spoon, and found the staggered chow line.

Some guys came up behind me and started shooting the breeze. "Hey, Donohue, when did you start playing hero?" one of them asked me.

I turned around. "What can I tell you? I would go to war for this meal."

"Without your flak jacket?" asked the soldier behind me.

I was taken back for a split second. Before my head jerked down and my chin hit my fatigue shirt, I knew. "Holy shit!" I said incredulously.

My eyes told the whole story. I thought they would pop out of my head. Slowly shaking my head with an 'how stupid can I be' grin on my face, I walked quickly off of the chow line and fought the urge to run. I passed looks that showed everything from amusement to empathy for my predicament. I walked away from my favorite meal and headed back to my bunker, wincing and waiting for the gook round to find me without my flak jacket on. How could I have been so careless?

"I wouldn't look so down if I was going home tomorrow," said a smiling Lieutenant Olsen coming toward me. I looked up, not sure what I had just heard. "You're out of here tomorrow with the morning mail."

I couldn't believe my ears. "I'm going home?"

"You are *sayonara*."

I liked the sound of those words. I kept repeating them to myself. One moment, I was running scared, and the next moment, I was running happy. I was going home! "Rotation done hit me," I said with a smile.

Pusan Harbor South Korea, September 1952

Waiting for transportation in Pusan assembly area

Truck route through slums of Pusan

Meeting Van Syckle, a fellow 40th Division replacement at Chunchon

Passing a quad fifty (four 50 caliber machine guns
mounted on a truck)

Meeting up with GIs from our 140th tank battalion

First assigned .50 caliber machine gun bunker on Heartbreak Ridge
with tank on top, October 1952

Front view of gun position

Checking the Perimeter around my Bunker

Corporal Colon, assistant gunner

Lieutenat Brewster, mortar platoon and Warrant Officer Kelly with
Lieutenant Donald Gottshall, Commander of "Mike" Company

Warning signs on Heartbreak Ridge

Firing Sector on Heartbreak

Aerial view of Heartbreak

Outside of Lyle Olson's bunker

Corporal Dee-jack-a-moe (right) with buddy

Company mess boys after bringing up chow

Eating hot chow on the line on a frostbiting day

Merry Christmas
and
Happy New Year
from
The Korean People's Army
The Chinese People's Volunteers

KOREA 1952-3

"Peace" Chinese Christmas cards

American Soldiers:

We are wishing you a Merry Christmas and a Happy New Year. We also have something to talk to you about.

Christmas is a day of peace and happiness. And a day for family reunions.

But this Christmas, for you, there is no peace. You are far away from those you love, in Korea, a country you never heard of three years ago—hundreds of thousands of casualties ago. Your family longs for you across the wide Pacific. Will they ever see you again? Will you ever see them?

You've been told you came here to stop "Communist aggression." But what do your own eyes and head tell you? The Koreans are fighting in their own country. The Chinese are defending their own nearby borders. Neither of these peoples ever dreamed of invading the United States. It is U.S. troops who have come here with bombs, napalm, germs and every other weapon of mass murder.

Bombs and guns can't break the spirit of the Koreans and Chinese, because they are guarding their homes. What about you? Is there any reason why you should be here instead of home with your folks? You are risking death or crippling wounds to hold one or two bare Korean mountains. What for?

The heartless men who sent you here have sent American soldiers to Europe. Those soldiers too are told that they must protect different countries from "Red aggression." But everywhere they go, they hear the people yelling, "Yanks, go home!" This wasn't the way the GI's were greeted everywhere in world War II, when they were really fighting against aggressors—the Nazis and Japanese warlords. Then they got

Letter to American soldiers

flowers. So something is wrong. What is it?

The truth is that American soldiers today are helping oppressors, not fighting them. You know how the Koreans "love" Syngman Rhee! You know how the Chinese "loved" Chiang Kai-shek whom they kicked out in spite of $6 billion worth of U.S. aid. In Japan the U.S. is letting convicted war criminals out of jail and giving them a new army to play with. In Germany, it's the same. In France, in Italy, they back governments which have sold out their own peoples for dollars, governments which order the police out every time working people strike for a living wage. Isn't this true? You know it is.

Why are Americans sent abroad to do this kind of dirty work, the exact opposite of every fine thing America ever stood for, in a way that would make Washington, Jefferson, Lincoln turn over in their graves if they knew it? Because the American government has been stolen from the American people by greedy Big Business which cares nothing about your life or anyone else's but only for its lousy profits. The corporations have made more money since the Korean war than they ever did before, out of arms orders for which the American people are paying through higher taxes, higher prices in every grocery store and the lives of their sons—YOUR lives. That's why the Brass Hats are throwing monkey wrenches into the talks at Panmunjom which could have succeeded a year ago. That's why they want more war everywhere, not peace.

Every people on earth is getting wise to this new kind of business— Murder for Profit. Americans at home are getting wise to it too. Millions are asking for peace and getting fed up with lies. American fathers and mothers have refused medals sent to them after their boys died in Korea. Hundreds of American pilots with decorations for courage in World War II have refused to fly in Korea. Tens of thousands of young men are dodging the draft. This is not because they are cowards. It is not because they

Continuation of letter

aretn't ptriotic. It's because they are beginning to understand that they've been fooled.

The patriotic thing is to fight for peace! The patriotic thing is to fight for friendship, not war, between peoples! What harm can peace do to any country, to America? What good does war bring to any nation, Americans included? The real traitors, the real criminals, are the few who send troops, thousands of miles away so they can rake in dollars. They think they own America, and for that matter the world. They think they own you. Who gave them the right? What kind of free American citizen are you when they can shove you into uniform, pack you in a boat, and send you to all ends of the earth for no other reason than this?

We, the Chinese People's Volunteers, are writing you this letter. We came here because, after we cleaned out the dirty grafter Chiang Kai-shek, you stormed into the land of our neighbor and threatened the first chance we ever had to build up our country. We don't want to fight anyone. We want to build in peace. We are in favour of peaceful coexistence and trade for every people in the world.

Don't believe the Big Money boys and politicians at home. They are no different from Chiang Kai-shek whom we ran out of China. Don't do what they want. Do what the people want.

We offer you peace and friendship. America for Americans. Korea for the Koreans. China for the Chinese. Why should not we all, Korean soldiers, Chinese soldiers, American soldiers join our efforts for peace? Then we don't need to be soldiers any more. Then next Christmas, if not this one, can really be merry. Then we can have a really Happy New Year in 1953! Let's make it so!

The Chinese People's Volunteers

Completion of letter signed by The Chinese People's Volunteers

LOVE LETTER FROM GI's SWEETHEART

Safe Conduct Passes

Warrant Officer Kelly and driver on supply road

Chuck Mason (left) 75 RR gunner with buddies

Bunker destroyed by Chinese artillery

Sergeants Dale West and Lyle Olson checking gun positions

Frank and Tim Sullivan of the 45th Infantry Division on the
Punchbowl, March 1953

Outside platoon tents at Inje river reserve, March 1953

Mike Company's 75 RR platoon after inspection,
before going back on line

Dee-jack-a-moe and Joe getting ready to go back on line

Lyle and Joe ready to go

Joe and Rock on the way up to the Punchbowl

Rock and Young on their water cooled .30 caliber machine gun

Lyle Olson MG Squad Leader

75 Recoilless rifle team

Lt. General J.D. White X Corps Commander and Lt. Col.Clement,
Commander 245 th Tank Batallion

40th Infantry Division Commander, General Joseph Cleland

Sleeping bunkers on the Punchbowl

Reverse slope of Punchbowl MLR

Radioman Clarance (Tiny) Meeks and Leahy outside of
communications bunker

Joe and George Reimer, on line, with tank in backgrounds

Tree stumps, with uniform shreds, in front of gun bunker

Sighting in on the 75 recoilless rifle with assistant gunner Elias on left

Outside of 75's platoon command post waiting for Jeep to R & R

Mac waiting for me to go on R & R with him to Japan, April 1953

PART 5—RETURNING

WAR VETERANS

CHAPTER 60

SEPARATION MANIA

I couldn't wait until morning. I knew I wouldn't be safe until I was off the front line. I saw too many war movies where the old veteran was told he had been discharged from the service only to get killed before he could leave. I figured there must have been some truth to that. Otherwise, it wouldn't have been a big part of so many movies. I didn't want to be that soldier, and I wasn't the only veteran who thought that way.

I said good-bye to my buddies. I guess I became an instant celebrity because there were guys whom I hardly knew that dropped by my bunker to wish me well. I was the lucky dog going home. I wished it was over, and I was gone. Each guy brought a special thought to me. Flashbacks of moments exploded from person to person. I smiled a lot and wisecracked with the Mule, Ole Tuck, McChesney, Martinez, Elias, Coleman, Van Syckle, Yang, Pak, and Choi. These were my men.

I gave away my books, precious cans of fruit and soup, tea crackers, flashlight batteries, and the rest of my stash to the guys in the bunker. They all had that "I wish I was going with you" look. I was sorry they were staying, but I wasn't sorry I was leaving. It was my time to go. Their time would come too. Finally, Dee-jack-a-moe's voice came over the intercom.

"Joe, get your ass and gear down here on the double. You're outta here, trooper. The jeep from battalion is coming up for you. It's *sayonara* time, old buddy."

I tried not to show my overeagerness. I gave some extra pairs of socks and Gil's M-1 rifle to Elias, my assistant gunner. "*Sayonara, amigo.*"

My departure was fast. I went down to the command post on the double. Lieutenant Blackburn, who was not one of my favorite soldiers, was the first to wish me well in the only way he could. "It was my pleasure to have you serve under me, corporal. Good luck."

I smiled, knowing he didn't care for the pleasure of my company. The flashback for him came easily. When he joined our company a few months ago as our first Negro officer, he tried to impress everyone with his superior knowledge of heavy weapons. Our 75-RR section often manned machine guns with our machine gun platoon. At the time, Blackburn came up. We were covering bunkers that housed .50-caliber machine guns. Admittedly, we were not specialists. Lieutenant Blackburn asserted himself immediately by demonstrating the proper way to check for the correct spacing and play of our gun barrels. He admonished us for being sloppy. There was no question that he was an expert in heavy weapons. We used the feeling/hearing method. In other words, we clicked off the tension on the barrel by feel and sound. He went by the book and was absolutely correct. He then proceeded to show us how to correct the tension on the barrels of two of our weapons by using a gauging tool. In his last demonstration, he pulled back on the bolt and pressed his thumbs to fire, and the barrel blew, sending a small piece of shrapnel into his thigh. It was ironic that in all the times we had used our own primitive way, we had never had an accident. That was an embarrassing moment for the lieutenant. He would never live it down in the eyes of the men. I knew he was glad to see me go because I was one of those who reminded him of that fiasco.

The driver of the jeep was a clean, neat, young soldier in freshly laundered fatigues. "Hop in the back. I have to pick up two more men," he said authoritatively.

A hundred feet up the road brought us to another rifle company. A beaming sergeant waved to us and rushed down to the road and made a bee line toward us.

"Battalion jeep?" he asked.

Both the driver and I shook our heads. "Get in the back," said the young private.

"Goin' home?" asked the sergeant as he jumped into the backseat with me.

"You got it," I said, and we shook hands.

He was the closest thing I ever saw to a young Groucho Marx. He would have been a perfect twin. Jack Farazzi was from Boston, and his thick accent left no doubt about it. He had quick movements and a hearty handshake. His black, Fuller Brush mustache and thick eyeglasses under bushy eyebrows reminded me of Colon, my assistant gunner who had pissed in his pants when I had told him to fix bayonets.

Our driver pulled away and started up the road to another part of the hill.

"What are you doing?" asked Jack.

"I have one more pickup," replied the driver.

"Where?" asked Jack.

"Up the road a way," said the young driver.

"You can't go up there," said Jack incredulously. "That's Skyline Drive."

"That's right," I said. "You can't go up there. It's a goddamn shooting gallery."

"Hey, I have my orders, man. It'll take a few more minutes."

"No way," blurted Jack. "Turn around."

"I can't do that. I have another pickup. Just cool it, man. We'll get there."

In a quick, jerking motion, the bolt of Sergeant Farazzi's carbine clanged forward, and he jammed the nozzle into the back of the soldier's neck.

"Turn this fucking jeep around now, or I'll blow your fucking, goddamn head off!" screamed Jack, which brought the jeep to a screeching halt.

There was a long pause and then a frenetic backup and quick U-turn on the narrow road. "Okay. No sweat, sergeant. No sweat. Take it easy," pleaded our impassioned driver.

The young soldier was totally shaken. "I'm just doing my job. Take it easy. I'm going back."

I got nervously giddy looking at Jack's wild, bulging eyes and spastic movement. I was taken aback myself, uncertain as to how this comic-tragic scene might end.

"Don't fuck with us," I said menacingly, drawing the bolt back on my .45 and putting my face close behind the driver's ear. "We're going home. We've been up here a long time, and we're a little edgy. We're going home over your dead body if that's the way you want it, but we're going home. No more stops. You understand?"

The young driver shook his head.

Jack looked at me and winked.

CHAPTER 61

NEAT AND CLEAN AND CIVILIZED

You just didn't rotate home by taking a cab from Heartbreak Ridge to Kimpo Airport for a flight to the States. It didn't work that way. You had to be processed. You had to be sanitized. Your appearance and demeanor had to be changed so you could make the transition from caveman to gentleman, from combat soldier to civilian.

My first night at Battalion was reassuring. Comparatively speaking, things were fairly neat and orderly. I stretched out on a cot and read one of my books. Before I racked out, I thought about my kid brother's eighth birthday that had just passed and that I had to bring him something special from Japan. My daydreaming was rudely interrupted by the crude whine of a siren and someone shouting, "Incoming! Incoming!"

I was totally taken by surprise. It was like a Chinese fire drill. Steel pots went on, and everybody started running like hell out of the tent. I followed suit and squeezed into a two-foot-wide trench outside my sleeping tent that wouldn't have protected a dwarf. The old fears suddenly came back. Despite the fact that I was several miles behind the front line, I was out in the open, surrounded by darkness with no cover or protection. I looked up at a beautiful, starry sky, anxiously waiting for the first shells to fall.

The bombardment never came. Twice during the night, false alarms occurred in the wee hours of the morning, ruining all chances of getting any sleep at all. Battalion rear wasn't very restful. It was within range of Chink artillery and too close for comfort. When I learned that I would be spending a second night in the area, I got a little paranoid. Joe Chink knew where I was. He was gunning for me. Although I wasn't in the game anymore, it didn't matter. I had a price on my head. I had thirty-six points. The enemy targeted all veterans who were on their way home. How come nobody knew that except us?

The next day was better. We boarded trucks and drove farther back to the rear. We moved to our regimental headquarters and out of artillery range. For the first time since coming off of the hill, I felt safe. Of course, there was always the threat of infiltrators, but I wasn't thinking negative anymore. When we off-loaded from the deuce and a half and I heard the familiar barrack soldier's orders, I knew I had made it.

"All incoming troops will fall in for roll call and tent assignments immediately."

We were informed of the time to assemble to be denuded, deloused, and showered before given a complete change of socks, skivvies, and fatigues. We were also told to bring any unissued items with us, including war trophies, souvenirs, personal weapons, and anything else we wished to bring home. We would be given claim forms for retrieval when we got to Japan. If we didn't sign a claim form, then any unissued items found in shakedown inspections would be confiscated.

"Don't believe it," someone said. "You give it up, and you'll never see it again. Better to try to smuggle it in. Hide it and find it later. If it can be broken down and separated out, then do it. You can always put it together at another time."

After these words of wisdom, it seemed like half the tent disappeared outside to hide their contraband. It was funny seeing guys try to figure out how they were going to outsmart the army and beat the system.

We lined up in two columns across from each other. Two tables were set up outside a large hut. For those guys who went by the rules, clerks collected and tagged all sorts of incredible stuff. There were fountain pen pistols, snub-nosed .38-caliber police specials, numerous handguns, hunting knives, brass knuckles, dummy grenades, and a real grenade in one case. The assortment of non-army-issued stuff guys carried with them on line was amazing. We stripped naked except for our boots. We carried our clothes in our arms.

There was a lot of joking and joshing around going on. There were a lot of skinny, scarred bodies on those lines. I talked to guys who had been wounded two and three times. I couldn't understand why replacements weren't found for these guys. They had paid their dues in blood, tears, and disfigurement, never mind the psychological pain, and their rewards had been purple hearts and returns to the front lines.

Near the tables to the entrance of the hut, two open-ended, fifty-gallon drums of steaming hot water were set on top of pits of burning wood and coal. On the sides of the drums were young Korean kids wielding six-foot-long bamboo poles. When I got to the tent entrance, I dropped my fatigues on the ground to one side and my socks and underwear on the other side. The boys scooped up the clothing with the poles and dropped them into the different vats of boiling water.

Except for my dog tags, I stood naked in boots without socks, and then I was sprayed with a powdered disinfectant before I could enter the tent. The pump-action cans made me think of an old commercial where bugs and roaches were invading a house and the owners yelled, "Quick, Henry, the Flit!" which instantly exterminated the dirty, little, pestering vermin.

Once inside the tent, my boots were collected, and a number was given to me so that I could pick them up later. After I showered, I received fresh underwear and socks. Clean fatigues were issued with noticeable bleach stains from some sort of liquid disinfectant with had a distinctive, strong, unpleasant odor. I got my boots back, wiped them off, stepped out from the other side of the hut, and joined my buddies who were getting dressed. It was a glorious, delightful, warm, sunshiny day. I felt as if I had been born again. I had been baptized, sterilized, and sanitized. I was neat and clean and civilized. I was ready to rejoin society as a normal member of the human race.

CHAPTER 62

GUARDING GI PRISONERS

I had been working my way slowly back from the line. I spent a few days going from company to battalion to regiment and then to division headquarters. My last stop in Korea would be Inchon Harbor and then a boat to California and a plane ride home to New York. I was now playing the waiting game of a part-time garrison soldier, so I wasn't too surprised at being called out for guard duty. I didn't expect to be given an assignment that was so distasteful and such a distraction from my journey home.

I was pretty much hanging around, waiting to be shipped out to Inchon. I couldn't wait to see Frank. Somehow, I found myself in a formation of replacements and rear-echelon troops from which a guard duty detail was to be selected. The only way to be exempted from this sleepless duty was to be the sharpest soldier in the formation.

I went back to my tent and went through my routine. I wiped my beat-up boots, donned my best faded fatigues, and shined my wings, CIB, and belt buckle. I oiled my old .45-caliber pistol, trench knife, and carbine. I went the whole nine yards. I was ready.

We were called out for inspection onto a floodlighted area. I was the only veteran in the group. I felt awkward. I shouldn't have been there. They should have left me alone. I could feel people ogling at me. It was only natural for nonveterans to check you out. They wanted to size you up and guess how they might compare in combat.

The uncertain-looking second lieutenant was obviously a green replacement. He came down the line in his new fatigues and inspected the troops. He stopped in front of me. I came to attention and wrist-twisted my carbine sling rapidly to port arms. I pushed back the slide on my rifle with my left hand, jerked my head up, and stared right through his face. I stood there at attention, thinking that I had executed the maneuver pretty well despite the fact that I hadn't done too many of these drills lately.

The young lieutenant gave me a slow, up-and-down stare. I continued to stand rigidly still. There was no movement except for a gentle breeze that brought the familiar odor of human excrement from the surrounding rice paddies.

I don't know when the thought came into my head, but my decision was made. I would go piss and vinegar airborne all the way. At the first sign of his hand coming up to swipe my rifle, I would immediately drop my hands to my sides. He was incredibly slow. His hand came up meekly and fumbled the takeaway. My rifle dropped to the ground. The lieutenant's face froze in horrid disbelief and then recovered. He quickly bent down and swiped the rifle up in his hands. I never moved.

I was made supernumerary. I was rewarded for being the sharpest soldier in the formation. This meant that I would have special privileges. I would be a reserve guard. I would be used as needed. In other words, I had it made. The lieutenant, who was the officer of the guard, had to clean my rifle because he had dropped it. That was the rule. You dropped it, you cleaned it. He was also my guard officer and superior and the one who made me supernumerary. The good deal didn't last very long. After he returned my carbine to me, he had a special assignment for me. I was to relieve a sergeant who was guarding GI prisoners.

The lieutenant drove me to a trailer-type office that was being used as a temporary guardhouse. The door was opened by a short, thin, bespectacled sergeant with a wire-brush crew cut.

Introductions were made, and the lieutenant made it clear that I was to relieve the sergeant so he could grab some chow.

The sergeant and I saluted the lieutenant as he left the room.

The sergeant brought me over to his desk, where a single lightbulb shone from under the cover of a wire-coiled, gooseneck lamp. Next to it was a double-deck bunk bed with two soldiers. The sergeant gathered some documents and put them into a file. He was quick and deliberate and all military.

"I should be back in an hour or so. You have a phone and a check-in time every half hour, but you can call in any time if you need anything. You have two prisoners," he said, quietly pointing to the two young men lying down on the double-deck.

"They're confined to quarters. There's no talking. They won't give you any trouble. They want to be on their best behavior."

"What did they do? I asked.

"Went AWOL off of the line," said the sergeant. "They got caught in Seoul in a whorehouse, could be charged with desertion, could get life, maybe they'll be shot. Who knows? Who gives a shit?" He shrugged as he turned to the soldiers. "Nobody leaves their bunk," commanded the sergeant.

"Hey, sarge, I have to go to the john."

"So do I," piped the other prisoner.

"One at a time!" barked the sergeant and turned to me. "I'm going. Don't take any shit. You have a phone. Use it."

"What if they give me a hard time?" I whispered.

"They won't. They're asses are on the line."

"What about a worst-case scenario?" I pressed.

"Hey, sarge, what about it?" said the prisoner on the bottom bunk.

"Just hold your water," said the sergeant, who was visibly getting annoyed. "If they try anything," said the sergeant, making a big show of exchanging his two fully loaded, .45-caliber clips with my empty ones, "shoot the motherfuckers." He then strode adamantly out the door.

Suddenly alone, I was hit with the silence of the situation. I felt very uncomfortable. I was pissed off at being put in this situation.

"What about it, corporal?"

"Hold on," I said and turned my back to the two young men and walked to the sergeant's desk to check phone numbers and names.

"Hey, corporal, I gotta go, man. I ain't gonna try anything," whined the soldier on the top bunk as he swung his legs over the side.

I took out my pistol, slammed a clip up into the handle, slid the bolt back, put a round in the chamber, slipped the safety on, and finally put it back into my holster as nonchalantly as I could. I turned to the prisoners and tried to look as tough as I could.

"Let's keep it simple. Don't do anything stupid. I'm rotating home. I've been through enough bullshit. One way or another, I'm out of here. I don't want to have to use this thing," I said, patting my pistol.

The soldier in the bottom bunk sat up. "Hey, don't get excited, man. We're veterans too. We ain't doin' anything. We don't want trouble. We wanna get home too."

"Good. Top bunk first," I said, placing myself in the open door facing the bathroom down at the end of the hall and keeping an eye on the bunk bed at the same time.

"Okay, go ahead," I said impatiently when the first soldier returned.

It was the longest two hours of my life. I sat sideways to the desk because I didn't want to turn my back on these guys. I tried to read an old *Stars and Stripes* newspaper, but I couldn't concentrate. I was sure it was obvious that I was uneasy with what I was doing. I was too distracted. I found myself listening for the sounds of deep breathing or snoring or anything that would allow me to relax somewhat. I was pleasantly relieved at the sound of a jeep stopping outside.

"How did it go? Any problems?" asked the sergeant.

"Nope," I said, clearing my pistol over the desk and giving back his two pistol clips. "Everything was fine. No problem," I said calmly, trying not to look like I was in a hurry to get the hell out of there.

"Good. The lieutenant and your ride are outside."

"Good," I said, thinking that I had been paid back for my rifle-dropping incident by a green second lieutenant who didn't like to look bad in front of the troops. I hoped this was the end of the bullshit, because in the next day or two, I would be in Inchon, my last stop in Korea, before I sailed home.

CHAPTER 63

CARGO OF PAIN

At last, I left Fortieth Division Headquarters at Chunchon and boarded a train for Inchon. The scuttlebutt was that the train was slower than the Pusan Express, the train I had taken north when I had first arrived in Korea. This time, I was headed west on a much shorter trip to the harbor at Inchon for a transport ship to California. The morning was a scorcher. It was uncomfortably hot and humid, but I didn't care because I was finally leaving this godforsaken place. For the less fortunate on another train, the ride would be a tortuous journey of pain and suffering.

We waited a good while before we boarded the train, and then we waited a good while more in our seats before the train got under way. It was stifling hot. We wanted to get going, but nobody seemed to be rushing. There wasn't much talking. Everybody seemed to be caught up in his own thoughts. When the train finally started to move, it was in slower-than-slow motion but managed to create a pleasant breeze.

The countryside scenes were lovely. Lush green paddies, peasants working in the fields, winding rivers, and deep ravines held your gaze. It was a different world from the sparse mountain foliage and ugly, barren spots that dominated the landscapes of Heartbreak Ridge, Bloody Ridge, Sandbag Castle, and the hills of the Punchbowl.

A couple of long hours later, we came to a stop at a train station with a water tower next to it. It was a pit stop to take on water for the steam engine. We were told that we'd be here for a while. Without the gentle breeze from our open windows, the heat suddenly became oppressive. It was a prompt to get up and stretch our legs and walk around a bit.

I stepped down onto the shaded platform and walked along the side of the train. GIs filled their canteens next to the train engine from a hand-operated pump. I hopped off of the platform into the blazing sun. I sauntered along a beaten path next to the tracks and joined the soldiers around the pump. I waited patiently in line as the sweat dripped down my body. When my turn came, I bent over and filled my canteen. I threw some purification pills into it and twisted the chained cap closed. I shook the daylights out of it before I unscrewed the top and took a slug and rinsed my mouth with the strongest water I had ever spit out of my mouth. I took off my cap and poured the putrid water over my head and down my shirt to cool off. I felt refreshed as I sang to myself, "I'm going home. I'm going home. I'm going home."

When they pulled the water spout away from our engine, it smelled like your car radiator after it had overheated. Hissing steam brought plummets of foggy white vapor pouring around the engine's huge boiler. We were ready to move out.

The train started up slowly. As it picked up speed, it sucked in air from the open windows and once again created a gentle breeze. The terrain flattened out, and things went great for a while before we came to unexplainable slowdowns and then squeaking stops. We'd hiccup with a lurch, pick up speed, and then come to a near stop like the train was trying to catch its breath before it jumped forward again only to maddeningly repeat the process all over again.

Eventually, we slid into an empty train station and came to a halt. We sat there and waited, and the bitching began. We didn't move for a long while, and our car became a steam bath. Everyone was cursing and pouring sweat. Relief came in the form of a sergeant who ordered us off the train. To a chorus of groans and moans, we gathered our gear and filed out along the platform, thinking that the train had died on its tracks.

In the hot sun, we were given a report. We were being bumped. There was a big battle raging around Luke, the gook's castle in the Punchbowl area. The Chinese had broken through the lines of the Twelfth ROK Division, which was to the right of us on line. Our Fortieth Division tankers had tried to help out and had blown them off of the hill a couple of times, but the South Korean soldiers had suffered heavy casualties as they tried to retake their positions. Fighting was still going on. They were bringing wounded off of the hill and needed trains to get them to hospitals. We were going to have to wait until the track was cleared.

Everybody was thinking the same unthinkable thoughts. Could the ROKs hold their own? Did they need reinforcements? How bad was the breach in the lines? Would we have to go back up? That was the real question gnawing at everyone's gut. The thing about the army was that you got information on a need-to-know basis, which resulted in a lot of speculation, innuendo, and rumor. At least it did for me. The second-guessing drove me crazy. Would I ever get out of Korea?

Someone cracked out loud, "Maybe the Chinese would reach Inchon before we did," which brought smiles and laughter and a light touch to the situation. We broke up and looked for any piece of shade we could find, which was none. We sprawled all over the platform, using our duffle bags as cushions against the station walls, trying to get as comfortable as possible. Smoking, drinking from canteens, reading, and small talk were carried out with as little movement as possible. The stillness of the hot afternoon air and staring at where the train tracks converged, hoping for movement and the telltale sign of a coming train, was like self-hypnosis. Eyes drooped, and heads came down slowly, succumbing to sleep. The siesta was suddenly rocked by an ear-splitting boom from above that shook the hell out of everyone. I looked up as an F-86 made a low pass, dipping its wings as it roared overhead. The entire platform of GIs got to their feet to gaze over the railing as the American fighter plane landed on the airfield below.

"Kimpo," said the soldier next to me. "It's one of our air bases in Korea." I watched the ground crew clamber up the plane. A tall, slim pilot climbed out of his cockpit and removed his flight helmet. A flash of white teeth and a thumb up came from the smiling lieutenant's black face, which brought a lusty reaction of applause, cheers, and whistles from his gazing audience.

A distant train whistle caught our attention and brought us back to the train station. We watched curiously as a slow-moving engine approached, hauling a long line of freight cars behind it. As it crept into the station, open side doors emitted a foul smell. Inside the dark caverns of the boxcars, bandaged South Korean soldiers lay strewn across blood-stained, straw-littered floors. The whiff of urine, stale body odors, excrement, and disinfectants was overpowering. I was transfixed by the slow-motion pictures gliding by. Momentary stops brought walking wounded to the open doors. The sights were nauseating to watch. Oozing wounds, bloody bandages, pain-ridden faces, and relentless, swarming flies made it a horror show.

Open hands asked for cigarettes and water. "Cigaretto! Cigaretto, hava, yes? *Mu-ul, mu-ul*, hava, yes?" Behind them came moans of pain and agony.

We threw cigarettes, candy bars, whatever we had. It was a pathetic scene. One moment, I was smiling and waving at the antics of a hotshot combat pilot, and the next moment, I was grimacing at the ugly sight of suffering, wounded, young Korean soldiers.

Hours later, a train with empty coaches chugged into the station and stopped to pick us up. It was received with muted appreciation and ambivalence by all of us. It was hard thinking about the wretched ROK soldiers going to a hospital with their wounded cargo of pain, while we were so fortunate to be going home in good shape.

In spite of everything, I was selfishly relieved when our train came in to pick us up. I was glad to be continuing my journey to Inchon, and I was looking forward to a happy voyage home.

CHAPTER 64

INCHON ICHI-BAN

Inchon was a madhouse of arriving soldiers. My machine gun buddy, Lyle Olson, got here just before me. We would be going home together. I couldn't believe Frank wasn't here yet. He had gotten his rotation home news before I had. Deuce and a halves and flatbed trucks packed with gleeful troops loudly made their way onto an open square in front of a pier of warehouses. The excitement in the air was so thick you cut it with a trench knife. I was looking for Frank. Sailing home together was the moment we had been looking forward to since we had gotten separated back at Drake.

The first thing that hit me when I came into Inchon Harbor was the delicious smell of salty sea air. It was like being at the shore in Rockaway Beach. It added to the euphoria of the moment, even though Inchon was just another war-torn port of South Korea. Every time a new shipment arrived, I stood outside my tent, anxiously scouring the trucks of smiling, yelping faces, looking for Frank.

I thought I spotted him on one of the flatbed trucks, holding on to the side, looking over at the barracks and tents of soldiers, watching the new men come into the depot.

The gate was lowered, and the men jumped off and lined up in rows. I went down to the formation for a better look. One soldier kept going up on his toes, lifting his head above the lines and craning his neck from side to side, looking around. It was Frank. What a delicious moment. I was ecstatic. I scooted around columns and ducked down low behind the soldiers in front of me so he couldn't see me. When I got to his row, I waited for him to look, and then I rushed through the line of soldiers, who all looked at me in surprise as I removed the helmet liner from my head and brought it down with a mighty swoop. Hitting his steel pot and ringing his bell with a bong definitely shook his brain and scared the hell out of him.

"Welcome to Inchon, baby!"

"Joe! I knew you'd be here," hollered Frank as we pummeled each other amid smiles and laughter.

"Frankie baby, we're goin' home."

We stayed up all night, swapping stories, bullshitting, and fantasizing about home. Two days later, Frank and I moved from tents into wooden barracks that had a prominent sign outside: "If you drip, you don't ship."

It wasn't the clap that we had to worry about. It was vermin. Our sleeping quarters were not *ichi-ban*, number-one, first-class accommodations. They were being used constantly by different soldiers every few days. They were worse than any bunker I had ever slept in. They were small, grimy hovels sleeping too many transient soldiers in the same bunks without the proper changes of bedding and clean linens. The night before we shipped out, Frank got lice. He was very upset.

"Look over here," said Frank, pointing. "They're even climbing up the goddamn beams. Can you see them? This place is crawling."

"Hold still!" I commanded, bringing my lit cigarette close to Frank's pubic hairs.

"Jesus, not too close," said Frank, wincing more out of wariness than out of pain. "You want to draw them out of my crotch, not burn them out."

"Don't make me laugh, or I'll end up branding you," I said. "Gee, I wish I had a flamethrower," I said, shaking my head slowly from side to side. "You're being invaded."

"Don't fuck around, Joe! Those are my jewels," said Frank, and we both howled.

We were so excited about going home together that nothing could dampen our high spirits. Inchon was the best. Lice or no lice, it was *ichi-ban*.

CHAPTER 65

INCHON HARBOR
JULY 22, 1952

HOME ON THE MEIGS

The troopship Meigs was not the *Queen Mary*. As far as Frank and I were concerned, it was our beautiful, luxury liner home. The hospital ship tied up next to us was a jolting reminder of the disparity between the well and the wounded, the living and the dead. We were happily going home while Bell helicopters, their two wounded soldiers strapped under their skids, kept landing and taking off from the hospital ship. The most unfortunate ones were the dead who slept silently in pine boxes stored deep in the bowels of our ship.

It was late afternoon when we boarded tugs to ride the shallow waters out of Inchon Harbor to the troopship Meigs. Frank and I were one of the first ones to scamper on board, our heavy duffle bags in tow. Below the waterline and without portholes, we descended ladder stairs to our sleeping quarters. Overhead, dull, wire-masked lightbulbs played off of side-by-side stacked, gray, canvas-stretched, iron bunks. The scene was reminiscent of the ship that had brought me to Korea.

Frank got the first bunk, and I got the one over from him. The paired bunks were so close together that if you rolled over, you would be sleeping with the guy next to you. Frank and I joked about the poor guy who would be sleeping next to an effeminate-looking first sergeant in the rack across from us. He was sashaying all over the place. He wore bright chartreuse zori slippers. His blond hair was rather long for Korea and was combed back in a duck's ass—style of cut. He certainly had had the opportunity to let it grow by the time he came off line and got to Inchon. It contrasted dramatically against his silk, embroidered, knee-length Japanese kimono with a fire-breathing dragon.

The bunks filled up fast as troops came off their tugboats. The more men, the noisier and hotter it became. Even with open hatches, the ship's hold became rife with the body odor of sweaty soldiers. When chow time came, it was a mob scene. Hordes of bodies seemed to emerge on deck, simultaneously inhaling the fresh sea air while waiting for a hot meal. Thousands of guys queued up and snaked along the decks, chatting and waiting to be fed. The lines moved at a snail's pace. Frank and I realized that this was going to be a major problem for the rest of the voyage. Hurry up and wait and then finally get served only to start lining up for the next meal. This was not a happy thought for the next week and a half. We could spend all day each day of our trip home just lining up for meals. When I suggested that we skip the dinner meal, Frank thought I was crazy. Frank was a big eater. He was adamant that we stick it out.

"I've got a stash, Frank."

"You have food?"

"Yeah, I've got some canned food I've been saving for an emergency or a celebration, and it's gourmet too."

"Serious?" he asked.

"Yeah, my aunt Anna sent it to me a month ago. It's cooked, boneless, sliced turkey breast. I got two cans and a box of tea crackers. We got canteen water to drink, and *bingo!* we have a 'bon voyage' party."

"Beats waiting on this line," said Frank with a great big grin. "How is your aunt?"

"Remember the money she threw out the window to us?"

"Of course I do. I bought a beer at the bus stop in New Jersey."

"Right. That was the day we got inducted into the service."

"Can you believe the shit we went through since then?"

"And here we are finally going home," I said.

We found a bulkhead that we could lean against and stretch our legs. It was perched on the upper deck and gave us a terrific view of the harbor. Small launches made lazy wakes as they came in at low throttle from other ships tied up in the port. Sampans glided across each other. It was a grand summer's evening. A warm, gentle breeze mixed with chatter and occasional outbursts of laughter erupted from happy passengers as they queued up for chow.

We took out our all-purpose knives with fork and spoon attachments, and I placed the box of crackers in between us. I then used a tiny metal two-inch can opener that I kept on a chain around my neck along with my dog tags to open the cans of turkey meat. It was a handy relic left over from my National Guard days which came in handy more times than I could count. Cups were filled and our banquet was ready to eat.

"Hey, let's say grace. Like old times!" I said suddenly.

Without missing a beat, we lowered our heads and recited in unison the prayer before meals, which we had learned from Sister Conception in our first-grade class back at Saint Stephen's of Hungary in our old neighborhood.

"Bless us, oh Lord, for these thy gifts, which we are about to receive from thy bounty through Christ our Lord . . . amen."

"I will never forget this moment, and I will never forget this meal," said Frank.

"I'll drink to that."

"Wait!" said Frank, holding up his hand. "I want to propose a toast."

We lifted our cups.

"To friendship and to going home. It was a hell of a ride, and we took it together, Joe. That's what made it so special. Pals to the end, babe."

"Pals to the end," I said. "Buddies all the way."

We had noticed the hospital ship before. It was moored right across from us. You couldn't miss it. It stood out among the others boats in the harbor. A bright red cross screamed out from its glistening white hull. At first glance, it could have passed for an elegant cruise ship except for the army ambulances that came racing up the dock and the frantic medics sliding stretchers off to eager hands that would carry the wounded on board.

As night fell, the ship lit up and took on a different look. It was a pretty sight in a macabre sort of way. Spotlights played on a marked bull's-eye on deck, casting the rest of the vessel in shades of shadowy lines. It became the center of attention for our ship. *Puckata . . . puckata . . . puckata . . . puckata* sounds grew louder as choppers circled and hovered over the ship before they started their descents. A beam of light would catch the Bell helicopter, momentarily highlighting the human cargo encased in a plastic bubble attached to its skid. Handheld strobes arched, darted, and danced, waving the chopper onto the targeted deck.

Mesmerized, we sat as these dramatic scenes unfolded before our eyes. The baritone twang of Hank Williams could be faintly heard in the background: "Your cheatin' heart . . . won't cheat no more" carried softly only to be drowned out by the rhythmic beat of a whirlybird's propeller blades.

"Aint life a bitch? Here we are going home, happy as pie, eating, drinking, and listening to music, watching guys in pain being brought to a hospital ship. They've got to be scared out of their skulls, not knowing what's in store for them. It's a weird feeling watching all of this. For the grace of God, it could be us out there," I said and shuddered.

"I know what you mean. I can remember getting the letter from my brother in the military hospital when he was wounded in Italy," said Frank. "My parents were beside themselves, not knowing if he would lose his leg or his life. When he limped home on a cane, we cried, laughed, and thanked the Blessed Virgin all at the same time."

We sat in silence, smoking and watching the scenes unfold dramatically in front of us before realizing we were moving ever-so-slowly away from the horror movie to begin our long-awaited journey home.

401

CHAPTER 66

SING FOR YOUR SUPPER

"Sweepers, man your brooms. Swabbies, man your mops," blared the boom box. The odd part about the cleaners was that they weren't sailors. They were soldiers. They were us. In an instant, GIs become day laborers. Over the extent of the voyage, considerable time was spent dodging work details. It became obvious that we were expected to "sing for our supper" to earn our passage home.

On a daily basis, the two biggest problems on board our troop ship were being put on work details and lining up for chow. The work details to be avoided were serving in the kitchen (KP), peeling potatoes, serving food, washing dishes, pots, and pans, cleaning trays, collecting garbage, sweeping/mopping the decks, cleaning the latrines (heads), emptying and filling butt cans, or any other menial jobs they could find for you on the Meigs.

The best deal was if you could play an instrument. Talented people got together and formed groups. They would entertain us with shows, so they always needed time to rehearse and were left alone. Of course, they were always rehearsing because they loved to perform.

Another creative group was the clothes cleaners. These guys cornered the market on deck. They tied a rope around your fatigues or whatever you gave them and threw them over the fantail of the ship into the ship's wake. The trick was how long to let them

402

be battered and skipped along the top of the water. You took a chance. If the cleaners left them in too long, you had tattered fatigues. Washed just right by the saltwater waves, all you had to do was squeeze them dry and lay them out in the sun.

Chow was a huge problem. As soon as you finished eating one meal, the lines were so long that you could find yourself lining up for the next meal. If you did this three times a day, you could suddenly find yourself ready for bed. To beat the system, you either skipped a meal or smuggled food out of the galley for your next meal. If you could afford it, you could buy snacks from the ship's tiny commissary. These daily annoyances interfered with your cruise time. They were undoubtedly a challenge to your leisure hours.

Hanging out on deck and working on your tan was what it was all about. Reading, writing, and rapping were by far the favorite pastimes. Pinochle, poker, and blackjack weren't far behind, and you could always find or start a craps game somewhere. At our last pay call, we turned in our script and foreign currency for dollars, so everybody had spending money.

Our on-board PX was small, but it had nice merchandise at the right price. A Longine-Whitnauer gold wristwatch with a blue suede band caught my eye. I debated with myself about whether I should buy it or not. It was real sharp, but it was expensive. It cost over thirty-five dollars, but I knew it was worth twice the price in a store. Every day, I went down to the PX and looked at it. I was always fearful that it would be gone. If it was sold, then my decision would have been made for me. Finally, I couldn't take it anymore. I bought it. It crushed me financially; however, it was the most elegant thing I had ever bought, and I was proud of it. Heck, I figured I had earned it.

Frank found me lolling on deck and reading an Agatha Christie paperback. He had gotten captured for a work detail that I had managed to elude. I greeted him with a smug grin. "How was work today, dear?" I asked in a falsetto voice.

"Better than yours," Frank said, giving me a superior, knowing look. "I had hot butter rolls and coffee for breakfast and freshly baked cookies with cold lemonade for a snack. I don't have to go to lunch now. I'm free for the rest of the day. No more hiding from work details. I got us a good deal."

"What do you mean us?" I asked, putting down my book.

"I got us a steady job in the bakery. It's only for the morning. All the coffee, rolls, and Danishes you can eat. It's a sweet deal—no pun intended. And it solves our food problem. We only have to line up for evening chow. It's a good deal, Joe."

"How did you work that out?" I asked, suspicious.

"I got nailed in the latrine. At first, I was pissed off. Again, no pun intended. But it's a natural setup. They've got everyone trapped in the same place. Now we can go to the latrine without worrying who's in there. When they marched us off to the bakery, it was heaven. The smell of baking bread and freshly brewed coffee is unbelievable. Joe, there's food all over the place. We lucked out."

"What's the drill?"

"You hang around the bakery, waiting for Pop to yell at you. He's the boss. When he wants something, you jump. It's a funny scene. He's got a German accent that's so thick you can cut it with a knife. When he starts giving orders, most of the guys just gape at him, trying to figure out what he wants. It was like old home week for me. He was like one of the old-timers from our neighborhood. I understood him pretty good. You bring up bags of supplies out of storage. There's heavy lifting but a lot guys to help. You set them up at the right stoves. You help out the bakers. You fill up baskets, clean trays, and things like that. He sounds like Hitler, but his bark is worse than his bite. He's a benevolent dictator," said Frank with a smile. "He's like Sister Ann with the altar boys from Saint Stephen's. Remember in the sacristy when she wanted us to light the incense, and she would yell, 'Make fire!' Well, it's time to make fire, Joe!"

"Remember Dopey Doyle?" I said enthusiastically.

"Yeah," said Frank, "and the time he grabbed the folding chairs and started throwing them in a pile and then lit a match, and Sister Ann screamed, 'Vot you doing? Vot you doing?' And he looked up at her innocently, 'You said to make a fire, sister.'"

"That was funny," I said, and we both laughed.

"Okay, okay," I said smilingly. "So how do I fit into this?"

"Well, just before I left, I thanked Pop for the food, and he thanks me for working so hard for him."

"Ach, I vish I hot more like you," said Frank, imitating Pop and the disapproving face that he had given him, nodding at the others as they left the shop.

"I tell him that I have a combat buddy from the old neighborhood who is half German and works even harder than me."

"Oh, thanks a lot for the buildup," I said sarcastically.

"It worked," said Frank enthusiastically. "Pop said, 'Get him here tomorrow. If he's dot goot, you both verk for me until vee dock.'"

"What can I say," said Frank. "We work a few hours in the morning. We get breaks. We drink coffee. We have juice; eat doughnuts, pie, whatever we want. We work until noon and *boom*, we're done. The best thing is we bring back food. No lining up for lunch. We have the rest of the day to ourselves. What more could you want? We have it made. Who's your buddy?"

At five in the morning, Frank introduced me to a balding man in his midfifties. The man wore a spotless white baker's cap, T-shirt, and apron, and he seemed to be in a race of some sort. He was in perpetual motion. He nodded to me and started rattling off orders in a heavy German accent. He reminded me of my grandfather, Emil, who was born in Rostock in the northeastern part of Germany. I understood my grandfather though.

"Effrey vun vashes dare hants. Effrrey vun vares T-shirts. Zen you come back und you," he said, pointing at me, "you take zis hart flowa und put it heer. Und zen you two take zee zoft flowa, und you put it in zair. Mach shnell!"

Frank and I looked at each other and giggled. Pop was a pisser, a pure dictator, an unforgettable character loaded with sarcasm and humor, which he dispensed with equal conviction.

405

"Vhy are you standing dare?" asked Pop. "Are you vaiting for a date or for the var to end? Comin' zee heer. Come! You in der sink! You over dare! Move! Move!" he said, clapping his hands.

He had us jumping from table to table, mixing batters, whipping cream, cutting fruit, measuring flour, rolling dough. "Goot, goot, everybody verks."

Pop was like an orchestra conductor. He had us emptying, cleaning, stacking cooking trays, stacking pans, opening sacks of supplies, and doing whatever was needed at the moment. Despite the fans and portholes, when the ovens got fired up, we started to sweat. The bakery got hotter than hell. Still, Pop took care of his men. He would have made a great top sergeant. He would always have a couple of men rotating on a break. He had a table always set up with coffee, juice, milk, cookies, cakes, and pies.

On one particular morning, I had my cap off while I was working, and Pop stopped me. "Ach, you scratched yourself," he said, looking into my flushed face.

"Oh, no," I replied, fingering the long, jagged scar down my forehead. Before I could explain that Frank and I had been in a head-on collision driving up to Montreal the summer before we had been drafted and that I had gotten my head split open, Pop answered his own question.

"You ver vounded," Pop said and pointed to my face.

The scar was still red and sore-looking. I started to explain, but for some reason, I hesitated and then shook my head slowly up and down.

"Come. Zit heir. Have zum tink to eat. No? Colt lemonade? Hot apple strudel mit shlag ya?"

I shook my head gratefully and sat down at the break table, which would be my new kitchen assignment for the rest of the voyage home.

On the way out of the bakery, I told Frank what had happened and how I had gotten my new job in the bakery. He was both pissed and pleased.

"Well, you earned your milk and cookies. You sang for your supper, Kemo Sabe."

CHAPTER 67

THE WAR ENDS, AND WE TURN BACK

On the early morning of July 28, Frank and I were on our bakery detail when the ship's squawk box suddenly came alive. "Now hear this! Now hear this! Last night, July 27, 1953, as of ten hundred hours, General Mark Clark, United Nations Commander-in-Chief . . . signed an armistice agreement . . . with the forces of the North Korean People's Army. The fighting in Korea is over. Repeat—the fighting in Korea is over."

At first, nothing happened. There was a long, stunned silence. Then there was some sporadic clapping, whistling, and outbursts of obscenities but no yelling, cheering, or wild applause. For the most part, we went about our business. There was lots of talking, comments, and quiet conversations but no enthusiastic bursts of exuberance.

"It's finally over," said Frank.

"Thank God. Even if it's only a truce, it's better than nothing. I just hope it lasts."

"Not too much excitement," said Frank, catching eyes with some soldiers and smiling triumphantly and giving the thumbs-up.

"I don' feel too excited either," I said. "More relieved I think, but I bet the guys on line are excited. Can you imagine what they're doing right now?"

407

"Yeah, they're going crazy," said Frank.

"They are one happy bunch of guys. They made it. I know that feeling. I can relate to that. I'm so glad for them. Coming off the hill and making it back in one piece was our excitement," I said. "I'm just happy we're going home together."

"You know," said Frank, "it's anticlimactic in a way. Everybody on this boat is going home safe and sound. We left all our worries behind once we came on board this ship."

"Yeah, well, now the guys on line can do the same thing," I said. "They can relax, knowing that they've made it. They've got to be excited, hootin' and hollerin' and raising hell."

"I would be too," said Frank, smiling in agreement. "The booze came out of the woodwork last night."

"It was party time on line," I said, grinning. "I can just see the happy faces of the guys in my platoon. Not that I would want to trade places with them, but it would have been nice to have shared the moment with the guys on line."

After evening chow, we went topside as usual to watch and enjoy another gorgeous sunset. As twilight turned to dusk, we waited for night to fall and another movie to begin under an evening sky of endless stars. We had a nice dinner. The war was over. We were heading home. It was a beautiful evening on deck, and we were watching a good movie. During the show, Frank turned to me and said, "We're heading in the wrong direction, Joe."

It seemed like everybody on deck heard our conversation. The hum of conversations grew louder. We had been watching the night sky since he had left Inchon. The ship hadn't turned dramatically about. It was a gradual shift in course, but it was pointedly noticed by the horde of stargazers on deck. Rumors were hatched on the spot.

The truce is broken. They need troops for the cease-fire. We're going to repatriate prisoners. We're going back to Cheju-do and Koje-do to guard prisoners. Unidentified submarines have been spotted, so we're heading for Japan.

You name it. The rumors were heard and passed on. Whistles and banging noises were mixed with curses and obscenities.

"Turn this tub around!" a soldier cried out, which was followed with howls of nervous laughter. A sing-song chant of "home . . . home . . . home" soon erupted.

The ruckus was interrupted by a lifeless, metallic drone. "Now hear this! Now hear this!"

The voice of God served the purpose of quieting the voices. The ship had changed direction. We were turning around. We were not going back to Korea. We were going to rendezvous with a merchant ship less than a half of a day away at sea. There was a seaman in need of immediate medical attention. We were going to transfer him to our ship because we had a doctor and medical facilities on board. San Francisco was a few days out, and he would go to a hospital there. This grateful news brought about instant sighs of relief, spontaneous backslaps, and a renewed interest from the sky watchers in the romantic singing and tap dancing of Fred Astaire and Ginger Rogers as they glided across the screen.

Early the next morning, cable lines were rigged between the two bobbing ships. The merchant man was strapped to a swing-like chair in a harness and slowly hauled across the water. Both ships swayed in place, signaling each other as their crews fought to keep their trim. Thousands of pairs of eyes followed the dramatic high-wire act unfold on center stage in the middle of the ocean. It was really a marvel to behold. The guesses going around ranged from a ruptured appendix to a fall to a stabbing at sea. At any rate, when he was finally hoisted aboard after his dips and numerous stops, he managed to feebly bring his arm up over his head, which produced a loud burst of cheers and applause. He didn't look too lively while he was put onto a stretcher and carried down the ship's infirmary.

After evening chow, every soldier went topside. They weren't anxiously awaiting the John Wayne movie as much as they were the stars to come out so they could reassuringly check our direction home. When I heard voices singing, "California, here I come, right back where I started from," I knew the Korean War had finally ended for us. The Meigs was back on track. We were heading home.

409

CHAPTER 68

PACIFIC OCEAN

AUGUST 3, 1953

AROUND FULL CIRCLE

The blasts from the stacks of the Meigs drew everyone's attention to the portside of the ship. To my delight and astonishment, an elegant, three-mastered schooner, complete with white sails, crew, and sunbathing women, waved to a lunatic ship of howling baboons. A surge of excitement swept over the deck like a jolt of electricity. That boat was just a couple of days out from California. Frank and I would go back to Camp Stoneham. We'd fly out of Oakland to New York, where we had started from, and complete our journey home. It was so close to happening I could taste it.

August 3 was the real thing. We sailed into San Francisco Harbor in a thick morning fog. I was all spit and polish, dressed in my class-A summer uniform, excitedly facing the bow of the ship along with everybody trying to spot land.

"Whales!" somebody yelled.

All at once, everybody rushed to the starboard side of the ship. Frank skidded on the wet, grimy deck and came up with a huge, black, dirt spot on his pressed, khaki pants.

"Shit, look at this," Frank said in disgust.

"Look at that!" I said excitedly as two small whales burst out of the water like miniature submarines and floated in front us.

"Look, behind the whales—sharks!" I said.

"No, they're porpoises," said our bunkmate sergeant who usually wore silk pajamas.

Frank and I did a double take. Our mouths hung open. Our blond-headed Adonis had ribbons up the wazoo. Silver and Bronze stars lined up next to a Purple Heart.

"You see what I see?" asked Frank in amazement.

"Shit, he can man my foxhole anytime," I said, and Frank nodded in total agreement.

The sun came out as if on cue to light up a beautiful picture of San Francisco Harbor and welcome us home. A small flotilla of sailboats, motorboats, cabin cruisers, and tugboats greeted us with funnel blasts, some darting across our bow and crashing through our wake or sailing alongside, waving and zigzagging across the harbor. It was as if the scene had been choreographed by a Hollywood director.

"I love it," said Frank, beaming. "It's like a three-ring circus."

I welled up. I was speechless. For me, it was an unforgettable moment. Seeing the Golden Gate Bridge loom bigger and bigger and the hills of San Francisco in the distance rising up from the bay made me feel more like a wondrous sightseer than a returning war veteran. I had been here before. I was happy, because the dock was coming toward me rather than going away from me.

The harbor master came out to us in a small boat. He was quickly followed on board by a television crew. They busily set up their cameras, wanting to capture the waving and smiling soldiers and to interview the first troops returning home after the war had ended.

"What's your name, soldier?" Where are you from? What's your outfit? How does it feel to be home? Who do you want to say hello to? What do you think of the truce?" We lined up by the number, torturously waiting on deck with our duffle bags to go down the gangplank and put our feet on American soil. Like racehorses at the starting gate, we were raring to go.

"You're on TV now. No show boating. Keep moving. No kissing the ground. Keep moving. Stay in line. Look good. You're soldiers." Blah, blah, blah. A long line of shoulders balancing duffle bags moved down the gangplank onto the dock while a band struck up "Boogie Woogie Bugle Boy," and we all started to move to the beat. Red Cross workers had set up snack stations and served and bantered with us as we stood waiting for the next set of orders to come down. A young woman came up to Frank and me and asked if we would like some doughnuts and coffee. Frank gave her his best smile. "What are you doing tonight, beautiful? How about a date?" he asked.

"How about a snack instead?" she said with a pretty smile.

It was silly banter, and we all laughed a little too loud and a little too much. We were having fun.

"I'm back in action," said Frank, deliriously happy playing Romeo and the returning hero and enjoying every moment of it. He suddenly got very serious and looked me square in the eye. "Joe, do you realize that's the first American woman we've seen or talked to in a year."

I nodded vigorously and smiled. "Hey, Frank, look behind you up on the middle deck," I said.

With his pipe in his mouth and a bemused look on his face, Pop raised his arm slowly and waved at us. Frank and I waved back and moved our mouths with great exaggeration, "*Zank you!*"

Pop's mouth was also moving. I think he said good luck, but in my head, I heard his voice say, "Zank you, boys, und goot luck!" Frank gave him a thumbs-up, and I waved and yelled back, knowing he couldn't hear me, "*Auf feider zane,* Pop, and don't burn the cookies."

I hoped that in all of the excitement, Pop hadn't noticed the absence of a Purple Heart among the ribbons across my khaki shirt.

Sharp, commanding voices brought us back. We lifted our duffle bags once again onto our shoulders and started to move. Small commercial ferries pulled up to the dock. My number was called, and I responded loud and clear, "Donohue! Joseph! 090245535." I hopped on board and was guided to my seat with helping hands. Frank plopped down beside me with a naughty grin on his face.

"Do you remember the last time we were here?" he said.

"We weren't laughing then," I added seriously.

In no time at all, we were going under the Oakland Bay Bridge, which connected San Francisco to Oakland and Camp Stoneham, the place where it had all began. The place from where I had made my great escape in going to Korea.

We had come full circle.

CHAPTER 69

SAN FRANCISCO, CALIFORNIA
AUGUST 3, 1953

AWOL #2: DÉJÀ VU

I went AWOL twice in the army. The first time had been the night before I had gone to Korea. The second time had been on the night I had arrived back from Korea. I got caught without proper passes in the same place, Pittsburgh, California, right outside of Camp Stoneham. You would think I would have learned my lesson. I knew the old saying, "Once bitten twice shy," but I didn't pay attention to it. Fortunately, the second time I screwed up, I came out smelling like a rose. Sometimes you just have to love the army way of doing things.

Our troop ship docked at San Francisco Harbor in the morning. At noon, I ate lunch at Camp Stoneham. I was one of the last guys to leave the mess hall after evening chow. On the way back to my barrack, I talked baseball with a vet from New York. His name was Jerry Aspesi. It was good to be talking New York baseball again.

We walked into a loud and lively barrack. Frank was in the barrack across the company street. We were billeted in alphabetical order.

"Hey, two guys in class A's!" yelled Guinea and Caccia, two guys from my neighborhood in Yorkville. Everyone was in a relaxed mode of dress. Some were reading or playing cards, and others were shooting dice or just shooting the bull.

414

"We're ready to party, and we got two camp cadre here playing dice who can make it happen. They're willing to give us their permanent passes for going on and off camp. We can buy beers and booze in town," said Guinea.

"You guys go now. You'll be back in no time," said one of the dice-shooting cadres.

Alarm bells went off in my head, but how could I be a party pooper?

"Sure!" said Jerry, interrupting my thoughts. "No sweat."

A list was written, and money collected. Jerry and I got the cadres' passes and instructions on what to do.

"Take a taxi going off camp and flash the ID. You won't have any trouble. Come back in the same cab after you load up. You go in. You go out. No problem."

"Just act natural," I said to Jerry, remembering Frank's advice ten months before when we had gone into the same town of Pittsburgh.

We got a cab and left Stoneham without a hitch. We bought the beer and whiskey without a hitch. The problem was we never saw the MP jeep pull up behind us as we were loading the trunk of the taxi outside the liquor store.

"You boys having a party?" asked the MPs.

"Just buying a few things," we said, and I guess Jerry and I didn't act very natural. We had Fortieth and Twenty-Fourth Infantry Division patches on our uniforms.

"Didn't you boys come in this morning? Let's see your passes and IDs."

We were caught bare-ass naked. The dark faces on the cadre IDs didn't match up well with our faces. The MPs loaded the booty from our taxi into their jeep and rode us back to camp.

The brig corporal was big. He was heavyset and bordering on fat. He had blond hair and a sallow complexion, and he wore brown-framed glasses. He sneered when we told him our stories. His reaction was angry as if what we had done had been a personal affront to him. He was a jerk, a perfect asshole. He was the type of stateside soldier who liked being a military policeman and wielding the power that went with it. He was your overgrown schoolyard bully.

We were told to empty our pockets. The corporal had us remove our belts and bootlaces. He made lists of what had been confiscated in the taxi and taken from our persons. Jerry and I read the lists and signed off on them. The corporal looked at us with disdain, as if he wanted to ask, "Who did these veterans think they were coming into his camp and disrespecting our rules and shoving it in our faces?" We were trespassers. We didn't belong here. We were bad-boy New Yorkers who were going to get the justice we deserved. The corporal read in a stern voice the charges against us: "Absent without leave, acting under false pretenses, impersonating US military personnel, and attempting to smuggle illegal contraband onto federal property."

Jerry looked bored like this was all bullshit. I wanted to tune the corporal out as well, but I couldn't. I kept thinking about the last time I had been here. I pictured myself sliding over the window in the officer of the day's room. I saw myself sneaking across streets and running like hell back to my barrack. I could see Frank at the top of the barrack stairs, looking for me. It was funny then and scary. Now it wasn't funny but still scary.

Sweet mother of God, I thought. *Did they have a record of my escape last year? Did they have a warrant out for me?*

Lastly, I heard, "Collaborating with camp cadre in an illicit money-making operation."

"This is crazy," I blurted out. "We just got here this afternoon."

"No one asked you!" shouted the red-faced corporal. "Open the cell door!"

"You fucking guys," was all I heard as a hand grabbed the back of my shirt and shoved me headfirst into the cell.

"What are ya doin'?" screamed Jerry, and for an instant, I thought the corporal was going to whack him. The corporal could easily provoke an incident, and we would have had more charges brought against us. Things were going downhill fast. What a way to come home! How dumb could I get?

The following day, Jerry and I were brought to the provost marshal's office. We spoke to a military police captain who was a noncombatant like the corporal and another real hard-ass guy. He wanted us to admit that we were part of a scheme to make money from soldiers coming back from Korea.

"No way!" I said. "We just got here!"

"Look, we admit we went into town without authorization. We wanted to buy some beer to celebrate coming home from Korea. Why such a big deal?" asked Jerry with a grin.

That turned out to be a mistake. The captain jumped on us.

"You soldiers think this is a joke? Did you read the charges against you? Is a court-martial funny to you men? How about getting busted down to private, a forfeit of pay, and maybe even some brig time? Do you think that's funny?"

We didn't smile anymore. This was serious shit. We were in deep *kimchi*. Our next stop was to the judge advocate general's office, where Jerry and I met our appointed legal counselor. He was a JAG captain and, much to our relief, a combat veteran. We hoped that he would have some understanding about our situation.

We lucked out. Our combat captain was a good guy. He was able to empathize with jubilant veterans who had just gotten back after they had fought on line for months and had gotten carried away on their first night home. He believed our story, and he wanted the best for us. He walked us through the whole thing. He told us how we should deport ourselves and what to say and what he thought the outcome would be. He was a good lawyer.

"There would be a court-martial—no question about it," said the captain. "The two cadres will be charged with running illegal crap games, selling their IDs for favors and profits like having a percentage deal with the package store on how much liquor and beer you bought, and things like that. The jury of officers would most likely drop the charges against you if you just tell them what you told me. It's honest and straightforward. They probably want to nail these guys. You and Jerry, in effect, would become witnesses on their court-martial trial. By the way, did you show the liquor store people ID?"

"Nope, we're not underage now, and they didn't ask us for our IDs."

"In California, you have to show your age before buying booze, and they didn't do that," said the captain.

"How much did you spend?"

"Around fifty bucks," I guessed.

"They probably had a deal with the store owner and made a percentage off that, but you don't know that. All you have to do is tell the truth. You'll have to identify under oath the two cadres who gave you their passes and hope they corroborate your story. Tell it plain and simple just the way you told it to me. Be very military. Stand tall. Look sharp. Speak loud and clear. Make eye contact. Respond with "yes, sir," "no, sir," and "no excuse, sir." Be polite. Try not to hesitate. Do those things, and you should be okay. Good luck!"

I nodded thankfully and almost told him about my first AWOL at Stoneham last August, the night before I had shipped out to Korea but thought it might complicate things, so I kept my mouth shut. I hoped it wouldn't come back and bite me in the ass.

Frank found me confined to quarters.

"I heard you got busted. What the fuck happened?"

I introduced Frank to Jerry and told him the story. "It was like the first time in the town of Pittsburgh. It was like déjà vu. Only this time, it was with a guy from the Bronx."

Frank's look was one of pained exasperation. "Did you know we're flying out the day after tomorrow?"

"No," I said dejectedly.

"How long will you be here for?"

"I don't know, as long as a court-martial takes. A few days, I suppose."

"I had a court-martial in basic training for taking food from the mess hall without permission. They called it stealing. It took a week. That means you'll have to wait for the next boat to dock. Damn, we get this far, and now we're not going home together?"

"I want to go home too, you know."

"I know. I know," said Frank glumly. "I'm going to speak to the chaplain. Maybe he can do something."

"Thanks, I appreciate it. If I don't see you, have a good flight home. I'll see you in New York," I said.

"We'll all get together in New York and have a ball," said Jerry, smiling and shaking hands with Frank. "Nice meeting you."

"I'm sure the chaplain can do something," said Frank, putting his arm on my shoulder.

I nodded. "There is one thing you can do for me though."

"Sure, what's that?

"For God's sake, don't let my mom know you're home!"

The next morning, Jerry and I reported to the judge advocate general's office. We were told to take a seat in the waiting room. There was no one there. We rehearsed what we were going to say and do. At one point, the door opened, and as incredible as it might seem, the two cadres who had given us their passes walked in. We all looked at each other in disbelief. The four of us were in the same room alone. It was the first time we had seen each since Jerry and I had gone into town to buy the booze.

"What's happening?" asked the cadre sergeant.

"They want us to tell what happened that night," said Jerry.

"What did you say to them?" asked the other cadre.

We went through the whole story and brought them up to date.

"They were accusing and threatening us and you with all sorts of things," Jerry said.

"Basically, what we told them was that you offered us your IDs with no strings attached to get through the gate and go into town to buy some liquor and beer for a little homecoming party. We loaded up the cab, and the MPs nailed us. Our patches and picture IDs gave us away. That was it," I said.

"That's the truth, and that's what we're swearing to," said Jerry.

"That's our story too," said the sergeant. "Don't worry, man. They can't prove anything. So they court-martial us. We only have a few months left, and then we're discharged. We made it through Korea. We'll make it through this. What can they do?"

"I'm sorry how this whole thing ended up," I said.

"Don't sweat it. We're not getting the firing squad," said the other cadre. "They're after us for other things. We'll be all right." The four of us leaned over our seats and shook hands and wished each other good luck.

Moments later, the door opened, and the captain from the provost marshal's office strode in and stopped dead in his tracks when he saw the four of us sitting alone together.

"Well, now isn't this cozy? I guess you men have your stories straight by now," he said with an annoyed look on his face. Our JAG captain came in behind him, and a coy smile played on his face when he saw us together.

My name was called, and I stood up. I was escorted to an open door. It was like going on stage. I was trying to contain the butterflies in my stomach. Now I know how Frank must have felt at his court-martial. You never knew what to expect. Frank was lucky. He got a severe reprimand on his army record. I only hoped I would be as lucky. I remember him telling me how scared he had been during the trial.

I took a deep breath and marched into the room. Several officers sat at a long table that faced the door, papers in front of them, looking very officious. I tried to look like a model soldier. I had spit-polished my boots, and I had shined my belt buckle along with my combat infantry badge and paratrooper wings. They sparkled. My campaign ribbons and battle stars showed prominently. A colonel was seated in the middle of a raised, long, rectangular table. I squared my shoulders, saluted smartly, and called out my name, rank, and serial number. I had never seen so many somber-looking, high-ranking officers sitting at one table before.

The stern-looking colonel started, "Do you know why you're here, soldier?"

I admitted to the wrongdoing, heard the charges against me, told my story, answered questions, and listened to the lecture and their decision of leniency because I was a Korean War veteran. I thanked the panel, saluted sharply, and marched out the way I had marched in. Only this time, I was a relieved and happy soldier. There were no other charges against me and no mention of my first AWOL in Stoneham last year. I really was only a witness in this court-martial.

Jerry went through the same routine. At the end of the trial, Jerry and I thanked our lawyer captain for all his help. It couldn't have gone better for us. We asked him about going home before the next ship arrived from Korea, which wasn't for another week or so.

"Flights out of here are booked days in advance," he said, "but you can try. If you get one, I'll cut your orders home."

I was never more motivated in my life. I called air transportation and spoke to the sweetest voice I had ever heard tell me she was booked solid through next week. I told her my sad story. We were two combat veterans returning home from Korea when we were requested to serve as witnesses in a big court-martial case through circumstances out of our control. As a result of doing the proper thing and seeing to it that justice was done, we missed our flight home. In effect, we were being punished for doing our duty. Couldn't she at least put our names on waiting lists?

They put our names on the waiting lists of every flight going to the East Coast in the next two weeks. Within an hour, we were rewarded with a commercial flight on TWA going to LaGuardia Airport tomorrow morning with a stop at Fort Worth, Texas.

She had to be the cutest corporal in Camp Stoneham. Jerry and I had a ball flirting with her. Our orders were cut for a thirty-day leave home plus four days of delay in route. Frank told me later that he and Guinea and Caccia went home by military transport and had to go to Fort Dix, New Jersey, for a couple of days before they started their thirty-day leave at home. I ended up going home on a free commercial flight right into LaGuardia Airport, which was close to Rockaway, with more furlough days than Frank had.

Sometimes you just had to love the way the army did things.

CHAPTER 70

"IT'S TIME TO COME HOME, SON"

"I'm coming home!" I yelled into the phone.

"Where are you?" the calm, measured voice asked.

"Ahm callin' from the big old state of Texas," I said in my best Western drawl. "I'm in Fort Worth on a stopover, Dad. I'll be home tomorrow for lunch." I gave my father my flight number and estimated time of arrival at LaGuardia.

"Your mother's working, but your brother and I will be there. It's good to hear your voice. Welcome home, son."

The trip from California was long but filled with great anticipation. Jerry and I got to know each other better. We exchanged telephone numbers and made promises for a double date on the town in the big city. We flirted with the hostesses, who couldn't do enough for us and made the flight an enjoyable one. It was a bright, bright morning, and our flight was on time. We'd be landing in New York in minutes, ready to spend the next thirty-four days with family and friends and have some fun. How sweet could life get?

Jerry and I used the restrooms on board the four-engine plane to wash up, shave, and change into fresh khakis before we landed. We sat in seats in the rear of the plane and were joined by the hostesses during our descent. We chatted away and exchanged telephone numbers before our plane landed outside our terminal gate.

423

We grabbed our overnights and waited in the aisle, anxiously looking out of the plane's windows for our folks and for the steep platform to be rolled up to our cabin. Jerry spotted his family. "There they are!"

When the door opened, Jerry scrambled down the steps and out onto the tarmac and started running. I heard god-awful screams as he rushed forward. A horde of people were being led by a pretty, shrieking, blonde girl. The two sides met, and the pretty blonde leaped into Jerry's arms with a squeal. They twirled around as they hugged and kissed.

I stood there and smiled and shaded my eyes from the sun to look behind them. Out of the crowd shot a charging figure in a long, brown habit scraping the ground and with a flopping white belt around her waist and bobbing eyeglasses, which kept reflecting the morning light as she ran. A smiling, crying face under a veil flying in the wind came racing toward me. My aunt, a Franciscan nun, crushed me with a hug, called my name, and praised the Lord for bringing me home safely. Sister Estelle, her sidekick, ran up behind her and smiled. "Thank God, and welcome home, Joe."

"Look over there," said my aunt and pointed up to the observation deck. My eight-year-old brother stood up on the deck railing, my father holding him from behind. Both were smiling and giving me big, slow, side-to-side waves of the arm.

I dashed up the stairs and rushed up to my father and brother, whom I hadn't spoken to or seen in a year. My dad extended his hand. "Welcome home! It's good to have you home, son."

"And how's my little brother?" I asked.

"Good."

"I think I can do better than that," I said, lifting up my eight-year-old brother and giving him a big kiss and a hug.

We went downstairs and joined the nuns. Aunt Mae was my father's sister and the principal of a Catholic school in Broad Channel across the bridge from Rockaway Beach, where we had our summer bungalow. Today, she was also our chauffer. She had borrowed a car for the occasion. Conversation centered on family and friends. Questions and answers were fast and furious.

"That's new," I said, pointing to an unfamiliar sight along the road. "That's a Carvel," said Aunt Mae.

"They serve all kinds of frozen custard," my father said.

"Would anyone like custard?" I asked.

"Sure," said Aunt Mae, who jammed on the brakes and backed up into the parking lot. *Only a nun would do that*, I thought. Everybody wanted to pay for the custards. I had to demand the privilege of being allowed to make my first purchase since I had come home. I had three hundred dollars back pay that was burning a hole in my pocket. It was so gratifying to be carefree. Here I was sitting in a car with a bunch of exuberant nuns, my little brother, and my father on a beautiful homecoming day, leisurely licking frozen custard. It was hard to believe that I was home. It was like a beautiful dream come true. I couldn't wait to see my mom.

My father worked the four-to-midnight tour at the post office in Penn Station, so he had to leave. Here was the game plan. My mother would leave work at Chase Plaza in Manhattan at five o'clock. My aunt and grandmother would stay home and cook dinner. Mom's bus arrived at the stop on 116th Street at around 6:15. Aunt Mae, Sister Estelle, and my brother would sit in the car just around the corner from the bus stop and out of sight. The surprise was as well planned as a military operation.

My heart skipped a beat every time I spotted an arriving bus. I would step back out of sight, peeking to see who was coming off of the bus. I did this a couple of times before I met the right bus. I saw my mom line up in the bus, carrying two big bags of groceries. She didn't see me. As she came off of the bus, I walked up to her, dressed in my fresh summer tans with pants over glistening cordovan parachute boots. Infantry powder blue piping outlined my cap, and green leadership swatches encircled the shoulder straps of my shirt, displaying regimental crests. A gold sunburst insignia blazed across the blue, diamond-shaped patch above my two gold stripes. Decorations and badges adorned my breast along with a great big, ear-to-ear smile on my face.

"Let me help you with those, Mom."

Nothing was said. The face contorted. The head moved silently, and tears rolled down her cheeks. One bag fell to the ground, and then the other. A scream of joy was followed by kisses and a long embrace.

Smiling passengers gathered around us. After she had thanked God and the holy family over and over again, my mom burst out, "My son . . . just came home from Korea."

Strangers patted us on the back. My mother was teary. I was teary. People shook my hand and welcomed me home.

I don't know how long we stood there. The groceries were picked up by passengers, and we thanked them as we went arm-in-arm back to the car. In the background, I caught some words to the effect, "Was he a prisoner of war? How long?"

It's amazing the way stories got started. I lived with them every day in Korea—one rumor more ridiculous than the next but always believable.

I called Frank and told him, "I'm home, so you can come out of hiding now."

We stayed on the phone for a long time, swapping homecoming stories. Frank told me what had happened when he had gotten off of the bus in Yorkville.

"So I'm walking down 82nd Street as happy as a pig in shit. I looked great in my uniform. With my six-foot-two height plus jump boot heels and my duffel bag slung over my shoulder, I was an imposing figure. I smiled and nodded to familiar faces who didn't respond. They didn't recognize me, Joe. I don't think my neighbors knew I was gone, never mind that I was off fighting in Korea. It was the strangest feeling. I got to my apartment house and let myself in the vestibule door. I went up stairs to the third floor, and my mother was on the landing, cleaning the doorknobs and hinges. I'll always remember that look on her face. It was unbelievable. It was a mixture of grief and joy. I can't describe it. I thought she was going to collapse. When my father came home, she greeted him in Croatian, 'Guess who is here?' My father welled up in tears as we embraced. My brother and sister were called, and they came over with food and wine and the whole bit. We sat down to dinner, and the schnapps came out. And we talked into the evening. My father and my brother, who was wounded in Italy during World War II, told me how proud they were of me and thankful to God for bringing me home safe. When my brother got up to leave, my father embraced the two of us. He smiled with pride and said, 'I've always regretted never being a soldier.'"

Frank and I had very different homecomings. After my phone call, I went into Irishtown to visit my old haunts. It was a year to the month since I had left Rockaway. The first place I went for a beer was Gildea's. I listened to the musicians go through their Irish-American medleys. Big John Gildea was still going through his routines. He worked the bar, cleaned, and picked up dirty glasses from the tables. Nothing seemed to have changed since I had been gone.

Next stop for beers was the Snake Pit and its Fifty-Beer Wall of Distinction displaying the names of those who had drunk fifty beers in one day. I was never one of those. I headed over to the Irish Circle and listened to real, hardcore, traditional Irish music and entertainers. My beer walk took me to the Dublin House, Inisfree, and Ireland's Thirty-Two, which had a full house, so I stayed there for a while. There was a smattering of uniforms among the summer crowd who were eating, drinking, dancing, and enjoying themselves. I couldn't believe that I had been one of them last summer. They seemed younger. I felt older, like I didn't belong. I felt like an outsider looking in.

I stopped into McGuire's on my way home. I always got a kick out of the liquor store across the street with the owner's name, "Donohue's," splayed in bright neon lights across the top of its sidewalk window. McGuire's was family owned and operated. It catered mostly to locals and an older crowd. Sometimes you might see one or both of the Maguire Brothers, Al and Dick, who had played basketball for St. John's University and then the New

York Knicks, working behind the bar. I remember a newspaper clipping my father had sent me in Korea. "I Can Stop Cousy," read the headline in the daily news. Al had been badgering the Boston Celtics before game time to sports reporters.

I had a few more beers before I headed home. My last stop would be my favorite bar. I was tired, and the beers were starting to hit me. The Seaside Inn often had Western as well as Irish music. I had really acquired a taste for country music when I had been stationed in the South, so it was the perfect last stop before I called an end to my bar-hopping, first night home. I could hear the music a block away and the twang of a hillbilly voice in the microphone. I was really tired, but hell, I was home. I finally made it. I was really home, and I was proving it.

"Detour! There's a muddy road ahead . . . detour." The music was getting louder. I staggered slightly. I breathed in the delicious sea air of Rockaway and smiled knowingly. Thank you, God. "Shud-a . . . read . . . that detour sign," I heard and then tripped on the sidewalk.

A hand came down out of nowhere and helped me to my feet.

"Thank you," I said, straightening up and looking into the face of my dad, who was coming home from working the night shift at the general post office in Manhattan and was right behind me. As he put his arm through mine, he whispered soothingly, "I think it's time to come home, son."

Happily playing "Catch" on the supply road. Rotation done hit me

Drinking 3.2 beer at battalion rear waiting to go to Chunchon,
July 1953

My buddies at 40th Division Headquarters in Chunchon

Waiting for the train at Chunchon station

Emergency stop at Kimpo Airport to allow train of ROK
wounded to pass

Bell hellicopter used to take wounded off of the battlefield

Inchon Rotation/Replacement Center

Boarding ferry, at low tide at Inchon, to take us out to our troop ship

Hospital ship in Inchon harbor

Ferry shuttles GIs to our troop ship the USS Meigs

Harbor master bids us farewell

Last ferry out of Inchon with hospital ship in background

Aboard the USS Meigs for our trip home

Lyle Olson sunbathing on deck during the journey home

Mustering out picture, 1953

Best man next to me at my wedding to Christine (Teenie), 1956

The Donohues—Jody, Ter, Teen & Christopher, 1980's

Frank's New Wife Sue & Son Mark, 1989

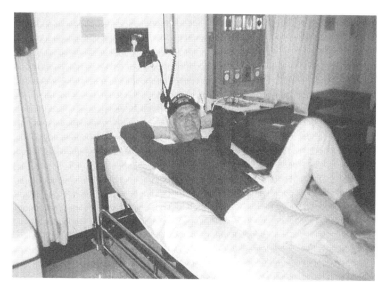

Frank at V.A. hospital in Boston, November 1993

EPILOGUE

In 1952, our combat mission was to hold the line until an end to the war could be worked out at the peace talks in Panmunjom. The parties eventually settled on a truce. Over sixty years later, the conflict in Korea continues. Episodes of violence still flare up. The recent sinking of a South Korean warship and the bombing of a fishing village emphasize the continued aggression of North Korea from Kim Il-sung, the founder of Communist North Korea, to Kim Jong-il, his son, and now Kim Jong-un, the grandson. Like a bad dream, the Korean War won't go away. "The Forgotten War" refuses to be forgotten. It remains our longest war.

In 2004, I read about a California tour being organized for Korean Veterans from the Forty-Fifth and Fortieth Infantry Divisions. The tour would visit our old battlegrounds of Heartbreak Ridge and the Punchbowl. Accompanied by my wife, Christine (Teenie, my girlfriend, in this memoir) and a handful of septuagenarians from these two divisions, I made an arduous fourteen-and-a-half-hour trip to Korea. Why? Why did a bunch of old graybeards pay big bucks to drag their spouses and loved ones to see relic battle sites and relive unpleasant memories?

The reality of war is impossible to describe. Over time, the intensity fades, but the blur of memory remains. Did those things really happen? I came to revisit places and sites that had become more like dream than fact. I came to reminisce and share my memories with other veterans who were a part of these battle sites and most likely the only ones who could really understand those moments. I came for myself and for my best friend, who is long gone and missed and would have loved nothing more than to have been part of this journey back to Korea.

My wife, Christine, was so moved by our Korean/China tour that she wrote an article that was published in a couple of military magazines that I have included as a proper ending for my memoir.

GOING BACK TO KOREA:
THE WAR THEY WOULDN'T FORGET
Christine Donohue, Spring 2004

Return Salute, Heartbreak Ridge, Korea, April 2004

"Present arms!" someone from the group called out, and the old veterans sitting for a group picture on top of Heartbreak Ridge saluted their young escorts and hosts for the day. The Republic of Korea soldiers were taking photographs and looking on in curiosity at their predecessors of more than a half century ago. Suddenly they stopped what they were doing and, as if on command, came to attention and returned the salute. One by one the old soldiers stood and applauded. It was a moment of respect and gratitude connecting soldiers generations apart who understood the importance of protecting, and fighting for if necessary, their country's freedom. We were on top of a desolate, windy, infamous mountain. A lump came to my throat and tears flooded my eyes.

It is April 2004, and I'm in Korea on a tour with my husband and fourteen other men from the 40th and 45th Infantry Divisions who fought here between 1951 and 1953. In July 1953, the truce ended the fighting but unfortunately not the war. Alex, our charming guide, was especially kind to her senior tourists. She smilingly reminded us how the Japanese and Chinese cultures are quite familiar to us and how the words Samurai, Kamakazi, Mah Jong, and Moo Shoo Pan are words that we probably know. This does not hold for Korean words and Korean culture, she said, except for the veterans on this trip. They're hearing snippets of the language of places they haven't been to for many years: Komapsumnida, Inchon, Seoul, Chorwan, Kimchi, Panmounjom. I notice the group, especially the veterans, listening intently to the guide and following the broad itinerary on their maps. Old Baldy, Pork Chop Hill, the Iron Triangle, Heartbreak Ridge, Sandbag Castle, and the Punchbowl are funny names for places that weren't so funny. I had heard the stories that went with these colorful names and places many times over the years, and now I was with the men who were part of those stories.

Who were they, these men? What were they like? Why did they, these seventy-year-olds, including an octogenarian, travel 14,000 miles a second time in their lives to revisit places of war and harsh memories that took a precious year or more out of their young lives? They had served their time, and now they were back. They were colonels, lieutenants, sergeants, corporals and a PFC. They all saw combat. They all wore their CIBs, Combat Infantry Badges, proudly. They drove trucks and tanks, commanded companies, led patrols, flew Cessnas as artillery spotters, manned machine guns, and fired rifles. They were shot at and did their share of shooting. They fought from foxholes, bunkers, and rat-infested trenches. They lived on mountain ridges and ate C-rations out of cans. They earned their in-country points the hard way to be rotated home and out of harm's way.

I was just along for the ride, but I was curious as to why these men came back after so many years. I knew why my husband was here. His best friend and the best man at our wedding, who is now deceased, was in the 179th Regiment of the 45th Infantry Division. Joe was in the 224th Regiment of the 40th Division. He and Frank were drafted together, graduated from jump school, went to Korea, and came home on the same ship together. My husband came in part because of a promise made to write the book that Frank had always wanted to write for his young son about the war in Korea. He also knew his buddy would have come with him to revisit battle sights and share old memories. Did these other men come for similar reasons?

We turned to Pork Chop Hill on our second morning out. Lieutenant Colonel Jack Rose, who was also a World War II veteran, was a company commander in the 279th Regiment of the 45th Division in Korea. Paul Elkins, one of his platoon sergeants, gave a moving account of the hills they were on and the battles fought in defending their positions against attacking enemy troops.

I roamed the assembly room and the observation deck, listening and trying to understand the men and their motives as they studied the display table which showed the topography of the land out front. Hill 270, 271, Hill 515, were such powerful episodes in their lives, and now it seemed they were trying to make sense of what it was like then and what they could piece together now.

"Hill 1240, where is it exactly?" someone asked.

"Over there between the two ridges."

"No way, it was over there," replied one of the veterans.

"No, no it was right here."

I don't know why, but I thought it was a little bit sad to see them trying to recapture the moment, to relive it. Was it real? What were they trying to feel? What were they trying to remember? They had their reasons for being here, that was for sure, and I wish I knew what they were. Could they put it into words? I certainly couldn't and wouldn't even try. I could try to understand, though.

I cornered one vet back on the observation deck, and referring to Jack and Paul, I asked him, "Arthur, what must it be like for them? What must they be feeling returning to Pork Chop?"

"It must be eerie, and they must be excited, but I'm not excited yet because I wasn't here at Pork Chop. I was at Heartbreak. When we get to Heartbreak, maybe I'll have an answer for you."

Now that gave me pause. They were all here to honor the Korean War and their fellow veterans but could they only get excited about their own piece of turf, their little piece of mountain where they were dug in for months and months? Was that what they knew best of their time spent in Korea?

"Why are you here, Jack? Why did you come back?" I asked later that day. "What were you expecting?"

"To tell you the truth, I didn't know what to expect, but I guessed that it wouldn't be the same. At least I knew the place would be covered with foliage today, and it was nothing but bare root back then."

"Have you been back to Korea since you left in '53?"

"No. Never wanted to," said Jack. "I had no desire. I never thought about coming back."

"Why now, Jack?" I asked.

"Why not?" he said. "I'm eighty-one and I don't have that many years left."

"What about you, Art?" I asked. "Why are you here?"

"Well, I saw the ad for the tour, and even though I never thought about coming back, I guessed this was as good a time as any."

"But why return?" I persisted.

"I guess you could say 'unfinished business,'" was Art's response.

In the Punchbowl we stopped at Air Strip AE-17 because First Lieutenant Al Gale had taken about eighty trips during his time with the 40th Division in Korea in a Cessna type plane (just pilot and observer) flying over enemy territory looking for emplacements and other information. Al was a spotter for division artillery. My husband often said the men on the ground loved to see those little single prop planes flying over enemy positions because they knew it would be a quiet time on the line for a while.

Al's son, Todd, who accompanied him on this trip, was equipped with a technologically sophisticated Global Positioning Device, and he had calculated the coordinates indicating exactly where his father's airfield site should be. Sure enough, what looked like a small farm plot was as he remembered it, and there we were taking pictures of Al and his son, Todd, and empathizing or identifying or doing whatever we do when we put ourselves in another person's shoes. We were all delighted that we, and he, were here to tell the story. I think I was beginning to figure out why they were in Korea, but I couldn't be sure I was right. There were the tears, swelling up again.

"What were you expecting, Charles?"

"I knew it would be changed, but I didn't expect the extent to which they've built up the country. I know one thing I learned while I was in the army here in Korea, and that was the thing you must always say to a sergeant."

"What's that, Charles?"

"You say, 'Yes, sir!'"

"Very funny," I said with a wince.

"What about you, Ed. What were you thinking when you decided to return?"

"I don't know what I was thinking. My daughter is the one who pushed me into coming, but I didn't object too much. As far as what I remember, I was a truck driver in the motor pool. One thing I remember well is the post sign with all kinds of arrows pointing in different directions right when we came out of our compound. I didn't know exactly where I was, but since I made regular trips to Seoul for supplies, I only paid attention to the arrow for Seoul, to Seoul and back to camp. Those were pretty much the only trips I made."

Our guide, Alex, said as we neared a city, "And this is Inje, a resort town."

A roar of laughter erupted from the veterans. "Yes, it's a little different from the way you remember it. It has six-story buildings, hotels with walls of glass, terraces, restaurants, and places to eat breakfast overlooking the Inje and Soyang Rivers. Just a little different from the meals you may have eaten fifty years ago." My husband reminds me that this is where his regiment went into reserve in January 1953, when they came off Heartbreak Ridge and were served eggs which had frozen into stones. It was a funny remembrance.

Over wine, before dinner in the Inje Skylark Hotel, we talked about Korea. I could see it was a powerful piece of each veteran's life. A ten-to-twelve-month period of time during which they learned to be fighting men, saw their buddies shot up, and bonded in ways they hadn't bonded before or since. They faced death and mortality, and they experienced survivor guilt, although they couldn't have identified it then. It was poignant to see pictures they brought along: fifty-year-old black-and-white photographs, some tattered and torn, of beautiful young men who were here for what? For their country, they would say. Their country needed them. They were here in Korea, in a war that their government didn't even call a war. It was a "Peace Action," but their country needed them. They weren't bitter, they weren't even regretful, they were just proud to remember.

My eyes welled up with tears, and I couldn't tell why. I confess I am someone who cries at kindergarten graduations when the CD player starts with "Pomp and Circumstance," not to speak of my three sons' high school and college graduations. Nonetheless, I was emotionally touched on our fourth day at the base of Heartbreak Ridge when we were greeted by a platoon of Korean soldiers and a Brigade Band dressed in brilliant red tunics, lustily playing the Star Wars melody. The colonel of the brigade saluted each one of us and solemnly shook our hands, greeting us in English by saying, "Thank you, and welcome." It was stirring and joyful, so why was I crying? I wasn't a veteran. I was married to one, and I guess I was living vicariously, but I was so moved to see all these veterans acknowledging the warm, respectful feelings generated in the air.

One of the biggest things I learned during this two-week tour of Korea and its significant battle sites was that there is a deep reverence and honor that the Korean population have for the veterans who fought in their war fifty years ago. All along the way we met South Korean people who openly acknowledged the debt they felt to the American soldier. The older generations especially remembered the pain of war and wished to show their appreciation. Everybody on tour knew that Korea was the "Forgotten War" except for the Korean people. Sharing thoughts on this, Tom Branch said he had marched in a parade only once in New York after the Korean War. Charles Brady said that in fifty years, nobody had ever said "thank you."

The young men of the Brigade, at the base of Heartbreak Ridge, somehow wanted to make up for this sentiment. They were so anxious to show their gratitude. They couldn't do enough for us. We were at a camp of about 120 soldiers spread out along the line so eager to accommodate us, to get us coffee, to test their English, and ever so courteous helping us into jeeps for the rocky, bumpy ride up Heartbreak. When we reached the top we were greeted by a colonel and a cadre of officers. The same thing happened. They couldn't do enough for us.

It was somber and dramatic as we struggled uphill and viewed the actual war site of so many years ago. As we went up we were briefed on each of the hills in the area. At the top we made numerous trips from the viewing site to the topography table and back again to realign binoculars and share clarifications and verifications of what we were seeing, and then it was picture time. What a photo opportunity. Five of the veterans on the tour, including my husband, were actually on Heartbreak during the fighting in 1952-53. We took pictures of them posing together even though they weren't together at the time. They didn't even know each other until they met on this tour. We took pictures of the South Korean soldiers, and they took pictures of us. Even the colonel posed with us and his men. On our way down from Heartbreak, we got off the bus to look at a natural waterfall. Bob Becker, one of the veterans, excitedly asked us all to look up. With photo in hand, he pointed up the mountain at a ragged, prominent, broken ridge line that was exactly duplicated in the faded old photo that he had taken of this exact same spot fifty years ago. It was mind-blowing. This was yet another joyful and gratifying moment of the tour.

Our next stop was the Kenneth Kaiser Kapyong High School, founded by soldiers of the 40th Division and named after the first soldier killed in combat from the division. My husband and I are educational consultants and had been working with the Fort Lee Public Schools in New Jersey, whose student population was almost 30 percent Korean American. Superintendent of Schools Dr. Anthony Cavanna, thought it might be educationally beneficial to begin a dialogue between the Korean high school students at Kapyong and the high school students at Fort Lee. With the approval of Roy Montgomery, the tour director, we decided to bring correspondence and gifts to Kapyong. We had no idea what to expect.

At one o'clock, as we headed to the high school, our guide was talking on the phone and holding up the bus, forcing our driver to go slowly. We learned later that she was talking to the principal of the school, who wanted us to enter the school grounds at precisely 1:05 p.m.

As we descended from the bus, a uniformed student band in their school colors filled the air with "California Here We Come" and other lively American music. Roy asked my husband to represent the veterans. My husband was astonished when the principal of the school presented him with a huge bouquet of flowers cascading with pink and blue ribbons. We were formally greeted with a speech, which the principal delivered in English, though he kept a translator close by. He then presented a five minute slide show about Kapyong High School. The principal was incredibly anxious to display his gratitude to the veterans who fought for his country. When he finished, Joe presented him with two yearbooks, a manila envelope filled with pen pal letters from Fort Lee students to the students of Kapyong, divided in half (by male and female students), and a T-shirt with "Fort Lee Tennis" emblazoned on the front. (It didn't matter that the school didn't have a tennis team.) The principal loved it.

On the school grounds there is a monument to Sergeant Kenneth Kaiser, who was an eighteen-year-old soldier from the 40th Division, California National Guard, who was the first to die in combat from the division. The school was built by donations from the men of the 40th in his memory. Interest from these funds was still being used to maintain the school, which had become the eighth highest academic scoring school in all of South Korea (not bad for a school where the boarding students go to school from eight a.m. to eleven p.m.). There was also a KATUSA war monument dedicated to Koreans who augmented the US Army. They were South Korean soldiers integrated into American units who fought alongside our soldiers during the war.

After a somber wreath-laying ceremony, it was time for fun. The students wanted to practice their English and the veterans wanted to see the school, so we were divided into groups led by the high school seniors, who acted as our escorts. The veterans interacted so positively with their shy, giggling, exuberant, respectful young guides that we concluded our visit with extensive picture taking of the principal, assistant principal, students, teachers, tour guides, and veterans. All agreed it was a delightful highlight of the trip.

The crowning moment of the trip was the farewell dinner. The Korean Veterans Association honored their American comrades-in-arms with the Korean Medal for Valor. They wanted to show their appreciation to these guys for what they had endured in 1951, 1952, and 1953. The Korean Veterans wanted to make sure the Americans understood that they hadn't forgotten. They remembered their sacrifices, and they wanted them to know that they would never forget the debt they owed these elderly gentlemen. They only wished more veterans of the war would visit Korea to be similarly honored. Yes, my eyes welled up with tears once more as each man was called upon and the ribboned medal was tenderly placed around his neck.

I'm so glad I made this trip. I know why I came. It wasn't just for the ride. I came to be with my husband and the men who fought with him. I came to honor these valiant, gray bearded veterans, and I delighted in seeing them acknowledged and appreciated for what they did. I even understood, to some degree, why they were there. They were soldiers who fought together for their country, each in his own way, each having personal moments and memories they will never forget. Some of the memories they had left behind, and so part of them will always be in Korea. They came back to reconnect. They came back to remember those who didn't make it home, buddies who died in the fighting. They came back to finish their own unfinished business.

As I write this piece, President Bush is preparing to go to Normandy for the anniversary of D-Day, June 6, 1944. Thousands of veterans will be returning to the beaches where they came ashore some sixty years ago. I can't help thinking of our men and women in Iraq. Where will they be fifty years from now? Will they go back? Will they be visiting Baghdad, trying to remember and trying to piece together the time they spent there? Is this what soldiers do? I'll stop here and let the reader reason why.

40th & 45th Division Korean war Veterans

Robert Becker	Richard Fink	Alfred Poeppel
Charles Brady	Dan Hughes	Jack Rose
Thomas Branch	Dudley Hughes	Allen Schroeder
Joseph Donohue	Alfred Gayle	Arthur Sokolow
Paul Elkins	Albert Juanitas	Edward Weatherwax

Veterans receiving Korean Medal of Honor from Korean War Veterans
Association in Seoul, 2004

Farewell dinner leaving Pusan

Arriving in China For Peiking Tour, May 2004

Part of the Great Wall of China

Walking the walk on the Great Wall

Boat ride in Peking Gardens in Beijing, China

Last Tango in the Gardens

Leaving Beijing Airport for home

Christine (Teen) and Joe Donohue—Home sweet home

A BRIEF HISTORY OF THE FORTIETH INFANTRY DIVISION DURING THE KOREAN WAR

(The following extract is an abbreviated overview of the history of the Fortieth Infantry Division taken from the commemoration service of the fiftieth anniversary of the Korean War.)

Just prior to annual training in July 1950, the Fortieth Infantry Division received an alert for mobilization. On August 10, 1959, the division was inducted into federal service, and at 1200 hours on September 1, 1950, guardsmen in the division were mobilized at their armories. Soon, the Fortieth Infantry Division (known as the Fighting Fortieth), with its assigned units, 140th Anti-Aircraft Artillery, Self-Propelled Automatic Weapons Battalion, 140th Heavy Tank Battalion, and the 160th, 223rd, and 224th Infantry Regimental Combat Teams moved to their new home at Camp Cooke, California, now Vandenberg Air Force Base, to conduct combat training and process the reception of draftees.

By September 5, 1950, the North Koreans had American and South Korean forces pinned against the sea at Pusan. On September 15, 1950, General MacArthur launched the "Inchon Landing" and the drive to the Manchurian Border along the Yalu River. By October 19, 1950, American forces had captured the North Korean capital of Pyongyang and over a hundred thousand Communist soldiers. The North Korean Army was in a general rout and ceased to exist. On November 26, 1950, four Chinese armies launched a counteroffensive with an initial 395,000 troops and entered the conflict on the Korean Peninsula. The Chinese forces pushed the outnumbered American and South Korean forces behind the Han River, abandoning Seoul, its capital.

On February 28, 1951 Major General Hudelson, the commanding general, addressed the division en masse to prepare for overseas deployment: "I am depending on your men of the Fortieth to (do), and do well, whatever duty we are called to perform. You will be ready to leave Japan in the latter part of

March." The division was assigned as occupation forces and reserves in Japan, replacing the Twenty-Fourth Infantry Division, which was fighting in Korea. (During World War II, the Fortieth also replaced the Twenty-Fourth Division in Hawaii and then the Solomon Islands and then fought side-by-side with them in those campaigns.)

The military band played "California, Here I Come" while the Fortieth Infantry Division was arriving and disembarking at Tokyo Bay, Honshu, Japan. The division boarded trains to military posts throughout Japan. The 160th Infantry Regiment was assigned to Camp Haugen, Mitsuichikawa. The 223rd Regiment was assigned to Camp Schimmelpfennig (Shemmie) in Sendal and Camp Younghans in Yamagata. The 224th Regiment was assigned to Camp McNair in Yoshiha, and the 140th Anti-Aircraft Artillery and Self-Propelled Automatic Weapons Battalion to Camp Whittington Air Field in Yokahama. The division assumed its occupation forces duties and conducted aggressive and extensive advanced combat training in those assignments.

In Japan, the Fortieth Infantry Division earned a reputation of unflinching tenacity. They were recognized as one of the best-trained and most competent divisions on active duty. It was clear to the soldiers of the division that they must be ready for deployment into Korea at any time. The division continued with its aggressive and extensive advanced training in combat, air movement, and amphibious landing.

On December 23, 1951, the division received orders directing it to Korea to relieve the Twenty-Fourth Infantry Division. On December 26, 1951, the division's advanced party deployed to Korea and reported to First (US Army) Corps headquarters. The division was ordered to assume immediate control of the Kumwha sector on the central front. An advanced party moved to the assigned sector, established a headquarters, and immediately took control from the Twenty-Fourth Infantry Division.

On January 11 and 22, 1952, the division's main body arrived in two echelons. Under the cover of darkness, units moved in and assumed control of the Kumwha sector on the central front.

Both units were under enemy pressure from their debarkation site at Inchon directly to their battle positions. When they assumed control of the sector and before the second echelon arrived, the division was engaged in fighting. The first casualty occurred on January 20, 1952, when Sergeant First-Class Kenneth Kaise, Jr. of the 160th Infantry Regiment was killed by communist mortar fire near Kumsong. On January 22, 1952, the division was officially assigned to the Eighth Army.

On March 1, 1952, the division defended the Kumwha sector. On April 1, the division completed relief of Second Republic of Korea (ROK) Division in the Kumwha-Kumsong sector. The 223rd Regiment deployed on the left of the sector with the 160th Regiment on its right. The 224th Regiment and 140th Tank Battalion were held in reserve. On April 3, the division effected a boundary change with the Second Infantry Division. The 224th Infantry Regiment inserted itself between the Second Infantry Division on its left, and the 223rd Infantry Regiment on its right. On April 6, the Fortieth Infantry Division assumed responsibility for the entire Second Infantry Division's sector.

During May 1952, as scheduled, the army started pulling guardsmen out of the front lines, which continued through August. As with their regular army counterparts, many guardsmen volunteered to remain and joined the active army. By September, the division's personnel rotations were the same as any other division's, which made for one-year combat tours and then a return home. During May, the Communists launched fewer ground assaults but fired over 2,722 mortar and artillery rounds into the sector. On May 19, Ninth Corps revised the left boundary to the rear of the Main Line of Resistance, and the Seventh Infantry Division relieved the Fortieth Infantry Division of responsibility for the Kumwha Valley sector.

On June 14, 1952, Sergeant David B. Bleak, medical aide of Medical Company, 223rd Infantry Regiment, near Minari-gol, was awarded the Medal of Honor for his actions while on a combat patrol to capture Chinese prisoners. Also on June 1952, Corporal Clifton T. Speicher, Company F, 223rd Infantry Regiment, near

Minari-gol, was awarded the Medal of Honor (posthumously) for his actions while he was participating in a company assault to secure a series of Chinese bunkers and trenches on key terrain.

On June 20, the Fortieth Infantry Division was relieved by the Second Republic of Korea and Twenty-Fourth ROK Divisions. The Fortieth Division moved to field training command #5 and was designated as Ninth Corps Reserve Elements of the Division, and they intermittently moved to front line, rendering proactive and direct support to the Republic of Korea (ROK) units. The 140th Antiaircraft (AW) and 140th Tank Battalion remained in combat positions attached to Ninth Corps and in direct support of the Second and Twenty-Fourth ROK Divisions. The Fortieth's logistical support elements were rotated forward in support of the divisional elements supporting the South Korean troops. On July 1, Third Battalion, 223rd Infantry Regiment was dispatched to the Sangdong Mine area to perform security missions.

On October 2, 1952, the Fortieth Infantry Division relieved the Twenty-Fifth Infantry Division in the Paem-ihyon-ni sector and assigned to the Tenth Corps, with the Fifth Infantry attached. Initially, the 160th Infantry Regiment was on the left, the 224th Infantry Regiment center (Kumsong sector), Fifth Infantry on the right, and the 223rd Infantry was designated reserves. Trying to exploit the relief, Chinese bugles signaled an attack at midnight along the division's front that lasted every night from October 2 to October 15 as well as November 3 to November 4. The Chinese's main effort came from the vicinity of Heartbreak Ridge to the Mundung-ni Valley. The division held fast and repelled the foe time and time again.

On March 6, 1953, the Fortieth Division was pulled back to the rear and designated as Eighth Amy Reserves. On April 27, the division relieved the Twentieth ROK Division in the Ihyon-ni-kalbakkumi (Punch Bowl) sector. The division defended part of the Main Line of Resistance (MLR) along the northern rim of the Punchbowl. On May 27, 1953, the 140th Tank Battalion was asked to "direct support" of the newly arrived Twelfth ROK Division in the vicinity of Nojop-Yong. When the ROK forces were routed, the 140th Tank Battalion defended four strategic hills on June 1—8 and July 16—18, 1953. For the battalion's heroism, it was awarded the Presidential Distinguished Unit Citation for single-handedly breaking the attack of a Chinese infantry division. After the battle, the Chinese division was completely demoralized and ceased to be an effective striking force.

On July 10, 1953, the Fortieth Infantry Division was relieved by the Twentieth ROK Division along the Punchbowl. The Fortieth Infantry Division quickly moved while they were under attack and relieved the Forty-Fifth Infantry Division (Oklahoma National Guard "Thunderbirds") on Heartbreak Ridge and Sandbag Castle from Paem to west of Ihyon-ni on July 11. The 223rd Regiment deployed on Heartbreak Ridge to the left. The 224th Regiment deployed in the Sandbag Castle sector to the right, and the 160th Regiment stayed in reserve. On July 19-20, 1953, Sergeant Gillbert G. Collier, Company F, 223rd Regiment near Tutayon, was awarded the Medal of Honor (posthumously) for his actions while on a combat patrol to determine Chinese strengths and dispositions along the regiment's front.

At 1000 hours on July 27, 1953, the Armistice Agreement was signed at Panmunjom, ending hostilities at 2000 hours. This started massive shelling and assaults along the entire front by the Communists. The division's sector was barraged by the Communists with over 4,700 mortar and artillery rounds. The division received a few casualties and only slight damage. In return, the division counterattacked with over eleven thousand artillery and mortar rounds. At exactly 2000 hours, the fighting stopped along the entire front. Captain Chuck Monges, commander of F Company 224th Infantry Regiment, gave the order of the day, "Cover your butts, and nobody is to move out of his hole." He also said, "The damnedest thing, after all that, not another sound." The silence was so peculiar that it was reported that many soldiers in the trenches whispered to one another and refused to speak aloud.

The Fortieth Infantry Division soon started its nation-building duties. Its members were credited with the building of roads, schools, hospitals, and orphanages and repairing some of those same structures that they had built after World War II. They also built defenses, helped train, and assisted with arming a formidable army and National Guards for South Korea. Several times during this period, this area was called to the demilitarized zone to enforce the tenuous armistice.

On May 8, 1954, the Fortieth Division conducted its final Pass-in-Review parade while the band played "California, Here I Come" and carried the colors and the California flag. By June 19, 1954, on behalf of a grateful nation, representatives of the president of the United States of America returned the division's regimental colors with the Korean Campaign Citation streamers during a ceremony in San Francisco. On June 30, 1956, the Fortieth Infantry Division, California's National Guard, was demobilized, and the federal recognition of the Fortieth Infantry Division (National Guards) was withdrawn. Officially, the two organizations combined and again became the Fortieth Infantry Division, California's National Guard.

Revised US Military Korean War Statistics (Released June 1, 2000)	
Battle Dead	33,686
Killed in Action	23,637
Died of Wounds	2,484
Died While Missing (MIA)	4,759
Died While Captured (POW)	2,806
Non-Battle Deaths	2,830
Total Deaths in Theater	36,516
Died Elsewhere (Worldwide during Korean War)	17,730

Unaccounted (Bodies Not Identified/Bodies Not Recovered)   8,176

Prisoner of War   2,045
Killed in Action   1,794
Missing in Action   4,245
Non-battle   92

Wounded   195,418

Wounded (Number of Personnel)   92,134
Wounded (Number of Incidents)   103,284

Prisoners of War   7,245

POWs Returned to US Control   4,418
POWs Who Died While Captured   2,806
POWs Who Refused Repatriation   21

Number Who Served Worldwide   5,720,000

Number Who Served in Korean War   1,789,000

GLOSSARY

This glossary includes military slang and phonetically sounded English, Korean, and Japanese *pidgin* (words) commonly used by GIs and KATUSAs in Korea.

Slang	Meaning
Ah-ri-ga-to	Thank you
AWOL	Absent without Leave
Baby-san	Young girl
Bandolier	Belt of ammunition worn around the body
Bera Bera	Blab, talk too much
Bero Bero	Lick vigorously
Boom Boom	Sexual intercourse
Boy-san	Young boy
Burp Gun	Chinese thirty-five-round sub machine gun
Cadre	Trained personnel
Cessna (Bird Dog)	Two-seater prop plane used to spot enemy artillery
CCF	Chinese Communist Forces
Clusterfuck	Jam up, a mess
CPVA	Chinese People's Volunteer Army
C-Ration	Combat ration of canned food eaten in the field
Chicom	Chinese Communists
Chimpo	Penis
Chin-gu	Friend

Choggie	Carry, haul, elderly Korean civilian laborer
Choke	Slow your motor down, take it easy
Chon-gee	Stop, halt
Chop Chop	Hurry up, food, eat
Cho-sum-nee-dah	Okay, all right
Cho-tah-mah-tay	Hold your horses, wait a minute
Commo Wire	Black communication wire strands
Deuce and a Half	Two-and-a-half-ton army transport truck
Dai-jo-be	Understand, okay
E-2	Enlisted man of lowest rank
E-dee-wha	Come here
FECOM	Far Eastern Command
Firefight	Small weapons exchange of fire
Fire in the Hole	Warning shouted before firing recoilless rifle
Friendly Fire	Unintentional firing on friendly forces
Gook	Korean slang for person, enemy soldier
Gung Ho	Overzealous
Helmet Liner	Plastic helmet worn under steel helmet
Hew-gee	Toilet paper
Honcho	Leader, boss
Hooch	Wood/sandbag sheltered structure
Ichi-ban	number one, the best
JAG	Judge advocate general, military legal advisor
Joe Toe	Okay, good shape
Jon Ju	Halt
Kamikaze	Japanese WWII suicide airplane pilot
Komapsumnida	Thank you
KATUSA	Koreans Augmenting the US Army
Kemo Sabe	Partner, friend
Kim-ichi	Trouble, Korean pickled cabbage with garlic
KP	Kitchen Police

Ko-ni-chi-wha	Good afternoon
Lifer	Career military army volunteer
LP	Listening Post
M-1	Army Garand, eight-round, .30-caliber, clip-fed rifle
M-2	Army fifteen-thirty-round magazine fed carbine rifle
MLR	Main Line of Resistance
Mah Jongg	Old Chinese solitaire game
Mama-san	Elderly Korean woman
MASH	Mobile Army Surgical Hospital
Maxim	Enemy water-cooled heavy machine gun
MP	Military Police
Moose-a-may	Korean mistress
Moo Shu Pan	Fried shaved thick noodles with pork
Mosh-skosh	Do it quick, in a little while
Muul	Water
Mush-ee-dah	Drink
Neh	Yes
Neem-shee-dah	You want to see my young sister Joe?
No-Man's-Land	Unoccupied territory between opposing armies
NK or NKPA	North Koreans, North Korean People's Army
Numbers One to Ten	Used to express good and bad. Number one is best. Number ten is worst. Hucking one is the very best. Hucking ten is the very worst.
OCS	Officer Command School
Oh-ka-nay	Money
On-na	Woman
OP	Outpost

Oh-sheep-she-oh	Welcome
Papa-san	Elderly Korean man
Pecker Check	Visual examination of genitals
Piss Tube	Vertical grounded shell used for urinating
POW	Prisoner of war
Quad 50's	Four mounted, .50-caliber machine guns
ROTC	Reserve Officer Training Corps
Samurai	Aristocratic Japanese warrior
Scrip	Military payment, monopoly or funny money
Seventy-Five	(75RR) 75-millimeter recoilless rifle
Sheck-shi	Male prostitute
Slicky Boy	Thief, butterfly boy, Steal from flower to flower
SOP	Standard Operating Procedure
Supernumerary	Stand by in case of need, extra
Su-ko-shi	Few, a little bit
Sy-o-nara	Good-bye
Tak-son	Much, many
Thompson	American submachine gun used by tankers
Toujours Pret	Always ready
Um-sheek	Food
Wan	Korean money
Watashi	I, myself
Willie Peter	White phosphorous explosive
Yen	Japanese money
Yakimoki	Anxious, impatient, on edge
YOYO	"You're on your own."

Made in the USA
Lexington, KY
12 December 2012